The Sociology of Religion

A Canadian Perspective

Lorne L. Dawson
Joel Thiessen

OXFORD
UNIVERSITY PRESS

OXFORD
UNIVERSITY PRESS

Oxford University Press is a department of the University of Oxford.
It furthers the University's objective of excellence in research, scholarship,
and education by publishing worldwide. Oxford is a registered trade mark of
Oxford University Press in the UK and in certain other countries.

Published in Canada by Oxford University Press
8 Sampson Mews, Suite 204,
Don Mills, Ontario M3C 0H5 Canada

www.oupcanada.com

Library and Archives Canada Cataloguing in Publication

Dawson, Lorne L., author
The sociology of religion : a Canadian perspective / Lorne L.
Dawson and Joel Thiessen.

(Themes in Canadian sociology)
Includes bibliographical references and index.
ISBN 978-0-19-542557-4 (pbk.)

1. Religion and sociology—Canada. 2. Religion and sociology.
I. Thiessen, Joel, 1981-, author II. Title. III. Series: Themes in Canadian sociology

BL2530.C3D39 2013   306.6'0971   C2013-902926-5

Cover image: Daniele Pietrobelli/Shutterstock.com

Oxford University Press is committed to our environment.
This book is printed on Forest Stewardship Council® certified paper
and comes from responsible sources.

Printed and bound in Canada

2 3 4 — 19 18 17

Contents

7   The Religious Life of Contemporary Canadians   154

8   The New Religious Diversity   186

9 Summary and Conclusions   222

Preface

This book was written with several simple objectives in mind. First, and most obviously, we have sought to provide a clear and concise introduction to many of the key theories, findings, and debates of the sociology of religion, for both students and scholars new to the field of study. Second, we tried as much as possible to relate these discussions to the situation, past, present, and future of religion in Canada. To our knowledge this is the first book-length study to do so. Third, we recognized that most young Canadians, unlike their parents and grandparents, will approach this topic from a more or less secular point of view. Consequently, more attention was paid to explaining the basic nature and relevance of religion, for the lives of individuals and the cultures of whole societies, including Canada. The very nature of religion as a phenomenon remains a topic of ongoing dispute (see Chapters 2 and 3). Fourth, this means the uniqueness of the Canadian situation relative to other societies is always kept in mind. Canada is one of a handful of nations that have become largely secular, and only recently so. We live, however, in a world of nations that are still largely religious. Canadians, much like Scandinavians, Germans, and the British, tend to assume that this places them in the vanguard of a dominant pattern of historical development, one that will slowly but surely transform the rest of the world. Religion, in this view, is emblematic of a bygone era and is thus incompatible with modernity. Most sociologists of religion held a similar view, and many were proponents of secularization theory (see Chapter 5). But things have changed and now the opposite view holds sway: largely secular societies like Canada may be more the exception than the rule, now and for the foreseeable future. Religions change with changing times, but there is nothing intrinsically incompatible between becoming modern and being religious. Even in Canada it is unclear whether religion is disappearing as a significant social phenomenon or just undergoing changes in form, function, and expression that defy easy assessment in terms of categories of analysis designed to study the most traditional ways of being religious and little else. Traditional churches, with their Sunday services, no longer dominate the religious or spiritual lives of Canadians. Less than a quarter of Canadians attend any kind of religious service with regularity, despite many more claiming to belong to a religious tradition. But does this mean many of the rest, the majority, are not religious in some way? There is reason to think otherwise, as we will discuss, but there is much debate among sociologists of religion about the nature and strength of the signs of religiosity, whether we are simply talking about more private ways of being religious or actual engagement in new and alternative ways of being religious. Fifth and lastly, to give some broader context for this discussion, we situate our thinking about the functions and future of religion in an overview of the social structural features of "late modernity" (see Chapter 6). This is the term used by many analysts to describe a sweeping set of social changes associated with globalization, changes that may be resetting the grounds for whether individuals and societies are religious, and exactly how they are religious. To adequately grasp the delicate balance of social and religious change, how each affects the other, we need to think about the changes to society as much as the changes religions are undergoing.

Of course in writing this small book we had to be selective in the issues covered, but we have provided everything someone would need to launch a more specific or sophisticated investigation of religion as a social institution, and hopefully you will be encouraged to pursue the sources and expand your knowledge of the fascinating role religious and spiritual beliefs and practices have played in human history. For good or bad, religions have guided the lives of most the people born to this world. They have provided true consolation and happiness, and they have fomented bitter animosities and violence. Rarely, however, have our beliefs and expectations about the ultimate meaning of things been irrelevant, at least in the long run, to how we have lived our lives and run our societies.

Acknowledgements

For Lorne Dawson: Many years ago, Lorne Tepperman and James Curtis (since deceased), encouraged me to write this book. Much in life and work got in the way, but with the able assistance of my co-author and past student Joel Thiessen the task was belatedly completed. I wish to express my gratitude to Joel for his invaluable knowledge and hard work. I extend a special thanks to Phyllis Wilson and Tanuja Weerassoriya of Oxford University Press as well for their patience and thoughtful assistance, and to Jennifer McIntyre for her efficient and cheerful work as the copy editor. Progress on this book was interrupted by the passing of Dianne Dawson and I dedicate this book with love to her, and the sweet memory of her smile and constant support.

For Joel Thiessen: Lorne Dawson's respect, trust, and enthusiasm toward me and my research interests as a graduate student extended that much further in this project, and I am immensely thankful for his role as a mentor, co-author, colleague, and friend. To my students at Ambrose University College—your insightful questions, observations, experiences, and discussions in the classroom about sociological phenomena reveal once more that teaching and research come alive when they feed into each other. Thank you for your ongoing interest in and encouragement of my research on religion; it is a joy to serve you.

Credits

The authors gratefully acknowledge their use of the following material:

Excerpts on page 37 from the Supreme Court of Canada, 2004. *Syndicat Northcres v Amselem*, http://scc.lexum.org/decisia-scc-csc/scc-csc/scc-csc/en/item/2161/index.do. Reproduced with the permission of the Minister of Public Works and Government Services Canada, 2012.

Excerpts on pages 32 and 50 from *Imagining Religion: From Babylonia to Jonestown* by Jonathan Z. Smith (Chicago: University of Chicago Press, 1982). Reprinted with permission.

1 Religion in Canada, the West, and the Rest of the World

Learning Objectives

In this chapter, you will learn:

◎ To understand that the role religion plays in Canadian society is in many ways atypical of what is happening in much of the rest of the world, including the United States.

◎ To start thinking about some of the fundamental reasons why people are religious, and the important role that religion has played, until very recently, in all societies.

◎ To recognize that the decline of traditional forms of religious practice sometimes gives way to the rise of new forms of religious life.

Introduction

The sociology of religion requires us to exercise our "sociological imagination." We need to suspend the certainty of our personal understandings and open ourselves to new and broader views of the world and the place of religion in it. The sociological imagination, as classically formulated by C. Wright Mills (1959: 14), illuminates the "intersections of biography and history within society." It allows us to grasp how our individual situations, our troubles and triumphs, are influenced by and also contribute to the larger course of events. These larger forces of history are embodied in social structures and patterns of social change that exert a strong influence on how we envision the world, in terms of what it is, and what it ought to be or possibly could be. In other words, we need to recognize that our own behaviours and attitudes are conditioned by larger social forces and, conversely, understand that our own activities cast light on the very nature of those forces at work in our society.

In terms of the study of religion in a contemporary context, this means we must do at least three things: (1) understand that the natural point of view of most Canadians on these matters is distorted by some specific features of our religious history that are not necessarily typical of the experience of people in other countries and parts of the world; (2) give some thought to the important role that religion has played in the daily life of most people in almost all societies until very recently; and (3) recognize that the future of religion in most developed societies is going to be conditioned by certain changes in the structural features of society and the social-psychological consequences of those changes, which have been characterized as a shift from modernity to late or post-modernity. These are the themes we will start to discuss in this chapter, which is designed to get us thinking about the intriguing issues currently being tackled by the sociology of religion.

Religion in Canada: The View from Here

When it comes to religion Canadians are prone to mistake their experiences in the late modern world of the twenty-first century for the fate of religion worldwide. We are inclined to think what has happened here is universal and will soon happen everywhere. We overlook the singularity of our experience and how it might bias our understanding. But the experience of most Canadians is not typical of most of the rest of the world. In fact, it is atypical in some important regards. We tend to overlook the discrepancy because the changes that have happened in Canada seem to be in line with what the intellectual and cultural elites of the Western world expected and desired. But the reality, here and elsewhere, is more complex and perplexing than anticipated, and our common assumptions about religion are more problematic than we think.

The way most Canadians view religion is marked by at least three prejudices that stand in the way of developing a full and adequate grasp of the nature and functions of religion. The first prejudice is that we tend to think that the process of modernization, whatever that means precisely, has led to the inevitable decline of religion. The urbanization and industrialization of Canada, and the spread of public education, science, and technology, have undermined the credibility of religion and set in motion a process of **secularization** (see Chapter 5). Where once much of community life was centred on the church and its activities, today people dedicate their time, money, and energy to other pursuits and institutions. The religious beliefs and leaders that once shaped the conscience and habits of most Canadians have been displaced by other leaders and influences of a decidedly more secular nature, whether political, economic, or social. Canada has become a largely secular society, a post-Christian culture. That is what the survey research and church membership figures show. Most simply, fewer and fewer Canadians are attending church on Sundays or choosing to identify with a specific Christian denomination. In fact, there has been a precipitous decline in traditional forms of religious involvement over the last five decades, and the number of Canadians who regularly attend church is now a distinct minority.

But what is more, our culture has become post-Christian in the sense that the basic principles of Christianity no longer provide a pervasive and widely accepted base for our values and norms. Historically the legacy is still in place and, like other Western societies, much of our way of understanding the world is implicitly influenced by our Christian heritage. But few Canadians can any longer correctly identify or explain even the most rudimentary aspects of Christian doctrine. They are hard pressed to identify a few of the four Gospels, the Ten Commandments, or the twelve disciples of Christ. The basic Biblical literacy that once loomed so large in our culture, and which informed our books, plays, music, and public rhetoric, is no more (Bibby, 1987; Prothero, 2007). The religious views that shaped people's lives are waning. Few people today believe, for example, in original sin. In fact, sin is not even associated with damnation and the concept of hell is fading out of existence. But does the decline of conventional Christianity mean the end of religion? If it does, then are we becoming more, or less, like the rest of the world?

All of this is rendered more complex by the emergence of other religious traditions in Canada as more and more people arrive from societies that are primarily Muslim, Hindu, and Buddhist. Overall the number of non-Christians in Canada is still relatively small, but in many large urban centres the presence of these religious alternatives is pronounced, and under the influence of our national policy of multiculturalism more and more Canadians are actively conceiving of Canada in post-Christian terms (see Chapter 7). But at this time the number of new Hindu, Muslim, Buddhist and other non-Christian immigrants arriving in Canada is not sufficient to compensate for the overall decline in the religiosity of Canada (see Chapter 8), and many of these immigrants or their children have started to conform to the dominant Canadian pattern of secularity.

The second prejudice stems from the ways we are conditioned by our history to think of religion in terms of going to church. This is still what most Canadians think being religious means. For three hundred or so years this has been the dominant public expression of religion in the Western world. To be "religious" in Canada, the United States, Britain, and Europe was to belong to a specific church and denomination; to attend Sunday services with some regularity; to give money to the church; to be baptized, married, and buried by the church; to participate in and support its missionary and charitable activities; and to teach your children about the basic beliefs and practices of your church. In other words, religion is strongly associated with one type of religious practice that is centred on the idea of being a member of a "congregation." But that way of organizing religious life is specific to the European heritage of our society and it was shaped by the legacy of the Protestant Reformation (1517–1648). Prior to the Reformation there were no churches per se; there was only the Church. Everyone in Europe was Catholic, at least nominally so. But the kind of practice that we have come to associate with religion was largely confined then to the upper classes. The bulk of the population would rarely be found in the churches except on special occasions, such as feast days and baptisms, and when they did attend there were many distractions from the solemn rites being performed, in a foreign tongue (i.e., Latin), by the clergy at the altar. Conversation, commerce, and even petty crime continued as people came and went. Marriage, as a ceremony taking place in a church, did not become a sacrament until the sixteenth century. Until then, private self-marriages were the norm for ordinary people in Christendom (Bullough and Brundage, 1982). It was the Protestant reformers, with their earnest desire to purify the church and increase people's piety, who created the traditions of church service and attendance that we recognize today, patterns of behaviour soon emulated, extended, and modified by the Catholic Church in its own efforts of reform (i.e., in the Counter-Reformation of 1545–1648). More specifically, in North America our contemporary way of understanding religion is the end product of a long campaign of evangelism by religious leaders, intent on gathering people into churches to save their souls. American sociologists speak of the "churching of America" (Finke and Stark, 2005) and the idea applies to Canada as well. The pioneers who settled Canada and the United States were won over to this form of religious life, but it is not the way religion was practised before, even in Europe, and it is certainly not how religion is practised in much of the rest of the world. We must be wary, then, of confusing a turn away from one way of being religious, as embodied in declining levels of church attendance, with the end of religion per se.

The third prejudice is that the dominance of this "church-style" religion is associated with the assumption that religion is first and foremost about individuals affirming specific beliefs, certain propositions about the true nature of the world and how we should live in it. Religion in this largely Western and modern understanding is about holding certain convictions, based on faith, that impose specific moral rules and expectations on our behaviour, and formally unite us with others who have adopted the same beliefs. Viewed in these terms, religion is a largely cognitive phenomenon; it involves understanding and accepting a certain body of ideas. It is also characterized by what sociologists call "voluntarism." People are thought to freely choose their beliefs and to willingly abide by the behaviour they dictate. True religion is voluntary; it is neither merely habitual nor coerced. Likewise, it is largely thought to be a private and personal matter, in part because it is presumed to be the result of our most serious reflections on life and our subjective self-understandings. But is this really why 80 percent of Canadians still say they believe in God? Throughout human history, with the exception of some "religious virtuosi" (Weber, [1920] 1963), people have been socialized since birth to the religious worldview dominant in their societies. No other options were even present for serious consideration, and being a believer was largely marked by participation in shared public rituals. Yet this way of being religious was every bit as authentic, moving, and important to the daily, and the overall, lives of the people. A religion based in unthinking conformity can be as meaningful and significant socially as one based in the modern preference for reflection and choice. Everything depends on the context.

These widespread and largely unexamined assumptions about religion characterize popular conversation about religion and have exerted a heavy influence on academic conceptions of religion. In them we see the influence, once again, of the dominance of Protestant Christian views. But is this how religion is actually experienced by most people in the world? Is it characteristic of how religion happened, how it functioned throughout most of human history? Or is this point of view primarily the product of the post-Reformation history of religion in the west, of the European cultural legacy brought to Canada and developed by those who first settled this nation? It is, in fact, a historically specific and normative conception of religion that we tend to mistake for a neutral and universal description of religion (see Chapter 2).

Religion in Traditional Societies

To the best of our knowledge, humankind has always been religious. Until very recently, every aspect of human social life was imbued with meaning and regulated by religious systems of beliefs and practices. People's very sense of time and space were organized by religious principles and marked by ritual activities. The cycle of the year followed the calendar of holy days and festivities, while the temple or cathedral lay at the physical heart of every town or city. Sacred places, where the gods or other supernatural forces were thought to reside, were secure refuges from the cruelties of nature and our enemies. In these special places people could call upon the strength of their gods to protect them and to assure them that there was meaning in life and life after death for the faithful. The time and space dedicated to making contact with and preserving the integrity of the sacred gave structure to the profane time and space around people. Birth, death, and every major life transition in between were understood in terms of religious rites of passage (for example, baptisms, initiations, marriages, and funerals) that made these events meaningful and legitimate. The great events of the world, from wars to the coronation of kings and the launching of ships, were marked by ceremonies designed to curry the favour of supernatural powers, while the events of daily living, from planting crops to cursing an uncooperative neighbour, were suffused with words and gestures that acknowledged and invoked a spiritual presence (Eliade, 1959). Religious beliefs and behaviours were so common that until a few centuries ago most societies did not even have a word like "religion." Religion was so much a part of everyday life that there was little need to distinguish it (Smith, 1962).

Throughout history those who could mediate between humanity and the gods, or other supernatural forces, whether by aptitude or training, were held in high esteem. Religious leaders were influential and consulted on most matters of importance. In fact, political authority clearly rested on a religious legitimation, and in the course of daily life ordinary people often sought the advice of the local shaman, priest, or clergy on everything from business decisions to the choice of a marriage partner. They had knowledge, both specialized and general, thought to be essential to the survival and success of individuals. This was the truth of the human condition for most of our existence.

To drive this point home, highlighting the hubris of our current secular self-conception, imagine that you are in a classroom where the front is covered with a set of black or white boards. Your professor enters and, taking the chalk or a marker, draws a line from one side of the boards to the other end. Then he or she marks a small vertical line a few inches from where the line ends. The line tracking across the front of the room represents the history of humankind, and the space of a few inches (if that) separated at the end represents the time during which people have seriously entertained the idea of creating societies that were not based on an explicitly religious worldview. If *homo sapiens* have been around for about 100,000 years, and the oldest evidence of religious rituals dates back to about 70,000 years ago (Research Council of Norway, 2006), then we have been **homo religiosus** for a very long time, and only in the last few hundred years have a few societies sought to be or actually become secular. With this simple truth in mind we need to be aware of the ways in which religion may be, as they say, bred in the bone. Socially, culturally, and perhaps even biologically (Boyer, 2001; Atran, 2002), we are the heirs to a legacy of religious thought and behaviour that is unlikely to simply disappear soon, if ever.

All the same, with the rise of science and the material comforts and security that came with industrialization, much of life has changed for the prosperous nations of Europe, North America, parts of Asia, and elsewhere. We do live in much less manifestly religious societies. Yet as the great sociologist Max Weber reasoned, the root causes of religious belief have not been significantly displaced by our recent progress in achieving either prosperity or knowledge. We may no longer sense as strong a need to curry the favour of the gods in our daily lives, but Weber ([1920] 1963) suggested there is an inner compulsion on the part of humanity to understand the world as a meaningful cosmos, and a consequent desire to take a consistent and unified stance toward this cosmos. Throughout most of our history humans have been unwilling to live in ultimate uncertainty about the meaning of life. This compulsion, which has taken on a life of its own in human history, is fundamentally driven by the need of humans, as a species and as individuals, to cope with the graphic realities of suffering in their lives.

In this sense, Weber finds at the heart of all religious systems what Christian theology calls "theodicies." A **theodicy** is an attempt to explain and justify why God or other supernatural forces would allow the suffering we all experience, from both natural and human causes. In particular, many people need some way to account for the suffering of the innocent and of the righteous. While today a mother can know how her young child died, that a specific disease was responsible, her need to reconcile why it was *her* child that died is as great as that of any mother in the past. The object is not so much to explain this suffering away as to place it in a framework of meaning that renders it bearable and that strengthens our resolve to face even more suffering in the future. Without this resolve, societies themselves would wither and die.

Over the course of human history, religious beliefs have changed, prompting sweeping changes in the social conditions of life. The world is a different place because of the past actions of great military and political leaders, figures like Alexander the Great, Genghis Khan, Saladin the Great, Napoleon, Hitler, and Stalin. But few figures have transformed the world so completely and lastingly as Moses, Confucius, the Buddha, Zoroaster, Socrates, Jesus, and Muhammad. In reshaping the thoughts and feelings of even the lowliest citizen of any society, religious and moral reformers have exerted more influence on human affairs than anyone else. People respond to the prophet's call, Weber argues, when their desire for greater meaning, order, and justice is frustrated. This frustration is the result of the discrepancies between the expectations and explanations we learn from our societies and our actual experiences. In the face of the seeming irrationality of so much that happens to us, the suffering experienced at the hands of nature and our fellow human beings, a plethora of religious views have arisen, some gaining acceptance and spreading, others disappearing, almost without a trace. Humans have been infinitely imaginative in fashioning a higher purpose for our being.

Religion in Contemporary Societies

The collapse of certain forms of religious expression in some societies of the advanced industrial West is indicative of a growing discontent with the existing religious institutions. The church-centred Christianity that satisfied the needs of so many Canadians from the founding of our nation through to the 1960s appears to be losing its relevance (see Chapter 7). But the data collected by sociologists continue to reveal a strong and ongoing need for some meaningful response to the ultimate issues of life. We undoubtedly live healthier and more materially happy lives than our predecessors, so our religious orientations have changed. We no longer turn to God so readily to help us survive a long journey or to make our crops grow. But the kinds of suffering that Weber saw as fundamental to the religious impulse remain an all too regrettable presence in our lives. Illness, accidents, heartbreak, loneliness, failure, and death still punctuate and disrupt, and sometimes even define our lives, and with the advent of the mass media, every Canadian is now embroiled, if only emotionally, in the catastrophic or senseless suffering of thousands of others around the world. The more our knowledge progresses, the greater the risks we seem to face as our awareness of global threats to our very existence keeps pace (see Chapter 6).

The force of this state of affairs was driven home by the public response to the tragic events of 11 September 2001. A hundred thousand Canadians gathered spontaneously on Parliament Hill in Ottawa three days after members of the terrorist group al-Qaeda crashed the planes they hijacked into the twin towers of the World Trade Center in New York and into the Pentagon in Washington, DC. Canadians gathered to share their grief and show their solidarity with their American friends and allies. Similar memorial services, redolent with religious symbols, prayers, and other invocations of God, happened across Canada.

In the United States, a much more religious society to begin with, the shocking attack upon innocent Americans spurred public officials from the president to the mayor of New York City to set aside the constitutional separation of church and state and call upon their citizens to pray as a nation for the salvation of the thousands who had lost their lives and for the future safety of their country. Levels of church attendance rose markedly for weeks after, and throughout Manhattan shrines of candles, flowers, and pictures honouring the dead were created spontaneously in parks, on church steps, and around the lampposts where pictures of missing loved ones had been posted. Strangers stopped and offered impromptu prayers, adding more flowers and candles to express their solidarity, grief, and love. These suddenly fashioned sacred spaces, and the informal rituals that accompanied the retrieval of bodies at Ground Zero, especially those of the hundreds of fallen police officers and fire fighters, focused and magnified the concern and bewilderment of the rest of the city, the nation, and the world.

It would be difficult to imagine how either Canadians or Americans could have responded to this disaster without religion, and in honouring the anniversary of this tragedy people continue to turn to their faith in a higher order, no matter how implicit or vague, to seek the appropriate words of solace and significance to commemorate the shocking events and tragic loss of lives. The first anniversary began with a moment of silence in the United States and ended with a plea from President George W. Bush to pray that God "will see us through and keep us worthy." The citizens of the most powerful and modern nation in human history struggled to cope with what had happened while listening to the stirring sentiments of traditional hymns such as "Amazing Grace" and "The Battle Hymn of the Republic" (see Box 1.1). These songs, known by almost everyone, related those who grieved to one another, to the struggles of their nation's past, and to the promise of a better future—in line with God's providence. Americans believe that this faith, variously defined, makes them stronger. Perhaps it does, but it would be difficult for sociologists to determine whether this is the case. What kind of evidence could be used to prove it is so? Émile Durkheim ([1912] 1995), another great sociologist of religion, thought that societies needed something like the unifying force of a common religion to succeed. Yet he could see that the complex societies of the future were very unlikely to share any one religious worldview, and he feared what the consequences might be of living without religion.

As a Canadian, especially if you are a young Canadian, it is probably hard to imagine how important religion once was, since we live in one of the few truly secular societies in the world (see Figure 1.1). Now the fads of pop culture, rather than religion, are more important in the lives of most Canadian teenagers, and the public presence of religion has dissipated dramatically for all Canadians. Until recently, the churches played a prominent role in educating Canadians and meeting their medical and welfare needs through the hospitals and charities they sponsored. You could not shop on Sundays or have an alcoholic drink at a table outside of a hotel, let alone have an abortion, because it offended religious sensibilities. In the last fifty years all this has changed, and with the spread of modernization most sociologists thought the same fate awaited the rest of the world.

We are inclined, naturally, to think that what has happened here will soon happen everywhere and, hence, that we need not pause to consider how our experience may be different and how it could bias our understanding. Other nations such as Sweden, the Netherlands, Britain, Australia, and Japan share our experience of secularization. But this is not the case in

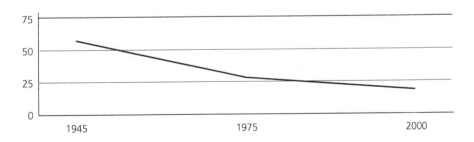

Figure 1.1 Declining Church Attendance in Canada
Source: Bibby, Reginald. 2006. *The Boomer Factor: What Canada's Most Famous Generation is Leaving Behind.* Toronto, ON: Bastian Books. Page 179.

Box 1.1: The Battle Hymn of the Republic

The stirring lyrics of this classic American hymn were sung by the soldiers of the Union Army as they marched into battle against the Confederate armies of the south in the American Civil War (1861–1865). The hymn was set to the tune of the popular song that had become the anthem of the American anti-slavery movement, "John Brown's Body." The lyrics were written in a flash of inspiration in the middle of the night when Julia Ward Howe woke from a mystical dream, prompted by the battle she had witnessed that day. The verses refer to the second coming of Christ to defeat evil and judge humanity, as foretold in the last book of the Bible, the Book of Revelation. It is easy to see why contemporary Americans could still find comfort in these words in the face of threats to their nation. Listen to one of the many different performances available online to get a sense of the expressive force of the song.

> Mine eyes have seen the glory of the coming of the Lord;
> He is trampling out the vintage where the grapes of wrath are stored;
> He hath loosed the fateful lightning of his terrible swift sword;
> His truth is marching on.
> Glory, glory, hallelujah! His truth is marching on!
> [repeat after each verse]
>
> He hath sounded forth the trumpet that shall never call retreat;
> He is sifting out the hearts of men before his judgement seat.
> O be swift, my soul, to answer him; be jubilant my feet!
> Our God is marching on!
>
> In the beauty of the lilies Christ was born across the sea,
> With a glory in his bosom that transfigures you and me;
> As he died to make men holy, let us live to make men free,
> While God is marching on!
>
> He is coming like the glory of the morning on the wave;
> He is wisdom to the mighty, he is succour to the brave;
> So the world shall be his footstool, and the soul of time his slave:
> Our God is marching on!

> — Julia Ward Howe (1819–1910),
> The Battle Hymn of the Republic (1862)

much of the Muslim world, South America, India, Africa, China, Korea, and most curiously the United States. In the last few decades many millions of Americans have experienced a revival of religiosity, and one need only turn on the radio or TV in most US cities to become aware of this stark difference. While the declining levels of religious involvement that began in the 1960s persisted in the 1980s in Canada, the trend was reversed in the United States, with a rising tide of "born-again" Christians and the emergence of the "new religious right" as a powerful new force in American politics (e.g., Capps, 1990; Smith, 1998). Other societies have recently experienced equally surprising and strong revivals of interest in traditional forms of religion, whether Islam in the Middle East, Pakistan, Indonesia, and Malaysia (e.g., Sutton and Vertigans, 2005), Hinduism in India, Buddhism in Sri Lanka, or Pentecostal and Evangelical forms of Christianity in Latin America, Korea, China and elsewhere (e.g., Jenkins, 2002).The world is still a largely religious place, though admittedly often in new ways, and the onset of modern ways does not mean religion will cease to be important. But it will continue to change in form and functioning, in ways great and small.

If the Canadian experience is analyzed in greater detail, and placed in comparative perspective with what is happening elsewhere, we can see that the reality is much more complex and interesting than sociologists first envisioned (see Figure 1.2). Most sociologists of religion speak now of the changing face of religion in societies living with the conditions of late modernity, not of its simple demise. Though the future of religion is murky, it is clear that the demand for a religious or spiritual aspect to our lives persists, and so complete secularization is unlikely. Billions of dollars are spent every year in North America alone on religious and spiritual books, and even a cursory consideration of blockbuster films from Hollywood and elsewhere reveals a plethora of religious, mythological, and spiritual themes, especially those dealing with end of the world, the struggle with evil, guiding spirits and saviours (e.g., the *Omen* series, *Contact*, the *Terminator* series, the *Star Wars* series, *Michael*, *End of Days*, *The Matrix* series, *The Lord of the Rings* series, *Constantine*, *Knowing*, *2012*, *Avatar*, *The Rite*, and many more).

But after we stop going to church, what is left of "religion"? Are the new practices emerging still "religious" or are they something else? It is common now for Canadians, like many Europeans and Americans, to carefully specify that they are "spiritual but not religious" (Zinnbauer et al., 1997; Fuller, 2001). What does this mean? The lines traditionally separating the sacred from the secular are blurring as people seek spiritual sustenance by doing yoga at their health club or buying Neal Donald Walsch's *Conversations with God* (1997) at Costco. Sociologists, struggling with the surge of new forms of "religion" since the 1960s—cults, sects, schools of meditation, spiritual therapy and so on—have coined new terms, such as **quasi- and**

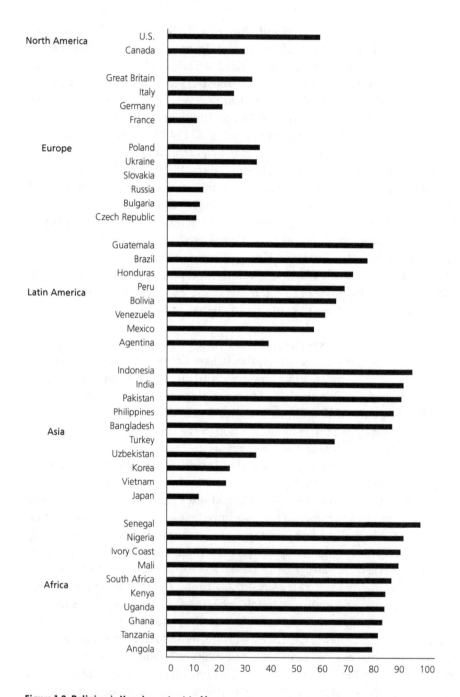

Figure 1.2 Religion is Very Important to Me
Source: Pew Research Center. Global Attitudes Poll 2002 (December 19). "Among Wealthy Nations: U.S. Stands Alone In Its Embrace of Religion." Available at www.pewglobal.org/2002/12/19/among-wealthy-nations/.

para-religions, to try to capture and make some sense of the emergent phenomena (Greil, 1993; Greil and Robbins, 1994). Quasi-religions are groups that deal with the sacred but are anomalous because they do not fit the existing folk conceptions of religion (e.g., Alcoholics Anonymous, Scientology, UFO cults such as The Raelians, and many New Age and Occult groups). Para-religions look a lot like religions; they are sometimes organized like religions, stress certain ritual-like practices, and are focused on ultimate concerns and the transformation of individuals. But they make few or no explicit supernatural claims and they choose for various reasons to not identify themselves as religions (e.g., Amway, Transcendental Meditation, Ramtha School of Enlightenment, various political ideologies such as the Nazis in Germany or Maoist communism at the height of the Cultural Revolution in China). In each instance, whatever the adequacy of this distinction, the key issue is the blurring of the traditional boundaries between things conceived as sacred or religious and things thought to be secular or non-religious.

Alcoholics Anonymous, for example, is an enormously successful treatment program for those whose lives have been ruined by alcohol addiction; it is a form of therapy. Yet at the core of its teachings is the principle of surrender of the self to the wisdom and guidance of a "higher power" or a generic conception of "God." Mao Tse-tung was the great political leader of the Chinese communist revolution of 1949. But the famous "Little Red Book" filled with inspirational quotations from Mao became far more than a political text during the "cultural revolution" that swept China from 1965 to 1968. It became a sacred text, used by the fanatical youth of the Red Guard to justify the spontaneous and radical reform of every aspect of life.

Less dramatically, but more pervasively, people who attend church services irregularly, if at all, but who still identify as religious, have been freely incorporating untraditional beliefs and practices into their worldviews since the 1960s, drawn from Buddhism, Hinduism, and Native American religions, or a wide variety of other folk and esoteric traditions such as witchcraft or Hermeticism (e.g., Hanegraaff, 1996; Cimino and Lattin, 1998). Some have more independently fashioned completely new spiritual lives for themselves, breaking with the churches of their parents to practise some form of "New Age" spiritualism (e.g., Heelas, 1996). The desire for alternative ways of being spiritual in the midst of our busy modern lives has spawned a substantial commercial market for books, magazines, videos, courses, and retreats promoting the revelations and therapeutic insights of a plethora of self-proclaimed gurus, sages, and mystics (e.g., Redfield, 1994; Schucman, 1996; Partridge, 2004). In these and many other ways, religious themes, aspirations, and behaviours continue to find expression in late modern societies, though the practitioners are often not counted amongst the religious.

Contrary to expectations, traditional forms of religion have also surged to the fore in international affairs with religious groups and conflicts playing a key role in the strife between Protestants and Catholics in Northern Ireland; the Iranian Revolution of 1978; the rise of the New Christian Right in American politics; the warfare and ethnic cleansing of Muslims in Bosnia-Herzegovina and Kosovo in the 1990s; the global spread of Christian Pentecostalism; the violent clashes of Christians and Hindus in India and of Muslims and Christians in Indonesia, Nigeria, and Egypt; and last but not least, the rise of al-Qaeda and the global spread of Islamist movements bent on waging holy war (jihad) though international terrorism (e.g., Thomas, 2005). Hard-core proponents of the progressive secularization of the world are hard pressed today to explain why religion continues to be such an important marker of identity in ethnic, nationalist, and social struggles. Religion is playing a more prominent public role in a globalized world than most sociologists would have presumed possible, prompting perhaps the equally surprising rise of the strident and controversial "new atheism" promoted in the bestselling books of Sam Harris (2004), Richard Dawkins (2006), Christopher Hitchens (2007), and others.

In these introductory comments it is not our intention to suggest that religion is simply about coping with pain, fear, and the unknown, or the assertion of parochial identities. Religion is not just a problem, a persistent source of tension and conflict in the world that needs to be controlled. It is easy, however, to fall into the trap of thinking so when the world is viewed from a contemporary Canadian vantage point. Most of what passes for religious activity in this world happens in a more mundane and daily context, and religions serve many other important and positive functions in society, in intended and unintended ways. But in the contemporary Canadian context, in a society in which secularization has made deep inroads, much of the conventional church-oriented religion that people experience seems increasingly tangential to their lives. So it is important to stress the ways in which a primal and ongoing need for religion persists at both the individual and societal levels. Moreover, there is reason to believe that even in Canada we may be on the cusp of a great shift in the form and functioning of religion as an integral part of social life. We have a better appreciation now that there have always been people who were not religious, who actively opposed the influence of religion on society. Atheism is not a modern phenomenon. But most sociologists of religion are now convinced that the outward appearance of secularization in many modern Western nations belies a deeper truth of continuity in the ways people will be religious, one that assures a significant, though somewhat different, role for religion in humanity's future. In exploring the possibilities, sociologists and other scholars of religion are reconfiguring their conceptions of religion, its nature and functioning. In doing so, the conceptual boundaries that have been used for the last several centuries to distinguish things religious and otherwise are beginning to give way. The neat distinction between the sacred and the secular is being blurred because

Box 1.2

Canada's "Highway of Heroes"

Canadian troops first landed in Afghanistan, to assist in the overthrowing of the Taliban regime that had supported al-Qaeda, in 2001. All troops are set to be home by 2014. Beginning in 2002, ordinary Canadians, veterans, soldiers, family, and friends have spontaneously gathered on Highway 401 bridge overpasses with Canadian flags, banners, and posters, paying tribute to fallen Canadian soldiers in Afghanistan as convoys of emergency vehicles and soldiers' families make the difficult journey from Canadian Forces Base Trenton to the coroner's office in Toronto, Ontario. This outpouring of public support led to renaming the stretch of Highway 401 between Trenton and Toronto the "Highway of Heroes" on 24 August 2007, and the inauguration of the annual Heroes Highway Ride, started by several motorcyclists in 2009. Unheard of even in the United States or Great Britain, two of the world's leaders when it comes to military and national pride, the "Highway of Heroes" represents a grassroots movement that affirms fundamental Canadian values of freedom, dignity, respect, and diversity. As structural-functional theorists note, group cohesion tends to arise in the face of tragedy and conflict and the "Highway of Heroes" is a stark reminder of how Canadian identity and nationalism are strengthened around a common ideology in difficult times. Luo DeVuono, one of the organizers for the Heroes Highway Ride, goes as far to say that the "Highway of Heroes" is "a collective group hug that has become the envy of the world." Incidentally, on 9 June 2011 the "Highway of Heroes" spread to Western Canada and the stretch of the Trans-Canada Highway between Langley and Abbotsford, commemorating the 13 British Columbian soldiers who lost their lives while serving in Afghanistan. It is difficult to say whether this spontaneous and collective effort to honour the dead is essentially "religious," but these gatherings undoubtedly include private prayers and pleas on behalf of the grieving families and the nation. At the same time, these public assemblies symbolize a nation's rejection of religious extremism and intolerance, locally and abroad, and the need to distinguish and celebrate those who made the ultimate sacrifice for their society, and hence the core values of that society.

people are behaving in ways that no longer fit into such a stark contrast of options. At the level of individuals and societies processes of secularization and of **sacralization** are happening simultaneously, and often in conjunction with each other (Demerath, 2007).

This new and permuting state of affairs has thrown the sociology of religion into disarray, in some ways. We can no longer rely on simple quantitative measures of the attitudes and behaviours of the members of largely conventional and formally institutionalized religious groups, of mainstream denominations, to gauge the extent, nature, or future of the religiosity of Canadians. We need to be more resourceful and sophisticated in how we look for the presence of religion or spirituality in late modern societies like Canada, and employ more qualitative and hands-on methods to develop the necessary familiarity with what is happening and why (see Chapter 3).

Conclusion

In summary, and in simple terms, we need to recognize that most of the dominant religious systems of the world emerged in traditional societies marked by the recurrent and highly stable rhythms of nature in largely agrarian societies where most people lived their lives in relatively small and close-knit communities. Differences existed in these communities, but they were minimized by a greater and more profound commonality of experience and shared values. The beliefs, practices, and norms of the religions born of these circumstances have changed with the times, but they still reflect the social world in which they were created and developed for centuries. In line with the Canadian sociologist Hans Mol (1976), we think this means that religion is intrinsically associated with the creation, maintenance, and defence of stable group identities, ones which frame and preserve the identities of individuals in the face of the inevitable threats and disruptions of life. But the social experience of these stable social worlds, which shaped these dominant religions, is disappearing under the impact of the processes of modernization and globalization. A need for meaning and order in the world persists, but it must adapt to a lived reality of constant change and magnified risks. So while more and more people are finding the traditional forms of religious expression irrelevant to the daily experience of their lives, to the socially conditioned patterns of their thought, many others are seeking and finding alternative ways of reinfusing a spiritual dimension into their lives. This is happening both in terms of a selective refashioning and use of traditional forms of religious life and the importation or innovation of foreign or new forms of religious and quasi-religious activity. The focus of this activity, we are supposing, is increasingly about the heightened integration of meaning, as grasped at the level of our most intimate relations and those of humanity as whole. There is a shift, in other words, from a concern with more local group identities, and their legitimation by various forms of religious expression, to what Durkheim ([1898] 1973) anticipated—a religion of humanity that finds its expression through the sacralization of the experience and potential of the individual. But we are getting ahead of ourselves, and the long-term consequences of the changes afoot are unknown. Too much is still in flux, and the implications for religion have yet to be fully studied.

Minimally, however, as the prominent American sociologists of religion Wade Clark Roof (1999) and Rodney Stark and Roger Finke (2000) argue, we now live in societies marked by a more permanent and profound religious pluralism. It is not just that there are more kinds of religion present in our societies than ever before, but there is also a fragmentation of the very market for religious ideas and services. It is highly unlikely that any one religion will ever again come to dominate our societies; rather, the population will be spread across various market niches. In this regard, even when people are of the same faith the nature of their affiliation will be more diverse. Different people will call upon the same tradition differently. Of course to some extent this has always been so, but never to this degree.

On the basis of a national study of the religious beliefs and practices of the Baby Boomer generation in the United States (i.e., those born between 1946 and 1960), Roof proposed that Boomer Americans are scattered over five categories: "born-again Christians" (about 33 percent of Boomer Americans), "mainstream believers" (about 25 percent), "metaphysical believers and seekers" (about 14 percent), "dogmatists" (about 15 percent), and "secularists" (about 12 percent). The profile has likely shifted since Roof did his research in the late 1990s, and it need not hold true for other generations (see Chapter 7), or for Canadians. Canada did not experience the wave of born-again evangelical Protestantism that swept the United States in the 1980s and 1990s. But while the precise pattern of fragmentation will differ, the reality of a fragmented religious populace undoubtedly applies to Canada as well.

Stark and Finke (2000) conceive things somewhat differently in their detailed analysis and theorization of many aspects of religious life, especially in America (see Chapters 4 and 5). Thinking in terms of the intensity of people's religious preferences, of their desire to abide by a strict or liberal pattern of religious life, they hypothesize a bell curve of niches running from the ultra-liberal, through the liberal, moderate, conservative, and strict niches, to the ultra-strict. The largest niches are those at the middle of the curve or spectrum, since there is a tendency for religious groups to gravitate from the margins of the curve to the middle. They do so because the success of any religious organization tends to generate a desire for more moderate views and demands. But the ultra positions at either end of the curve will always exist since the process of moderation reduces the capacity of these religions to satisfy the more intense preferences of some congregants. In other words, they "postulate the existence of a stable distribution of diversity of religious demand" that will result in "clusters of persons with shared preferences as market niches," and they observe that this will "make it impossible for one religious organization to satisfy demand" (2000: 198). There are systemic reasons, then, for assuming that the contemporary ecology of religion is more complex and fluid than is apparent from the vantage point of our still fairly traditional understandings of religion.

To understand the debate over the fate of religion in late modern societies like Canada, then, we need do three things. First, we need to get back to basics and begin to discuss what religion is, its elements, and their functions. This will be done in Chapters 2, 3, and 4. In Chapter 2 we tackle the old and still thorny issue of defining religion. In recent years our very use of the word "religion" has been called into question by scholars adopting a critical postmodernist perspective. In Chapter 3 we take time to consider the different and essential elements or dimensions of religion: belief, ritual, experience, and community. We need to understand that religions involve both cognitive and affective elements; they are about beliefs and actions and they are rooted in individual and collective, as well as ordinary and extraordinary, experiences. In Chapter 4 we sample the thinking of some of the most influential sociologists to theorize about religion, its nature and primary social functions. We start with the views of the great classical figures of sociology, Karl Marx, Emile Durkheim, and Max Weber, and then turn to an overview of two of the most important contemporary theories of religion, those proposed by Peter Berger and Rodney Stark and their colleagues.

Second, we need to tackle the dominant discourse about secularization which has framed almost all discussions about the fate of religion for many decades now. In Chapter 5 we will examine the dominant theories and call attention to some new ways of thinking about how the face of religion seems to be changing in Canada, the United States, and elsewhere. Is religious America the exception in a world destined to be ever more secular? Or is secular Europe the exception in a world that continues to be quite religious (e.g., Davie, 1999; Berger, Davie and Fokas, 2008)? Where does Canada fit in, and are the options actually so limited? In the pursuit of answers we will examine the divergent views of influential sociologists of religion, such as Peter Berger, Bryan Wilson, Jeffrey Hadden, Rodney Stark, Steve Bruce, and Jose Casanova.

Third, we need to set our analysis in a larger context by explaining what we have in mind in talking about "late modernity." If our religious beliefs and practices are changing rapidly, it is because our society is changing in dramatic ways as well. Religion both mirrors what is happening in the rest of society and, in some cases, acts as a creative response to the stresses, strains, and new opportunities born of those changes. One way of grasping the sweeping nature of the changes rippling through our societies is to use theories of late modernity (e.g., Beck, [1986] 1992; Giddens, 1990; Bauman, 2000). In Chapter 6 we use aspects of this prominent theoretical perspective to make greater sense of the shifts in religious sensibilities sociologists are detecting.

With this foundation in place, we can turn in Chapter 7 to a consideration of the nature and role of religion in the life of contemporary Canadians, and consider in particular how recent and innovative research on the views of younger generations is exerting an influence on discussions of the future of religion in North America, Europe, and elsewhere. The puzzle of secularization and the emergence of new understandings of the role of religion in society and in people's lives, especially those of the younger generations, highlight the intriguing challenges presented by the study of religion. Those challenges increase when we take into consideration some of the new forces for change and diversity at work in Canada and the rest of the world: the new cultural and religious pluralism that comes with globalization and increased immigration, including the growth of the religious "nones" (i.e., those claiming to have no religion); and the rise of new religious movements—all examined in Chapter 8.

Throughout, where appropriate, we will also reflect on the gendered nature of religion, since it appears religion has always functioned somewhat differently for men and women; indeed, many of the changes in the nature and role of religion in the contemporary world are both a reflection of and (in some cases) a catalyst for changes in the relations of men and women—both in the private and public spheres. Of necessity, however, our comments will be limited, since, as Linda Woodhead (2007b: 566) states:

> the Sociology of Religion has lagged behind many other fields in taking gender seriously. Whilst small-scale, ethnographic studies have been most likely to recognize the significance of gender, dominant theoretical frameworks within the Sociology of Religion often remain gender-blind. Although there has been some debate about why women, in the West at least, are more religious than men, this has largely taken place in isolation from what are still considered to be the "big" issues in the sociological analysis of religion, most notably issues concerning the growth and decline of religion in modern societies.

As will become apparent, though, religion is intimately wrapped up with issues of social order and social change in general, and more specifically issues of personal and group identity, and the related power differentials in society. The socially constructed and deeply engrained distinctions between masculinity and femininity in all societies, of the norms guiding the behaviour deemed characteristic of men and women, at home and at work, are a foundational feature of social life. As such they have been a focal interest of religious organizations and their belief systems. But as critics associated with the second wave of feminism in the 1960s and 70s began to assert, the dominant religions of the world all tended to obscure the crucial role played by women in the daily operation of those religions, while reinforcing cultural assumptions about the social and spiritual superiority of men. Consequently, there does appear to be a correlation between the liberation of women, as marked by such things as the use of birth control and their entry into the work force, and the decline of traditional religions. But as we will see, the reality is far more complex and women, like men, now have a diverse array of relationships with diverse types of religion and modes of religious expression.

In the end, then, whether one is sympathetic to religion or not, it is likely to continue to be a significant force for both good and evil in human affairs in the twenty-first century. This reality compels us to learn more about its nature and functioning, and how it is changing and yet staying the same.

Critical Thinking Questions

1.   Will (did) you get married in a church or will (did) you use some other traditional ceremony for your wedding? Why or why not, and what are the implications for the future of religion in our society?

2.   Is the "Highway of Heroes" (see Box 1.2) a religious activity? In what sense is this the case, and what does it say about the future of religion?

3.   Is the fear of death, at the level of the individual, or of social destruction, at the collective level, the most important reason for the existence of religion?

Suggested Readings

Bibby, Reginald. 2011. *Beyond the Gods and Back: Religion's Demise and Rise and Why it Matters.* Lethbridge, AB: Project Canada Books. Every five years since 1975, Bibby has run national surveys examining the religious beliefs and practices of Canadian adults, providing us with one of the most detailed overviews of the religious life of any country. This book is one of the latest in a series of publications that provides easy access to a compendium of data and insights into the religious life of Canadians.

Eliade, Mircea. 1959. *The Sacred and the Profane: The Nature of Religion.* San Diego, CA: Harcourt Brace Jovanovich. This classic text by one of the leading scholars of comparative religion was designed to introduce students to a basic understanding of the way ancient societies structured their worlds, their fundamental sense of the nature of time and place and the meaning of events in terms of the intrusion of the sacred into the profane, and the legacy of this traditional way of thinking for the rest of human history.

Roof, Wade Clark. 1999. *Spiritual Marketplace: Baby Boomers and the Remaking of American Religion.* Princeton, New Jersey: Princeton University Press. Basing his work on excellent national survey data, Roof presents a clear and comprehensive description and analysis of the sweeping and unprecedented changes in the religious views and practices of Americans since the end of the Second World War. While over a decade old, the book still provides one of the best guides to the nature of the changes working their way through the most religious modern nation on the planet.

Related Websites

www.sociologyofreligion.com

The Association for the Sociology of Religion is the flagship organization for sociologists of religion around the world to disseminate their theoretical, methodological, and empirical conclusions on an array of topics to do with religion. This website provides information regarding journal articles in the field (*Sociology of Religion*), past and upcoming conferences, and funding opportunities, as well as ways for students to get involved in the association.

www.theglobeandmail.com/commentary/the-future-of-religion-in-canada/article 1322000/?page=all

The *Globe and Mail*, a national newspaper in Canada, regularly invites religious leaders to discuss various things to do with religion. This website contains a lengthy conversation between "public" figures from the Roman Catholic, Hindu, Evangelical, Jewish, and Muslim traditions regarding the possible future of religion in Canada. There is also a link in this article to the first four articles in this five-part series on the "Future of Faith in Canada."

2 Defining Religion

Learning Objectives

In this chapter, you will learn:

◎ To understand the comparative advantages and disadvantages of various definitions of religion.

◎ To recognize that the process of defining religion is an activity with scientific and academic implications and social and political consequences.

◎ To understand the postmodernist critique of "religion" as an ethnocentric social construct.

◎ To see how the lack of a consensus on the definition of religion poses problems for the law in Canada and elsewhere.

Introduction

Few tasks have proved as troublesome as answering the simple question "What is religion?" We all have our working notions of "religion" that serve us reasonably well in daily life. We can talk fairly easily about religious beliefs and practices with our friends and others. But, as indicated in Chapter 1, our naïve view is based on limited experience. It is derived largely from what is normally considered religious, at any time, in our society. Most Canadians realize, however, that going to church, listening to sermons, and singing hymns, is only one way of being religious, and that the sheer diversity of ways people are religious around the world, and now in Canada as well, poses problems for our traditional views. In our increasingly global and pluralistic societies we are encountering situations where the boundaries of our unexamined folk conceptions of religion are being challenged.

Some of these instances are fairly common and may not overly concern us. The Church of Scientology, a new religion founded in the United States in 1954, for example, has been the focus of controversy for decades and it is often in the news as a result. At the heart of the controversy is the ongoing dispute over whether it is a religion (Melton, 2000; Lewis, 2009). Legally the matter was decided in the favour of the Scientologists, in the United States at least, when the Internal Revenue Service granted the group religious status for tax purposes in 1993. But that decision came only after a prolonged, expensive, and acrimonious legal struggle. Many other nations, including Canada, have yet to offer the same status to the group or have chosen to deny the request when it was made. Scientology is a religion in the eyes of the law in Sweden, for example, but not in Germany. It is interesting to note the variation since it points to the lack of agreement on what does or does not constitute a religion from society to society. The consequences for the Church of Scientology are significant, since the legal designation brings with it a host of rights associated with the various constitutional provisions assuring the freedom of religious expression in most Western nations. More pragmatically, it can also mean, as it does in the US, that donations made to the group are tax exempt, a significant financial benefit not shared by the Church of Scientology in Canada.

But this is likely of little concern to most Canadians or to you direct-ly. Things might change, however, if one of your close friends became a Scientologist and started dedicating a great deal of their time and money to the organization. Then, depending on your circumstances and attitudes, the determination of whether the group is a legitimate religion will matter. It will influence how the balance of the rights of the group and individuals are protected by your society. What you can or cannot do to address the concerns you have about your friend's involvement will be shaped by the of-ficial status of the group, and to some extent by the popular understanding of the group's legitimacy.

The same concern applies to all other groups who may wish to do things in your community that you are not comfortable with or in principle find unacceptable, from the public celebration of religious rites to the practice of polygamy. The guarantees of religious freedom ensconced in the Canadian Charter of Rights and Freedoms and the Constitution are designed to pro-tect religious minorities from the unwarranted interference of the majority, and everyone's religious beliefs and practices from the coercion of the state (e.g., Moon, 2008). These rights were first won in Europe and the Americas after centuries of turmoil and strife stemming from the persecution of one religious group by another or by the state. Put simply, a great deal of blood has been spilled to win the right of individuals to practise their religion free-ly. Democracy itself depends on the creation and protection of these rights, yet they are explicitly denied at times and in various ways in almost all na-tions, and more flagrantly so in some. Despite constitutional provisions for religious freedom, there is little real freedom for most religions in contem-porary Russia, for example, where the influence of the Russian Orthodox Church holds sway over the government (e.g., Richardson, Krylova, and Shterin, 2004; Richardson, 2006). But even in Canada, a society that in-creasingly takes pride in its pluralistic and multicultural nature, the reli-gious rights of individuals and groups can become the focus of public and legal dispute. The issues may range from the right of male Sikhs to avoid wearing helmets while riding motorcycles, because of their religious obligation to wear turbans, to the right of certain Muslim women to remain veiled while testifying in court, or members of certain new religions to import various hallucinogenic and illegal substances for use as a sacrament in their religious services (e.g., Santo Dame, The Church of the Universe). As more and more Canadians will be practitioners of religious or spiritual activities that fall outside the easy confines of what has conventionally passed for religion in Canada the need, academically, legally, and just personally, to determine what is a "religion" or is "religious" will become more urgent and significant. But the sheer diversity of what people have considered religious through the ages and around the world has stymied scholars for a long time, and hundreds of articles and books have been written on how best to define religion.

To cast some light on this complex issue and help you to start thinking more critically about the nature of religion we do four things in this chapter. First, we discuss the pros and cons of the dominant ways sociologists of religion have tried to solve the definitional problem. Second, we examine how recent late or postmodern approaches to the question have reconfigured the debate by highlighting the unique historical and social influences that have shaped the academic discussion and framed the conception of "religion." Third, we propose a pragmatic way out of the dilemmas posed by the current debate on defining religion by reverting to Wittgenstein's notion of **"family resemblances."** Fourth, we highlight the serious social implications of the lack of a clear definition of religion by examining the problems it poses for the resolution of legal disputes involving religious beliefs and practices.

Traditional Approaches and Problems

So when we refer to something as a "religion," what exactly do we mean? Regrettably, there is no easy answer to this question because there is no consensus in sociology. The diversity of things that people have held sacred through the centuries, and the practices they have adopted relative to these sacred things, are so vast as to defy easy inclusion under any one definition. But to determine what, if any, role religion plays in any society we are studying, or how significant a presence religion continues to have in late modern societies in general, we have to know, provisionally at least, what we mean by religion. How else can we find it and have some basis for saying how it differs from society to society (e.g., between Iran and Canada) or has changed over time (Canada in the 1890s and the 1990s)? Luckily there is considerable agreement on some key theoretical and methodological issues bearing on the creation and use of definitions of religion, and much can be learned by getting to know them. When pressed, most sociologists revert to a pragmatic definition of religion suited to their immediate empirical task or theoretical interest. These definitions tend to reflect a range of possibilities configured along a continuum anchored by **substantive definitions** at one end and **functional definitions** at the other. In thinking about what religion is we need to be aware of the advantages and limitations of these two definitional options.

Substantive definitions try to delineate the presumably crucial features of all religious activity. They focus on what religion "is," or its essential nature. A classic and simple example is provided by the British anthropologist Edward Tylor (1871), who succinctly defined religion as "belief in Spiritual Beings." Alternatively, functional definitions focus on what religion "does," or how it functions in society, and a simple and classic example is provided by the American sociologist of religion Milton Yinger: "Religion [is] a system of beliefs and practices by means of which a group struggles with [the] ultimate problems of human life" (1970: 7). Each approach has its well-known limitations, and many sociologists have devised definitions that attempt to blend the two perspectives while minimizing their liabilities.

Substantive definitions tend to be too exclusive. Tylor's definition, for example, has been criticized on three counts. First, the definition suggests that religions are primarily sets of beliefs. Critics have found this problematic in two different ways. Some critics note that it is often not the case, in any strict sense, for the religious practices of most preliterate peoples and even the followers of some other historically important and contemporary forms of religious expression. They have in mind such groups as the Quakers (i.e., The Religious Society of Friends) and the Wiccans (adherents of various forms of modern witchcraft). In both cases, their beliefs are quite fluid and not encoded in any definitive set of texts accepted by all as authoritative. Moreover, holding certain beliefs is often secondary in some traditions (for example, Hinduism and Daoism) to participating in specific rituals and other shared activities. Orthopraxis (right practice) may take precedence over orthodoxy (right belief).

The stress on belief may manifest an ethnocentric bias since it is so characteristic of the great religions of the West—Judaism, Christianity, and Islam, the so-called religions of the book (that is, the Bible and the Qur'an)—and most particularly of the Protestantism dominant in Britain at the time Tylor framed his definition. Protestants rebelled against the emphasis on the mediating role of the church, priests, saints, and the sacraments in the Catholic Church, in favour of an emphasis on the direct relationship of each believer to his creator, as mediated by an understanding of the Bible. They advocated "the priesthood of all believers." The focus on practice, or salvation by works as the Protestant reformers characterized the traditional Catholic approach, was displaced by a focus on the piety of the individual and the saving grace of God. Ritual, in other words, took a back seat to belief, in the form of knowledge of the word of God, as recorded in the Bible, and the profession of allegiance to a set creed.

Other critics of Tylor's definition are bothered more by the emphasis he places on the cognitive aspects of being religious. They prefer to stress the role the emotions play in religious life—in other words, the affective aspects of religion. Religion is about what we feel and sense first, and only secondarily about how these feelings become associated with certain beliefs (e.g., Riis and Woodhead, 2010). In most instances people learn to be religious, whether it lasts or not, through exposure to activities as children. This happens long before a full comprehension of the relevant beliefs is even possible, and people tend to continue to practise the rites of their religious traditions with limited real knowledge of their doctrinal meaning. Ask anyone in the pews during a Catholic mass or participating in *puja* at a Hindu temple in your community, at random points, why the priest is performing specific ritual acts, and you will discover, as many quizzical teenagers do, that few adult believers understand what is happening and why. Yet this lack of specific understanding impeaches neither the sincerity of their religious convictions nor the efficacy of their faith in their lives.

Second, the specification of "Spiritual Beings" in Tylor's definition of religion also works to questionably exclude some forms of religion. Contemporary neo-pagans and some Buddhists, for example, either see such a belief as optional or they formally deny it. There is no absolute God, or strictly any gods at all, for example, in the foundational teachings of Theravada Buddhism of southeast Asia. In all other regards, however, Theravadin Buddhists appear to be practising a religion, and little is gained empirically by denying that fact. Émile Durkheim ([1912] 1995: 28–31), for instance, uses this very case to refute the validity of Tylor's definition.

But many others argue, rejecting Durkheim's line of reasoning (e.g., Spiro, 1966; Stark and Finke, 2000), that the popular practice of Theravada Buddhism, in Sri Lanka, Thailand, Myanmar, Cambodia, Vietnam, and elsewhere is suffused with worship of the Buddha as a god-like figure and the extensive use of rites to propitiate various lesser spirits and demons. Are the ways in which common people misunderstand or mis-practise a religion grounds, however, for discounting the canonical creeds of a group? Can they be used to deny the relevance of Durkheim's criticism of Tylor? The activity in question does not alter the fact that Theravada Buddhism formally repudiates the existence of such gods and declares the Buddha to be merely an extraordinary man. It is common in most religions for devotees to acknowledge certain doctrines while contradictorily engaging in other practices. Canadian Catholics recognize the authority of the Pope, yet they regularly defy his teachings on birth control, divorce, and other social issues. The contrast between formal doctrine and actual practice may be more pronounced in the case of Theravada Buddhism, but that fact does not refute the argument made by Durkheim and others (e.g., Herbrechtsmeier, 1993; Hamilton, 1995). Is a religion to be judged by what it formally says are its beliefs and practices, or by what many ordinary believers happen to do?

Third, Tylor's substantive definition raises a problem that is common to almost all definitions of religion: it relies on terms that are themselves in need of further definition. In this case, we might simply ask "What constitutes a 'spiritual' being?" Can you define "spiritual" without reverting to other terms whose meaning is equally vague and problematic?

Attempts to circumvent this problem by substituting other similar terms have not proved very successful. The anthropologist Melford Spiro (1966: 96), for example, proposed defining religion as "an institution consisting of culturally patterned interaction with culturally postulated superhuman beings." The reference to "superhuman" does allow for the formal inclusion of the Buddha, and hence Theravada Buddhism, but what are we to make of the prefix "super"? Is the reference to "superhuman beings" any clearer than "spiritual beings"? Malcolm Hamilton asks (1995: 15) "How powerful or extraordinary does a human being have to be to be considered superhuman?" Does Hitler qualify? His accomplishments, no matter how ultimately reprehensible, were certainly remarkable and he was the object of intense and consequential adoration by tens of millions of people. Moreover, as the example shows, the conception of what is superhuman varies too much from culture to culture, if only because the essence of being "human" is also extremely relative cross-culturally (Herbrechtsmeir, 1993).

Functional definitions suffer from the opposite tendency of substantive ones: they are often too inclusive. Their terms of reference tend to be so broad that it is difficult to distinguish true religions from what sociologists call functional equivalents (e.g., an intense involvement in a political ideology). In addition, they too frequently invite an infinite regress of definitional questions. Yinger's definition focuses on struggles with the ultimate problems of human life, but what constitutes an "ultimate" problem? Further specification is needed, and disagreements are likely with any list of ultimate problems or criteria for what is "ultimate." Plus, who is to say what is ultimate: the believer or some outside observer? Is it appropriate to suggest, for example, that the worldview of radical environmentalists is their religion? What if they display an abiding concern with being a good environmentalist, perhaps even at the cost of laying down their lives to protect some endangered species or ecological niche? Risking one's life is surely an indication of the ultimate nature of their concern, but is their sacrifice religious? Expanding the criteria used to judge something religious helps to attune us to forms of religious life that defy conventional notions of religion, which is beneficial, especially in a late modern context. But in the last analysis does the inclusion of such activities within the bounds of religion help, or does such talk simply blur the boundaries between phenomena in ways that are analytically unhelpful? If everything is potentially religious, is anything actually religious? Functionalist definitions, Spiro charges, make it "virtually impossible to set any substantive boundary to religion and, thus, to distinguish it from other socio-cultural phenomena" (1966: 89). But how then could we determine whether any society is more religious than another or becoming more secular? Too many things become religious, the critics charge, when the functionalist perspective is adopted.

In framing their definitions of religion, sociologists must seek to balance the relative strengths and limitations of these options in the service of their immediate research objectives. Some of the most famous definitions of religion have incorporated elements of both the substantive and the functional approaches. Durkheim, for instance, defined religion as "a unified system of beliefs and practices relative to sacred things ... which unite into one single moral community ... all those who adhere to them" ([1912] 1995: 44). The substantive element is concern with the sacred, which is used to differentiate religion from other activities. The functional element is reflected in the identification of religion with the creation of moral communities. Does this approach, however, dissolve the definitional dilemma or merely compound it? It is difficult to say in principle, and much will depend on how it is used.

Certain limitations in Durkheim's approach, however, should stand out by now. First, we can ask, "What does Durkheim mean by the 'sacred'?" This is yet another notoriously slippery term (Segal et al., 1991; Idinopulos and Yonan, 1996). Can we define what is "sacred" any better than terms like "spiritual," "supernatural," or "superhuman"? Durkheim refers to the sacred as "things set apart and forbidden" ([1912] 1995: 44), and he suggests that the distinguishing feature of religion is its very division of the world into two categorically opposed orders of existence, the sacred and the profane. The latter is simply all that is not sacred, and the sacred can be almost anything. People, places, objects—crafted and natural—of every type, have been sacred at one time or another, in one place or another, in the course of human history. Nothing intrinsically distinguishes sacred things. Rather, sacredness is something people attribute to different things, which then gives them a wholly other status that is revered and feared. Durkheim's theory of religion rests on understanding why this happens (see Chapter 4). Some scholars, however, have questioned whether the division of the world into sacred and profane spheres is as universal as Durkheim supposes (Worsley, 1968).

One of the other great founding figures of the sociology of religion, Max Weber, refused altogether to settle on a definition of religion (Weber [1922] 1964: 1). Perhaps he feared it would introduce an unwarranted theoretical bias into his studies, one which might restrict his gaze artificially. Weber's own masterful work ranged over the cultures of the world—both geographically and historically—in ways few other scholars have dared to emulate. He aspired, moreover, to a value-free sociology and recognized that the act of defining social phenomena often involved, wittingly or unwittingly, the exercise of power in society. Minimally, as we have seen, setting a definition involves a process of either inclusion or exclusion, and good sociologists would always ask who benefits from imposing these parameters? We must be attuned not only to the critical assessment of the intrinsic merits of definitions, but also in many cases to the social and cultural reasons for imposing them. As indicated at the start of this chapter, disputes over the legitimacy of the claims of different groups to be a religion are becoming increasingly common. Consequently, as Arthur Greil and David Bromley suggest (2003: 5):

> It may be useful . . . to view religion, not as a characteristic that inheres in certain phenomena, but as a cultural resource over which competing interest groups vie. From this perspective, religion is not an entity but a claim made by certain groups and—in some cases—contested by others, to the right to the privileges associated in a given society with the religious label.

We will have more to say about this perspective below.

Durkheim would disagree with this view, arguing that no matter how leery we are of making incorrect generalizations or imposing our will, we are always working with some implicit conception of religion. So it is best to make our definitions explicit in order to avoid falling prey to unintended biases and untested assumptions. Thus, in the end, framing a specific definition at the beginning may well serve the ideal of value neutrality in the social sciences better than Weber's reticence to do so.

There is no simple way to resolve this clash of views. In truth we are facing a hermeneutical (i.e., interpretive) circle. Any definition we frame will be tested by the new knowledge we acquire, leading us sometimes to modify it. But in the absence of an initial definition we are less likely to note the anomalies that call our attention to new information in the first place. We need the definition to bring some order to the confusing array of data and possibilities. But the inherent limitations of the frame will point us to new things to be considered. In negotiating this feedback loop between data and theory (i.e., our definition of religion) we must keep a critical eye on the social and legal implications of our reasoning.

So, in the end, should we define religion or not? Should we use a substantive or a functional approach? On the whole, we agree with Hamilton when he argues that functionalist definitions tend to be framed in ways that render them non-falsifiable and hence of limited scientific merit. With the functional aspect of Durkheim's definition clearly in mind, Hamilton says (1995: 18):

. . . such definitions [seem] to prejudge the important empirical question of the role or effects that religion does have in society by stating in the very definition of it what ought to be demonstrated empirically. This allows defence, for example, of a functionalist theory which claims that religion is a universal factor in social life because it is essential for the integration of society and the promotion of social stability, against any evidence that could be cited in refutation of it. If a society were to be described in which there did not appear to be any system of religion, the functionalist could reply that absence of something which looked like religion in the conventional sense does not invalidate the theory because any set of values and beliefs which promote integration and stability is, for such a theorist, religion. By defining religion at the outset as that which promotes stability the theory cannot be wrong and no evidence can count against it. It becomes a non-empirical statement which would be true not as a matter of fact but by definition. The possibility of it being false is ruled out of consideration with the consequence that it becomes immune to the test of evidence and loses its explanatory value.

This is an important criticism, so with Hamilton we favour working with a more substantive approach (e.g., Dawson, 1987), one that draws a line in the sand around all those things meant to be considered religious. We favour, however, a very minimal definition to capture as much as possible of the diverse array of phenomena conventionally conceived as religious. From this perspective other things may be religious-like, yet still not religions *per se*. The trick is to find a criterion or set of criteria that are methodologically sound (i.e., that can be empirically detected and assessed), make a real difference (i.e., that truly differentiate things), and avoid the infinite regress and ethnocentrism typical of most of the substantive criteria proposed so far (and functional ones as well). That is a tall order. But it is a worthy and feasible aspiration and the resultant definition can be useful if it is applied in a pragmatic and not doctrinaire way. We will return to what we have in mind in saying this, after pausing to consider the more strident critique of the whole effort to define "religion" that has developed in recent years.

In the interim, however, we encourage you to take a try at resolving the definitional puzzle, with the further assistance of the examples provided in Box 2.1. Are these definitions characteristic of substantive or functional approaches, or both?

The Late or Postmodern Critique of "Religion" as a Category

Recently, under the influence of the late modern impetus to reflexivity, many researchers have chosen to stress the contextual nature of all our conceptions of religion. The ideas and practices that get called religious are social

Box 2.1   Six Well-Known Definitions of Religion

In his famous Gifford Lectures, published as *The Varieties of Religious Experience*, the American philosopher and psychologist William James states ([1902] 1994: 31): "Religion therefore ... shall mean for us *the feelings, acts, and experiences of individual men in their solitude, so far as they apprehend themselves to stand in relation to whatever they may consider the divine.*"

In his book *Dynamics of Faith*, the renowned German-American theologian Paul Tillich defined "faith," which he thought to be the core of religious experience, as "the state of being ultimately concerned." (1957: 1)

In one of the best known essays on defining religion, "Religion as Cultural System," the American anthropologist Clifford Geertz says ([1966] 1973) that "a religion is: (1) a system of symbols which acts to (2) establish powerful, pervasive, and long-lasting moods and motivations in men by (3) formulating conceptions of a general order of existence and (4) clothing these conceptions with such an aura of factuality that (5) the moods and motivations seem uniquely realistic."

In his book *The Invisible Religion*, the German sociologist Thomas Luckmann boldly asserts (1967: 49): "It is in keeping with an elementary sense of the concept of religion to call the transcendence of biological nature by the human organism a religious phenomenon."

In *Acts of Faith: Explaining the Human Side of Religion* the prominent American sociologists of religion Rodney Stark and Roger Finke assert (2000: 91, 278): "Religion consists of very general explanations of existence, including the terms of exchange with a god or gods." "Explanations," in their theory of religion, are defined as "conceptual simplifications or models of reality that often provide plans designed to guide action" (2000: 87, 277).

The British sociologist Steve Bruce says (2002: 200): "I see no great difficulty in defining religion as beliefs, actions, and institutions that assume the existence of supernatural entities with powers of action, or impersonal powers or processes possessed of moral purpose."

constructions born of specific times and places, and in line with postmodernist sensibilities; it is futile to search for any universal or essential features or functions. "Religion," it is argued, is more a category of thought and discourse, with specific historical and social roots and implications, than it is a thing. It cannot be assumed to exist as an entity independent of human interaction and social definitions. In the words of Greil and Bromley (2003: 5): "In this view, religion is a term that social actors have used in certain societies and at certain times to understand and describe an important aspect of their experiences." When scholars of religion talk about "religion," and not the specific aspects of some religious traditions *per se*, they are creating and using an abstract concept, much like "social class" or "social system," that does not have a simple ostensive reference.

Jonathan Z. Smith provides one of the best known statements of this point of view at the very beginning of his well-known book *Imagining Religion* (1982: xi):

> That is to say, while there is a staggering amount of data, of phenomena, of human experiences and expressions that might be characterized in one culture or another, by one criterion or another as religious—*there is no data for religion*. Religion is solely the creation of the scholar's study. It is created for the scholar's analytic purposes by his imaginative acts of comparison and generalization. Religion has no existence apart from the academy.

Wilfred Cantwell Smith (1962), Peter Byrne (1989), Peter Harrison (1990), Jonathan Smith (1998), and others have clarified the specific historical and socio-political context in which the very notion of "religion" was developed in European society. Talal Asad (1993), Russell McCutcheon (1999), Peter Beyer (1998, 2003a, 2003b), Dubuisson ([1998] 2003), Timothy Fitzgerald (1999), Masuzawa (2005), and others have established its ideological role in social and cultural disputes, the context of imperialism and globalization, and the creation of the discipline of religious studies.

Put simply, these studies demonstrate things that help put our discussion of the nature of "religion" into proper historical perspective. They reveal that the concepts "religion," "religions," and "religious" are relatively new, in the historical scheme of things. They also are distinctly European in derivation. For much of the history of Europe there were no religions, just religion and non-religion. In other words, there were Christians and heathens. This changed as Europeans experienced more encounters with other societies and Christendom itself became more divided and torn by the religious wars set off by the Protestant Reformation (1517–1648). As Jonathan Z. Smith succinctly states (1998: 271): "It is the question of the plural *religions* (both Christian and non-Christian) that forced a new interest in the singular, generic *religion*."

This conclusion is born of several insights. First, during the several centuries that Europeans explored and colonized the globe, repeated attempts were made to map and classify the new forms of belief encountered. These efforts culminated in the notion that there are several so-called "world religions" (i.e., Christianity, Judaism, Islam, Hinduism, Buddhism, Confucianism, and Daoism), as well as many other lesser religions (e.g., Jainism, Zoroastrianism, Inuit aboriginal beliefs, Cargo Cults). But this system of classification gives priority to belief systems that resemble what the West considers "religions."

Second, the terms "religion" and "religious" were adapted for this purpose from their more restrictive usage in earlier periods of European history. Some scholars argue that the term was originally used to designate only the formal expression of cultic rites and piety, and not as a "name for a system of ideas and beliefs" (W.C. Smith, 1962); others (e.g., J.Z. Smith, 1998) argue that it referred only to those who dedicated their lives to the quest for salvation and the service of the Church by becoming monks, nuns, or priests. It was these specialists who were identified as "religious" and the rites they performed that were "religious." Ordinary people, however, did not think of themselves as belonging to certain "religions." That idea only emerged much later in Europe during the seventeenth and eighteenth centuries, in the age of exploration, fledgling international trade, and religious strife. Only then, and later under the critical gaze of Enlightenment philosophers, did the idea emerge of an independent thing called "religion" whose essence could be discerned (e.g., Hume, [1757] 1976; Feuerbach, [1841] 1957) and to which people belonged. Ironically, by then talk of "religion" was often actually driven by the desire to free society from the tyranny of religious authority by differentiating the realms of the state and civil society from that of "religion." It was the Enlightenment quest for a less religious society that established our notion of religion as a set of religious beliefs and practices to which people commit voluntarily and which is distinct and set apart from the rest of society.

Third, in developing the new analyses and classifications of religion and religions, scholars struggled with the fact that most other cultures seemed to lack any equivalent words and distinctions. Religion, as an activity, was not segregated, either conceptually or in practice, from the rest of cultural life, and indigenous lexical equivalents were often missing. As the European and American missionaries and colonial administrators who descended on South America, Africa, India, China, and elsewhere discovered, there were no equivalents to their religious notions of "belief," "experience," "sin," and "salvation." But many of these and other concepts were imposed on these societies through the cultural influence of the more economically and militarily powerful European nations.

Fourth, this cultural conquest included the introduction of the idea that people have "religions"—distinct from the simple and relatively unthinking expression of their native culture. It was the local political and cultural elite, however, who adopted and propagated this idea (Beyer, 1998, 2003b). They did so to bring their societies more in line with the dominant foreign powers and reap the material benefits of such alliances, and to inoculate their own religio-cultural heritages against being impugned by Western scholars as primitive, idolatrous, or not truly religious. In the process they rewrote the histories of their own "religions" in the image of Western conceptions, importing many ideas that Indian, Chinese, and Japanese scholars had learned from their exposure to Western philosophy, theology, and culture. These somewhat distorted versions of the other "religions" of the world were then, ironically, introduced to the West by Eastern scholars, confirming many Western assumptions, though often in a rather romanticized form (Sharf, 1998; Masuzawa, 2005).

Social and historical research of this kind has led to an increased recognition that Christianity provided the prototype for conceptions of "religion." The meaning of this term has been shaped by a uniquely European history and by the expansion of European colonial power (Dubuisson, [1998] 2003). Consequently, some scholars (e.g., Fitzgerald, 1999), think the very word "religion" is too ideologically tainted to be academically serviceable anymore. It is too ethnocentric and modern. But the terms "religion" and "religious" are now almost universal in usage, and others argue that there is little to be gained from abandoning them at this point (e.g., Saler, 1993; Beyer, 2003a). Andrew McKinnon observes (2002: 77), for example, that

> "[r]eligion" has become part of the global political-economic discourse, enshrined, for example, in Article 18 of the Universal Declaration of Human Rights. This has been translated (more or less adequately, no doubt) into more than 300 different languages, from Abhkaz to Zulu, suggesting the concept has a kind of global currency.

The word "religion" has a history. It has its origins in a specific set of historical and cultural circumstances and it is important to know something about this history so we may guard against the reification of the term or smugly assuming it has a universal application. But like all words, it now functions independently of its origins and history, and the current meaning and use is as valid as any other. As the Canadian scholar Peter Beyer concludes (2003a: 151), "religion in contemporary global society seems to be an ineluctable reality at least as important and real as a number of other abstractions like culture, race, nation, and gender on the one hand, and sport, health, and art, on the other."

We are left, then, with a potentially paradoxical state of affairs: on the one hand, it seems, everyone knows what religion is, but on the other hand, when pressed, no one really does. So how should we to proceed? Minimally, much is to be gained from setting the definitional debate aside for a time and considering instead the basic dimensions of religion (see Chapter 4). In describing the dimension or elements of religion, however, much of the late modernist critique of the language we commonly use to talk about "religion" is replicated. Similar critiques apply to the very categories commonly used to organize the discussion, namely belief, ritual, experience, and community. There is no escaping this dilemma, but it does not block comprehension of the issues, which is imperative for any meaningful discussion of religion today.

The Family Resemblance Approach

In the end can we simply say that whatever people call religion is religion? It is tempting to do so, but then we lose the ability to make systematic comparisons and generalizations about this phenomenon, let alone be critical. If we are going to ponder whether religion is growing, declining, changing, or staying the same in late modern societies, then we need to be able to meaningfully differentiate between religion and its functional equivalents, between religion and a political ideology such as Communism, and between religion and a fanatical commitment to protecting the environment. Yet we also need to stay open to new forms of religious life. In the end most sociologists seek to strike a balance between the exclusive and inclusive tendencies of substantive and functional definitions, and are content to follow the lead of the great philosopher Ludwig Wittgenstein. Wittgenstein began his career trying to rigorously reduce all knowledge to the formal principles of logic (Wittgenstein, [1921] 1974), but in his maturity he famously reversed his position and advocated what became known as ordinary language philosophy. Philosophers seeking wisdom would do well to pay attention to the way words are used in everyday life to best discern their actual meaning and significance (Wittgenstein, [1953] 1958). Specifically, he suggests that almost all of our concepts operate through a principle of "family resemblance." This approach is still substantive, but there is no definitive list of criteria for saying when something is or is not a religion, any more than there is for other things, such as music, medicine, or murder. To use one of his examples, do all "games" share a distinguishing feature that makes them a class of things? In what sense are playing golf, football, and solitaire with cards all games? In the practice of science, just as in life, we make sense of things by bringing a cluster of related attributes to bear on a situation and then making a judgement about whether something belongs to that category. Some things display more of some of the features we have in mind; others display more of other features. But as long as there is sufficient overlap we are inclined to identify them as being the same kind of thing. Benson Saler (1993), Peter Clarke and Peter Byrne (1993), Alan Aldridge (2000), Andrew McKinnon (2002), and others, have argued the merits of taking a similar approach to the problem of defining religion. We will do so in combination with an emphasis on four features or dimensions of religion—belief, ritual, experience, and community—which are universally characteristic of religion, as discussed in the next chapter.

For most sociologists the term *religion* is a social construction. But once again, saying so does not mean either that the phenomenon is not real in its consequences or that the concept is not useful in making sense of the world around us. It merely means we must exercise due caution in treating the phenomenon and using the terms, and that we must try to avoid reifying them (i.e., making them into independently existing things) and launching a search for their true meaning and essence, when they are in fact only useful social constructions.

The Problematic Relationship of Religion and the Law in Canada

As we have indicated several times, the issue of determining what is and is not religious can have significant legal implications. In dealing with disputes involving religious claims, actions, and institutions the courts face a structural dilemma (at least in most democracies): by law they must uphold the principle of freedom of religion, yet some religious acts, or at least one's claimed to be legitimately religious, may be in conflict with the enforcement of laws established to protect the best interests of the public. Some of the obvious points where there may be contention are marriage regulations; military conscription; sexual, educational, and disciplinary practices involving children; the religious use of illicit substances (i.e., drugs); the use of public spaces for religious purposes; various conflicts between forms of religious expression and the interests and regulations of corporate bodies, both private and public (e.g., with regard to land use and building regulations); and health issues (e.g., the rejection of certain types of medical treatment). The courts in Canada and elsewhere are repeatedly asked to adjudicate between these fundamental and competing interests. In doing so they are compelled, explicitly and implicitly, to grapple with the definition of religion. In the absence of a scholarly consensus on which judges can rely, the law has proceeded to decide cases on a more ad hoc basis, resulting in a rather confusing set of judgements (see e.g., Moon 2008). We cannot address the history of precedents here, but we wish to delineate some of the difficulties commonly encountered to further highlight the broader social significance of the issue of defining religion.

In Canada the freedom of religion is constitutionally protected by Section 2 (a) of the Charter of Rights and Freedoms, which specifies that everyone has the fundamental freedom of conscience and religion. The most influential current precedent guiding the court is the Supreme Court's decision in Syndicat Northcrest v. Amselem (2004). The case involved a dispute between a group of Orthodox Jews and the business running the condominium apartment building in which they lived. Several of these individuals had built *succahs*, small dwellings to be used during the holiday of *Succot*, as prescribed by the Hebrew Bible, on the balconies of their apartments. The company running the buildings said this violated the by-laws governing the condominium property and they sought to stop this practice. The Jews responded that this restriction violated their rights under the charter. In framing a decision in favour of the Orthodox Jews the Supreme Court made two stipulations that have been used to guide many later decisions. First, in paragraph 39 the judgement proposed:

> In order to define religious freedom, we must first ask ourselves what we mean by "religion." While it is perhaps not possible to define religion precisely, some outer definition is useful since only beliefs, convictions and practices rooted in religion, as opposed to those that are secular, socially based or conscientiously held, are protected by the guarantee of freedom of religion. Defined broadly, religion typically involves a particular and comprehensive system of faith and worship. Religion also tends to involve the belief in a divine, superhuman or controlling power. In essence, religion is about freely and deeply held personal convictions or beliefs connected to an individual's spiritual faith and integrally linked to one's self-definition and spiritual fulfilment, the practices of which allow individuals to foster a connection with the divine or with the subject or object of that spiritual faith.

Second, in paragraph 46 the Supreme Court concluded:

> [F]reedom of religion consists of the freedom to undertake practices and harbour beliefs, having a nexus with religion, in which an individual demonstrates he or she sincerely believes or is sincerely undertaking in order to connect with the divine or as a function of his or her spiritual faith. Irrespective of whether a particular practice or belief is required by official dogma or is in conformity with the position of religious officials.

In reverting to a largely substantive and rather common-sense definition of religion in the first paragraph cited, the court displays the common tendency to reify the mainstream Christian conceptions of religion dominant in Canada. In this regard legally legitimate religions have "comprehensive systems of faith and worship" and they are about belief in "the divine" or some equivalent. Moreover there is an assumption that the spheres of the sacred and secular can and should be neatly separated, which is a modern and Western notion. But as we have seen this is not universally the case, especially for many new religions. Some religions do not favour or have yet to develop codified systems of beliefs and practices, or their beliefs may place little or no stress on the idea of worshipping deities (e.g., Quakers, Unitarian-Universalists, neo-pagans, Scientologists). It may also be the

case that they categorically reject the subordination of religious authority to any kind of secular sphere of influence. Yet it is precisely these more
unconventional groups that are most likely to come under suspicion in society, meet with resistance, and need the protections of religious freedom
afforded by the law. In other words, there is a structural bias against many
new forms of religious expression in the law, yet it is the introduction of religious innovations to Canadian society, either through the importation of
non-Christian views or the invention of new religions, that often sparks the
conflicts that require legal adjudication (e.g., the right of young male Sikhs
to wear the *kirpan* in school). Holding to a too conventional conception
of religion will fail to protect the new and often eclectic spiritual rich-
ness of the lives of many Canadians. But the courts cannot serve the
interests of its citizens by simply adopting the lessons of the postmodernist
critique of "religion" and abandoning the search for a definition of religion.
Such a move, as the Canadian sociologist Lori Beaman notes (2008: 198),
"could eviscerate 'religious freedom' at a time when religious minorities are
particularly vulnerable."

The courts are caught in a paradoxical situation, for as Beaman as-
tutely observes (2008c: 197): "All of the categories of protection in the
Charter—race, sexual orientation, and gender, for example—rely to some
extent on the reproduction of the very category they name as being protected. Paradoxically, categorization in this context problematizes at the
same time as it protects. The discursive working up of categories and the
power relations and their sedimentations within it work to construct and
reinforce disciplinary practices." In other words, the very act of designating things to be protected calls into question their nature and how different social interests are served by the extension or restriction of the scope
of the protection offered under the law. We are forced to debate issues that
we might otherwise shirk or allow more amorphous social processes to
eventually resolve.

In implicit recognition of the difficulties of defining religion and in
the face of conflicting expert testimony about this issue, judges have relied increasingly on the second "sincerity" standard to reach decisions. As
the second paragraph cited indicates, a religious belief or action warrants
protection if the people involved truly believe it, whether or not it is required by or in conformity with the dictates of some officially recognized
religious authority. But in most cases this approach only appears to avoid
the definitional problem. The courts can choose to focus on this aspect of
belief, but it is difficult to see how they could test for the sincerity of beliefs
without learning about the contents of the beliefs and passing a judgement
on whether they seem plausible in some regard. This entails, of necessity,
seeking expert advice on the nature of specific religious traditions and religions in general.

In doing so it regrettably raises a second and perhaps even more problematic situation for the courts: How can they avoid being drawn into disputes about the actual nature of specific beliefs and whether they are theologically or doctrinally correct? This is particularly the case when legal disputes hinge on clashes of religious viewpoints, as when two parties are disputing the requirements for continuing to be a member of a specific religion. Likewise it arises when religious people dispute whether something individuals are doing is actually emblematic of the religion they claim to be "sincerely" practising. Is any claim, no matter how outlandish, to be accepted just because someone believes it to be true? Do the courts have the right, in essence, to strip religious groups of their capacity to regulate the behaviour of their own members and even determine who is or is not a member of the religion? In addressing the issue, even indirectly, the courts risk jeopardizing the very freedom of religion they wish to protect by becoming arbiters of what constitutes "good" and "bad" religion. The legal system cannot protect all religions by becoming the ultimate authority on the legitimacy of the beliefs and practices of specific religions.

More generally, how is sincerity to be determined? Should the courts be examining the actions of those claiming protection? Are the beliefs of individuals who attend church or other religious services regularly necessarily more sincere than those who attend less often, or even not at all? What are the relevant criteria for measuring sincerity? We think we know how to make such determinations, in an everyday sort of way. But how would we make the distinction when faced with alternative, but equally plausible, criteria—say, someone's relative knowledge of their religious tradition versus the amount time someone spends participating in its rites?

Lastly, both paragraphs from the Amselem case presuppose and prioritize the autonomy of the individual. This is a foundational value of Western social systems that has become ensconced in their legal systems. In many respects it grew out of the emphasis, born of the Protestant Reformation, placed on the right of people to choose their religions. But autonomy in these matters has not been the norm for most of human history and it is still not the norm for many other cultures and religious traditions, where the needs of the collective often take precedence over the rights of the individual (e.g., India, China, Japan, and many African societies). It is also true of many new religions (e.g., Mormons, Krishna Consciousness, Scientology). This is not taken into consideration sufficiently in the Canadian legal system's approach to religion. Individuals may prefer to defer to the authority of their traditions, even at considerable personal cost. To deny religions the right, in principle, to impose their will on deviant or recalcitrant individuals and groups, may amount to a denial of the right of their members to practise their religion.

Box 2.2   Mormons, Polygamy, and the Law in Canada

Polygamous practice among a tiny sect of fundamentalist Mormons in Canada has long been a contentious issue in the Canadian legal system. Historically, fundamentalist Mormons have defended polygamous relationships on several grounds including that they prevent husbands from seeking extra-marital affairs, keep older males feeling and looking young, and fulfill God's call to replenish the earth with many "righteous" children. They cite prominent figures in the Old Testament involved in polygamous relationships and assert that the greatest glory in the celestial realm after death is reserved for those in polygamous relationships (see e.g., Hansen, 1981: 156, 165; Ivins, 1992: 175–76; Quinn, 1993). Opposition to polygamy in Canada is based on beliefs that it creates disharmony in the family, it devalues women, it exploits children as child brides, and it condones or conceals physical and sexual abuse (see e.g., Ivins, 1992: 178; Beaman, 2004). In Canada's formative years, strict immigration controls ensured "desirable" immigrants, resulting in the 1890 anti-polygamy laws that banned "what among the persons commonly called Mormons is known as spiritual or plural marriage." Offenses were punishable by imprisonment. Mormons are no longer singled out in Section 293 of the Criminal Code, but anti-polygamy laws remain in Canada.

Legal debates surrounding polygamy are notoriously complex because of conflicts between Canada's emphasis on freedom of religion and personal privacy and other social values to do with gender, family, and safety. When in conflict, which Canadian values should gain saliency? The presence of fundamentalist Mormons who practice polygamy in Bountiful, British Columbia, is well documented and contested. The RCMP launched an investigation in Bountiful in 1991, but British Columbia's attorney general declined to lay charges against the group's leaders (Winston Blackmore and James Oler) because of anticipated legal conflicts with Canadian rights to liberty and privacy as well as religious freedom. In 2004 the RCMP received allegations of abuse among the sectarian community, prompting the attorney general to appoint a special prosecutor to the case. In 2007, the prosecutor discouraged laying charges in favour of exploring, through the British Columbia Court of Appeal, the constitutional validity of anti-polygamy laws. The attorney general disagreed and appointed a different prosecutor to the case, who arrived at the same conclusion as his

Conclusion

In many respects, then, we can study religion without worrying too much about defining it. We can examine its dimensions and their impact upon people's behaviour. But in our age in particular, when the very persistence and importance of religion is in doubt, we cannot side-step the hoary question predecessor. In 2008, the attorney general pursued a third prosecutor who eventually laid charges against Blackmore and Oler; however, the case was dropped in 2009 because of the attorney general's questionable process of selecting special prosecutors. In 2011, the British Columbia Supreme Court ruled that while anti-polygamy laws do conflict with religious freedom, the laws are constitutional because polygamy causes "harm to women, to children, to society and to the institution of monogamous marriage" (Smith, 2011). This ruling suggests that charges could still be laid against Blackmore and Oler, but this has yet to occur.

Without taking sides, it is important to recognize the role of power in this debate, both within and outside the community of Bountiful. Internally, men are extremely powerful, especially within family life. Women are without decision-making power in the religious organization as a whole and they appear to lack control over their own bodies and homes (though within the group they are socialized to believe they do have some control over such decisions). Young girls are denied a full education, the education they do receive is not in line with the provincial curriculum, and they are sometimes married-off as child brides. Accusations of physical and sexual abuse have been levelled by some women in Bountiful and in other polygamous Mormon families, and there appears to be reason for advocates of women's rights to be concerned about the treatment of some women in the community. Power dynamics are also at work, however, between the religious sect and the state. In this case, and many others in Canada, the state has the power to determine what is meant by religion, harm, and freedom, and to place the protection of certain Canadian values above others (see Beaman, 2004). In the process the constitutional rights of religious minorities are circumscribed and impaired. The Bountiful example reveals that political and legal spheres are not as neutral in their dealings with religious groups as is commonly claimed, a conclusion magnified when one asks why our society tends to accept the right of individuals, married or otherwise, to have several sexual partners simultaneously and to have children with more than one partner, while resolutely condemning similar activities in polygamous settings. If harm is the key issue, then the alleged crimes can and should be prosecuted, as they are in others circumstances. Is there further need for recourse to laws proscribing specific religiously sanctioned ways of life? Is there one law in Canada for mainstream religions and another for non-conformist and less "desirable" ones? As things stand, Muslims in polygamous relationships also are penalized, and they are not allowed to immigrate to Canada. Should the government and the courts be the ultimate arbiters of which religious beliefs and practices are legitimate in Canada?

of definition altogether. Hence the need to appreciate the differences between the basic definitional options before us, between the relative clarity but exclusivity of substantive approaches and the vagueness yet inclusivity of functional ones. We have recommended the overall scientific and pragmatic merits of combining a substantive orientation with a Wittgensteinian family resemblances approach. But in doing so, we all must now recognize the historical and ethnocentric heritage of many of our most basic conceptions of religion, of the very terms we so commonly use to talk about this complex and difficult to specify social phenomenon.

In the next chapter we look at some of the basic dimensions or elements of religious life. We may not be able to agree on a precise definition of religion, but in order to even talk about religion we need to at least share an awareness of certain pervasive features of religious phenomena. Our thoughts about and experiences of these basic elements or dimensions will inevitably determine our definitional proclivities and whether we think religion is consequential at all.

Critical Thinking Questions

1. Before reading this chapter, what was your working notion of "religion" and what limitations do you now think it had, if any, and why?

2. Given the many hurdles standing in the way of framing a truly universal definition of religion, can the term be used meaningfully and without prejudice in the contexts of legal disputes and international relations?

3. Is there something unique about the debate over the definition of religion as opposed to many other terms (e.g., social class, justice, health, or sport)? What is it and does it matter in the long run?

Suggested Readings

Geertz, Clifford. 1973 [1966]. "Religion as a Cultural System," in *The Interpretation of Cultures: Selected Essays*. New York: Basic Books. Geertz's famous essay still provides one of the most comprehensive and thoughtful introductions to the many defining elements and functions of religion, despite the criticisms of Talal Asad and others that it imposes a modern Western conceptions of religion on other cultures.

Greil, Arthur L. and David G. Bromley, eds. 2003. *Defining Religion: Investigating the Boundaries Between the Sacred and the Secular. Religion and the Social Order, Vol. 10*. New York: JAI. This is an excellent collection of essays by sociologists of religion and religious studies scholars surveying and assessing most of the recent arguments about the socially constructed character of our conceptions of "religion" as an analytical category, and about the social and political uses and implications of how we define religion.

Moon, Richard, ed. 2008. *Law and Religious Pluralism in Canada*. Vancouver, BC: University of British Columbia Press. The thoughtful essays in this book demonstrate the uneasy and complex nature of the relationship between the law and religion in Canada with regard to the role of religious values in public decision making, government support for religious activities, and the restriction and accommodation of religious minorities.

Related Websites

http://www.huffingtonpost.com/religion/
> The Huffington Post, a news website, provides comprehensive and engaging coverage of current events to do with religious beliefs and practices from around the world. Many of the stories depict tensions between different social groups over what exactly religion is, what its function is, and what role religion ought to play (or not) in society.

http://ccla.org/our-work/fundamental-freedoms/freedom-of-religion/
> The Canadian Civil Liberties Association is a national organization designed to promote respect for and observance of fundamental human rights, which includes religion. This website monitors, provides details about, and offers commentary regarding current "religious" legal cases before the Canadian courts (e.g., the role of religion in schools or the place of head coverings in courtrooms).

3 The Dimensions of Religion

Learning Objectives

In this chapter, you will learn:

◎ To think critically about the range and nature of the basic dimensions or elements of religion (e.g., belief, ritual, experience, and community).

◎ To understand how scholars have conceived and analyzed the basic dimensions of religion, and how they are related.

◎ To gain a sense of the complexity of these dimensions and their partial resistance to conventional social scientific study.

Introduction

There is much to be gained from thinking about the basic attributes we associate with any phenomenon. In this case, educating ourselves about the different possibilities makes for better judgments about what should and should not be included in our working notions of religion, though there will always be debate. However you decide to differentiate religions from non-religions, there are certain dimensions or elements that all religions seem to share, though some non-religions have them as well. These dimensions have been conceived in different ways (e.g., Glock and Stark, 1965; Smart, 1989; McGuire, 1997), but every religion of which we are aware has a set of beliefs and some rituals, makes claims about special experiences, and is a shared or communal activity. By briefly considering each of these dimensions of religious life we can identify some of the things sociologists must bear in mind when studying religion and gain a sense of the complex nature of religion as a subject of study. Moreover, these dimensions more or less denote the things that sociologists and other scholars of religion spend their time studying—they represent the forms of empirical data available to us.

Belief

Most obviously, religions are systems of beliefs. To be religious is to "believe" something about the nature of the world that you have been taught by others who hold similar beliefs, based on the authority of some respected teacher—a priest, guru, prophet, or saviour. There is a "cognitive" aspect to religious life, then. It is about knowing certain things and thinking in certain ways. Religions provide people with highly generalized understandings of life that can be called worldviews. These worldviews explain why things are the way they are, and they tell us what can be done, accordingly, to make our lives better or more complete. As indicated in some of the definitions of religion, in particular religions provide guidance in understanding and coping with the ultimate questions in life—its meaning, beginning, and end. An ultimate frame is provided for interpreting the fate of every individual, the groups we belong to (e.g., families, nations, sports teams), and humanity. More often than not these teachings are grounded in some kind of primary belief in the existence of another level or type of reality, of another world—of supernatural beings, heaven, nirvana, or the complete blissful unity of all things—that is ultimately more important than this world and that can and often does exert a significant influence on how things happen in this world.

Table 3.1 Canadian Belief in God or a Higher Power: Adults and Teenagers (%)

	Adults		Teens	
	1985	**2005**	**1984**	**2008**
Yes, I definitely do	61	49	54	37
Yes, I think so	23	32	31	31
No, I don't think so	10	11	9	17
No, I definitely do not	6	7	6	16

Source: Bibby, Reginald. 2011. *Beyond the Gods and Back: Religion's Demise and Rise and Why it Matters.* Lethbridge, AB: Project Canada Books. Page 49.

It is irrelevant whether this presumed other world, whatever its features, is real. In line with the **Thomas theorem**, made famous by the American sociologist W.I. Thomas (Thomas and Thomas, 1928: 572), "If men define situations as real, they are real in their consequences." As long as people believe something is true, there will be consequences for their behaviour that sociologists are interested in studying. If a person believes in the existence of evil spirits, then they will use this "knowledge" to explain how and why bad things befall them and undertake prescribed actions to ward off the evil, such as saying special prayers, undertaking penance, or wearing special amulets. If they believe God knows everything, and that there is life after death for the virtuous, then they will be moved to think good thoughts and do good deeds. In other words, the social effects are real, whether or not the beliefs are true.

The very word *religion* normally calls to mind the formal creeds and sets of doctrines that people hold. Buddhists differ from Christians because they believe different things, as laid out in their respective teachings. The Buddha taught that there is no God, and that we must seek our salvation from a world of perpetual rebirth by discovering the right way to live through the practice of meditation. Jesus taught that we can only find salvation by placing our faith in God and living by his teachings during our one brief life on this earth.

Yet for most believers the daily practice of their religion is less about its formal teachings than it is about the lessons learned about how to lead the good life that are found in the myths, stories, images, and music of a tradition. It is this other less formal kind of knowledge that shapes people's values and guides their behaviour on a daily basis. The great religious leaders of the world set an example for us, and we practise religion as much by honouring and emulating how they lived as by knowing what they said or how it has been interpreted through the ages. In this way it is often the feelings evoked by the sights, sounds, and experiences of our childhood, from our first exposure to religious activities, that are more important in determining whether and how we are religious, than our later assent to formal sets of doctrines. In any one religious service, whether it is the *pūjā* (ritual) performed before a Hindu deity such as Shiva or a Christian baptism, religious knowledge is conveyed in myriad ways: through words, deeds, and settings that are laced with symbols; through ritual repetition; through the symbolic ways we move, speak, sing, and even eat—all shape the way we think, in both conscious and unconscious ways.

But it is the related myths and stories—of the exodus of the Israelites from bondage in Egypt, the Buddha's struggle with Mara (the embodiment of evil), Krishna's display of his true magnificence to Arjuna, Jesus walking on the water, or Mohammed ascending to heaven—that do most of the real work in conveying the meaning of our religious traditions to us. The stories are commonly used to legitimate the later actions of leaders, and their power persists, ingrained in the cultures in which we live, long after some of us lose our faith or choose not to believe. The values the stories embody are codified in the customs and laws enforced by our societies, while the moral logic of the myths continues as well, embodied over and again in myriad more ephemeral yet moving popular tales and entertainments.

As Weber ([1915] 1958b; [1922] 1964: Chapter 9) and others (e.g. Berger, 1967) have stressed, foremost amongst the beliefs that religions have developed are theodicies. As religions developed and sought to make ever greater sense of this world, a preeminent concern was the provision of an ethical explanation for what Weber calls "the incongruity between destiny and merit" ([1915] 1958b: 275). Why is it so often the case that the good die young or experience misfortune while the wicked prosper and live long? If the gods care, or the world is just, as the call to belief in God implies, then how can we account for this grievous disparity between the ideals that the religious espouse and the harsh realities of our experience? In Christian theology a theodicy is an explanation of why suffering and injustice are not an indictment of God's love for humanity, of his promise of reward for virtue. Weber broadened this term to discuss all similar ultimate explanations of seemingly undeserved woe, the world over. A brief consideration of the nature and diversity of such theodicies illustrates the nature, role, and variation of the beliefs found in religions.

As indicated in Chapter 1, Weber argued that the very need to account for suffering, to make it meaningful and hence manageable, especially at the societal level, provided the impetus for the creation of religious beliefs, practices, and institutions. We will have more to say about this in Chapter 5. The efforts of the intellectuals in any society, from the most primitive to today, to provide ever more comprehensive and resilient explanations were the motivation for developing ever more metaphysical conceptions of God and the world. The religious impulse instigated and sustained the creation of concepts for analyzing and making sense of our experience, and these ideas in turn framed our future interpretations and expectations, and hence how the world was actually experienced. But as the complexity of our understanding grew, so did our powers of analysis, renewing the demand for better explanations of what remained fundamentally at odds with our expectations. In the history of humanity, Weber argued, the drive for more "rationally satisfactory answers" resulted in three forms of theodicy: "the Indian doctrine of Kharma, Zoroastrian dualism, and the predestination decree of the *deus absconditus*" ([1915] 1958b: 275).

Believing in the reincarnation, or the migration of souls through many lifetimes, Hindus and Buddhists believe that the injustice that strikes an individual now is brought on by sins committed in a past life, and the reward for virtuous behaviour in this life may only come in a future one. Karma is the term used to identify, yet never really explain, this cosmic force or process of eternal retribution and justice. In the ancient religion of Persia, Zoroastrianism, there are two primal supernatural forces at work in the world: God and the devil. They are contending for power and the evil that befalls us is simply the work of the devil. We can reduce the devil's role in our lives by strengthening our bonds with God, but only in some distant future, at the end of time, will absolute good finally triumph over absolute evil. These views penetrated deeply into Judaism during the Babylonian exile and then eventually into Christianity, where they gained credence and influence in the Middle Ages and beyond. Alternatively, as also stressed in Judaism (see the Book of Job in the Bible), an emphasis was increasingly placed on the absolute majesty and transcendence of God. God is omnipresent, omnipotent, and omniscient. As such he is the source of all things, good and evil, and it is not our place, as flawed humans, to question his ways. In fact to do so, is to fall into error and lose faith. In the Protestant Reformation the Calvinists carried this line of reasoning to its logical extreme and declared that the fate of everyone is predestined by God. He has known since the dawn of time who is saved and who is damned, but we are commanded to have faith that we are saved and act accordingly.

None of these theodicies exists in "pure form," as Weber cautions, and there is a constant pressure to modify and mix them as the vagaries of the human condition and social circumstances demand. But one thing is clear: to this day, if people are asked why they no longer believe in or belong to some religion, it is common for them to refer to "the 'injustice' of the order of this world" (Weber, [1915] 1958b: 276). There is a telling but complicated relationship among the order one needs to find in this world, and the disorder one can tolerate, and the capacity or desire to believe in the things that religions teach.

Finally, in discussing beliefs as a dimension of religion we must guard against a particular modern prejudice. In Western societies, and now elsewhere as well, we are too inclined to associate belief—especially true belief or faith—with an interior psychological condition marked by a conscious knowledge and intention that motivates our actions. This view, however, is once again the legacy of the Protestant Reformation and certain currents of thought characteristic of the Judaic-Christian tradition which culminated in the Protestant worldview (see Weber, [1922] 1963; Berger, 1967). Most people, even in contemporary Canada, let alone the rest of the world, actually experience religion in their lives as some form of reassuring customary practice, and this has been the case throughout human history. Not much critical thought, let alone interior contemplation, goes into their daily prayers or participation in ceremonies and rites. Simple expressions of love, hope, fear, and duty figure more prominently in people's motivations and responses. But does this mean their engagement with religion is any less authentic, sincere, or significant? Much of social life happens at this habitual and taken-for-granted level, a phenomenon that in some ways speaks even more to its fundamental importance for individuals, and for their families and communities.

Ritual

This leads us naturally to our second dimension, ritual. As children we often participate in the performance of rites even before we have a grasp of what they mean. Being religious entails more than holding certain beliefs. It is about doing things, especially certain kinds of actions meant to arouse affective states, to engage our emotions. Religious meanings are given concrete form: they are enacted through the repeated use of certain bodily gestures and actions, from crossing oneself before the altar as a Catholic to prostrating oneself on the floor during prayers at the mosque. Rituals can be simple, barely attracting notice (e.g., saying "bless you" after someone sneezes), or elaborate and conspicuous (e.g., the coronation of a king or queen). The range of rituals humans have devised is enormous and varied, and the study of rituals—what they are, how they operate, why they matter—is a complex field (Bell, 1992; Grimes, [1982] 1995). Here it is sufficient to note that it is hard to imagine a religion without some regular, repeated, and proscribed actions that are meant to symbolically remind us of the teachings of our faith, or elicit the response of the other-worldly powers at the heart of religious belief, or induce in us the emotions, whether of solemnity or ecstasy, that are traditionally linked with a sense of the transcendent in our societies.

Much as with religion itself, the sheer variety of forms of ritual, and the diversity of ways in which rituals are present in our societies, poses serious problems for their study. There is no more agreement on what rituals are, on a definition of "ritual," than there is for religion. There are many opinions on the purpose and functioning of rituals, and the problems posed are compounded by the fact that there are both religious and non-religious rituals. In fact, life seems to be suffused with ritualistic acts and behaviour, from the hitter in professional baseball carefully repeating the exact same gestures each time he goes to bat to the precise rules governing the performance of a Catholic Mass.

Some religions are characterized by a profusion of ritualistic elements, of ceremony and symbolism. In a Western context one might think of the lengthy and elaborate rites followed by the Greek, Russian, and other Orthodox churches, whether for a wedding, a funeral, or the celebration of Easter. In an Eastern context some Hindu rites come to mind, like the fire (*havan*) ritual, especially in its ancient communal form, which entailed the sacrifice of many animals and other goods over several days in a precisely prescribed way (Staal, 1983). By contrast, one may think of the marked simplicity of many Protestant services, such as an evangelical prayer meeting or the rituals of Zen Buddhist meditation. It is far from clear why some cultures and religions are more flagrantly ritualistic than others. The styles are obviously the product of history, of differences in the experiences of these people—differences that the rituals themselves have helped to shape and magnify.

As with religion in general, however, we must be careful not to mistake simplicity of form for diminished presence and significance. Rituals can lose their force with time through their simplification, perhaps out of gradual accommodation to secular views and demands (e.g., to save time for other activities). But the complex elaboration of rites into cumbersome and ossified ceremonies, which ordinary people can no longer understand, is equally deleterious. The simple elegance of the Japanese tea ceremony can be as evocative and moving as the grandeur of the inauguration of the President of the United States. The functional merit of a ritual does not reside in its scope or complexity so much as in the manner in which it is undertaken and the attitude brought to bear on it. It is about performing a set of actions with great care and in the same way every time. Minimally this basic aspect of ritual points to the ordering and stabilizing function of ritual, and perhaps of religion as well. Over and against the unpredictability, and perhaps also the danger, of much of life, rituals announce there is an established way to invoke a controlling force, an unchanging reality, that transcends yet intersects with this world. This is true whether we are soliciting help in hitting a curve ball or preserving the lives of soldiers marching to war.

Thinking in terms of the social-psychological impacts of ritual activity, anthropologists have noted that rituals play a role in both relieving and inducing anxieties, at the individual and collective levels. When Bronislaw Malinowski (1948) studied the Trobriand Islanders of New Guinea he famously noted that they employed magical rites in contexts where chance played a greater role in achieving success. When fishing within the lagoon, where they are protected from the ravages of the ocean and the chances of success are high, little ritual is involved. But when venturing out onto the open seas, where both the catch and the weather are far less predictable, a ritual regime is invoked. The magical rites are used to supplement the stock of seafaring knowledge, not replace it, but they are considered essential. They are used, Malinowski proposes, to fortify the courage and commitment of the fishermen. In other words, the rituals help to quell and manage the anxieties of the fishermen, their families, and the community as a whole. In this scenario, rituals perform important psychological, social, and even instrumental functions, helping the people to survive.

Studying the Andaman Islanders, A. R. Radcliffe-Brown ([1939] 1972) suggests that this explanation only captures half the story. Rituals can also function to induce new anxieties that help to reinforce the social rules that bring order to society. Taboos—ritual prohibitions against doing certain things, such as touching the body of the king or eating certain foods when your daughter is about to give birth—create new sources of anxiety in society. The violation of taboos is strongly associated with misfortune, for the guilty party and often for the groups they belong to as well. To avoid the negative consequences, the offenders and their groups must perform a secondary set of rites of purification or expiation.

The role of such rituals in regulating behaviour is conveyed well in Jonathan Z. Smith's description of circumpolar hunting societies (1982: 58):

> The hunter and the hunted play out their roles according to a predetermined system of relationships. This system is mediated, according to the traditions of many hunting peoples, by a "Master of the Animals," a "Supernatural Owner of the Game," who controls the game or their spirits, in northern traditions most frequently by penning them. He releases a certain number to man each year as food. Only the allotted number may be slain in a manner governed by strict rules. Each corpse must be treated

with respect. The meat must be divided, distributed, and eaten according to strict rules of etiquette, and the soul of the animal must be returned to its "supernatural Owner" by ritual means. If the system is violated, game will be withheld and complex ceremonies, frequently involving the mediation of a shaman, are required to remove the offense and placate the "Master."

On first assessment the very existence of the taboos appears strange and inexplicable. Why must such rites be respected? Radcliffe-Brown argues that the fear of misfortune, of supernatural punishment for ignoring the taboo, focuses attention on and elevates the significance of the social phenomena shrouded by such taboos, whether it is the sacredness of the body of the king, the birth of a child, or the way humans interact with the animals on which they are dependent. The taboos act as mechanisms of social control, in other words, helping to persuade people to behave in ways that are functionally advantageous for society as a whole. The anxiety created by taboos motivates people to regulate their own behaviour, making for a more orderly society, in ways that could never be achieved by brute force alone.

In both cases, when an individual feels anxiety in the face of threatening circumstances or when a society imposes rules to cause an individual to feel anxious, partial relief is provided by following the traditional ways of expressing and countering that anxiety. Psychologically, then, a ritualistic response serves to make life easier for the participants, and sociologically, it unifies the group by bringing members together, physically and mentally, and by reducing the occurrence of deviance. The ritualistic orientation asserts the mutual dependency of nature and morality, of the way things are and how we act, and of the individual and society. It provides a framework, moreover, for doing something, at least symbolically, to influence these crucial relationships in positive ways.

Durkheim ([1912] 1995) stressed the foundational role of ritual in religion. Studying the practices of Australian Aboriginal tribes, he argued that at the heart of religion is the experience of people doing rituals. He argued, in ways we will discuss in Chapter 4, that though we think of beliefs as giving shape and meaning to ritual performances, in fact the sacred itself is continually created and sustained by ritualistic acts. The "reality" of religion is what people experience in the communal enactment of rites. Rituals constitute ways of symbolizing and reinforcing a group's sense of its own existence, its identity and unity. In the early history of humanity, rituals offered the means for recurrently remembering, recounting, and revitalizing the collective memories of the people. The co-operative enactment of rituals lifts individuals out of their immediate condition, and exposes them to the collective action and wisdom of their tribes. Such acts serve an important function, strengthening the individual by strengthening the solidarity of the groups to which they belong. Rituals act as a kind of mirror for society.

Through the constant repetition and gradual modification of rituals, societies have an opportunity to adjust and reset their conception of themselves, symbolically, and this benefits individuals and the group in a hostile environment.

In the days following the Allied victory in the first Gulf War against Iraq (1990–91), for example, the American government did something rather unusual for modern democracies. Americans had not witnessed such an event in decades. The government staged a grand military parade on the streets of Washington, DC. Reminiscent of the triumphal marches of the armies of ancient Rome, thousands of American troops and military vehicles marched passed the cheering crowds that lined Pennsylvania Avenue, symbolically marking the victory over Iraq. In the process, however, they were also helping to erase the lingering stigma of America's inglorious defeat almost two decades earlier in the Vietnam War (1964–75). The parade appeared to be a ritual act, on a grand scale, of collective redemption, designed to reset the ethos of the United States and restore its pride in itself as "the greatest nation on earth."

Humans have been infinitely creative in devising rituals. There are sacraments and rites of worship, sacrifice, atonement, purification, personal devotion, and divination. Rituals are used to make oaths; cure bodies and minds; cast spells and curses; bless or dedicate places, things and people; exorcise demons; memorialize events; invest chiefs, judges, and other kinds of officials; crown kings and queens; and inaugurate presidents. Catherine Bell, one the foremost scholars of rituals, suggests that rituals can be divided into six categories: (1) calendrical rites; (2) rites of passage; (3) rites of exchange and communion; (4) rites of affliction; (5) feasting, fasting, and festivals; and (6) political rites (Bell, 1997: 94). The sheer diversity and abundance of rites, rites related to so many of our activities, attests to their profound role in human social life—something we are inclined to forget in the late modern world. We do so at our peril, however, since there is every reason to think Durkheim's understanding of the essential social function of rituals remains salient.

Some of the most common kinds of rituals, widely performed in Canadian society, are **rites of passage**. These rituals, which entail the symbolic stripping of an old identity and the welding of a new one, are used to mark, commemorate, and sometimes legally accomplish various transitions in life, ranging from baptisms, through graduations and marriages, to funerals (van Gennep, [1908] 1960; Turner, 1969; Grimes, 2000). The rites provide a structured context for encouraging and experiencing certain strong emotions, whether of pride, shame, or obligation, that it is beneficial for society to associate with certain common but important changes in life. Clearly they function to both guide and control the thoughts and motivations of those experiencing the transitions (in most cases), but also, and perhaps even more importantly, of those witnessing the event, who will be affected by the transition—family, friends, and whole communities. While only a minority of Canadians now regularly attend religious services, the majority of Canadians continue to celebrate these life transitions with religious rites. We still feel the need, it seems, to legitimate these changes with some kind of ultimate blessing (Bibby, 1987). It is comforting to do so, even if we no longer fully believe, and the outward act of formally marking the change may still be the best way to adjust and reset our self-conceptions and social relationships.

Arnold van Gennep ([1908] 1960) pointed out the tripartite character of these rites of passage. They characteristically involve some kind of initial rite of separation by which the people in transition are symbolically and sometimes physically removed from their previous groups and statuses. Those on whom the rite is focused then enter into a state of "liminality" in which they are neither what they were nor what they will be. This period of transition is considered very precarious and the participants are thought to be vulnerable. In some cases the liminal state may be very brief, only minutes in length. The bride in Christian wedding ceremonies, for example, is formally in a liminal state from the moment her father gives her away until she is ritually united with her husband. In other cases, like the vision quest pursued by adolescent boys becoming men in many Native American tribes, the liminal state may last for several days. This betwixt and between state is followed by the third and final phase, rites of aggregation, that formally mark the incorporation of the participant into his or her new status. The entire process is often cast as a type of rebirth, as symbolically represented by passing through a tunnel, crossing a threshold, or receiving a new name.

Scholars have been paying close attention to the detailed and comparative study of ritual behaviour since the mid-nineteenth century, and the work done by historians of ancient civilizations, anthropologists, and religious studies scholars is too vast to attempt to survey here (e.g., Smith, [1889] 1969; Hubert and Mauss, [1898] 1964; Fraser, 1922; Eliade, [1958] 1963; Gluckman, 1962; Douglas, 1966; Driver, 1997; Rappaport, 1999). It is worth noting, however, that much of the early and formative scholarship, based on studies of the rituals of primitive societies and those of the ancient Near East (e.g., the Israelites, Egyptians, Greeks, Romans, and others) emphasized the centrality of sacrificial rites. For these scholars, as Bell aptly says, "ritual is the heart of religion and sacrifice the heart of ritual" (2006: 401). In many instances this meant that the killing of individuals for the sake of the community was at the core of religious life for many centuries. With time animals and other objects became sufficient symbolic substitutes, but we must recognize the cultural basis of the powerful imagery of Christ's sacrificial death, and that of other heroic figures throughout the world.

Today many of the religious rituals of worship or rites of passage that people experience seem empty of meaning, leading, as Meredith McGuire says (1997: 17) "to the notion that ritual itself is deadening." There is too much of a disconnection now between the meaning of many rituals, of the symbols, stories, and gestures used, and the knowledge possessed by most people. The very pace and character of the rites, established long ago in largely agrarian and simpler societies, can also seem intuitively out of step with the hectic character of today's urban and technological lifestyles. The messages conveyed may still resonate with us, at some basic human level, but the images created in our minds by the ceremonies, and the staid actions inscribed by the rites, may strike us as being just too archaic to be relevant.

Ironically, many contemporary rituals are sapped of their energy by the very convenience of modern life and religious practice. Rituals are used to build bonds between people and to pass on and reinforce collective memories. For millennia people have recognized that suffering helps to forge and fortify those bonds and memories. Referring to humans as creatures with the unique right to "make promises," the German philosopher Friedrich Nietzsche stressed the role the ritualistic infliction of pain played in human history in burning group loyalties into the consciousness of our ancestors (Nietzsche, [1887] 1967). Initiation rituals, a universal type of rite of passage, commonly entail the imposition of trials and tribulations, if not the straightforward infliction of pain (physical and psychological). Whatever the rites, whether initiating boys into adulthood in traditional hunting societies or pledges into fraternities and sororities on college campuses, suffering has been used to disrupt initiates' ties to their previous lives, sharply focus their attention on the new norms they must learn, and cement the bonds of camaraderie with all those who endured the same rites before them. Few rites today, however, call for such sacrifices, which may well account for their lack of lasting meaning.

Noteworthy exceptions exist, though, pointing to situations where strong loyalties and commitments are still seriously prized. Stressful initiations are common in such groups as youth gangs, military and paramilitary units, and some sports teams, especially at the higher levels. They are also typical of some prestigious professions. In the training of physicians, for example, hazing, long hours, and excessive demands still are used to test the mettle of initiates and determine whether they are worthy of the respect that comes with the new status. More importantly, other kinds of "ritualizing" activity continue to permeate even late modern societies, from the invention of new forms of initiation rituals and spiritual pursuits to marriage ceremonies, funerals and so on in New Age and other alternative religious groups, and even in the case of supposedly secular individuals. The formally non-religious memorial services held in funeral parlours that are increasingly becoming the norm in much of Canada, for example, continue to be conspicuously ritualistic in some basic ways. But how else could we honour a loved one, say a final goodbye, begin preparing to live life without them? Is this kind of perpetuation of "ritual" consonant with the survival of "religion"? As we have seen, for many reasons, there is no easy answer to that question.

Experience

To be religious is not just to think in certain ways; it is about feeling certain ways as well, and not just during the performance of rituals. If religions were only sets of beliefs and rites, with little other effect on us, it would be hard to imagine why religions exist or persist. In fact, as discussed, many Canadians no longer find the rituals performed in their churches, synagogues, and temples meaningful because they experience them as empty and boring. They seem dead, in part, because we can no longer relate the messages conveyed to the contexts of our lives, and the ritual forms used seem equally strange and limited. The sights, sounds, and impressions created in a bygone and much simpler era no longer resonate for many in our media-saturated and much more sophisticated times. As such we are unmoved by our experiences during religious services. But one assumes this was not the case in the past, and it is still not the case for many Canadians, and other people around the world. Durkheim was impressed with the reality of religion, sociologically, because he was convinced that rituals had power. "The believer who has communicated with his god is not merely a man who sees new truths of which the unbeliever is ignorant," he said, "he is a man who is stronger. He feels within him more force, either to endure the trials of existence, or to conquer them" ([1912] 1995: 419). However we may choose to characterize this feeling, all religions rest on claims of access to a special kind of experience of great force and significance. The subjective experience, we are told by the great religious leaders, is analogous to the excitement we associate with sex, love, or being in the presence of great beauty, but it exceeds any of these comparisons and involves some hard-to-explain element that is **sui generis**—unique, that is, to religion. We can know it, and even induce it in others, but we can never really capture it in words. As William James ([1902] 1994: 123-124) declares, it has a noetic quality but is ineffable. Yet claims about these ultimate experiences, expressed differently in different cultures, are part of what bonds people together in loyalty to certain traditions, and religious mystics have been rather prolific in trying to describe what supposedly cannot be described (Happold, 1970; Katz, 1983).

In speaking of religious experience it is common to first think of the extraordinary visions and revelations reported by the founders, prophets, and mystics of the great religious traditions, the altered states of consciousness induced by tribal shamans to communicate with the spirit world, or the myriad forms of spirit communication, channelling, automatic writing, and out-of-body experiences described by many esoteric movements and new religions in modern times. At the heart of Buddhism, for example, lies the extraordinary experience of Siddhartha Gautama, a prince from a small kingdom in northern India who achieved enlightenment while meditating under a pipal tree by a peaceful river. Islam is founded upon an extraordinary experience as well. Muhammad encountered the angel Gabriel while meditating in a secluded cave on Mount Hira, just outside of Mecca. Gabriel tells Muhammad that he is the chosen messenger of God, and inspires him, though Muhammad is illiterate, with the beautiful verses of the Qur'an. On the road to Damascus, on his way to persecute Christians, a Jew named Saul is blinded by a light and has a vision of Jesus. He is commanded to change his ways and begin to spread the good news about Christ to the rest of the Greco-Roman world. Saul becomes St. Paul, the great founding father, missionary, and martyr of the Christian church. On a Sunday in 1775, a young Canadian, Henry Alline, returns home from wandering in the fields where he has been struggling to discern his fate. He opens the Bible randomly to the 38th Psalm and is swept by a powerful feeling of "redeeming love." He immediately decides to dedicate his life to preaching the gospel and becomes the inspirational leader of a Christian "new light" revival that spreads like fire across the Maritime provinces. In the late 1820s, in rural upstate New York, eighteen-year-old Joseph Smith Jr. is confronted by an angel named Moroni, who reveals the secret location of a set of golden tablets that are translated by Smith as the Book of Mormon, the new gospel of the Church of Jesus Christ of Latter-day Saints (i.e., the Mormons). Near Fatima Portugal, in 1917, three young shepherds see the Virgin Mary six times. Three secrets are revealed during the apparitions, which become the famous prophecies of Fatima, and Fatima becomes a major site of Catholic pilgrimage. These, and other extraordinary experiences too numerous to count, are the very substance of religion. Claims of such experiences are a regular and perplexing feature of life, even in the late modern world, where they are discouraged and devalued.

But the full range of subjective states identified with religious involvement is more complex. These experiences may be momentary or prolonged, curious or profound. In content they may entail a sense of abiding peace, joy, and well-being or they may be marked by terror and instil anxiety. Upon first encountering the angel Gabriel, Muhammad was stricken with fear and doubt. He only came to accept his new prophetic role with the encouragement and support of his family and friends. In the famous eleventh chapter of the great holy book of Hinduism, the *Bhagavad Gita*, the god Vishnu, disguised at first as a mere servant, reveals his true nature, in all its awesome glory, to the terrified warrior Arjuna. In these instances, and so many others throughout human history, the encounter with the sacred is overwhelming and shocking. It is also almost instantaneously transformative. The power of the experience changes the participants permanently. In other cases, ones we all have probably experienced, the sense of being humbled and awed in the face of the ultimate may be more transient and have less lasting effect, but is no less moving at the moment. It may come upon us while walking on an ocean beach at low tide on a glorious summer morning, staring at the vast beauty of the a range of mountains from the top of a ski hill on a blustery winter day, or watching with quiet and intense love as our child first discovers the wonder of a butterfly in the garden. They are moments of special connection with the world that often invoke a sense of true gratitude for being alive and a sense that it all has some meaning that exceeds our understanding but is a blessing to experience.

Some religious groups encourage these experiences, the more ecstatic ones, that is. Some religions do not; they may even seek to suppress them for fear they are too disruptive or potentially misleading. Some groups differentiate between types of experiences, developing procedures for cultivating only some (e.g., Zen Buddhism, Santiera), while others exercise much less care and perceive the experiences as spontaneous and largely beyond their control (e.g., Pentecostal Christians, contemporary Pagans). Great care is taken, in many traditions, to determine whether the experiences are divine or demonic. Some groups use various hallucinogenic substances to facilitate mystical experiences (e.g., Santo Dame, Native American Church). Other groups categorically reject the legitimacy of visions induced in such a way (Zaehner, 1972; Smith, 2000). Some groups think the experiences should be open to all, while others confine the practices associated with the experiences to religious *virtuosi*—special classes of priests, prophets, or other visionaries. In Inuit society the shaman alone has the power to enter into the trance states in which he communicates with the spirits to seek their help.

But whatever the case, it is hard to imagine a religion that is not grounded in some promise of extraordinary experiences, of ecstatic or transformative states. In most cases, however, the daily experience of the devotee is much simpler, yet still essential. For centuries ordinary people have quietly asserted that they feel the presence of the Lord when they pray; they may even claim to speak with God. No matter what we believe personally, we have no credible reason, as social scientists, to discount these claims (see Chapter 2). In 1981, for example, "66 percent of Americans claimed to have had a religious experience and 25 percent said this was something that happened to them frequently" (Stark, 1991: 241). When asked if they have experienced God's presence, 40 to 50 percent of Canadians consistently say either "definitely" or that they "think so" (Bibby, 2002: 147). This response has held constant for decades, even though the conventional signs of religious involvement (e.g., church attendance, saying grace before meals) have plummeted. It is not necessarily clear what these responses mean, since no further study has been done in the Canadian context. But the web of religious life is constituted equally by both kinds of experiences, the great and transformative visions and more subtle yet profound feelings that colour how we see the world.

Basic questions about the nature of these experiences have been the subject of scholarly debate for a long time. On the one hand, philosophers and others question whether we can actually say there is some form of religious experience that is independent of the interpretations given to the experiences (e.g., Stace, 1960; Katz, 1983; Sharf, 1998). We only know the experiences from their description, but the descriptions are shaped by the cultural expectations and presuppositions of the mystics and devotees (see Reimer, 2003). Is there a pure or unmediated experience, as is commonly assumed, behind the interpretations? It is difficult to be sure when there is nothing we can point to that exists independent of our thoughts. The "reality" of religious experience is profoundly subjective, so how can we ascribe an objective significance to it? Moreover, as with the very notion of "religion," how can we really know if there is some common experience underlying the plethora of culturally diverse accounts subsumed under the category? Sociologically, we can dodge these questions by once again invoking the Thomas theorem: all that matters is that those who make the claims about religious experience do so sincerely. But of course, in some cases, it can be difficult to judge whether the accounts given are sincere (whatever that means).

On the other hand, some prominent scholars of religion argue that the study of religion requires researchers to have some prior personal knowledge of these unique and mysterious phenomena because they are so significant (e.g., Otto, [1917] 1958; Smith, 1959; Eliade, 1969). From their perspective, all sociological accounts of religion, based exclusively on empirically available data, are inevitably incomplete and reductive. They tend to reduce religion to those things that can be observed, measured, and compared in some way. But to do so is to miss the heart of religion—the experiential component that differentiates it from all other things. Most sociologists are willing to admit that their claims are limited, and that an element of mystery remains. But, they ask, how can we base the scientific study of religion on such highly subjective claims about the supernatural, the sacred, and the transcendent? How can we test the credibility of statements made by those who appeal to such privileged and idiosyncratic sources of knowledge (e.g., Idiniopulos and Yonan, 1994; Flood, 1999; McCutheon, 1999)?

Contrary to our modern conceptions of divinity, Otto argues that humans first experienced the holy as an object of extreme fear. Playing on the double meaning of the word "awfulness," Otto argues the holy is experienced as both awesome and awful. In its most primitive forms the numinous are associated with "demonic dread" and an unsettling sense of the "uncanny," "eerie," or "weird." "It is this feeling," Otto asserts, "which,

Box 3.1 Otto and the Irrational Heart of Religion

In *The Idea of the Holy* ([1917] 1958) the German theologian, philosopher, and historian of religion Rudolf Otto argues that the experience of the holy, or what he called the "numinous," lies at the heart of religion. While much of religion is rational or conceptual in nature, the concepts merely point to a deeper and more universal "nonrational" phenomenon. Examining an array of scriptures and mystical texts Otto sought to describe this core experience of religion, which he claims is the *sui generis* basis of all religions. His insights into this phenomenon were captured by the Latin phrase **mysterium tremendum**, *fascinans, et augustum*, but the substance of his argument is found in the first two terms. What is this *mysterium tremendum*, this "terrifying element of mystery"?

In Otto's own evocative words ([1917] 1958: 12) it is

> the deepest and most fundamental element in all strong and sincerely felt religious emotion. Faith unto salvation, trust, love—all these are there. But over and above these is an element which may also on occasion, quite apart from them, profoundly affect us and occupy the mind with a well nigh bewildering strength. . . . The feeling of it may at times come sweeping like a gentle tide, pervading the mind with a tranquil mood of deepest worship. It may pass over into a more set and lasting attitude of the soul, continuing, as it were, thrillingly vibrant and resonant, until at last it dies away. . . . It may burst in sudden eruption up from the depths of the soul with spasms and convulsions, or lead to the strangest excitements, to intoxicated frenzy, to transport, and to ecstasy. It has its wild and demonic forms and can sink to an almost grisly horror and shuddering. It has its crude, barbaric antecedents and early manifestations, and again it may be developed into something beautiful and pure and glorious.

emerging in the mind of primeval man, forms the starting-point for the entire religious development in history" ([1917] 1958: 14–15).

The numinous, like the wrath of God in the Hebrew Bible, is dangerous. As Otto says, reading the Bible, "it is patent ... that this 'wrath' has no concern whatever with moral qualities. There is something baffling in the way in which it 'is kindled' and manifested. It is ... 'like a hidden force of nature,' like stored-up electricity, discharging itself upon anyone who comes too near" ([1917] 1958:18). The sense of power in the presence of the holy is "overpowering." In the face of the transcendent we are stricken with by a profound awareness of our mortality, of our "createdness," over against the eternal, the uncreated. The presence of the holy, as mystics throughout the ages testify, annihilates the self. In part this is because the numinous is experienced as sheer "energy or urgency," movement, and force, and the encounter with it ignites a "burning consuming passion" in mystics to be in the presence of this energy.

But these powerful feelings can find no real focus, for substantively the numinous is experienced as "wholly other." It is a complete "mystery." Its presence induces a state of "stupor," "blank wonder and astonishment," since the thing we sense exceeds our reason ([1917] 1958: 26). The mystics, prophets, and visionaries are compelled to describe the holy in terms of what it is not—it is not this, not that; it is the void yet also everything. The numinous is unlike all other objects of our experience and hence it escapes the grasp of our metaphors.

The numinous repels and attracts us at the same time. In Otto's words (1958: 31), "The daemonic-divine object may appear to the mind an object of horror and dread, but at the same time it is no less something that allures with a potent charm, and the creature, who trembles before it, utterly cowed and cast down, has always at the same time the impulse to turn to it, nay even to make it somehow his own." Throughout history people have sought to harness the prodigious force sensed in what is sacred. To this end humans have been willing to undertake the most extreme forms of asceticism and sacrifice, to demonstrate their selfless virtue to the wrathful gods, and conjure the most elaborate rituals and magic to secure some kind of access to the numinous. In the end, Otto asserts, a familiarity with the history of humanity's struggles with the numinous reveals "that above and beyond our rational being lies hidden the ultimate . . . part of our nature, which can find no satisfaction in the mere allaying of the needs of our sensuous, psychical, or intellectual impulses and cravings" ([1917] 1958: 36). The press of civilization has covered over this primordial truth, encasing the experience in the refined and rationalized veneer of religious systems of belief and morality. But the simple and horrible reality—the irrational heart of religion—still pulses beneath these many layers of rational contrivance. Or so Otto would have us believe.

Community

Religion seems to be an inherently social phenomenon. It is a community-forming activity, whether it intends to be or not. In the first place, religious beliefs and practices gain their very plausibility from being shared, and they are the kinds of ideas that are meant to be shared. In principle one could have a private religion, but it is extremely unlikely that an individual's private religion would be of much significance—at least from a sociological point of view. Deeply held but totally personal beliefs will undoubtedly have an impact on the behaviour of the individual who holds them, but to influence others these ideas will have to be shared, understood, and accepted by others. One might also ask whether any religion can truly be private. Surely a person's religious views will be reliant on the content and authority of existing traditions, and in that sense it too would be a social phenomenon. In fact, when people agree about the ways of ultimately making sense of this world it is natural for them to bond together, and if they believe they have found a truth that is beneficial, especially in some ultimate sense, there is an equal compulsion to persuade others.

Of course, as we have been highlighting all along, the communal character of religion has been shrinking in the face of the social changes associated with modernity and late modernity. With each passing decade since 1960, fewer Canadians have been participating in the collective activities, ritualistic and social, at the heart of most traditional religion. But even those practising a more privatized form of religion, those marginal affiliates and independent thinkers who rarely darken the doorway of a church, are drawing their ideas, usually, from a larger popular culture of spiritualism which is being systematically developed and disseminated by networks of like-minded people (i.e., authors, movements, and publishers). The links among people may be looser and more transient than before, but they are still quite social and marked by a sense of common cause and fraternity.

Second, almost all religions are concerned with ethics. They are systems of beliefs and practices focused on the regulation of our behaviour and relations with one another. Religions tell people how to lead a good life, a life that protects and promotes what is thought to be in everyone's best and ultimate interests. In particular, religions tend to be preoccupied with guiding and when necessary sanctioning, how we behave in our most intimate relationships: those with our families—immediate and extended—and local communities. For it is here, around issues of love, sexuality, loyalty, work, and authority, that we are most prone to abusing others, or being abused. It is these relationships that religions have traditionally tried to control through the imposition of taboos and moral rules designed to encourage and compel us to behave well. In fact religions offer the ultimate means of controlling our actions. The gods, or other supernatural forces, can know what we are thinking, so we must sincerely strive to do what is expected of us, to be honest, compassionate, and wise in our thoughts as well as our words and deeds. In this sense religion has long been a primary means of exercising what sociologist call "social control." More importantly, it is a means of assuring the kind of self-control necessary for the success of any society, since sheer coercion is a most ineffective and costly way of guaranteeing the orderly interaction needed to navigate traffic, run a classroom, play a sport, make a business transaction, or get a parcel delivered successfully.

The legacy of this aspect of religious life continues to loom large for many people, even though they have more or less ceased to practise their religion. Today it is common for people to assert that one does not need to be religious to be moral, to be a good person. Yet many parents continue to send their children to religious schools and services because they are convinced it will help their children to become better people. Even while the particulars of belief and practice may be rejected because they are no longer relevant, a strong sentiment remains that some exposure to religion is a good thing. Sociologists of religion commonly encounter this paradox in the people they interview.

Before the onset of mass communication, mass media, and mass transportation, in a time when most people lived their whole lives in one, usually small community, the church, synagogue, or temple was the hub of social life. It was the place where people gathered with regularity to share meals, meet potential mates, learn the news and gossip of the neighbourhood, ask for advice, or seek help in times of trouble. It was even a primary source of entertainment, exposing people to music, sermons, stories and plays that were otherwise not available. Today all of these things are available elsewhere, but religious institutions still serve many of these functions, and many people find the kind of social support they need to be happy in the communities created by participating in religious rites. New immigrants, for example, are often more religious in their adopted homeland than they were in their native lands, because the religions help them to preserve some of their old ways, and hence their identity, while adapting to a strange new place. How many people, however, will continue to satisfy their desire for a sense of community and support in the late modern world in the confines of a church, temple, or synagogue, especially when there are so many other secular or quasi-religious options available to them (e.g., sports teams, Alcoholics Anonymous, yoga, even Facebook)?

Gender and Religion

Of course the sense of community traditionally reinforced and promoted by most religions is itself founded on an unequal distribution of power prevalent, until very recently, in most societies: the dominance of men over women. Because religious groups and systems of religious beliefs and practices have been so intertwined with all other aspects of social life they are part of the interlocking cultural, social, legal, and political practices constitutive of the "gender order" (Bourdieu, 2001) in every society. In fact, as the discussions of Marx's and Berger's theories of religion in the next chapter will highlight, religions have played a key role in legitimizing the status quo in most societies. Historically this has entailed the subordination of women to men, and the power that is unique to religions, the sacred, has been used to bolster the social differences each society deems to matter between men and women as god-given and natural. In most societies until just decades ago, to question the right of men to largely determine the fate of women was interpreted as a challenge to the will of god (or gods). It constituted a heretical defiance of the right and transcendent order of the world. To this day, religious conservatives, whether Christian, Muslim, Hindu, or otherwise, act as bulwarks against cultural change in the relations of men and women. They favour women staying at home and finding their purpose in serving the needs of their children and their husbands, and they are usually preoccupied with the imposing strict standards of sexual morality, especially for women, as a safeguard of the purity of the male lineage and inheritance (Turner, 1991). But the beliefs, practices, and symbols of all religions convey a cultural coding for defining, regulating, and circumscribing women as such, and in ways that bar them from privileges and powers granted exclusively to men, such as being a Catholic or Hindu priest or a Muslim Imam (Juschka, 2005: 230).

Beginning in the 1960s a number of feminist scholars of religion, most notably Mary Daly (1973), Rosemary Radford Reuther (1974), and Elisabeth Schüssler Fiorenza (1983), began to delineate and call into question the unthinking sexism endemic to the religions of the West. In their insightful and scathing analyses of the teachings, history, and texts of Judaism and Christianity they documented the patriarchal assumptions and dictates of these religious traditions. They also traced the systematic erasure of the creative role women in the creation and operation of these communities from the official records of their history—the records written and kept by men. A challenge was issued to re-evaluate and re-write the history of the Christian church and debates broke out in many denominations, with both sides turning to the Bible for support. As the Canadian sociologist of religion Nancy Nason-Clark summarizes (1993: 220):

> The testaments provide materials for debate and controversy concerning the scriptural record as it relates to the role and status of women in the familial, societal and religious spheres. Those who argue for restrictive gender relations base their position on the books of the law, the story of the fall into sin, and the Pauline instructions contained within the pastoral epistles. Others conclude their biblical search by justifying an expanded role for women in all facets of life, and root their arguments in the equality of men and women at creation, report examples of women in the Old Testament who broke through traditional moulds, view the life and teaching of Christ as exemplifying the highest esteem for women and cite Paul's openness to equal and free participation in the body of Christ for all people, regardless of sex, race or social standing.

Box
3.2

Can Religiosity be Measured?

If there is no common definition of religion, and religion is understood to be a complex multi-dimensional phenomenon, and many argue that a strictly empirical grasp of the phenomenon is inevitably deficient, then measuring the degree to which people are religious—what sociologists call **religiosity**—is going to be difficult. Can we actually compare how religious people are in different places and across time? That is precisely what sociologists wish to do, especially if they want to track changes in religion and its social role and significance. On the whole sociologists have relied extensively on a few simple measures of people's behaviours and attitudes, such as their religious affiliation and identification, attendance at religious services, belief in God, and how important religion is to them. But as most of us know, being a member of a church or attending services may not be very sound indicators of the piety or spirituality of individuals. There are many reasons for conforming to social expectations about religion, such as family pressure or making useful business contacts, which have little to do with being religious in any more profound sense. Psychologists have sought to tease out the difference by distinguishing between extrinsic and intrinsic forms of religiosity (Allport and Ross, 1967; Kirkpatrick and Hood, 1990). But all attempts to use survey questions to assess the religiosity of groups are hampered further by the problems of self-reporting. In most societies it is still considered desirable to display a degree of religiosity. Thus people are inclined to exaggerate their religiosity when approached by social scientists. In the United States C. Kirk Hadaway, Penny Long Marler, and Mark Chaves (1993) found serious discrepancies between the head counts they did on Sunday mornings in a sample of Protestant and Catholic churches and the levels of church attendance commonly reported by Americans.

Consequently, sociologists have sought to devise composite measures of religiosity that address many different aspects of religious beliefs, attitudes, and behaviour. Charles Glock and Rodney Stark (1965), for example, favour gathering data on at least eight different dimensions of religious life:

1. The experiential—whether people think they have had contact with the supernatural
2. The ritualistic—whether people participate in public rites

This, however, is not the place to dwell on the details of these and other theological arguments. In general, as Nason-Clark (1993: 219–221) stresses, the members of many Canadian denominations became sensitized to the inherent ambiguity and harmfulness of the age-old prejudices against women in the Christian church as women were unnaturally and

3. The devotional—whether they participate in more private rites, such as prayer or saying grace before meals
4. Belief—whether they agree with the doctrines of their stated faith
5. Knowledge—whether they recognize and understand the beliefs of their religion
6. The consequential—whether their religion affects daily life
7. The communal—whether they socialize with other members of their faith community
8. The particularistic—whether they believe that their religion is the one true path to salvation

Ideally, the higher a person scores on each of these dimensions, the greater their religiosity.

Multi-dimensional approaches of this type are used widely in the research literature. But the research shows that it is rare for anyone to score high on all counts. Most often, individuals score high on some measures while scoring low on others. For example, high levels of church attendance among Canadians and Americans are not matched by a sound grasp of the basic tenets and texts of Christianity: there is a very weak correlation between the ritualistic and the knowledge dimensions of religiosity. Application of the measures can tell us something important, then, about the nature and degree of religiosity of individuals, groups, and whole societies. But if one person or group scores high on one set of measures and another on another set, how can we gauge which is actually more religious? There is no way to truly measure the relative religiosity of different groups since the differences detected may often be more reflective of different ways of being religious, different 'styles' of religiosity, than "degrees" of religiosity (see Davidson and Knudsen, 1977). This is particularly the case if we are seeking to make cross-cultural comparisons, say between Hindus and Christians. Moreover, it has proven notoriously difficult to devise criteria for making the measurements characteristic of each dimension without introducing some implicit religious bias. Glock and Stark's original efforts appear to display an unintended bias in favour of more conservative styles of Christianity, resulting in devout Quakers scoring lower than indifferent Baptists.

Nevertheless, some measures must be used, and the problems attendant on the measure of religion are but an extreme example of the problems faced by social scientists relying on people's stated views on a wide range of complex social phenomena and issues (e.g., prejudice, sexual behaviour, mental health). But methodological rigour requires that caution be exercised in making any pronouncements about religion.

stereotypically forced to choose between the equally problematic cultural ideals of the "sinful Eve" and the "sinless Mary." More pragmatically, the heightened awareness of these issues culminated in the push for the ordination of women—an ecclesiastic reform that carried the day in the major Protestant denominations in Canada, but which remains a deviant aspiration in the Roman Catholic Church and many smaller Protestant sects and evangelical churches.

The debates over the patriarchal nature of Christianity led sociologists of religion to recognize two things: (1) the need to better understand how religions have long served the ideological function of constructing and maintaining worldviews that systematically favour one gender over the other; and (2) that their analyses of religion needed to more honestly and accurately reflect the divergent worlds of religious meaning that women and men inhabit. While women and men subscribe to the same beliefs and engage in the same practices, it is incorrect to assume they experience religion in the same way.

Across cultures, by any standard measure (see Box 3.2), women are more religious than men (Beit-Hallahmi and Argyle, 1996: 139–142; Inglehart and Norris, 2003: 58), and North America and European surveys consistently show that more women than men go to church, by about a ratio of 3:2 (see Walter and Davie, 1998; Woodhead, 2008). What men and women believe, moreover, differs in subtle but important ways. If women are asked to describe God, for example, they "concentrate rather more on a God of love, comfort and forgiveness, while men tend to prefer a God of power, planning and control" (Cox, 1967; Nelsen et al., 1985; Sered, 1987; Simmons and Walter, 1988). In her seminal study of women's religiosity, *Priestess, Mother, Sacred Sister* (1994), Susan Starr Sered notes that, cross-culturally, women of all social strata tend to share a religious orientation to coping with the demands and risks, physical and social, of childbearing and motherhood. As the primary care-givers in their families much of their religious attention is directed at rituals of healing and protection, at efforts to supernaturally fend off the threats to the well-being of their children and families. But does this emphasis mean that the gender differences in religion are a result of biological differences between the sexes or just a reflection of the contrast in the social conditions of the lives of men and women? What matters more, nature or nurture? Many of the religious, especially those from conservative groups, tend to stress the former, aligning their discriminatory practices with the natural and god-given order. The feminist critics, on the other hand, stress the role of social conditioning and cultural influence. Either way, the differences in the degree and kind of religiosity between women and men are real, and they pose a conundrum for those convinced that most religions tend to serve the interests of men over women. For if this is the case, then why are women usually more religious than men?

In fairness it must be noted as well that women today are also significantly over-represented in the alternative forms of spirituality we have mentioned, most of which explicitly or implicitly reject the invidious forms of gender hierarchy characteristic of traditional societies and religions (Heelas and Woodhead, 2005). In fact, some of the new ways of being religious in the West explicitly invert this hierarchy, prioritizing the divine feminine in us all and/or the worship of goddesses (e.g., many forms of neo-paganism, the Rajneesh/Osho movement; see Griffith, 1995; Goldman, 1999). So we must be careful to realize, as indicated in Chapter 1, that the relationship of women and religion is more complex than the debate between conservative believers and feminists indicates. We explore this issue of complexity further in our summary of the analysis offered by the British scholar Linda Woodhead in Chapter 7 (see Box 7.2).

Conclusion

Different religions, even different traditions within a religion, give more emphasis to some dimensions of religion than others. Catholics commonly tend to see participation in certain rites as more important, while most Protestant groups stress matters of doctrine and belief. Theravadin Buddhists place more emphasis on meditative experience, while Mahayanist Buddhists favour ritual and worship. Pentecostal Protestants highlight the role of intense religious experiences, with exuberant worship services, while Anglicans prefer decorum, giving a priority to formal ceremony. Each dimension, however, is present in each these religious traditions, and in studying religious life sociologists must be attentive to both its cognitive and affective aspects, as well as its individual and collective expressions. As the anthropologist Clifford Geertz points out ([1966] 1973: 90), religious systems equip people with a conception of how the world really works and what really matters, and they reinforce this worldview with intensely cultivated sentiments. Neither the ideas nor the sentiments may stand up to sharp scrutiny, but each is sustained by the "borrowed authority of the other." This makes religions powerful motivators and justifications for all kinds of important social actions, especially those involving self-sacrifice, from serving the needs of the poor to defending one's country or even becoming a suicide bomber.

Critical Thinking Questions

1.   Is all ritual activity intrinsically, or at least implicitly, religious? If not, then what distinguishes religious rituals from non-religious ones?

2.   What is the relationship between belief and ritual? Can there be religion without one or the other?

3.   Do you think people living in late modern societies can have numinous experiences like the ones Otto describes?

4.   Can one have a fully private religion?

Suggested Readings

Turner, Victor. 1969. *The Ritual Process: Structure and Anti-Structure*. Ithaca, NY: Cornell University Press. This seminal book provides an analysis of the symbolic structure and meaning of rituals of the Ndembu of Zambia followed by an innovative theory of their social nature and significance. It provides an excellent introduction to the complexity and power of the rites humans have created throughout the ages.

James, William. 1994 [1902]. *The Variety of Religious Experience: A Study in Human Nature*. New York: The Modern Library. This old book by one of America's greatest philosophers is still hard to surpass for its classic insights into the nature of religious experience. It is chock-full of colourful and intriguing accounts of people's experiences of the divine and other supernatural phenomena. The book remains essential reading for anyone studying religion.

McCutcheon, Russel T., ed. 1999. *The Insider/Outsider Problem in the Study of Religion: A Reader*. New York: Cassell. An excellent collection of classic and contemporary essays debating the perennial issue in the study of religion: Do you need to be religious to really understand religion, its nature and significance?

Related Websites

www.thearda.com
The Association of Religion Data Archives offers free access to raw data sets from studies on religion mainly in the United States, but also in Canada and around the world, that allow for regional, national, and international comparisons. This website also contains many resources for students and teachers alike, such as videos, dictionary items, bibliographic references, and working papers from leading scholars who draw on social science to study religion.

www.religionandgender.org/index.php/rg/index
Religion and Gender is a publicly accessible online international and interdisciplinary journal devoted to studying the intersection between gender and religion in contemporary society. Covering an array of religions and topics, authors deal with the many facets of religious belief, ritual, experience, and community that confront those studied in their projects.

4 Insights from Sociological Theories of Religion

Learning Objectives

In this chapter, you will learn:

◎ To develop a better sense of the fundamental character and social functions of religion, the ones associated with the persistence and significance of religion as a social institution.

◎ To understand the important roles the great classical figures of sociology assigned to religion in terms of the processes of social control, social cohesion, and social change.

◎ To sample two of the most comprehensive and influential contemporary sociological theories of religion, those of Peter Berger and Rodney Stark.

◎ To understand how sociologists have imagined that religion is uniquely rooted in the human condition, yet like all other social phenomena subject to our choices in ways that are perhaps quite predictable.

Introduction

Religion is a curious subject for sociological reflection. No one thinks it is necessary to question the reason for the existence of most other social institutions—the military, the family, systems of education, or forms of prostitution. The function of such institutions seems self-evident, whether this is in fact the case or not. But the enormous time and effort individuals and societies have dedicated to religious activities, throughout human history, is perplexing. At least it is a source of wonder to most of people living in the late modern world. Of course, at one time religious practices were just part of the web of social and cultural life, and few thought to question "religion" as a phenomenon. Rather, debates about which religious beliefs and practices were most efficacious, or simply true, were more the norm. Today we can itemize and measure (to some degree) the benefits of religion, both in terms of the well-being of individuals and the social solidarity of societies. But no one is quite sure why the beliefs and practices most characteristic of religion—the belief in invisible gods and other non-material forces that have the power to intervene in both the natural order of things and human affairs, or the rites by which these supernatural forces can be known and appeased—came into being or continue to be in demand. Perhaps the gods do exist and otherworldly forces are at work in our world?

If we are not willing to assume this to be the case, at least not as social scientists, then we must find at least a partial explanation in the needs, desires, and capabilities of humans, both as individuals and in the groups they form. Many of the apparent social benefits of religion are delivered by other social systems as well. Science and philosophy, for example, tell us about the nature of the world and its meaning. Doctors, hospitals, and psychologists treat the ills of our bodies and minds, while governments and legal systems work to safeguard our bodies, our property, and even our virtue. Yet in the face of the challenges of life a sizable and often influential segment of humanity feels the need to posit the existence of something more, and to seek some stronger sense of purpose in the midst of coping with the vagaries of the human condition.

It is hard to think about the social function of religion without speculating about the most rudimentary and compelling reasons for being religious in the first place—for believing in and adapting one's behaviour to things that cannot be seen, heard, tasted, or smelled in the way we normally sense other things. This holds true both for the classical figures of sociology, Marx, Durkheim, and Weber and for such influential contemporary sociologists of religion as Peter Berger and Rodney Stark, all of whom will be discussed in this chapter. Many sociologists have developed theories about many aspects of religion, but Berger and Stark have equipped us with some of the most clear, systematic, and compelling ways of conceiving the nature and functions of religion as a whole. Their impact on how we conceive religion has been profound and lasting.

Classical Theory: Marx, Durkheim, and Weber

The great founding figures of sociology, Karl Marx (1818–83), Émile Durkheim (1858–1917), and Max Weber (1864–1920), were not personally religious. In fact, Weber declared himself to be "religiously unmusical," while Marx was a scornful critic of the Christian heritage of Europe. Yet each saw the analysis of religious life as being essential to his work. Durkheim and Weber, indeed, dedicated much of their lives to its study. The great common concern of these theorists was the investigation of the sweeping changes in social conditions gripping their societies as they were transformed into modern industrial states. In the societies they lived in, in late nineteenth century and early twentieth century Europe, religious institutions still played a prominent role in the regulation of social life. But things were changing rapidly.

The traditional social order of every society prior to the modern era had been suffused with religious institutions, symbols, and sentiments. Religions legitimated the dominant institutions of the day and provided a cosmic sanction for the norms that guided almost every aspect of daily life. One of the seeming marks of modernity, as first experienced in Europe, was the declining presence and influence of religious symbols and institutions. Nationalism and a pragmatic stake in economic interests seemed to be displacing religion as the unifying forces of society. Religion became increasingly a private matter, a personal concern, of diminishing significance in the lives of an ever-growing number of people. Secularization appeared to be a hallmark of the modernization that Europe, and much of the rest of the world, was experiencing.

Comprehending the social functions of religion, Marx, Durkheim, and Weber realized, might improve their grasp of the causes of the social discord and alienation so characteristic of modern life. To know the contours of the emerging new social order and to ease the sufferings it imposed, they sought to understand the foundations of order on which societies had always relied—which most certainly included religion. Could societies be strong without the presence of a common religion?

In simple terms, it can be said that the studies of Marx, Durkheim, and Weber enhanced our appreciation of religion's intended and unintended contributions to three fundamental aspects of social life: Marx examined the ways in which religion can act as an agent of social control, Durkheim examined the role of religion in promoting social solidarity, and Weber showed how religious beliefs and practices may prompt sweeping social changes. In these and other regards their sophisticated insights into the nature and social functions of religion remain influential in the sociology of religion.

Marx and Social Control

Contrary to the Biblical view of the world, Marx ([1844] 1957) insisted, God did not make humanity: humanity made God. This atheistic proposition was nothing new when Marx penned it (e.g., Feuerbach [1841] 1957). But few others had expressed it more forcefully or stipulated so well the social sources of the human need for an illusion like God. Religions exist, Marx primarily argued, to legitimate the right of the wealthy and powerful elites to rule, and to make that rule possible by distracting the poor and oppressed masses from grasping the real causes of their suffering. The ideology and rites of religion provide people with a harmless way of venting the fears, hopes, and grief they feel in the face of the hardships imposed on them. In the pithy and famous phrase of Marx, religion is **"the opium of the people"** (Marx, [1844] 1957: 38). The promises of rewards for good behaviour in the next life and the admonitions to cultivate humility and forgiveness in the face of hardship act like a powerful sedative, subduing and diverting the people's attention from the social and economic sources of their lowly lot.

But Marx's understanding of religion was not one-dimensional. He also appreciated that religion has played an important and positive role in human history, giving voice to the distress of people and providing some much-needed comfort by infusing life with a greater sense of order and purpose and cultivating and reinforcing communal bonds. In Marx's colourful language:

> Religion is the general theory of this world, its encyclopaedic compendium, its logic in popular form, its spiritual *point d'honneur*, its enthusiasm, its moral sanction, its solemn complement, and its universal basis of consolation and justification.
>
> *Religious* suffering is, at one and the same time, the *expression* of real suffering and a *protest* against real suffering. Religion is the sigh of the oppressed creature, the heart of a heartless world, and the soul of soulless conditions.

In the end, however, he stresses, the struggles with temptation and sin, and the worship of God or gods, will do little to end the political and economic exploitation that is the real reason for people's suffering. Reasoned insight into the political roots of the real evil that afflicts us must come to supersede religion.

The classes who rule, Marx argues, those who "own the means of production," and hence also the "means of intellectual production," are equally deluded. They tend to fervently support the religious institutions of their day, believing in a cosmology that conveniently justifies their authority and material comfort as either their God-given right or just part of the natural order of things. Church and state collude to the mutual benefit of each other and of the ruling classes that are dominant in each set of institutions.

The first step, Marx asserts, to the communist revolution, which will usher in the classless society and finally liberate humanity, is the critique of religion. In order for the revolution to begin, enough people must realize that their religious beliefs and practices are fantasies in the first place, and that they constitute a harmful system of social control. But only with the ultimate overthrow of the political tyranny founded on the wage slavery of the modern capitalist state will the suffering of humanity be relieved sufficiently to end the condition of need that fosters the illusory compensations of religion in the first place. When equality is achieved, the church will simply wither away. Its primary purpose will be at an end (see Box 4.1).

Durkheim and Social Solidarity

Durkheim, like Marx, was essentially an atheist. But he was more keenly aware of the role played by religion in holding societies together in the face of adversity and, even more, of the destructive anti-social impulses of their own members. Religious beliefs and practices, he argued (Durkheim, [1912]

1995), have been instrumental in protecting the moral integrity of social relations and hence assuring the very survival of societies. Divine sanctions serve to suppress the natural selfishness of individuals and to encourage the unselfish behaviour that all groups need to prosper. The members of any society must be willing to make personal sacrifices, perhaps even lay down their lives, for the benefit of others or of future generations if that society is to survive in the struggle for resources with others. Religion provides the ultimate reasons and justifications for such sacrifices.

These reasons, with their supernatural cast, may well be illusory. But Durkheim thought he had discovered why people continue to believe in the special powers of the sacred to protect humanity. At the heart of religion lies a real experience of power, he argues, that people find exhilarating and comforting. They may attribute this feeling incorrectly to the various sacred objects they worship. But the experience is real, as are its benefits. The testimony of human history points overwhelmingly to the truth of this simple observation, one that irreligious modern social scientists struggle to understand. But in fact, Durkheim proposes, social scientists need not be perplexed by the force of religion in human history if they realize that it is the experience of society itself, in its most fundamental form, that inspires the religious convictions that serve society's needs so well. But how is this the case?

Durkheim's theory of religion rests on a set of interrelated observations and assumptions. He begins by stipulating that the unique mark of the religious worldview is the division of reality into two kinds of phenomena, the sacred and the profane. The sacred is that which is thought to possess tremendous power, and it is set apart and treated with special awe and respect. Throughout the course of human history, a great many things have been deemed sacred, from natural phenomena like trees, rocks, streams, animals, and stars to objects crafted by human hands. The sacred is not marked by any intrinsic features. What marks the sacred is our attitude toward it, and the consequences of that attitude. Put differently, nothing is actually sacred as given; it only becomes sacred when a group of people begin to treat it as such. Thus while Mount Fuji is sacred for followers of Shintoism and Buddhism in Japan, it has no significance for Christians, or even Buddhists in China. For Christians the sign of the cross is sacred in all contexts, but it carries no special meaning for Hindus. For Muslims everyone faces Mecca in their daily prayers, but for Buddhists and Christians no one direction or place is honoured in this way. In each instance, however, whatever is designated sacred acts as the fixed and eternal, yet volatile, focal point of reality, around which the chaos of the profane world happens. Religious rites and the institutions that provide them offer people a stable and safe way to contact this power and to harness it to stave off the threatening uncertainties of profane existence. But how, Durkheim asks, could this extraordinary division of reality into the sacred and the profane have arisen "though nothing

Box 4.1

Pentecostalism and the Marginalized: The Debate

From your own experience, would you agree with Marx that religion chiefly serves as a coping mechanism for those who are economically or socially deprived? Sociologists have long thought that sectarian religious groups draw disproportionately from society's oppressed (Lanternari, 1963). There is some research to suggest that Pentecostalism, for example, the most successful Christian sect of the twentieth century, appeals principally to the outcast and displaced in society (see e.g., Block-Hoell, 1964; Nicol, 1966; Anderson, 1979). In more recent research Donald Miller and Tetsunao Yamamori (2007) note that not everyone who joined the early Pentecostal movement came from the lower class, but a significant segment did. In the early twentieth century Pentecostalism seems to have thrived amongst the mass of people who moved to the cities from the country and were suddenly confronted with the instability and disorder caused by unstable employment and housing, vices such as gambling, prostitution, alcohol and drugs, and increased loneliness. Pentecostalism, it is believed, provided individuals "living precarious lives" with "order, stability, and hope" (Miller and Yamamori, 2007: 23). Today, Philip Jenkins (2002) argues, the overall centre of gravity of Christianity is shifting away from the Northern and Western parts of the globe where it has been dominant for years to the Southern and Eastern parts, where economic, political, and social instability are the norm for many. In places like Africa, Latin America, and Asia, charismatic and Pentecostal churches are filled to the brim with people from the lower classes seeking to improve the quality of their lives, not through mass political action, but rather by way of their own redemption and salvation and the conversion of others. It is believed, in the same way that the early American and Canadian Pentecostals believed, that social problems are the offspring of individual sin and collective temptation, and not the result of poverty and politics *per se*. In some of the Southern and Eastern

in sensible experience seems likely to suggest the idea of such radical a duality" ([1912] 1995: 39)? The answer lies, he proposes, with two other observations derived from his study of (what he mistakenly took to be) the most primitive religion in the world: that of the Australian aborigines. In studying their seemingly simple beliefs and practices, which he identified as forms of totemism, he thought he had gained an insight into the core nature of all religious experience.

When the aborigines perform their sacred rites, Durkheim notes, they are moved by feelings of heightened strength. In his words, "[t]he believer who has communed with his god is not simply a man who sees new truths. . . . he is a man who is stronger. Within himself, he feels more strength to regions of the world (e.g., Iraq, Nigeria and Malaysia) where martyrdom and exile are more common experiences for Christian communities, Jenkins asserts (2002: 219), "many Christians look for promises that their sufferings are only temporary, and that God will intervene directly to save the situation."

Other scholars, however, have raised doubts about this rather reductionist interpretation of the appeal of Pentecostalism for the marginalized (e.g., Cox, 1995; Wacker, 2001; Althouse, 2010; Stewart, 2010). In the United States, Grant Wacker (2001) asserts that early Pentecostals were economically representative of all Americans, drawing members across the class lines. Further, he cautions against confusing being on the margins of society because of one's religious values, which Pentecostals were, with being economically on the margins of society. Adam Stewart (2010) suggests that the empirical data in support of the Marxian interpretation of the success of Pentecostalism are insufficient. The poor socioeconomic status of some people, he notes, may have been a catalyst for joining the Pentecostal movement, but this explanation fails to account for why other poor people did not join and why many in the middle or upper classes did. While objective social structures such as social class may influence one's religious inclinations, so do other more subjective aspects of the human condition (e.g., family background, personality), as Stewart highlights; hence, we must give due consideration to the positive features of Pentecostalism that attracted followers as much as to the negative features of life that pushed them to see the benefits of joining. Overall, he argues, the presumed causal link between social class and religion is too deterministic and simplistic.

Marxian interpretations of religion likely carry some truth for a segment of the religious population around the world, yet we must heed the advice of critics and recognize that this view only tells part of the story. The debate over the links between economic deprivation and religious belief will continue and sociologists of religion need to carefully discover and weigh the quantitative and qualitative evidence available to determine how applicable Marx's theory of religion is in each case studied.

endure the trials of existence or to overcome them" ([1912] 1995: 419). This feeling of empowerment, Durkheim argues, is marked by three features: the strength is felt to come (1) from a source greater than the people themselves, and (2) from outside of themselves, and (3) is independent of their will. It has a kind of sovereignty over them. These features provide a crucial clue, Durkheim reasons, to the true source of their experience. If as scientists we discard the possibility of a supernatural source, then we must find the cause in the social character of religious activity itself. By participating collectively in the performance of religious rites of worship and sacrifice, people are brought into dramatic contact with two powerful aspects of social life: **"collective conscience"** and **"collective effervescence."** It is the social aspect of being human that is the real source of the sense of empowerment imparted by participation in religious rites and attributed to gods and other sacred things.

Religion, unlike magic or mere superstition, Durkheim insists, is always a social undertaking. It is a shared activity. In fact, for most of human history, the enactment of religious rituals marked one of the few regular occasions when relatively large numbers of people would purposefully gather together. The small hunting and gathering clans of the Australian aboriginals, for instance, came together several times a year in *corroboree*, lavish festivals of song, dance, and ceremony that punctuated the drudgery and isolation of much of the rest of the year. In the performance of solemn and elaborate rituals, often entailing specific attempts to induce ecstatic states through rhythmic drumming, chanting, and the use of incense and colourful imagery, people would be lifted out of their ordinary existence and worries. Through symbols and myths they would be exposed to a larger horizon of understanding and the cumulative wisdom of their society—to the collective conscience. They would be imbued with a profound sense of their participation in a cultural whole that transcends them and that seeks to instruct and protect them. The reassurance this provides is reinforced by a contagious emotional enthusiasm set in motion by the sheer presence of so many people united in an activity of celebration. They are gripped by a collective effervescence that inspires a sense of power and possibility far outstripping their solitary experience. Like soldiers marching to battle amidst cheers and bands playing, or participants in boisterous political rallies or large sporting events, they feel transported for a time to a place where their personal woes are of little consequence and their collective strength is unimpeachable.

People mistakenly believe that the mythic entities they are worshipping at these times are the source of these feelings, of their strength, when in fact it is society itself that they are really worshipping through the sacred symbols. So at the heart of religion, for Durkheim, lies a great error. But the illusion serves a worthy and most important social function: it boosts and maintains the social solidarity of a people. It is the unifying result that counts. In circular manner, the practice of religion bonds people together; these bonds fortify the strength of every individual, and this feeling of empowerment helps to perpetuate the belief in the sacred that in turn bonds people together. By Durkheim's reasoning, society is the "soul of religion," but then religion is the soul of society. When people worship their god(s) they are in fact acknowledging and honouring the society on which they depend, as represented in all its complexity, the good and the bad, by the subtle symbolism of religious stories and actions. This makes it difficult to imagine a stable society in the absence of religion, yet that was the very nature of the society that seemed to be emerging around Durkheim in France at the dawn of the twentieth century (see Box 4.2).

Weber and Social Change

Weber devised a comprehensive sociological theory of religion encompassing an encyclopedic range of historical information. He wrote books and essays on the religious history of the Western, Chinese, and Indian civilizations, as well as on ancient Judaism and Islam. In his famous essay "The Social Psychology of the World Religions" ([1915]1958b), the basic principles of his understanding of religion are discussed, but in its scope and critical insight, Weber's analysis of religion defies easy summary. At the core of his thought, however, is a famous and reasonably simple argument that has become part of the canon of sociological knowledge, what is known as the **Protestant ethic** thesis. We will confine our attention largely to this important argument and its ramifications.

Weber's chief concern was the origin and nature of modernity. Like Marx before him, he identified modernity with the emergence of capitalism. He recognized that many factors contributed to the creation of the capitalist economic, social, and political order of Western Europe—the driving force of modernity around the world. The capitalist system was dependent on the discovery of everything from double-entry bookkeeping to the steam engine. There could have been no capitalism without the growth of a large pool of labourers free to leave the land and take jobs in the new factories of the eighteenth and nineteenth centuries, or without the new resources and markets opened up by colonialist expansion. But capitalism, and modernity in its diverse forms (such as bureaucratic administration and autonomous legal systems), was also marked by an attitude, a motivational pattern, that was equally unique and essential. Weber identified this "spirit of capitalism" as the "ascetic ethic of vocation" (Weber, [1904] 1958a).

In his famous book *The Protestant Ethic and the Spirit of Capitalism* ([1904] 1958a) Weber argues that the early capitalists were distinguished from their more traditional predecessors by a proclivity to resist spending the profits of their labour on the luxuries of life. They favoured instead reinvesting their profits in their businesses. In other words, they peculiarly chose to deprive themselves in the present—to be ascetic—in order to establish ever-growing businesses, and hence more profits to invest as capital. With constant reinvestment, their enterprises prospered, and the substantial capital required to lay the foundation for the modern industrial economy accumulated.

But what could have led people to adopt this new approach to their work, to turn to an ascetic ethic of vocation? Prompted by studies indicating that Protestants, when compared with Catholics, were disproportionately employed in business and other related professions, Weber turned to the legacy of the Protestant Reformation for an answer (Weber, [1904] 1958a). He traced the spirit of capitalism to the unique influence of two religious doctrines advanced by the Protestant reformers in their rebellion against the

Box 4.2 Civil Religion

In 1967 the American sociologist Robert Bellah published a seminal essay, "Civil Religion in America." Inspired in large measure by Durkheim's understanding that as long as people join together to forms groups there will be a tendency to sacralize the beliefs and values they share and that bond them together, Bellah proposed that the formal separation of church and state in the First Amendment of the Constitution of the United States set the conditions for the spontaneous creation and spread of a "religion of America." This folk religion of American-ness borrows its symbolic cadence from the Christian heritage of the nation, but it is independent of any one denomination. In essence the formal disestablishment of any one religious group in the United States, to prevent a repetition of the religious persecution so many of those who settled in the new world had experienced in Europe, compelled Americans to ingeniously find a substitute for the established religions that served to unite and strengthen other nations (e.g., the Catholicism of France or Spain). Like all religions this "civil religion" is part of the symbolic self-understanding of American society and it has grown with the great crises faced by the nation, from its birth in the turmoil of the American Revolution through the Civil War, the Second World War, and 9/11. In these kinds of crises this civil religion helped to fortify the will of the people and to heal its wounds. At its core is the notion that America is a blessed nation imbued with a special and divine purpose: to bring its dream of a society founded on the ideals of "life, liberty and the pursuit of happiness" to the rest of humankind.

This American civil religion has its own sacred rites and symbols, a ceremonial calendar, prophets and martyrs, sacred texts and sites. It is ritually celebrated and reinforced on the Fourth of July, Memorial Day, Thanksgiving, and during every presidential inauguration. Its prophets and martyrs include the founding fathers, such as George Washington, Thomas Jefferson, and Benjamin Franklin; important and charismatic presidents such as Abraham Lincoln, Franklin D. Roosevelt, and John F. Kennedy; other inspiring leaders such as Martin Luther King Jr. and Robert Kennedy; and countless celebrated war heroes, great (e.g., Ulysses S. Grant) and small (e.g., winners of the Congressional Medal of Honour). Its sacred texts are

Catholic Church. The first was Martin Luther's concept of the calling. The second was John Calvin's doctrine of predestination.

Seeking to return people to the purity of the primitive Christian church, free of what he saw as the institutional corruption of Catholicism, Luther proposed that all people are called, in their ordinary walks of life, to the service of God. He announced "the priesthood of all believers," whereby each person, in completing their calling to the best of their ability, as farmer, the Declaration of Independence, the Constitution, and the Gettysburg Address; some of its sacred places are the Washington and Lincoln memorials, Gettysburg, Arlington National Cemetery, the Vietnam War memorial, and the 9/11 memorial. The ceremonies and visitations associated with these sites serve to invoke and renew the moral vision and fervent patriotism of Americans—all Americans, whether Protestant, Catholic, or Jewish, or, more recently, Hindu, Buddhist, or Muslim. The simple framework of this shared civil religion "provides religious legitimation to political authority, gives the political process a transcendent goal, serves as a carrier of national identity and self-understanding, and serves as a resource for morally judging the nation" (Cristi and Dawson, 2007: 272).

In Durkeimian terms, it works to cement the solidarity of a nation of immense diversity, culturally, racially, and geographically, by calling the people to a higher purpose through which the perfection of the nation can be achieved. It is invoked every time a president ends a speech with "God bless America," and no contemporary American politician would ever think to end any speech of significance otherwise.

Yet since the 1980s many commentators have worried that this tradition has actually become a source of cleavage in America as the increasingly polarized conservative and liberal factions in the nation have fashioned their own competing civil religions (Cristi and Dawson, 2007: 274–6). The civil religion of the conservatives stresses the Judeo-Christian heritage of America and the divine nature of its mandate. The liberals lay more stress on the responsibility of Americans to share their blessings of freedom and prosperity with the rest of the world. Like priests, the conservatives are more inclined to celebrate the unique virtues of America and issue calls to defend them against detractors and interlopers. Like prophets, the liberals are more likely to extol the egalitarian and democratic aspirations of America and admonish Americans for failing to live up to their ideals. Should the phrase "one nation under God" in the Pledge of Allegiance be understood, then, "as a proclamation of God's blessings or as a reminder of God's judgement" (Canipe, 2003: 309)? This ideological tension speaks to the inherent ambiguity of the concept of civil religion. But Bellah's small essay has spawned a vast literature, seeking to expand, modify, and criticize his ideas (see Cristi and Dawson, 2007). Of course if the underlying insight of Durkheim is true, then other societies will have fashioned other types of civil religions (e.g., Hammond, 1980; Liebman and Don-Yehiya, 1983; Cha, 2000), including Canada (Kim, 1993), and much might be learned about these societies by interpreting what has happened.

lawyer, carpenter, or whatever, was doing the bidding of God. The religious virtuosi—the monks praying in their cells or the bishops ruling the church—no longer had a special status in the eyes of God. Everyone was elevated in importance, in principle, while the church's role in intervening with God was demoted.

But this change had two unforeseen and related consequences. First, it made Protestants more acutely aware of the significance of all their daily deeds, most particularly their work. They became more methodical in their labours and more careful and honest in all their dealings. If one should fall into sin, there was no escape from the consequences, because the Reformation had cast off the rites of confession and priestly absolution in rejecting the Catholic Church. Second, this inducement to dedication to one's calling understandably helped businesses to thrive. A new "work ethic" came into being, elevating the motivation to excel. But other factors limited the impact of these developments until later in the Reformation, when the social consequences of Luther's innovations were reinforced by Calvin's doctrine of predestination.

If God is all-knowing, present everywhere, and all powerful, Calvin reasoned, then all things must have been determined by him from the beginning of time. God knows who is saved or damned, and all efforts to influence our fate are not only futile, they are an affront to God, calling into question his majesty. Our fate lies in his hands alone; it is predestined. Our duty, as prescribed by his teachings, is to have faith in God and to believe in our salvation. To doubt our salvation reveals that we are susceptible to temptation, and it may even be evidence that we are not saved. But how could doubts not arise, faced as we are with the threat of eternal damnation and the daily reality of human sinfulness? This spiritual conundrum, Weber surmises (Weber, [1904] 1958a), meant the very devout and sincere Protestants of the early modern era were driven to find some psychological relief in the discovery of covert, unofficial signs of salvation. Agonizing over their fate, Protestants were advised by their pastors to allay all doubts by redoubling their labours at their callings. Idle hands, as the saying goes, are the devil's helpmates. With time, success in one's calling became an unofficial sign of salvation, while the humility required of true believers helped to further assure that the wealth accrued from this success was ascetically reinvested and not squandered on ostentatious displays of self-importance or the corrupting pleasures of the flesh. Those who succeeded appeared, by this reasoning, to be blessed and to gain prestige in the community, further reinforcing the illicit logic lying behind the influence of the Protestant ethic.

Thus, the conditions required for the accumulation of capital sufficient to lay the foundations of the modern industrial order grew out of the religiously motivated desire to secure peace of mind and social status in the community of believers. By this means, Weber concludes, religion unintentionally played an instrumental role in the birth of capitalism, and thus in the eventual spread of modernity around the world. It had become a world-transforming agent of social change, but in ways quite contrary to the original intentions of any of the leaders of Christianity. In this instance, religion was the agent of a series of unintended and sweeping changes that, ironically, would eventually push religion itself to the periphery of social life—or so most sociologists believed until recently.

Weber tested his theory in many ways, examining how the traditions of other major religions—Hinduism, Confucianism, Taoism, Buddhism, and Islam—had influenced the "practical ethics" of the societies they dominated in Asia and the Middle East. While the material, technological, and political conditions were often present for the rise of something like capitalism in these parts of the world, he argued, the emergence was blocked by the adverse impact of aspects of their ideologies on the social motivations of the business, labour, and ruling classes. The accuracy of these sweeping comparative studies may be called into question, and the details of the entire Protestant ethic thesis have been criticized (e.g., Green, 1973), but scholars remain indebted to Weber's acute insight into three processes: (1) the often unintentional consequences of our actions and beliefs; (2) the powerful role that religious ideas have played in laying the foundations for the modern world; and (3) the way in which history has been shaped by the "**elective affinity**" (Weber, [1915] 1958b: 284) that can occur between a powerful set of ideas and specific material circumstances. We are the product of unintentional convergences of inspiration and opportunity that few, if any, can even recognize, let alone anticipate.

Contemporary Theory: Berger and Stark

In the late nineteenth and early twentieth century many anthropologists, sociologists, psychologists, and others were willing to try their hand at developing quite general theories of religion. In addition to Marx, Durkheim, and Weber, there was Edward Tylor (1871), Herbert Spencer (1886), Max Müller (1889), William James ([1902] 1994), and Sigmund Freud ([1913] 1950), to name just a few prominent figures. But as the social sciences matured and the sheer complexity of religious phenomena worldwide become more apparent, few have been willing to venture beyond the formulation of more delimited theories of specific aspects of religious life, such as the nature of ritual (e.g., Turner, 1969; Bell, 1992) or how religious groups are socially organized (e.g., Niebuhr, 1929; Yinger, 1970; Dawson, 2008). Two influential exceptions are the American sociologists Peter Berger and Rodney Stark.

Peter Berger's Theory of Religion

In 1967 Peter L. Berger published the seminal book *The Sacred Canopy*. In this work he laid out a theory of religion and a theory of secularization. We will examine the theory of secularization in Chapter 5. Here our focus is his theory of religion. This theory stems from a masterful synthesis of the insights of many other important thinkers in the social sciences (e.g., Karl Marx, Émile Durkheim, Max Weber, George Herbert Mead, Sigmund Freud, Max Scheler, Karl Mannheim, Alfred Schutz, Arnold Gehlen, and others), and has shaped the thinking of sociologists of religion for decades.

For Berger, religion grows out of a fundamental human predicament. Unlike most other animals, humans are born unfinished. We lack the biological programming, the instincts, to survive. Each of us requires a long period of instruction and protection to learn how to cope with our environment. Our species created culture to provide for this possibility. It is the humanly fashioned realm of culture that stands protectively between us and the cruel realities of nature. It is only through interaction with significant others, with our parents, siblings, friends, and other close community members, that we learn the cognitive, linguistic, and social skills needed to overcome the forces pitted against us, including other human groups competing for the same resources. In other words, it is culture that constitutes the true ecology of most of our behaviour, and not nature *per se*, and the quality of our lives depends on the stability of our cultural creations. Social order is a prerequisite of our survival and prosperity.

The success of a culture, in providing a stable environment for human development, depends, in part, "upon the establishment of symmetry between the objective world of society and the subjective world of the individual" (Berger, 1967: 15). The upshot of this symmetry is that the institutions of society and the roles these prescribe for individuals strike us as "factual," which is to say that we think we must abide by their dictates, by society's traditional ways of doing things, because these are seen as somehow belonging to reality itself. Under such conditions people do not merely perform their assigned roles in social life; they freely identify with these roles. They seek what another sociologist, Ralph Turner (1978), calls "role–person merger"—they become their roles—and in the process they impart great stability to the received social order. Human activity becomes very regular and predictable, providing practical and psychological reassurance to everyone about their own behaviour and that of others. Hence, under ideal circumstances, which are never actually achieved, most aspects of the social order come to be "taken for granted." The relatively stable human environment that results is what Berger calls a **nomos**, a meaningful world order.

But the stability achieved is in some sense illusory, because human cultures are inherently unstable. The world we live in, the world as perceived by humans, is constantly being created and re-created by us through a "dialectical process" of world construction that has three aspects: "externalization, objectivation, and internalization." Our thoughts become embodied in the things we make and do in the world—they are externalized. Once out there, these products of our thought (e.g. machines, art forms, belief systems, institutions) take on an independent existence as objects of our awareness— objectivation occurs—and they act back upon us, shaping and changing our behaviour and our further thoughts. We internalize the lessons of living in the world of these objects (physical, social, and cultural), adapting ourselves in thought, word, and deed to the presumed requirements of "reality." We are socialized to the reality of these objects and the norms associated with them. Thus, while we are ultimately the creators of our world, we are also just another of its creations, objects in the world that humanity has collectively fashioned. But because the world we live in is the ongoing product of human externalizations, it is subject to constant flux and change. This is our predicament. We are biologically driven to create culture in order to secure a stable and hence safe environment, yet our cultures are at heart only fragile social constructions.

Religion is the ultimate response to this predicament. The collective effort to fashion a nomos is "totalizing"; that is, it wishes to encompass all things to assure its stability. But it cannot. On the margins of everyday life are less predictable experiences that resist being incorporated, that threaten some primal chaos. The experiences threaten us with **"anomie,"** an anxiety-inducing sense of normlessness. Dreams, sickness, death, defeat, and unexpected events repeatedly threaten us with separation from the social world and the loss of the meaningful order of our lives. In Berger's words (1967: 23), "every nomos is an edifice erected in the face of the potent and alien forces of chaos." Religion seeks to provide the "ultimate shield against the terror of anomie" (1967: 25) by supplying the social order with the **ultimate legitimation**.

Religious myths, rites, doctrines, and practices seek to assert that the social order is in fact the natural order, the way things are meant to be. Religions institute a higher order of symmetry between the worlds of objective and subjective experience by merging the nomos with the cosmos. The social order, in Berger's words, is "cosmosized." It is no longer a human construct, subject to change, but a divinely given order subject only to the will of the gods (or other supernatural forces). In this world where the human microcosm has been merged with the natural macrocosm, where social roles become reiterations of cosmic realities, the experience of anomie is much more tolerable. It is not eliminated, since death, nightmares, and unanticipated twists of fate persist. But these events are given a meaning in light of some larger divine scheme, whether through reference to the will of a supreme God, the struggle of supernatural forces of good and evil, or the consequences of karma. This meaningfulness helps individuals to maintain hope and endure suffering. The promise of ultimate order provides comfort and, furthermore, it ensures that individuals will continue to willingly sacrifice themselves and their own selfish interests for the benefit and survival of the group, the social system, and the culture.

This stability and security is purchased at a price, however: a mode of forgetfulness called **"alienation."** For the illusion of culture to work, humans must forget their own ongoing creative role in the dialectic. They must become estranged from their own responsibility for the nature and fate of their society. To consider one's creative role would be to question the objectivity of the social order and hence the ultimate meaning attributed to life. Religions socialize us to this "forgetfulness" and place the creation of the world in the hands of others, the gods. In this sense, Berger says, religions are the consummate agents of alienation. They estrange us from an important aspect of our own nature in order to harbour us from the effects of another—the experience of anomie. In Berger's theory, every society strikes some balance between the evils of anomie and alienation. The former can only be staved off by a certain amount of the latter. In traditional societies, religions function as sacred canopies, unifying groups and sheltering their members from the anomic chaos lurking at the margins.

In late modern societies the pendulum has swung far in the opposite direction. We have become de-alienated as our reflexive grasp of the creative role we play in structuring our world grows. The sacred has shrunk as the authority of secular expert systems has grown, but at the price of a heightened sense of anomie and global risk.

Berger recognized that religions exist in dialectical relationship with the societies they serve. Their success depends on certain "plausibility structures." Just as religious beliefs may justify certain habits or institutions of society, a social system can provide a kind of material validation of its religious beliefs. A powerful, viable society lends credence to the belief system associated with it. Conversely, the military defeat or social disruption of a society may discredit its religious ideology. Conquests are commonly followed by mass conversions of those conquered to the faith of the conquerors. But given the historical function of religion this is not the only means by which it can be discredited or rendered implausible.

The plight of religion in the modern world is a plausibility crisis brought on by social and cultural pluralism and the privatization of religion. Following Weber, Berger highlights the role of the Protestant Reformation (1517–1648) in bringing about this situation. In casting off the religious monopoly of the Catholic Church, the Protestant reformers placed a premium on the faith and practice of the individual believer. With time, this emphasis transmuted religion into a private matter. In principle, at least, religious beliefs became a matter of individual choice. Such beliefs cannot be legitimately imposed on populations from above, and people should not take the beliefs to which they have been socialized for granted. Religious beliefs can and probably should be subject to critical scrutiny. These new norms, in combination with the exposure to other cultures and religions that accompanied the global spread of Western capitalism, made it possible for a plurality of religious systems to either develop in or be imported into the cultures of North America and Europe. So we live in societies where there are a large number of quite different and seemingly equally valid religions. But the relative plausibility of all religious systems today impairs the ability of any one religion to offer the kind of absolute protections against anomie that Berger thinks brought religion into being in the first place. Privatized conceptions of religion will not support a common universe of meaning for the members of a society, a lack of support that severely ruptures the traditional function of religion. The sacred canopy of the past has been dissolved, Berger laments, by the acidic rain of new and voluntary religions.

When *The Sacred Canopy* first appeared, Berger's critics accused him of sounding the death knell of religion. But Berger is also a Christian and he rejected this conclusion. He went on to write several books formulating a new experiential and even sociological justification for the persistence and importance of religion in the late modern world (e.g., Berger, 1969, 1979, 1992, 1999). But the religion he has in mind diverges in one important respect from its traditional counterparts: it is a more subjective and individualistic expression of the role of the sacred in people's lives, and as such it will never be able to sustain the collectivist agenda of the religion of our ancestors. In this he struck the theme that dominates the thinking of contemporary sociologists of religion: contrary to the fears or the aspirations of early modern social theorists, religion is unlikely to disappear as a significant social force; but it has undergone a fundamental transformation in its nature, in conjunction with other sweeping changes in the character of social systems. Understanding the processes of religious and social change, and how they are related, is the big question underlying research in the sociology of religion today.

Rodney Stark's Theory of Religion

Rodney Stark formulated another highly influential theory of religion, one that is remarkably simple and appealing in its premises, especially for those living in modern, capitalistic, and individualistic societies. Often labelled a "rational choice theory of religion," it was developed in collaboration with several colleagues, most notably William Sims Bainbridge and Roger Finke. This theory starts off where *The Sacred Canopy* leaves off: it seeks primarily to explain why a significant interest in religion persists in late modern societies. "At least since the Enlightenment," Stark and Bainbridge note (1985: 1), "most Western intellectuals have anticipated the death of religion as eagerly as ancient Israel awaited the messiah. . . . But, as one generation has followed another, religion has persisted." If scholars were to grasp the simple essence of religion, Stark insists, and the implications that follow for the sociology of religion, they would cease to mistake the demise of certain traditional forms of religious life for "the doom of religion in general" (Stark and Bainbridge, 1985: 3). There can be no doubt, Stark admits, that secularization is "a major trend in modern times" (Stark and Bainbridge, 1985: 1). But we cannot simply equate the advancement of reason, science, and technology with the death of religion. The conjoined processes of secularization and religious revival are much more complex. The discussion in this chapter, however, is limited to the rudiments of Stark's theory of religion, leaving the discussion of his theory of secularization to Chapter 5.

Stark's theory of religion, as first formulated with Bainbridge (1985, [1987] 1996), grows out of four simple premises. The first is that any meaningful discussion of religious phenomena must acknowledge the pivotal role of the "supernatural." Religions, they argue (1985: 5), "involve some conception of a supernatural being, world, or force, and the notion that the supernatural is active, that events and conditions here on earth are influenced by the supernatural." Some scholars are inclined to see many things as religious, even though they lack any explicit reference to the supernatural (for example, the fanatical cult of personality surrounding the Communist Chinese leader Mao Tse-tung in the 1960s, or the life-consuming commitment of certain radical environmentalists). But these can only be deemed "religions" insofar as they resemble activities that actually do refer to the supernatural; the description is the result of drawing an analogy, but an incomplete one.

The second premise is that "humans seek what they perceive to be **rewards** and try to avoid what they perceive to be **costs**" (1985: 5). Stark and Bainbridge claim that this simple utilitarian adage accounts for most human action, including religious acts. At its core religious behavior is no more intrinsically "irrational" than other kinds of social behaviour and the decisions people make about religion are analogous to those studied by economists. There are more similarities in how people choose cars, for instance, and how they choose religions, than there are differences. The modes of reasoning involved are analogous in important ways.

The third premise is that the rewards people seek are often scarce. Throughout human history some of the most desired rewards seem to be things that are not readily available at all, like life after death or an end to suffering. Religions exist to meet the persistent demand for these most scarce rewards.

The fourth and last premise is that, in the absence of real rewards, people often create and exchange what Stark and Bainbridge call "compensators," promises of reward at some later time or in some other place. These range from the specific to the highly general. When a child is promised a future trip to the amusement park in exchange for chores done now, a specific compensator is being invoked. The promises of a happy life, knowledge of the meaning of life, or immortality, which are common to the religions of the world, are obviously very general; these can be provided only, Stark and Bainbridge assert, with the assistance of some supernatural agency.

Combining these four ideas, Stark and Bainbridge (1985: 8) propose that religions should be viewed as "human organizations primarily engaged in providing general compensators based on supernatural assumptions." With this view in mind they see little reason to be pessimistic about the future of religion, arguing that history suggests that

> so long as humans intensely seek certain rewards of great magnitude that remain unavailable through direct actions, they will be able to obtain credible compensators only from sources predicated on the supernatural. In this market, no purely naturalistic ideologies can compete. Systems of thought that reject the supernatural lack all means to credibly promise such rewards as eternal life in any fashion. Similarly naturalistic philosophies can argue that statements such as "What is the meaning of life?" or "What is the purpose of the universe?" are meaningless utterances. But they cannot provide answers to these questions in the terms in which they are asked. (1985: 7–8)

Implicitly, like Weber and Berger before them, Stark and Bainbridge are positing that humans need to live in a meaningful world and that neither the wonders of modern science nor the material abundance of advanced industrial societies has displaced this need and the consequent quest for supernatural reassurances. The way in which these reassurances are offered is another matter. Religion, in their opinion, is changing, not dying.

Stark and Bainbridge rather remarkably developed these simple ideas into a complex and systematic deductive theory of religion, framed in terms of 344 testable propositions (Stark and Bainbridge, [1987] 1996) about everything from why people are religious to the process of religious conversion and the organization of religious groups. In 2000, in collaboration with Roger Finke, Stark published a further simplified and revised statement of the elements of the theory in *Acts of Faith: Explaining the Human Side of Religion*. Several interesting changes were introduced at this time, largely in response to some of the criticisms of the earlier version of the theory (e.g., Young, 1997; Bruce, 1999). In its basic orientation and reasoning, however, the theory remains much the same.

The first change Stark and Finke make is an acknowledgment that every process of decision making is qualified by certain parameters that limit its rationality, in an ideal sense. People will attempt, they state (2000: 85), to make rational decisions "within the limits of their information and understanding, restricted by available options, [and] guided by their preferences and tastes." This change introduces a much more realistic conception of rationality into their theory of religion. This is commendable but it highlights a suspect element of circularity in the theory. Given these parameters, could we not fashion an argument for the "rationality" of even the most outlandish or extreme religious decisions or actions, such as the mass suicide of the members of The Solar Temple, and of Heaven's Gate, in the

1990s (see e.g., Hall, 2000)? These acts of violence are deeply disturbing, and they defy our common-sense notions of what is reasonable. But, given the qualifications introduced above, how could we differentiate between these mass suicides and other religious acts worthy of our respect without reverting to value judgments that are extrinsic to the theory? If all religious acts are conceivably rational, relative to the circumstances and preferences of individuals and groups involved, then are any acts "rational" in a meaningful sense? Stark's theory is simply asserting that people think about the benefits and costs of religious decisions, which is something we need to keep in mind in explaining religious behaviours and groups. But without applying some set standard of rationality it is difficult to determine whether these decisions are any more or less rational than others. The approach does, however, correct the common tendency to cast all aspects of religion as intrinsically irrational.

Second, in *Acts of Faith*, Stark and Finke repudiated the use of the term **"compensators"** in the earlier version of their theory, saying the word "implies unmeant negative connotations about the validity of religious promises." It suffices instead, they assert, to speak of religious "explanations" (2000: 289), with explanations defined as "conceptual simplifications or models of reality that often provide plans designed to guide action" (2000: 87). Religions offer people explanations of a high general order, which are commonly about "otherworldly rewards" and "supernatural forces." These explanations are rewards in themselves, giving meaning and purpose to life, quelling fears and affording us greater peace of mind in the face of life's hardships. In doing so, they are also indirectly valuable, motivating and guiding the attitudes and behaviours that increase our likelihood of securing many more immediate and this-worldly rewards (by motivating us, for example, to be ethical and work hard).

Third, Stark and Finke choose to place a new and more specific activity at the heart of religion: the process of **exchange between humans and gods**. In the pursuit of the most scare and valuable rewards, humans will seek to strike a deal with the supernatural agents thought to control access to the rewards. Accordingly, they recast the definition of religion in this theory, saying that "[r]eligion consists of very general explanations of existence, including the terms of exchange with a god or gods" (2000: 91). With the new focus on the exchange, they delineate some criteria that determine when and why people will be willing to incur a high cost, in terms of the commitment of their time, energy, and resources to the religious groups through which the exchanges with the gods are thought to occur. In doing so they develop an understanding of how participation in prayers and rituals binds people together through their common exchange relationship with the supernatural beings at the heart of religion, reinforcing in turn their confidence in the validity of the religious beliefs framing the exchange.

The details of the theory vastly exceed the needs of this introductory analysis. But the chief virtue of the theory, relative to Berger's theory, for example, is the way in which Stark and his co-theorists have been able to logically frame many propositions about religion that are systematically related and open, in principle, to empirical study (see Box 4.3). Many things are assumed in the framing of these propositions and they are limited, in essence, to advancing our understanding of a key concern of sociologists of religion, especially in an age of mounting secularity, namely, "What are the basic conditions that influence the decision of individuals to make a commitment to a religion?" There is much that is commonsensical in the formulation of these propositions. But by the same token no one has thought to state the obvious before, and in such an interrelated manner, which highlights the need to clarify and test our often unspoken assumptions. Spelled out in this manner it becomes apparent that other factors should be taken into consideration as well, and in most instances they are considered elsewhere in Stark and Finke's theory, with its staggering array of 36 definitions and 99 propositions.

The chief weakness of the theory is that most of Stark and Finke's propositions have yet to be properly tested, and in part this is because testing them would require the controlled comparison of different religions or religious organizations with regard, for example, to such notions as "otherworldliness" (see propositions 13 and 15 in Box 4.3, p. 90). It would be difficult to operationalize (i.e., to define and measure) this variable and the entire attempt points to what might be an unacceptable ethnocentric bias in the theory. Is the Protestant conception of God more otherworldly than the Catholic? Is the Islamic conception more otherworldly than the Hindu? There are ways of arguing they may well be, as proponents of the religions themselves advocate. But what are the relevant indicators of greater otherworldliness, and are we willing to conclude that some of these religions are somehow superior religions *per se*? Stark and Finke's theory implies certain religions are more "successful," because these religions are more capable, in principle, of fostering the strong commitments to specific religious organizations that are systematically prioritized by this theory as indicators of success. In other words, Stark and Finke have implicitly elevated the chief concern of post-Reformation Western denominations, namely the competition for congregants, as the hallmark of "religiousness." The implicit ethnocentrism of this assumption is objectionable, and it imparts another suspect element of circularity to their entire theory of religion. The criteria used to delineate all religions are too skewed from the start to the preoccupations of American evangelical forms of religion, so it is not surprising that their application in comparative analyses tends to reveal the inherent religious superiority of these forms of religion, with their prioritization of proselytism and group commitment. This kind of implicit circularity, born of the largely Western and Christian roots of the

Box 4.3   Stark and Finke's Conception of Our Terms of Exchange with the Gods

Stark has developed his theory of religion into large sets of deductive propositions, most of which could be tested empirically. To provide a sense of this important and appealing aspect of his work let us consider, for example, some of the propositions Stark and Finke delineate for the human side of the exchange with the gods, the exchange they posit as the heart of religion. The propositions are listed here without seeking to elaborate on the discussion of each proposition that Stark and Finke provide in their theory (see Stark and Finke, 2000: 96–102 and 106–13). The list provides a good sense of the reasoning employed by the theory. The numbers assigned to each proposition are those used in Stark and Finke's theory.

Proposition 8. In pursuit of rewards, humans will seek to exchange with a god or gods.

Proposition 9. The greater the number of gods worshipped by a group, the lower the price of the exchange with each.

Proposition 10. In exchanging with the gods, humans will pay higher prices to the extent that the gods are believed to be more dependable.

Proposition 11. In exchanging with the gods, humans will pay higher prices to the extent that the gods are believed to be more responsive.

Proposition 12. In exchanging with the gods, humans will pay higher prices to the extent that the gods are believed to be of greater scope.

Proposition 13. The greater the scope (and the more responsive they are), the more plausible it will be that gods can provide otherworldly rewards. Conversely, exchanges with gods of smaller scope will tend to be limited to worldly rewards.

Proposition 15. In pursuit of otherworldly rewards, humans will accept an exclusive exchange relationship.

Proposition 16. People will seek to delay their payment of religious costs.

Proposition 17. People will seek to minimize their religious costs.

Proposition 18. A religious organization will be able to require extended and exclusive commitments to the extent that it offers otherworldly rewards.

Proposition 22. An individual's confidence in religious explanations is strengthened to the extent that others express their confidence in them.

Proposition 23. Confidence in religious explanations increases to the extent that people participate in religious rituals.

Proposition 25. Confidence in religious explanations will increase to the degree that miracles are credited to the religion.

sociology of religion, is extremely difficult to avoid, and it is characteristic of much of the work still done in the field.

Nonetheless it would be intriguing and helpful, for example, to see if there is a correlation among an organization's active promotion of the belief in miracles, Stark and Finke's proposition 25 (see Box 4.3), and the confidence people have in their religions. In seeking the correlation, however, it might be hard to determine the cause-and-effect relationship. Do miraculous claims reinforce confidence or does prior confidence, based on other factors perhaps, lend credence to claimed miracles? In truth there is probably a feedback loop among these variables, and among many other related variables Stark and Finke have not noted, that we cannot break down into a more linear model of causation. But it is still important that we seek to hypothesize and demonstrate the correlations, and Stark and Finke's overall theory amply demonstrates the complex and over-determined nature of the interactions of numerous variables in the formation and operation of religions. Patient reading of the theory can pay dividends in terms of framing worthwhile theses that can be tested empirically.

Conclusion

Peter Berger's theory of religion probably still stands as the most comprehensive explanation of the root reasons for the human interest in religion and the fundamental nature of its social purpose. There is something about the very human condition, about the emergence of our very consciousness, with its unique reflexive awareness of our position, as individuals and a species, in a vast array of relations with other humans, other animals, and even the natural world in general, that inclines us to almost compulsively search for a greater sense of order and meaning in the ebb and flow of our days. Berger's theory rests, of course, on the previous seminal insights of Marx, Durkheim, and Weber, whose complex observations on the nature of religion we have only been able to sample here. With Weber he posits a fundamental need for meaning that drives humanity and inspires the religious imagination (see Chapter 1). Yet like Marx, Berger links religion strongly with the need to legitimate the existing social order, justifying in the process the distributions of power and privilege present in any society. As Weber stressed in his work, the kinds of "domination" that social systems require to function can only be achieved, in the long run, if those with power are deemed to be worthy. Their domination must be transformed into what Weber calls "authority" (Weber, 1964: 324–329). Systems of religious beliefs and practices have provided the ultimate legitimation of authority throughout human history, anchoring the order we have created in the world, thorough our collective interaction (i.e., Berger's dialectic), in images of a superior and otherworldly source that transcends the uncertain, transitory, and threatening nature of our daily experience.

For both Berger and Durkheim, however, there is a real source for the sense of empowerment people feel in the face of this imagined other order, and this is the collective presence of society itself in our lives. Or more accurately, the source is our creative capacity, working together, to build a safer and more stable world in which to live. It is this collective capacity to fashion an environment in which the potential of our species can be maximized that is symbolically represented, periodically celebrated, and regenerated in the stories and rituals of religions. In doing so, however, as Weber's study of the larger social consequences of the Protestant ethic reveals, we may alter people's behaviour in ways that are unanticipated, helping to set in motion social forces, such as the capitalist economic system, that may ironically undermine our confidence in and need for the very religious ideas that inspired these developments in the first place.

Stark and his colleagues introduce into this mix of ideas about the more or less compulsive force of religion in human affairs a key emphasis on the element of choice. He too posits a basic human demand for the things that religion has to offer, but infuses the situation with the agency of reason. At least in the modern context, people have the right and the opportunity to make choices amongst an array of religious options and we can discern the conditions that influence these choices, just like any other. In doing so Stark frames the variables and correlations that shape religious life in ways that are more open to empirical study and assessment. In this way grand theorizing about the reasons for being religious and the social functions of religion is anchored in much more specific propositions about the operation of religion in our societies. The overarching reasons for humans being religious may exceed our grasp, but as Stark's theory highlights, building on Weber, how religions actually tend to work, and hence which ones will succeed or fail, is more predictable than is commonly realized.

Critical Thinking Questions

1. Marx called religion the "opium of the people." Thinking in sociological terms (i.e., what is functional for society), is this necessarily a bad thing?

2. Is the sacred/profane distinction Durkheim sees at the foundation of religion meaningful any more for individuals living in late modern societies? If it is, how is this the case? Can you provide an illustration?

3. Can you provide an example that illustrates the three phases of the social dialectic of world construction (i.e., externalization, objectivation, internalization) as delineated by Berger?

4. In Berger's theory of religion, pluralism is problematic for religion. Why is this the case and need it be so?

5. Do we choose our religious beliefs and practices largely in the same way we make other choices? If that is not the case, then what precisely is the difference?

Suggested Readings

Anthony Giddens. 1971. *Capitalism and Modern Social Theory: An Analysis of the Writings of Marx, Durkheim and Weber.* Cambridge: Cambridge University Press. This is still one of the most accessible and accurate overall presentations of the sociological theories of Marx, Durkheim, and Weber. Reading it will help to flesh out their full theories of religion and place them in the context of their broader analyses of the nature of modernity and social systems in general.

Linda Woodhead, Paul Heelas, and David Martin, eds. 2002. *Peter Berger and the Study of Religion.* New York: Routledge. An excellent collection of essays examining the nature and legacy of Berger's work on religion and the discontents of modernity, providing an assessment of the overall merits of his theoretical work for the debates over secularization, new religious movements, the interface of sociology and theology, and other topics.

Lawrence A. Young. 1997. *Rational Choice Theory and Religion: Summary and Assessment.* New York: Routledge. A collection of essays by leading proponents and critics of Rodney Stark's theory of religion that reiterates and develops many elements of the theory and provides a well-rounded sense of its relative strengths and weaknesses.

Related Websites

http://hirr.hartsem.edu/ency/index.html
The Encyclopedia of Religion and Society contains in-depth descriptions and summaries for hundreds of key terms, concepts, theories, and theorists in the social scientific study of religion, including each of the theorists and theories explored in this chapter.

www.ted.com/talks/tags/religion
Technology, Education, and Design (TED) Talks contains a series of lectures given by some of the world's most inspiring voices on many important issues of the day, including religion. This website includes several talks from different religious, philosophical, and scientific traditions on religion and themes such as inequality, group cohesion, or meaning and purpose in life—themes all explored by the theorists summarized in this chapter.

5 Arguments For and Against Secularization Theory

Learning Objectives

In this chapter, you will learn:

◎ To understand the difficulties encountered in defining, measuring, and analyzing secularization.

◎ To understand that there are different kinds or levels of secularization, and recognize that these distinctions must be kept in mind in evaluating the state of religion in the late modern world.

◎ To identify the social, cultural, and historical causes and correlates of secularization.

◎ To comprehend the similarities and differences of the theories developed in support or rejection of the theory of secularization.

Introduction

How religious are people around the world today? Are we more religious than in the past? Are we less religious? Are we about the same? When thinking about these questions, what measurements of religiosity do you have in mind? What social, cultural, and historic variables should be considered in making your judgement? These are the simple but important questions at the heart of what has been the core concern of much of the sociology of religion since its inception. They are component parts of the debate over the "theory of secularization"—the widely assumed correlation between the modernization of societies and the decline of religion as a significant social phenomenon. Some knowledge, then, of the different theories of secularization is essential to understanding the role religion may or may not play in the late modern world.

In this chapter we address some of the most influential theories about secularization. Each defines secularization somewhat differently, but to get us thinking about this topic let us just say that secularization refers to the process by which religion and the sacred gradually have less validity, influence, and significance in society and the lives of individuals. For almost a hundred years most sociologists have assumed that as societies became "modern" they would inevitably become more secular (i.e., non-religious). As noted in the previous chapter, Marx, Durkheim, and Weber all predicted that religion, as traditionally known, would more or less disappear from the modern world. In the last few decades, however, the balance of opinion has shifted, with many sociologists calling this assumption into question. In many instances, though, the theorists involved in this debate are talking past each other, since they are using different terms of reference.

Clearly many individuals, and entire societies, continue to invoke the supernatural in their everyday lives. But there is great dispute over just how religious individuals and societies are today, relative to the past. Some scholars, mainly from Europe, argue that individuals and nations are less religious today and they point to the impact of certain large processes of social change that we will address: processes of **structural and social differentiation, rationalization**, societalization, **pluralism, individualism,** and subjectivization (e.g., Wilson, 1982, 1985, 2001; Davie, 1994; Bruce, 2002, 2011; Voas and Crockett, 2005; Crockett and Voas, 2006; Voas, 2009). Conversely, there is a school of thought, mainly from the United States, which rejects secularization theory and points to ongoing signs of religiosity in the contemporary world. They see the emergence of new religious movements, the resurgent public presence of religion in some parts of the world, and the continued persistence of some form of popular "spirituality" as evidence of religion's continued strength (e.g., Hadden, 1987; Casanova, 1994; Stark and Finke, 2000; Finke and Stark, 2005).

At its core, the secularization debate intersects with our discussion of the elements of religion and the methodological problems of measuring religiosity (see Chapter 4). Disagreements arise because scholars define and measure religion and secularization differently, and consequently their interpretations and explanations about the current state of religion vary (see Demerath, 2007). Karel Dobbelaere (1981, 2002), a sociologist from Belgium, has examined the ambiguities found in the research literature and fruitfully suggested the need to distinguish three different levels or types of **secularization: societal, organizational, and individual**. He encourages researchers to specify what level of secularization they are defining, measuring, and analyzing.

Societal secularization is "the shrinking relevance of the values, institutionalized in church religion, for the integration and legitimation of everyday life in modern society" (Dobbelaere, 2002: 19). For many centuries, for instance, the teachings and institutions of the Roman Catholic Church and various Protestant churches dominated the way the educational, political, judicial, and health needs of the citizens of most European nations were understood and met. The provincial government of Quebec, for example, had no departments of health or education until the early 1960s, since these responsibilities were left in the hands of the Catholic Church. With the onset of liberal democracies and industrial societies in Europe, North America, and elsewhere, most of these responsibilities were transferred to various government agencies that operated independently of religion.

Organizational secularization refers to the "modernization of religion" from within (Dobbelaere, 2002: 21) as with, for example, the liberalizing of religious beliefs (e.g., the acceptance of gay marriage) or the inclusion of "contemporary" music (akin to secular music in the minds of some) in worship services.

Individual secularization includes any "decline in involvement in churches and denominations" (Dobbelaere, 2002: 18), and one could add personal belief and practice (e.g., belief in God, the power of prayer, life after death). This last level of secularization is especially contentious if we consider that many individuals, in Canada and elsewhere, continue to profess belief in God (or a supernatural being) and identify with a specific religious tradition, even though they rarely attend religious services. How should we interpret the behaviour of these individuals? Is their decreased involvement in the activities of their churches, temples, and synagogues emblematic of secularization? If so, how do we account for their continued belief in God and many other religious ideas (e.g., an afterlife)? Are such beliefs and the strong interest many still display in the spiritual and moral issues associated with religion merely residual? Or are these interests indicative of a near-universal need for something like religion?

In this chapter we highlight the clash of views over secularization theory, turning to the influential arguments of Peter Berger, Bryan Wilson, and Steve Bruce, proponents of secularization theory, and Jeffrey Hadden, Rodney Stark, and Jose Casanova, opponents of the theory. The discussion of secularization theory can be exceedingly complex, but in its rudiments it need not be so. As we survey the opposed views we encourage you to ask what "type" of secularization is being discussed and to consider the relevant ways of measuring the changes being postulated. Doing so will help to minimize the ambiguities that have plagued discussions of secularization theory.

None of the theorists we are surveying directly broaches the question of late modernism. Their focus remains on the impact of a more generic modernism. As such, however, it is not hard to extend many of their observations and conclusions to the features of late modernism. A handful of other sociologists have already done so, in various ways (e.g., Beckford, 1992, 1996; Roy, 2004; Dawson, 2004, 2006b, 2007; Campbell, 2006; Heelas, 2008). Some comments on this relationship will be made throughout our discussion, and we will return to the question in our concluding comments.

The Case for Secularization Theory

Peter Berger

One of the most influential theories of secularization was developed by the American sociologist Peter Berger in his book *The Sacred Canopy* (1967). In line with Dobbelaere's notion of societal secularization, Berger defines secularization as "the process by which sectors of society and culture are removed from the domination of religious institutions and symbols" (1967: 107). He argues that secularization is a consequence of processes of rationalization in industrial societies that sharply reduced the influence and control of religion over most aspects of social life. On the societal level, for instance, the increasing specialization and fragmentation of social functions meant that Christian churches gradually lost control over the social institutions delivering many social services, such as education, healthcare, and relief of the poor. This is the process of structural and social differentiation mentioned above. As societies have become larger, more complex, and successful, they have been subject to a progressive division of labour, both at the levels of institutions and individuals. Where individuals living on the farm in largely agrarian societies once took care of many of their own needs—growing their own food, building their own homes, making their own clothing, for example—the urban workers of industrial societies work at one task. They are specialized and rely on the work of others, with special abilities and training, to meet most of their basic needs, in exchange for the money they earn at their own singular labours. Such is the way of the differentiated and practically integrated societies in which we live. Similarly, at one time the church (i.e., the predominant religious institution of any society) once dominated the other spheres of activity in society. In the Middle Ages in Europe the Catholic Church regulated and often actually provided whatever education, healthcare, and social welfare existed, and they exerted tremendous moral, practical, and financial influence over the provision of the arts and entertainment, and the political life of these societies. With the growing complexity of these societies and their progressive rationalization the dominance and control of the church was broken and specialized institutions, both private and governmental, arose to independently meet the diverse needs of the populace. Culturally, of course, this meant that secular themes and ideas started to increasingly displace religious ones in the art, music, and literature of these modernizing societies. As the environment in which people lived changed the very consciousness of individuals became more secular too, as they looked upon the world less and less through the lens of religion.

In considering how and why secularization develops, Berger distinguishes between internal and external causes of secularization. The development of certain features of Christianity had the unanticipated consequence of setting the conditions for secularization, just as Weber had argued that the Protestant ethic unintentionally paved the way for capitalism. These developments are the internal causes of secularization. In this regard Berger has the impact of the Protestant Reformation most in mind. In protest against the perceived corruption of the church, and in an attempt to place more emphasis on God's majesty and sovereign grace, Protestants abolished many of the sacraments of the church, gave less significance to miracles, eliminated intercession of saints for sinners, and reduced the role of the priest in the lives of individuals. "If compared with the 'fullness' of the Catholic universe," he notes, "Protestantism appears as a radical truncation, a reduction to 'essentials' at the expense of a vast wealth of religious contents" (1967: 111). The beliefs and practices discarded by the Protestants were deemed to be without Biblical justification and to be hindering, and not enhancing, the relationship of individuals with their Creator and saviour. The streamlined worldview and practice of the Protestants, however, had the unintended effect, Berger suggests, of actually widening the gap between God and humanity, as it stripped so much of the sacred and supernatural from the human and natural worlds. It reduced the sway of religion over other aspects of life, created a cognitive opening for other views, and rendered the faith of the individual more exposed and precarious in a largely desacralized world (1967: 111-112):

> The Protestant believer no longer lives in a world ongoingly penetrated by sacred beings and forces. Reality is polarized between a radically transcendent divinity and a radically "fallen" humanity that, ipso facto, is devoid of sacred qualities. Between them lies an altogether "natural" universe, God's creation to be sure, but in itself bereft of numinosity. In other words, the radical transcendence of God confronts a universe of radical immanence, of "closedness" to the sacred.

Weber famously referred to this process as the "disenchantment of the world."

The Protestant revolution in religion temporarily increased the piety of the faithful, creating societies of great devotion and dedication (e.g., the Puritans in England and New England), but it formally granted us the right to explore and exploit much of the natural and social world free from the control of religious ideas and institutions, and it narrowed the channels of communication between God and humanity to God's word, as embodied in the Bible and the redemptive action of God's grace. "As long as the plausibility of this conception was maintained," Berger observes, "secularization was effectively arrested, even though all its ingredients were already present in the Protestant universe. It needed only the cutting of this one narrow channel of mediation, though, to open the floodgates of secularization" (1967: 112).

But this process did not originate with the Protestants of the sixteenth century. In line with Weber ([1922] 1963), Berger traces the internal causes of secularization back to the religion of ancient Israel, as embodied in the Old Testament (see Box 5.1). The more immediate causes of secularization, however, are the changing social conditions in which religions must operate. Berger focuses on two key developments as the external causes of secularization: pluralism and privatization. He contends that the structural differentiation of religion from all the other sectors of society sets the conditions for religious and social pluralism. Once the state, and the institutions of political life in general, gained their independence from the church (at least formally) in the early modern era, the call rose for greater freedom for religious minorities. Without the state endorsing any particular religion, religious groups all shared the equal right to hold and practise their beliefs. But this meant they were all equally left to fend for themselves as multiple religions emerged in such societies. Moreover, the loss of privilege experienced by the dominant religious tradition meant all religious groups must contend with non-religious voices in society, vying for the time, money, and attention of people. In this setting of religious and social pluralism, "religion," which was formerly a leading institution, plays an increasingly peripheral role, both for the organization of society as a whole and the provision of meaning in the lives of individuals (Berger, 1967: 130). With time religious beliefs and practices lose much of their "natural" or "taken-for-granted" status as an essential feature of social life. Prayers continue to be offered before soldiers march off to war, but fewer and fewer people think the prayers have much real influence on their fate, relative to the decisions of the government and their commanders.

Pluralism opens the door to increased religious choice for individuals, which undermines the seeming objectivity of any one religious system of belief and practice. The presence of many forms of religion relativizes the absolute truth of any one religious commitment. Since religion (or at least a single religion) is not reinforced throughout the many institutions in society, individuals and families are left with immense freedom to decide for themselves if they will be religious, how they will be religious, and to what degree they will be religious. This is an extraordinary situation in the course of human history. Only recently has such freedom of religious thought and expression been possible, let alone prized as a social good. With the pronounced surge in immigration to Canada, the United States, and Western Europe since the 1960s, from countries in Asia, Latin America, the Middle East, and Africa, the complexion of our societies, especially in the large urban centres, has been transformed. They are marked by a range and type of pluralism that is unprecedented. Just a few decades ago it would have been very unlikely and difficult for a Canadian raised as a Protestant, Catholic, or Jew to even think of becoming a Buddhist or, say, a Muslim Sufi, let alone succeed in doing so. Such is no longer the case in Vancouver, Edmonton, Winnipeg, Toronto, Montreal, or Halifax today. In fact, with a little effort, significant communities of non-immigrant Canadian Buddhists (i.e., converts), for example, can be found and seekers actually have their choice from among an array of forms of Buddhism, hailing from various parts of the world (e.g., Japanese or Korean Zen, Vietnamese or Sri Lankan Theravadin traditions). Presumably, then, by Berger's reasoning, it should

Box 5.1

The Origins of Secularization in Ancient Israel

Peter Berger (1967), building on the insights of Max Weber ([1922] 1963), traces the beginnings of the process of secularization to three innovative aspects of the Judeo-Christian heritage of the West, starting with the ancient Israelites and culminating in the Protestant worldview: "transcendentalization," "historization," and "ethical rationalization."

Transcendentalization refers to the Israelite belief that there is a clear distinction and gap between a monotheistic God and human beings, where God is completely transcendent and outside the empirical world (Berger, 1967: 115–17). Although the Israelites believed that God was actively involved in the events of the physical world, they were keenly aware that he existed beyond the universe. For instance, God had no genealogical ties to the Israelites and he could not be coerced with magic. He commanded obedience from his followers, yet he was not dependent on their obedience in order to exist. He was entirely self-sufficient and without need for human companions. This perspective stands in stark contrast to the dominant cultures of the day, the Egyptian and Mesopotamian belief systems of the ancient Middle East. Their polytheistic deities were physically and locally present in human affairs, and the supernatural and physical worlds were closely intertwined. Humans could seek to ritualistically manipulate the gods to do their bidding, and events in the physical world influenced events in the supernatural realm. Berger discusses, for example, how human disobedience toward the god-king of Egypt was thought to negatively impact the divine realm. In response, such defiance evoked punishment, not only of the individual offender but often of the entire society. Such punishment might come in the form of defeat at the hands of an enemy or drought and famine. We can, of course, still see elements of this worldview in the Old Testament, but here too we have evidence of a more sophisticated and complex relationship pointing to the greater transcendence of God.

Historization builds on the idea of a transcendent God who stands outside this world yet acts in human history, giving it a grander meaning and purpose (Berger, 1967: 117). The Old Testament is filled with historically specific events where God intervenes in human affairs, such as delivering the Israelites out of Egypt, forming a covenant with Moses and the Israelites on Mount Sinai, and crushing the Canaanites in battle to deliver the "promised land." But these interventions are not portrayed as the recurring acts of idiosyncratic gods responding, more or less spontaneously, to things happening in this world. Rather, they are conceived and presented as manifestations of a larger divine plan for God's chosen people. There are three primary consequences that flow from this new understanding of time as the progressive intent of a single all-powerful being.

First, as indicated, the Bible became essentially a historical text, and not merely a mythological one. It is a memory of God's specific interactions with humanity, designed to shape how humans will interact with Him in the future. It transformed the cyclical pattern of time characteristic of most cultures, one modelled on the course of the four seasons, and in which the world was symbolically created anew each year in the rituals of the New Year (Eliade, 1959: 68–113), into an extended historical record of God's plan for humankind. Cycles were displaced by a sense of the linear progression of time. Second, the religious rituals and festivals of the ancient Israelites, such as Passover, mark past events in history when humanity and the divine achieved a new bond of mutual obligation, one which became the basis for people's faith in God. This historical orientation to the world is unlike the Egyptian and Mesopotamian worldviews in which the many gods are only bound by some highly general notions of cosmic order in their seemingly quite arbitrary dealings with humanity. The God of Israel was singular and more truly transcendent, yet he freely chose to enter into a partnership with humanity, one that imparted extraordinary significance to the acts of individuals in history. This brings us to the third consequence. In the world envisioned in the Old Testament, Berger surmises (1967: 118–19):

> individual men are seen less and less as representatives of mythologically conceived collectivities, as was typical of archaic thought, but as distinct and unique individuals, performing important acts as individuals. One may think here of such highly profiled figures as Moses, David, Elijah, and so forth. . . . This is not to suggest that the Old Testament meant what the modern West means by "individualism," nor even the conception of the individual attained in Greek philosophy, but that it provided a religious framework for a conception of the individual, his dignity and his freedom of action.

Ethical rationalization, the third process of internal secularization initiated by the ancient Israelites, is the culmination of transcendentalization and historization. Once more departing from the dominant Egyptian and Mesopotamian polytheistic religious practices, the God of Israel did not act erratically or inconsistently with humans, and he could no longer be appeased through simple rites of sacrifice and worship. Instead, God provided a set of unwavering commandments and ethical laws that followers needed to obey in return for his love and protection. These were moral prescriptions and not mere taboos. They demanded that believers not only perform the right rites but also think, speak, and act in accordance with God's commandments at all times. As the Israelites were aware of their separation from the transcendent God, mindful that the covenants made with God in the past would impact their ongoing relations with God, and cognizant of the need to police not only their actions but their intentions, they developed a system of norms to guide their attitudes and behaviours, to prevent them from falling into sin (Berger, 1967: 120). The Israelites were encouraged to devote their lives to serving and pleasing God, so they became methodical in their exchanges with God and, ideally, each other. In effect, they began the process of rationalizing all facets of life.

In these ways, Berger argues, building on the insights of Weber ([1904] 1958a; and [1992] 1963), the roots of the secularization recede far into the unique cultural heritage of Western civilization. The dominant and unique motif of a fully transcendent God interacting with individual humans, on the basis of ethical commitments, in the context of a profane and linear history, created the cognitive conditions for the emergence of the modern individual who conceives of religion as a matter of private faith and personal choice. This includes the choice not to believe, in a world ruled primarily by reason, which is the cornerstone of the secular reality that characterizes life for most Canadians and Europeans, many Americans, and others around the world today.

come as no surprise that our societies are also, on the whole, much more secular.

One consequence of the freedom born of pluralism is the privatization of religion, where individuals increasingly identify religion as a personal and private matter (Berger, 1967: 133–135). When religion is privatized, even very religious individuals choose to keep their religious perspectives separate from their public lives, whether at work or in politics. Recalling his theory of religion (see Chapter 4), Berger ruefully remarks that in modern societies "religion manifests itself as public rhetoric and private virtue. In other words, in so far as religion is common it lacks 'reality,' and insofar as it is 'real' it lacks commonality" (1967: 134). It is no longer acceptable in Canada for politicians to even suggest that their religious convictions might inform their policy decisions. Such is the case as well in most of Europe, while the United States is another matter, to be discussed below. Under conditions of pluralism and privatization, then, which have become normative in Canada, religion is robbed of one of its primary functions: to provide a "common world within which all of social life receives ultimate meaning binding on everybody" (1967: 134). In these conditions, as indicated, the plausibility of everyone's private beliefs suffers. In the face of the mounting competition from alternative and presumably equally valid worldviews, how can one claim a greater validity for one's own faith? Plus, if there is no common and dominant worldview, we might begin to seriously wonder what will hold the members of society together? The resultant sense of social and cultural fragmentation experienced by significant segments of our societies heightens the sense of risk people encounter in the late modern world. It challenges their ability to trust in the national institutions of their society, which seem to have come unhinged from the traditions and values on which, rhetorically at least, they were founded (i.e., Christian and European). This situation causes some to place even further emphasis on the private cultivation of faith (e.g., the surprising growth of born-again Christians and the Pentecostal-Charismatic movement) and others to abandon religion altogether (e.g., the "new atheism"). Either way, in the long run, the process of secularization may be strengthened.

In the context of pluralism and privatization, Berger (1967: 140–49) argues that religious groups are compelled to market themselves to remain competitive. In economic terms this means they fall subject to the process of "standardization and marginal differentiation" that we will discuss in Chapter 6. The products of religion are standardized: they become increasingly similar to satisfy the same set of perceived consumer preferences. To remain competitive, however, marginal differences in style and approach are emphasized to stand out from the crowd of products available (1967: 148–49). The emphasis falls on preaching, music, and social activities, and away from real theological concerns and differences. The net result is a plethora of similar yet slightly different religions, like toothpastes or shampoos, which focus primarily on the private needs of individuals and families and are careful to be consonant with the largely secular consciousness of the citizens of modern societies (e.g., by accepting the pre-eminence of the methods and findings of science). Contrary to expectations, this competition of many look-alike religions further undermines the plausibility and appeal of any one and pushes them all further to the margins of society.

The privatization of one's religious commitments in the face of social and religious pluralism has one further consequence of note: the subjectivization of religion. In this social context "emotionality takes the place of objective dogma as the criterion of religious legitimacy" (Berger, 1967: 158). When one set of religious beliefs is neither formally more truthful than another nor the preferred system of the state or the populace, then the veracity of one's commitments becomes increasingly a matter of subjective conviction, based on personal experience. Religious choices are about what feels right and being religious is increasingly a psychological state of affairs. But since, as Berger puts matters (1967: 158), "the 'heart' of one individual may say different things from the 'heart' of another," the belief commitments of everyone are again relativized. Some may also argue that they are trivialized as well, with religious choices being reduced to mere preferences, which are difficult to articulate, let alone impose on others. In these circumstances it is understandable why many religious groups and individuals have experienced a crisis of legitimacy.

In *The Heretical Imperative* (1979) Berger discusses three possible responses to this crisis of religious legitimacy. Some religious groups or individuals may choose the deductive or Neo-orthodox approach, which entails simply staunchly reaffirming the authority of an existing religious tradition (e.g., the New Christian Right in the United States). By bringing people of like mind together through new socio-religious organizations and movements (e.g., the Moral Majority, the Promise Keepers, and so-called mega-churches) a sub-culture is created that lets people find the certainty and stability they crave in their religious tradition despite pluralism. Others pursue the reductive or modernizing response, seeking to reinterpret their tradition in light of modern realities (e.g., the United Church of Canada). The benefit to this approach is that it reduces the cognitive dissonance that individuals experience between the religious and modern worldviews. This means that people feel less tension between their most important ideas about religion and the related emotional convictions and the way we are expected to behave in a late modern world. If the Bible, for example, is understood as a set of helpful stories imparting sage advice on what matters most in life, and not as the literal word of God, then believers can better accommodate living with the findings of science or the idea of allowing homosexuals to become ordained ministers of the faith. But this approach may also boomerang on the proponents, leaving participants wondering why the continued commitment of time, energy, and money to specifically religious institutions is warranted. Finally, some turn to the inductive and experiential approach to authority, which ultimately accepts personal experience as the sole authority over one's worldview.

Berger expresses the inductive approach this way (1979: 32–3):

> When the external (that is, socially available) authority of tradition declines, individuals are forced to become more reflective, to ask themselves the question of what they really know and what they only imagined themselves to know in the old days when the tradition was still strong. Such reflection, just about inevitably, will further compel individuals to turn to their own experience: Man is an empirical animal . . . to the extent that his own direct experience is always the most convincing evidence of the reality of anything. The individual, say, believes in X. As long as all people around him, including the "reality experts" of his society, ongoingly affirm the same X, his belief is carried easily, spontaneously, by this social consensus. This is no longer possible when the consensus begins to disintegrate, when competing "reality experts" appear on the scene. Sooner or later, then, the individual will have to ask himself, "But do I really believe in X? Or could it be that X has been an illusion all along?" And then will come the other question: "Just what has been my own experience of X?"

Berger concludes that individuals will inevitably rely on personal experience as the source of authority in modern pluralist societies, reinforcing in the long run the crisis of legitimacy that undergirds the secularization of social life. This pessimism about the ongoing significance of religion in human affairs is characteristic of Berger's early and most influential work, and his critics have taken him to task for it. His view of the modern condition does not seem to leave room for the logical possibility of a form of religious practice that would continue to have much in the way of social significance. Yet personally Berger remains a believer, and to the surprise of friends and foes alike he later recanted much of his theory pointing to the resurgence of religion in many societies around the world (Berger, 1998, 1999).

Bryan Wilson

Bryan Wilson, a British sociologist, defines secularization as the "process by which religious institutions, actions, and consciousness, lose their social significance" (1982: 149). He expands on this, saying secularization refers to "the decline in the significance of religion in the operation of the social system, its diminished significance in social consciousness, and its reduced command over the resources (time, energy, skill, intellect, imagination, and accumulated wealth) of mankind" (1985: 14). His concern, then, is with both the societal and individual levels of secularization, and his argument is similar to Berger's, but with three differences. First, Wilson makes the important point that the seeming secularization of our society means neither that a golden age of faith existed before (though that may be the case), nor that secularization is inevitable or irreversible. Second, like Durkheim before him, he is more explicitly leery of the consequences of secularization for the moral well-being and social cohesion of our societies. Third, he stresses that the rate and magnitude of secularization differs depending on the historical and social conditions of specific societies. A point David Martin (1978) forcefully made in his comprehensive comparative study of data on religion and the process of secularization in an array of countries (see Berger, Davie, and Fokas, 2008 as well). What binds all forms of secularization, however, is a process Wilson identifies as "societalization."

Societalization occurs when "a collectivity of communities and individuals are drawn into complex relationships of interdependence in which their role performances are rationally articulated" (1982: 154). In making this argument Wilson draws on the classic *Gemeinschaft-Gesellschaft* distinction introduced by Ferdinand Tönnies (1957) in the late nineteenth century. *Gemeinschaft*, or traditional community, is described as a society in which trust, loyalty, respect for seniority, clear patterns of authority, goodwill, and morality are vital to everyday interactions and social stability. This type of society is marked by a common understanding that the values that guide behaviour are rooted in an absolute and numinous power. Thus religious buildings are central to the local architectural landscape of these societies, issues of life and death are interpreted in supernatural terms, the authority of political leaders is divinely ordained, and strong community bonds unite people out of a concern for the welfare of children of the same God or gods. This is contrasted with *Gesellschaft*, or modern society, which is built on impersonal associations, the coordination of skills, formal and contractual patterns of behaviour, role obligations, and duty and role performances that are based on the demands of a rational ordering of society. In this society, people rely on individualism and rationalism, instead of custom and tradition, to legitimate their beliefs and practices. Social control is based on the socially constructed laws of humanity and not the divinely inspired rules of the Bible, Qur'an, or other religious records of revelations.

In agreement with Tönnies, Wilson suspects that societalization leads to the "demoralization" of society. By demoralization he has in mind decreased respect for moral behaviour and principles in favour of mere conformity to rules, and technical standards of competence and performance (2001: 44). We live in times, he fears, when everyone has abdicated their responsibility to socialize children to the moral standards that lay at the foundation of our societies in favour of merely teaching them the skills required to succeed and satisfy other more immediate needs. As a result, children are left without any strong moral guidance. The consequences are catastrophic, and Wilson (2001) points to increased selfishness, individualism, hedonism, poor manners, social division, and crime in post-industrial societies. This is not an uncommon view, and other studies similarly highlight the strong link between religiosity and individual and social well-being (see e.g., Piché, 1999; Reed and Selbee, 2001; Campbell and Yonish, 2003; Nemeth and Luidens, 2003; Smidt, Green, Guth, and Kellstedt, 2003; Bowen, 2004; Wuthnow, 2004, 2007; Berger, 2006; Bibby, 2007, 2011; Zuzanek, Mannell, and Hilbrecht, 2008; Hall, Lasby, Ayer, and Gibbons, 2009; Putnam and Campbell, 2010). Some sociologists have alternatively argued that non-religious societies are actually amongst the most civil in the world (e.g., Zuckerman, 2008), and the "new atheists" continue to press home the age-old lament that religions have played a leading role in fomenting hatred and social discord (e.g., Dawkins, 2006; Harris, 2006; Hitchens, 2007; see also: Piché, 1999; Wuthnow, 2005; Putnam and Campbell, 2010). But in the end, Wilson concludes, "the societal system relies less on people being good (according to the lights of the local community), and more on their being calculable, according to the requirements of the developing rational order" (1982: 165). Is this enough? You might ask yourself, for instance, whether it is enough while you are negotiating the busy traffic of our cities or seeking help at a hospital.

Cast in the more contemporary framework of late modernity theory, this is a tale of the growing imbalance in the risk/trust dialectic, of our decreased ability to "find an abiding sense of security in the routines of everyday life and taken-for-granted assumptions about the way things are and should be" (see Chapter 6). The resultant anxiety experienced by at least some members of our societies fuels efforts to push back against the forces of change by either reasserting, at least privately, a more traditional and religious world order or augmenting their daily secular existence with private experimentation with new forms of spirituality and alternative religious ideas. Either or both responses may be read as evidence, on the one hand, that secularization is not inevitable and irreversible or, on the other hand, that religion will never again play a significant role in society. Deciding which is true will depend on answering two related questions, not adequately pursued by Berger, Wilson, or other theorists of secularization. First, just how comprehensive or all-encompassing are the social structural changes that are identified with the process of secularization? Second, even if the changes in the social conditions that religion must live with are pervasive, are there not ways in which a more privatized expression of religion could play a significant role under the new system of social relations instituted in late modernity? It is difficult to imagine how we could "measure" the effects of structural differentiation or pluralism so that we could side-step relying on more subjective and speculative interpretations. But some sense of what we mean by the latter suggestion will be indicated in the next two chapters.

Steve Bruce

The single strongest contemporary proponent of secularization theory is probably Steve Bruce, a British sociologist who studied under Bryan Wilson. He begins his well-known book *God Is Dead* (2002: xii) by claiming that "liberal industrial democracies of the Western world are considerably less religious now than they were in the days of my father, my grandfather, and my great-grandfather." Reminiscent of Berger, he later elaborates (2011: 2–3):

> The declining power of religion causes a decline in the number of religious people and the extent to which people are religious. As religious faith loses social power, it becomes harder for each generation to socialize its children in the faith. It also becomes progressively harder for those who remain religious to preserve the cohesion and integrity of their particular belief system. As religion becomes increasingly a matter of free choice, it becomes harder to maintain boundaries. Alternative reworkings of once-dominant ideologies proliferate, and increasing variation encourages first relativism—all roads lead to God—and then indifference as it becomes harder to persuade people that there is special merit in any particular road.

In short, Bruce contends that rising levels of pluralism and individualism facilitate a widespread societal vulnerability to attitudes and behaviours that delegitimize traditional, universal, and exclusive religious beliefs and practices. Bruce also suggests that unless religious beliefs and practices are reinforced in many social settings on a regular basis, it is unlikely that the existing remnants of religious belief will survive.

Bruce substantiates his claim by pointing to steady declines in the levels of church attendance, church membership, and Sunday school attendance, as well as the decreasing number of full-time clergy, in Britain (2002: 62–73). He cites recent data showing that fewer people are turning to religious groups for rites of passage, and smaller numbers of people are indicating an attraction to any type of religious belief. Contrary to the impression sometimes created by the media, he asserts that interest in so-called New Age forms of spirituality is declining, hand in hand with belief in various kinds of superstition overall. Likewise, the number of other new religious movements may be growing, and some specific new religions may be growing in size, but their growth pales in comparison to the losses experienced by mainstream religious groups. Catholics and Protestants in Britain are not leaving the church to take up alternative spiritual practices. Rather, most are simply ceasing to be religious, he stresses, in any socially meaningful way.

Bruce formulates a complex theory of secularization based on a wide array of variables, historic, economic, social, and cultural (see 2002: 5–37). The approach is far too complex for our purposes. The emphasis falls, however, on two related factors that have been discussed already: structural

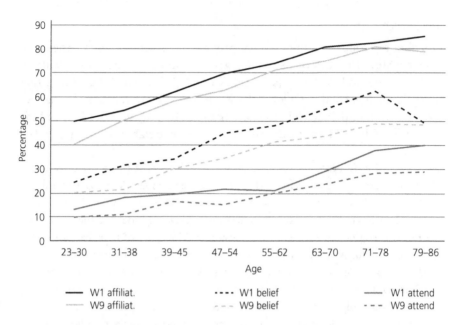

Figure 5.1 Generational Religious Decline in Britain: Affiliation, Belief, and Attendance
Source: Voas, David and Alasdair Crockett. 2005. "Religion in Britain: Neither Believing nor Belonging." *Sociology* 39 (1): 11–28.
Page 16.

Figure 5.1 accounts for the same individuals in 1991 (Wave 1) and 2000 (Wave 9) who identify with a religion, attend religious services once a month or more, and claim that religion makes a difference in their life. The data suggest that, on the whole, each generation is less religious than the previous one, as evidenced by younger people being less religious than older people and Wave 9 respondents being less religious than Wave 1 respondents.

differentiation and social differentiation. Similar to Berger and Wilson (and others like Durkheim), Bruce (2002: 8) identifies structural differentiation with the fragmentation of social life among a variety of institutions, to the degree that social features and functions once controlled by a single institution, namely religion, are now divided among many specialized institutional spheres of activity (e.g., politics, economics, education, entertainment, and the family). In and of itself, structural differentiation is synonymous with societal secularization. Building on Karl Marx, Bruce (2002: 9–10) further highlights that structural differentiation gives rise to social differentiation. The new social order born of structural differentiation, and which in turn promotes it, is also characterized by more extensive social differentiation. In pursuit of new economic and life opportunities, people either acquire or are compelled to accept a greater measure of geographic mobility, and they are enlisted in new systems of social stratification linked to the emergence of industrial societies. As more people leave their traditional communities, separating themselves from their families and the customary beliefs and practices of life at home, and as they take on new and more specialized roles in a variety of institutional contexts in burgeoning cities, it becomes harder and harder for them to share a common worldview. The traditional set of religious beliefs and practices that once unified them as a community become less and less relevant as the important daily experiences of people, of construction workers, lawyers, computer programmers, and teachers, deviate more and more from one another and from the nature of life in the past. As the division of labour advances, elevating educational levels and expectations, and life in our increasingly diverse cities fragments the experiences we share with others, it becomes harder and harder for traditional religions to remain relevant.

In line with Berger, Bruce reverts to a form of internal secularization argument to deflect many of the attempts made to call the reality of secularization into doubt by citing recent developments in the religious life of the West that are thought to be indicative of a revival of interest in religion. In particular he tackles those who are optimistic about the implications of the New Age Movement, the surge of Eastern religious movements in the West (e.g., offshoots of Hinduism and Buddhism), and the dramatic world-wide spread of Pentecostal-Charismatic forms of Christianity. In each case his primary concern is that these movements are geared pre-eminently to the individualism and subjectivism of the dominant society, which accounts for their popularity. As such, in the long run, the "epistemological individualism" at the core of these new ways of being religious works against establishing the kinds of unified systems of belief and practice and strong institutional expression that he thinks are required to become a force to reckon with in our complex and diversified societies. In Dobbelaere's terms, they are more likely to further the "organizational secularization" of religion than they are to offset the general advance of secularization by reversing its impact at the individual level. Many of the beliefs espoused by New Agers and Westerners who adopt Eastern religions, for instance, highlight the innately holy nature of the individual and elevate the authority of personal experience (e.g., in meditation) over all external authorities. This means that individuals can select the beliefs and practices that work for them, largely on the basis of their experience and intuition. The focus, moreover, of these movements is on the spiritual means of achieving better health, greater wealth, and heightened self-esteem (Bruce, 2002: 82–85, 120–121; 2011: 100–140). Thus, as many commentators have lamented, they are turning religion into a form of therapy, and in doing so undercutting, even trivializing, the more otherworldly, demanding, and collective purposes of religion.

In Bruce's eyes, much the same holds true for the Pentecostal-Charismatic movement. He (2002: 179–181) scrutinizes the emphasis on personal experience over shared doctrine, the importance placed on developing a personal relationship with Jesus Christ, and the reduced sense of awe which marks the interactions between the divine and humans (e.g., Jesus is viewed by some as their "homeboy"). The secularizing and troubling aspect of this type of religion for him (2011: 112–119) is the seeming lack of commitment to and consensus around a common set of values and behaviours, other than the implicit respect for the principles of autonomy and diversity, that make it difficult for religious groups to compel members to adopt and maintain ideals that bind the group together. In Durkheimian fashion, Bruce suspects the groups lack the cohesion required to motivate and sustain attempts to evangelize outsiders or to even effectively socialize their children to the religion, since their first allegiance is to the notion that "each of us is the best judge of what is true for us" (Bruce, 2011: 117).

Bruce's critique, of course, hinges on a conception of the foundational nature and purposes of religion that others may not share. It carries us back to the definitional disputes of Chapter 2 and the struggle to discern the basic elements of religion surveyed in Chapter 3. No one disputes that religious change on a fairly sweeping scale is happening in the contemporary West. The question is, What do the changes portend?

In addressing the higher levels of religiosity in the United States, as compared with Britain (and much of the rest of Europe) Bruce (2011: 160–6) extends the internal or organizational secularization thesis, noting how much many American churchgoers now look like their non-churchgoing friends and neighbours. Many smoke, drink, dance, visit movie theatres, divorce, and dress pretty much the same. In other words, being religious does not seem to make much of a difference anymore, undercutting the traditional grounds for the social significance of religion. Here too the force of individualism, of the independence of the believer from institutionalized forms of religious authority, has won the day. People are no longer willing to pay the personal price required, in terms of discipline and sacrifices, to meet the traditional obligations of Christianity or most other religions.

In sum, Bruce (2002: 148-150; 2011) argues that without constant religious socialization and reaffirmation from others, religions (and religious individuals) will struggle to exist in the face of an individualistic, diverse, and relativistic culture. So long as people favour individualism, secularization will continue (Bruce, 2011: 55-56). This individualism acts as a force stripping society of many of its traditional ways of conceiving and living life, the taken-for-granted assumptions that have long bound people together in communities. What he does not consider, however, is the offsetting impact of the heightened anomie people experience in our societies or the strains placed on our personal relationships by the loss of many traditional communal ties and supports. He correctly discusses the ways in which the freedom of thought and expression associated with the rise of individualism undercuts the relevance and viability of traditional group-oriented (i.e., church) forms of religion in the West. But he may have underestimated the ongoing need for something more than mere individual liberty and self-expression in making life meaningful. In part this is because, with Berger and Wilson, Bruce contends that religion must be shared for it to have individual or societal meaning and significance, and the dominant features of modern society make it very difficult (though not impossible) for this to occur. These are themes and tensions in late modern life that are pertinent to understanding how and why religions are changing, and the future of religion in Canada and elsewhere, to which we will return in detail in Chapter 6.

The Case against Secularization Theory

Jeffrey Hadden

The contemporary criticism of the secularization was prompted in many respects by a seminal essay by the American sociologist Jeffrey Hadden (1987). Hadden begins his challenge of secularization theory by arguing that sociology carries an inherent bias in favour of the process of secularization, born of the discipline's origins in the Enlightenment commitment to transforming society by replacing superstition and tradition with reason and science. This intellectual heritage has prevented scholars from critically, systematically, and empirically evaluating the secularization thesis to the same degree as any other theory. In Hadden's words (1987: 588):

> Secularization theory has not been subjected to systematic scrutiny because it is a doctrine more than it is a theory. Its moorings are located in presuppositions that have gone unexamined because they represent a taken-for-granted ideology rather than a systematic set of interrelated propositions.

Drawing on a landmark study of American scientists and scholars done by psychologist James Leuba ([1916] 1921), Hadden notes that few sociologists believed in God. But more importantly, in their desire to establish the new discipline of sociology as a science, sociologists strove to establish a clear line between sociological aims and religious aims in what was then a very religious America. Hadden's point is that the secular agenda and professional culture of science and sociology in particular inclined sociologists to "sacralise" secularization theory as a given reality rather than an idea requiring further examination.

For most of the twentieth century, what passed for the theory of secularization, Hadden observes, was really a series of related but purely descriptive statements correlating modernization with religious decline. Aside from the conceptual ambiguity that exists among the different proponents of secularization (i.e., secularization means different things to different people and is measured in different ways), few sociologists actually offer a thorough and systematic set of hypotheses that are testable across time and place. Thus, once again Hadden asserts, secularization is more of a proposition than a theory.

To demonstrate the need to handle the debate over secularization in a more systematic and empirical manner, Hadden points to three developments that should give pause to proponents of the theory. First he calls attention to data from the United States revealing that levels of religiosity have been more or less stable for decades, as evidenced in belief in God, church membership and attendance, acts of personal devotion, and financial giving (e.g., see Greeley, 1989). Recent studies add some support to this argument. Stanley Presser and Mark Chaves (2007) found that evidence from several surveys demonstrates that "weekly attendance at religious services has been stable [in the United States] since 1990." In this time American religion has also changed, of course. This is apparent in the fluctuating percentages of Americans who believe that the influence of religion on society is increasing and in the decreasing numbers of those who believe that the Bible should be interpreted literally. But change is not synonymous with becoming more secular. This is a position that more and more scholars are adopting, questioning the assumption that a softening of traditional beliefs and practices necessarily entails a blurring of lines between the religious and non-religious worldviews (see e.g., Heelas and Woodhead, 2005; Houtman and Aupers, 2007; Wuthnow, 2007). Contrary to Bruce, they argue, we must not confuse the inevitable adaptation of modes of religious expression to the prevailing social norms and cultural idioms with the actual demise of religion as a social phenomenon. The English sociologists Paul Heelas and Linda Woodhead (2005), for example, use their study of the religious life of the citizens of one small English city to more or less invert Berger's worries about the "subjectivization" of religion. They argue that the marked turn away from churched forms of religion toward new forms of spirituality, or so-called New Age types of activity, are indicative of the continued need for religion. In simple terms, they hypothesize that religions that emphasize the subjective life, a prominent feature of modern western culture, will succeed. Religious institutions that stress hierarchical and authoritative dogmas and obligations are struggling to survive because they are out of sync with the times, while broader non-institutional cultural appeals to subjective forms of spirituality, and more personal, subjective, and socially aware forms of traditional Christian practice, are expanding (see e.g., Miller, 1997; Lynch, 2007).

Second, Hadden discusses the influence of the rise of new religious movements on both the American religious landscape and the sociological study of religion itself. Scholars of religion under the sway of the dominant theory of secularization were taken aback by the sudden surge in new religions, some invented and many imported, that have swept the Western world since the 1960s. Mainstream society recoiled in shock in the 1960s,

70s and 80s, when college students in America and elsewhere converted in unprecedented numbers to such groups as the Children of God, the Hare Krishna movement, the Divine Light Mission, the Moonies, the Church of Scientology, and literally thousands of other previously unknown religious groups. The social turmoil brought about a renaissance of interest in the sociology of religion and for decades the study of these more exotic forms of new religious life exerted a strong influence on the discipline (see, e.g., Bromley and Hadden, 1993; Lewis, 2004; Dawson, 2006a). As Stark and Bainbridge (1985) demonstrate, new religious movements are more likely to emerge in places where conventional forms of religion are least common (e.g., the West Coast in Canada and the United States). This suggests that their appearance is compensating for the effects of secularization, or at least that the complete disappearance of religion is unlikely. We are in a time of transition, and the next great world religion may now be an unknown or persecuted minority amongst us, as Christians once were in the Roman Empire.

Third, Hadden questions the validity of assumptions about secularization by pointing to the central role that religion continues to play in politics around the world. One need only consider the role of religion in the Civil Rights Movement of the United States, the violence between Protestants and Catholics in Northern Ireland, the Jewish–Muslim–Christian tensions in the Middle East, the clash of Hindus, Muslims, and Sikhs in India, the Islamic Revolution in Iran, and the rise of the Christian Right in American politics, to illustrate the profound influence that religion seems to exert on world affairs. Religion is inextricably linked to significant global challenges and hence it would be foolish to conclude that religion has become nothing more than a private and personal affair with minimal social significance. Jeffrey Hadden and Anson Shupe (1989), Jose Casanova (1994), Peter Berger (1999), David Martin (2005), and Peter Berger, Grace Davie, and Effie Fokas (2008), and many other influential scholars have driven this point home as well.

Rodney Stark

Once sociologists of religion began to openly question the inevitability of secularization, one of the most vocal critics of secularization theory to emerge was Rodney Stark. Examining the factual record more carefully, as Hadden advises, Stark argues there is good reason to be sceptical about the merits of the theory (Stark, 1999). In the book *Acts of Faith*, written with Roger Finke, he summarizes and rejects five arguments commonly used to support claims about secularization (2000: 57–79).

The first argument is that modernization is the causal engine of secularization. As societies modernize in areas of economic development, urbanization, or education, levels of religiosity inevitably decline as the material security of people increases and individuals realize that they no longer need the supernatural to explain how and why things happen in the world. Stark and Finke reject this claim without reservation, citing evidence from both the United States and Europe. In their book *The Churching of America* (2005), Finke and Stark demonstrate that Americans actually appear to have become more religious as their society has modernized. Rejecting the notion that people have fallen away from a prior "golden age" of religion, they document noticeable increases in the number of seminarians, clergy, congregations, missionary efforts per congregation, and new religious movements over the course of American history. They also show that there is an increase in the number of religious adherents, church attendees, and those who hold religious beliefs. In Europe, Stark and Finke (2000: 62–3) contend there is no solid evidence to support the claim of long-term decline in religious involvements. Levels of church membership and attendance may be low, compared with the United States, but there is clear evidence that Europeans continue to be religious, at least nominally, with many continuing to believe in God or a supernatural being, life after death, and so on (also see Davie, 1994). Reversing the argument for a golden age of religion, Stark and Finke (2000: 63–8) question how religious Europeans really were during the Middle Ages and the Renaissance. In the past, much as today, people mainly attended church for rites of passage, and many of those who did attend more regularly, attended for non-religious reasons (e.g., to make and maintain social ties, to meet potential mates). Contrary to our assumptions, records show that many congregations had no regular clergy, and there were very few seminaries to train new religious leaders. In the end, they conclude (2000: 68): "The evidence is clear that claims about a major decline in religious participation in Europe are based in part on very exaggerated perceptions of past religiousness."

Second, although secularization proponents are mindful of the different levels or types of secularization, they are most interested in declining levels of individual piety and religious belief. Stark and Finke (2000: 71–2), however, point to the notable presence of subjective religiosity in Western society. Turning to Grace Davie's (1994) popular characterization of contemporary British attitudes to religion as "believing without belonging," Stark and Finke question the emphasis Bruce and other proponents of secularization lay on the declining levels of church attendance. Alternatively, they argue, there is considerable evidence that most Europeans continue to believe in God and many of the other basic teachings of Christianity, even though they no longer attend church with any regularity. Stark and Finke highlight the strength of measures of subjective religiosity in Iceland, for example, one of the supposedly most irreligious nations in the world. Despite very low levels of church attendance, most people in Iceland continue to turn to a church to observe rites of passage, many believe in life after death, some even in reincarnation, most pray sometimes, and very few claim to be committed atheists. Much the same can be said for Canada (Bibby, 2002, 2011). With these kinds of societies in mind Stark and Finke challenge the tendency to draw too simple an equation between levels of church attendance and secularization, documenting instead the ways in which many non-churchgoers continue to be quite religious (see e.g., Stark, Hamburg, and Miller, 2004).

Bruce (2011: 16) has sought to counter this line of reasoning by arguing church attendance is a critical indicator of religiosity. Aside from the obvious fact that most religious groups identify attendance at religious services as an important measurement commitment, Bruce notes that attending church requires significant effort on the part of the individual. Consequently it is a more reliable and objective indicator of people's devotion to their faith. More than this, church attendance is highly correlated with other measurements of religious activity and the relative importance of religion in one's life. These correlations are a function of the social nature of church attendance, and in the absence of this social encouragement, Bruce does not believe that the mere presence of largely private beliefs is sufficient to cast doubt on the spread of secularization (see Putnam and Campbell, 2010: 468, 472).

The third argument commonly advanced by secularization theorists that Stark and Finke wish to refute is the assumption that the advancement of science is antithetical to continued belief in religion. The fundamental principles of science, such as rationality and empiricism, are thought to conflict with the superstitious notions and faith requirements of religion. But Stark and Finke (2000: 52–5; 72–3; 77) draw on several studies of the levels of religiosity of American professors and scientists to show there is no simple correlation between the adoption of a scientific worldview and the demise of religious belief. In fact, a high percentage of American professors describe themselves as religious and attend religious services regularly. American professors are as likely to be regular attendees at religious services as average Americans. Moreover, Stark and Finke emphasize, those in the so-called "hard" sciences (e.g., mathematics, physical sciences, and life sciences) are more religious than those in the "soft" sciences (e.g., sociology, psychology, and anthropology). Citing a study by Smith, Emerson, Gallagher, Kennedy, and Sikkink (1998), they further note that very few people question religious claims because of the findings of science. Instead, people are far more likely to cite the influence of personal tragedies, the continued presence of evil in the world, or human hypocrisy, as the cause of their doubts.

Fourth, Stark and Finke take secularization theorists to task for assuming, more often than not, that the process of secularization is irreversible. In this regard they simply point to the prevalence of movements of religious revival and religious innovation in America and elsewhere. Building on the principles of his theory of religion (see Chapter 4), and his related ideas about the supply of religion (examined below), Stark notes that religious groups are not always effective in supplying religion to people (Stark and Bainbridge, 1985: 435). Over the course of time, he argues, religious groups relax their beliefs and practices to appeal to an ever wider audience. In the process, however, they lose their distinctiveness and their ability to demand the kind of strict adherence that assures the high levels of commitment and co-operation that made the religions attractive to new members in the first place. The result is a widespread decline in the religious fervour of congregants, as manifested in their declining attendance. While some interpret this as a sign of secularization, Stark takes a larger historical view and argues that the decline acts more often as a catalyst for religious revival and innovation.

Religious revival happens when new religious groups come into being that re-assert the fundamentals of an existing religion, the basic values and beliefs that the dominant religious groups seem to have strayed from (Stark and Bainbridge, 1985: 444–8). Commonly referred to as "sects," these revivalist groups are very demanding and in high tension with the surrounding culture (e.g., the early Mormons and Pentecostals). Religious innovation refers to the creation of new religious groups that focus on beliefs and practices that are quite different from mainstream religion in the local culture (e.g., Eckankar, Scientology, Growing in Grace). They are culturally sensitive to, and cater to, more current changes in the beliefs and interests of the culture (1985: 435–9). These groups are commonly identified as "cults." But otherwise they commonly possess the same qualities as sects, and in both cases they are successful because individuals desire the more definite rewards, of a spiritual, social, and material nature, that can be gained from participating in such committed and demanding groups.

With time and success, of course, Stark and colleagues hypothesize that most sects and cults (but not all) will moderate their beliefs and demands. They will become indistinguishable from the very dominant religions they once replaced. Consequently, they themselves will become the targets of criticism and competition from other and newer sects and cults (Stark and Bainbridge, 1985: 437–44; Stark and Finke, 2000: 205–07). The entire process is cyclical, which means that secularization is as well. Conventional religious groups give way to new sects and cults, which over time evolve once again into dominant traditions that prompt the formation of new and more rewarding competitors. The precise reasons for this are delineated further below, but at base this theory rests on Stark's assumption that there is a steady state demand for the things that religion uniquely offers (see Chapter 4). From this point of view society cannot be fully secularized because the cycle of new religious groups rising and falling will never cease. Secularization theorists are mistaking the current down-cycle of dominant religious groups (e.g., mainstream Protestant churches), or perhaps even a historically specific form of religious expression (e.g., "churched" religion), for the demise of religion altogether.

Fifth and finally, Stark and Finke note that most secularization theorists tend to apply their theory universally. Yet Stark and Finke, and Stark and Bainbridge, offer ample evidence to the contrary. Atheism did not flourish, they note (Stark and Finke, 2000: 73–6) in Eastern Europe or Russia even under the sustained and forceful policy of atheism enacted by the communists. Since the fall of the Soviet Union in 1989, moreover, fewer people claim to identify as atheists and more people attend church on a monthly basis. In Islamic countries, commitment to Muslim beliefs and practices is positively correlated with levels of education and occupational prestige. The same can be said of those who practice Asian "folk" religions. In Japan, Shinto religious traditions are more commonly adopted today than in the past. In Taiwan there are more folk temples than any previous time in history and more people are frequenting those temples. In Hong Kong and Malaysia, Chinese folk religions are also increasingly popular. As in Islamic nations, it is the well-educated and urban folk who are turning to religion, not the poor, uneducated, and rural peasants. In the United States and Canada, as noted, Stark and Bainbridge (1985) document that sects and cults prosper where conventional religions are weakest (e.g., the West Coast). This suggests that instances of secularization in society tend to be offset by new processes of "sacralization" (see Demerath, 2007).

Stark's overall theory of religion, secularization, and the supply-side approach to religious growth (see Box 5.2) were greeted as a breath of fresh air in the debate over secularization. Stephen Warner heralded it as a "new paradigm" for the sociology of religion (Warner, 1993). Stark and his colleagues, and many others, tested aspects of the theory in a series of empirical studies, and the findings were initially impressive (e.g., Stark and Iannaccone, 1994; Hamburg and Pettersson, 1994, 1997; Finke, Guest, and Stark, 1996; Stark, 1997; Jelen and Wilcox, 1998). But many criticisms have been levelled as well (Young, 1997; Becker, 1999; Bruce, 1999; Lawson, 1999). Is it realistic, for example, to think of religious leaders and groups as entrepreneurs and companies engaged in competition to market their wares to religious consumers? Studies of pastors and congregations have not found evidence of this competitiveness. Rather, they continue to find a theological impetus to "save souls" and encourage people in their religious and spiritual journeys, whether in their own congregation or in another. Consequently, we had best exercise caution in thinking of religion in economic terms. In an analysis of nearly thirty articles dealing with the relationship between religious pluralism and religious participation, Mark Chaves and Philip Gorski (2001) argue that few studies support the rational choice position that religious pluralism leads to higher levels of religiosity. In fact, the opposite may be

Box 5.2

The Supply-Side Theory of Religious Vitality

Stark and colleagues' critique of secularization theory grew out of a sub-aspect of their own rational choice theory of religion, which came to be known as the "supply-side theory of religion" (e.g., Stark and Iannaccone, 1994). This sub-theory was developed in response to the presumed problem of "American exceptionalism": If secularization theory is correct, then why was the United States, one of the most modern nations in the world, also one of the most religious? In a foundational sense rational choice theorists of religion assume that individuals have a never-ending demand for religion. This assumption inevitably works against secularization theory, and in part accounts for their inversion of the problem of American exceptionalism, asking alternatively why Western Europe is so irreligious, seemingly, in a largely religious world. In either case, if the demand for religion is more or less a constant, then how can we account for this variation? The rational choice theorists are well aware that some people are more religious than others, that an individual's beliefs and practices wax and wane with time, and, further, that religiosity levels vary between nations. The question for Stark and others becomes how we should explain the varying levels of religiosity, both within and among nations.

In line with the economic reasoning underlying their micro-level analysis of religious belief and behaviour, rational choice theorists claim that the answer lies with differences in the supply of religion (see Stark and Iannaccone, 1994; Finke, 1997; Stark and Finke, 2000; Finke and Stark, 2005). The very separation of church and state enshrined in the First Amendment of the Constitution of the United States set the conditions for religious pluralism in America. In contrast to many European nations, such as Britain, France, Germany, or Sweden, no one religion was allowed to be "established," that is, designated as the official religion of the state. So in America many religious groups competed to secure people's allegiances, under the constitutional protection provided for the freedom of religious expression. In effect, the United States set the conditions for the first true religious market or economy. Recalling the analogous observations of Berger, like any other economy, "religious economies consist of a market of current and potential followers (demand), a set of organizations (suppliers) seeking to serve that market, and the religious doctrines and practices (products) offered by the various organizations" (Stark and Finke, 2000: 36). Within this framework, if demand is assumed to be constant, then variations in the success or availability of religion must be the result of differences in either the nature of the suppliers or their products. Similar to McDonalds or Coca-Cola, religious groups succeed or fail based on their ability to effectively create, maintain, and promote a product that people are interested in, which includes, in Stark's theory of religion, supervising and motivating people's exchanges with the gods (Stark and Finke, 2000: 103–13).

If this is the case, however, then why have European religious organizations been so unsuccessful, relative to their American counterparts? The answer to this question is already implied, of course, in the principles of the theory. By legally creating the conditions for greater religious pluralism, the United States introduced more market options for religious consumers, and as economists believe, this means more competition among suppliers, which stimulates greater investments in the products and their delivery to gain a competitive advantage in the market (Stark and Iannaccone, 1994; Stark and Finke, 2000; Finke and Stark, 2005).

We see this every day as fast food chains, car companies, and hotels compete for people's loyalty. Companies set themselves apart from their competitors by distinguishing their product through technical improvements, better marketing campaigns, reduced prices, free upgrades, and prizes. These companies believe that if they constantly improve their product, people are more likely to consume their merchandise. Religion, Stark and company argue, is no different. On the world stage, Christians, Muslims, Hindus, and others are in competition. Within religious traditions the competition is between denominations or sects within dominant traditions (e.g., Anglicans, Baptists, and Pentecostals). Growth in the market share, so to speak, of any group can be traced to changes in their product, in the form of adjustments made to the preaching, rituals, music and programs offered, and perhaps even their very doctrines—changes that resonate better with the current preferences of the populace being served by these religious companies.

Rational choice theorists posit that the result is that people not only turn to organizations that sharpen their supply, but they also respond with higher levels of commitment (Iannaccone, 1994), which in turn increases the competitive advantage of these organizations. Why is this so? Following the economic analogy, Stark argues that people are willing to pay higher costs (i.e., commitment) when they believe the reward is of greater value. Yet somewhat circularly, Stark also asserts that the value of the religious rewards is primarily conditioned by the levels of commitment demanded by a group. Technically, for example, Stark and Bainbridge state that "the value of a reward is equivalent to the maximum cost a person would pay to obtain the reward" ([1987] 1996: 34). Commitment is a cost because it entails a willingness to forgo the use of time, money, and energy doing other things. In the case of high-demand religions, such as many sects and cults (e.g., the Jehovah Witnesses, Mormons, the Moonies), it may also entail putting up with the stigma experienced by members or, in the case of converts, the hostility and ridicule of family and friends. But Stark and Bainbridge (1985) and Iannaccone (1994) claim that people are drawn to sects, as opposed to churches, because of the high rewards offered, in the form of the confident assurance that one is part of the chosen few destined to be saved and the sense of belonging to a strongly supportive group, a new and extended family, with all the psychological, social, and even material benefits that stem from belonging to such a group. Stark and Finke reiterate this reasoning when they say (2000: 145, 147):

> Among religious organizations, there is a reciprocal relationship between expense and the value of the rewards of membership. . . . [T]o the extent that one is motivated by religious value, one must prefer a higher priced supplier. Not only do more expensive religious groups offer a far

continued

more valuable product, but in doing so, they generate levels of commitment needed to maximize individual levels of confidence in the religion.

If individuals come to value a particular religious brand, and if they associate strongly desired rewards with that brand, then they are more likely to pay higher costs to ensure that they receive those rewards, and their investment motivates them to work harder to convince others of the value of their choice, further contributing to the success (i.e., growth) of the group. This is what Stark and Finke conjecture has happened in the United States because religious groups exist in a free market in which they openly compete and are driven to offer better rewards to retain current members and attract potential new members.

Conversely, in many European countries religious monopolies arose through the course of history. One church became aligned with the state, and with the assistance of the state was allowed to suppress all competitors. Examples include the Anglican Church in England, the Presbyterian Church in Scotland, the Lutheran Church in Germany and Sweden, the Roman Catholic Church in Italy, Ireland, Spain, and Poland, and the Orthodox Church in Greece and Russia. The resultant lack of competition removed the impetus for European religious organizations to sharpen their supply of religion (Stark and Finke, 2000: 228–39). For when the state pays for the salaries of clergy and the upkeep of church buildings, Stark argues, the clergy will become lazy and complacent about improving their services and attracting more people. After all, why would it matter whether there are ten or a thousand people in pews, when there are no financial consequences? In fact, monopoly conditions did even more, since state support for an established religion allowed that religion to become ever more liberal and less demanding in its beliefs and practices, in part because this lessened the likelihood of clashes occurring between the interests of the church and the state over matters of religious principle. Under monopoly conditions the established churches had little to fear in terms of losing valuable social or financial support to other religious organizations. But in the end, actions taken in the name of protecting the religious interests sapped the organizations of vitality, and hence viability, given the long-run realities of the religious market. It is this situation, Stark and his colleagues argue, that accounts for the secularization of Europe.

true (see Norris and Inglehart, 2004 as well) (see Figure 5.2). Bruce (2011) goes so far as to accuse rational choice theorists of "cooking the books" in their favour. At this point it is safe to say, however, that the jury is still out on this heated debate.

Keeping the criticism in mind, it might be wise nevertheless to think of the process of secularization as more cyclical than linear, at least in the long run. In some circumstances sociologists may be mistaking a down-turn in the fortunes of certain forms of religion, and of certain specific suppliers, for a collapse of the market altogether. We may be dealing with fluctuations

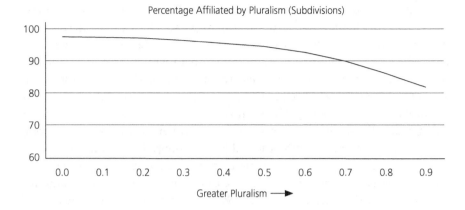

Percentage Affiliated by Pluralism (Subdivisions)

Greater Pluralism ⟶

Figure 5.2 Religious Pluralism and Affiliation in Canada
Source: Olson and Hadaway. 1999. "Religious Pluralism and Affiliation among Canadian Counties and Cities." *Journal for the Scientific Study of Religion* 38 (4): 490–508. Page 497.

Sociologists have conflicting views on the relationship between religious pluralism and secularization. Berger contends that pluralism weakens levels of religiosity because a shared society-wide religious framework is missing, while Stark argues that pluralism fuels levels of religiosity due to competition and more effective religious supply between religious groups. Figure 5.2 supports Berger's theory, demonstrating that as religious pluralism increases, levels of religious affiliation decrease.

and periods of transition rather than absolute changes in the presence of religion. In saying this, however, the opponents of secularization theory are somewhat indiscriminately calling on information about the continued or renewed strength of more traditional forms of religion (i.e., various churches and sects in the West) and more diffuse forms of new spirituality, ranging from the popularity of writers like Deepak Chopra, and the practice of yoga, to the rise of Neo-Paganism and Scientology. They are talking about revivals and innovations, to use Stark's labels. Will both persist under the conditions of late modernity, and if so in what specific ways and why? The picture of the future of religion must be more complex than that afforded by Stark and others and not just a simple reliance on a constant demand for religion that creative suppliers will seek to satisfy. Admittedly, Stark and Finke (2000: 196–203) do at one point speak of a spectrum of religious niches in the overall market for religion. But the niche markets they have in mind are based only on differences in the level of intensity of people's desire for religion.

Jose Casanova

Similar to Dobbelaere, Jose Casanova, who teaches sociology in the United States, identifies three levels or types of secularization: "secularization as differentiation of the secular spheres from religious institutions and norms, secularization as decline of religious beliefs and practices, and secularization as marginalization of religion to a privatized sphere" (1994: 211). Casanova agrees that the first level of secularization is present in many modern societies, for the reasons outlined earlier in this chapter. He also sees the second level of secularization at work, though mainly in nations that resist the first type of secularization. For example, similar to rational choice theorists, he attributes higher levels of religiosity in the United States to the acceptance of differentiation in society. Denominationalism and religious volunteerism mean that religious groups are freer to experiment with how they supply religion as they compete with other religious groups. The result is a product that is more enticing for individuals to consume and thus higher levels of religiosity emerge. The same cannot be said of places where state churches exist and resist the differentiation of society, such as in Scandinavia.

Casanova departs from secularization proponents when he rejects assertions that the third type of secularization is present in the modern world. Instead, he argues that we are witnessing the "deprivatization" of religion in the modern world. By "deprivatization" he means "the fact that religious traditions throughout the world are refusing to accept the marginal and privatized role which theories of modernity as well as theories of secularization had reserved for them" (1994: 5). Since the 1980s Jose Casanova (1994, 2007, 2008) has seen many signs of the strong public (and global) presence of religion. In his own work he explores such examples as the Islamic Iranian Revolution, the Solidarity Movement in Poland, the involvement of the Catholic church in Latin American political conflicts, and the influence of the conservative Protestant right and fundamentalists on American politics.

Casanova claims that "deprivatization" arises for a variety of reasons. Some groups, such as the Roman Catholic Church, hold the doctrinal conviction that God has commanded them to assert Christian principles in the public sphere (e.g., to speak out against abortion). Some, like the Christian Right in the United States, are motivated by a mounting fear that their influence, which they presume to be fundamental to the cultural heritage of the United States, is being eclipsed by a new and dominant culture of "secular-humanism." To revitalize and reform their religious tradition and its influence, they have reasserted themselves in the public square (e.g., by organizing campaigns to get the conservative Christian vote out for candidates aligned with their values, and lobbying the government). Other transnational groups, such as the many movements of Islamic fundamentalism, have used the new tools of global communication, political mobilization, and terrorism, to spread their influence (e.g., the Muslim Brotherhood in Egypt, movements like Hizb-ut-Tahrir in Europe and elsewhere). Even in nations that are considered more or less secular (e.g., Canada and France), Casanova (2007, 2008) argues that religion is playing an important role in the recurrent debates over immigration issues and the impact of religious diversity (e.g., the controversy over Muslim headscarves in France, or about Sikhs wearing the *kirpan* in Canada).

Not everyone agrees on the ultimate significance of these instances where religion has reasserted itself in the public life of late modern societies. But almost everyone was taken aback by the re-emergence of religion as a significant factor in global politics after the heady sweep of secularism in the modernizing societies of the post–World War II era. Some have made the case for re-introducing religion as an important consideration in international affairs (e.g., Dark, 2000; Toft, 2011). Others though, such as Bruce (2002), argue that religion will continue to play a significant role only in situations where people sense their socio-cultural identity is threatened. Religion remains part of a rearguard action in the face of the forces of cultural and political imperialism (e.g., Poland under the Communist rule by the Soviet Union) or more generally of globalization (e.g., Islamic, American Protestant, Jewish, and Hindu forms of fundamentalism). As such, the resurgence of religion is reactionary and temporary. The movements are revivals that will pass away as social and political conditions change and these societies are integrated more thoroughly into the highly differentiated system of social relations (structurally and socially) characteristic of late modern societies. Is Casanova's vision of the future more accurate, or is Bruce's? Only time will tell.

Conclusion

The arguments for and against secularization theory are more complex than simply considering whether levels of church attendance or belief in a supernatural being are falling or rising. Rather, as Dobbelaere clarifies, there are at least three different levels or types of secularization—the societal, organizational, and individual—which may or may not co-vary. To accurately discuss the past, present, or possible future state of religion in late modern society, sociologists need to be careful that they are talking about the same things, and recognize that even nations that have become largely secular may be full of citizens who are still religious (in some sense). In countries like Canada, as we will see in the next chapter, there are mixed signs of religiosity and secularity. So while many proponents and opponents of secularization theory may be talking past each other, their respective theories attune us to the multi-faceted nature of religious belief and practice around the world, in the past, present, and future.

Simplifying the arguments of Berger, Wilson, and Bruce, we can say there are two related ideas at the heart of the theory of secularization: (1) the growing religious and social pluralism, and the individualism, of the late modern world is making it very difficult for individuals and entire societies to share a common religious worldview; and (2) the significance and impact of religious beliefs and practices depends on them being shared.

Under this framework pluralism is consistently bad for religion. In contrast, Hadden, Stark, and Casanova argue, in essence, that diversity and pluralism strengthen the place of religion in society by promoting competition, and the relative demise of some of the more traditional ways of being religious is not synonymous with the demise of religion *per se*. Rather, they argue, either the privatization of religion has been exaggerated (in most of the world) or privatized religion can still be strong and socially significant. Individuals around the world continue to believe and behave in ways inspired by the supernatural, religious groups constantly adapt and re-create themselves to the needs of those around them, new religious groups continue to form and flourish, and religiously inspired movements and conflicts continue to be consequential in many parts of the world today. Pluralism, under this framework, has changed the face of religion in North America, Europe, and elsewhere. It is very unlikely that one religion will become dominant in any of the advanced societies again. But as Beckford argues (1989, 1992; see Chapter 6), religious ideas and symbols may remain potent "cultural resources" and pluralism may act as a stimulus for new religious life, assuming, that is, that a basic demand for religion persists.

Is there an ongoing demand for what religion has to offer? To what extent is this so, and for what reasons? Can religious worldviews be influential even when people recognize the legitimacy of many different religions? We must have a better grasp of the answers to these questions before we can embrace or reject secularization theory. In addition, we need a more nuanced explanation of the kinds of religion/spirituality most likely to develop in response to a demand for religion under the conditions of late modernity. The investigation of this issue is in its infancy.

While people in late modern societies may no longer share a common commitment to a specific set of doctrines and rituals, they may well share a set of circumstances that motivate them to seek structurally similar kinds of religious-like solutions to their personal and collective dilemmas. Dawson observes (2006b: 113–14):

> The expectation that modernity would be synonymous with the near complete secularisation of society was short-sighted. It failed to take into account the full social psychological consequences of modernisation. True, as Bruce stresses, the detraditionalization of society undercut the place of religious institutions in the social order. Yet in line with Stark's suspicions, the inability of the reflexive institutions of late modern societies to manage the fateful moments and core existential experiences of human existence has implicitly kept the door open to religious worldviews.

The problems of death, illness, disaster, and misfortune continue to stalk us, no matter how sophisticated the structure of our societies becomes.

To cope with these inescapable realities we still need to make sense of them, to render them somewhat meaningful. What is more, we need to believe that we can exert some influence over our fate, especially in the extreme exigencies of life when our expert systems come up short. It is true, on the one hand, that in some societies our encounters with some of these dilemmas may be postponed or less frequent today. The threat of death and violence is far less prevalent in Canada, the United States, and South Korea, than it is in Haiti, Somalia, or North Korea. But, on the other hand, the very infrequency of our encounters with fateful moments may increase their poignancy, while simultaneously undermining our cultural capacity to cope with them.

But in the end, if it is only the challenge of theodicy that continues to foster the need for religion (as suggested in Chapters 1 and 2), then it could be argued that religion has been pushed to the margins of life and society. We encounter it at weddings and funerals and in times of national and personal crisis. After all, even dyed-in-the wool atheists have been known to spontaneously utter a prayer when they think their plane is about to crash, or their child falls grievously ill. But religion is about much more (see Chapter 3).

Alternatively, is it not strange to think of this essential function as marginal to the interests and operation of society, especially under the conditions of late modernity? Living in a heightened risk environment, in terms of our daily awareness of an unprecedented range of "high consequence risks" (e.g., nuclear war, pandemics, global warming, international financial crises), is our need for ultimate reassurance more or less than, or the same as, before? The old forms of religious expression may no longer fit with our more complex and reflexive interactions with the world. But does "religion" die with the demise of its current forms, or does it transcend them?

Ironically, the dialectical flip-side of the very individualism that gutted the appeal of the traditional ways of being religious intensifies the need to explain and give significance to each individual's experience of tragedy in their life. What happens to each of us as individuals matters more, to us and others, than it did in the past. In our scientific age we might be able to tolerate more ambiguity and anomy than our ancestors, but as Giddens observes (1990: 141): "Our acts and convictions are often only partially warranted by the information at hand and we are compelled to trust that our good deeds will be rewarded" (Dawson, 2006b: 114). The comment calls to mind Wilson's concerns about the demoralizing effects of secularization.

Can we be satisfied, however, with religious assurances that are not shared by almost everyone in the groups to which we belong? The very pluralism that undercuts the foundational claims of traditional religions, as it becomes a new universal reality, may be setting the conditions for the emergence of new ways of being religious, more reminiscent of the ways people practised religion before the rise of the so-called "world religions," and more specifically, the dominance of congregational or church-forms of religion in the West. These new ways of being religious may manifest themselves as shared worldviews and social movements more than institutionalized religions *per se*. They will be "cultural resources" shaping the lives of thousands of individuals in recognizable, though more indirect and flexible, ways. This is a thought to which we will return in Chapters 7 and 8.

Critical Thinking Questions

1. Is it only a matter of time before the rest of the world is as secular as Canada?

2. What is it about heightened individualism that undermines the role of religion in society? Is individualism intrinsically incompatible with strong religious beliefs and practices?

3. Is pluralism the friend or enemy of religion?

4. Do you think the new linkage forged between religion and politics in many parts of the world will continue into the future, or are modern states destined to be secular?

Suggested Readings

Berger, Peter. 1967. *The Sacred Canopy: Elements of a Sociological Theory of Religion*. Garden City, NY: Doubleday & Company. In the second half of this seminal book Berger develops the theory of secularization briefly delineated above. Few books in the last half century have been as influential in shaping the thinking of sociologists of religion and others. It provides a concise and lucid rendering of complex ideas, and a brilliant synthesis of a sweeping array of theoretical insights. It is essential reading in the field.

Wilson, Bryan. 1985. "Secularization: The Inherited Model." Pp. 9–20 in *The Sacred in a Secular Age*, edited by Phillip Hammond. Berkeley, CA: University Of California Press. This brief essay by one of the best-known sociologists of religion provides a succinct and clear statement of the most common way in which the process of secularization has been understood by sociologists and others for decades. It is an excellent introduction to the subject.

Rodney Stark. 2000. "Secularization RIP." Pp. 41–66 in *The Secularization Debate*, edited by William H. Swatos, Jr. and Daniel V.A. Olsen. Lanham, MD: Rowman and Littlefield. First published as an article, this essay summarizes Stark's scathing critique of secularization theory. The essay is marked by the creative flair, brilliance, and combativeness so characteristic of this prolific author's work.

Related Websites

http://pewforum.org
    The Pew Forum on Religion and Public Life provides surveys, demographic analyses, and other kinds of social scientific reports and discussions of a wide range

of issues where religion and public policy concerns intersect, both in the United States and around the world. It is an excellent source to help evaluate whether or not secularization, in any or all of its forms, is occurring, where, and at what pace.

http://nsrn.net

The Nonreligion and Secularity Research Network is an international and interdisciplinary research network devoted to studying positions defined in reference to religion, but which are considered to be not religious (e.g., atheism, agnosticism, humanism, or religious indifference). This website includes a list of key researchers in this area of study, a bibliography of academic research in this field, videos and recordings from group events, resources for teachers and students, and an online journal titled *Secularism and Nonreligion*.

6 Religion and Late Modernity

Learning Objectives

In this chapter, you will learn:

◎ To gain some insight into the key features of "late modern" society in which we now live.

◎ To consider the ways in which the changes characteristic of late modernity may be related to the changes, on a global scale and in Canada, in the nature and practice of religion.

◎ To understand how the conditions of late modernity suggest that the common assumption that modernization leads to increased secularization is far less warranted than most sociologists have thought until recently.

Introduction

But what is this "late modernity" to which we have now referred at several points in our discussions of the ongoing role of religion in Canada? Over the last several decades social theorists have argued that we are in the midst of a transition into a new form of social life. It is widely thought that the basic structure of our social system has changed, with real consequences for the conceptions we have of ourselves and our society. The analyses parallel those that ushered in sociology as a field of study more than one hundred years ago. Then it was in response to the sweeping social changes that marked the final stages of the transition from a more traditional social order to something new called "modernity" (see Chapter 4). Now we are talking about a shift from modernity itself to something qualitatively more. The changes in religion we are discussing in this book are taking place in the context of this larger pattern of social changes. In some cases they simply reflect these social changes: they are instances of how society acts on religion. In other cases the religious changes might be seen as harbingers of things to come for the rest of society, because religion is the forum in which many people struggle to find meaning in their lives, to cope with the changes happening around them (e.g., Dawson, 2004b). Either way, no one can talk about the sociology of religion anymore without at least implicitly and repeatedly addressing the larger currents of social innovation and turmoil we are about to discuss.

Many terms have been used to characterize the changes we have in mind, from John Kenneth Galbraith's (1958, 1967) initial formulation of an "affluent" and "new industrial" society to Daniel Bell's (1973) "age of information" and "post-industrial society," or the "consumer society" of Jean Baudrillard ([1970] 1998) and others (e.g., Bauman, 2007). These influential ideas were followed by various more abstract and theoretical pronouncements about the emergence of a "post-modern" or "liquid" society and culture (e.g., Lyotard, [1979] 1984; Lyon, 1994; Bauman, 2000). Many of the ideas were also addressed in less grand fashion in discussions of the processes of **"globalization"** (e.g., Robertson, 1992; Scholte, 2000) or the emergence of the "risk society" (Beck, [1986] 1992).

The range of complex ideas presented in these important discussions far exceeds our needs here, but we can delineate five common themes that indicate the broader patterns of social and religious change we have in mind. In doing so, we will lean heavily on the views of the British social theorist Anthony Giddens. In a series of influential books Giddens presents a unique synthesis of many of these ideas (1990, 1991, 1992) and scholars have started to use his theoretical analyses to gain a better understanding of the impact of the changes in question on the presence and functioning of religion in contemporary societies (e.g., Beckford, 1992, 1996; Mellor, 1993; Beyer, 1994; Hervieu-Léger, 2003, 2006; Dawson, 2004, 2006b; Campbell, 2006; A. Dawson, 2007). The five themes are: (1) the process of de-traditionalization, (2) globalization, (3) the rise of expressive individualism and the new tribalism, (4) the **risk/trust dialectic**, and (5) the transformation of intimacy. These themes are intersecting, as they refer to processes that are intimately intertwined in real life. They are separated here to help us simplify the issues at stake.

In line with Giddens we have chosen to frame these developments in terms of the emergence of "late modernity." Rejecting the radicalism of much that has been said about "postmodernism," Giddens favours the term *late modernity*, or what some others call "high modernity" (e.g., Hervieu-Léger, 2006; see Beckford, 1996). Regardless of which term is used, however, the essential point is that the social changes we are experiencing are more a product of the extreme development and spread of trends begun in the modern period (roughly from the late sixteenth to the mid-twentieth century), than of some rejection or reversal of these features of modernity. There is an important element of continuity between the modern era and contemporary times that we need to keep realistically in mind, especially when we are dealing with religion as a social phenomenon. While appreciating that we are dealing with new circumstances of significance, religion remains an institution preoccupied with bringing order to our lives, with imparting meaning by pointing to something more permanent and important than the many new changes and troubles assailing us.

De-traditionalization

The notion of de-traditionalization encompasses several things (Giddens, 1994; Heelas, Lash and Morris, 1996). It refers to the ways in which our lives are no longer so strongly anchored in age-old understandings of time and space. Most of us are no longer destined to live our lives bound by the cycles of nature or the place we happen to be born. With the invention of clocks and the re-ordering of life around chronological time schedules, in conjunction with the social and geographic mobility introduced by the development of modern industry and technology, in particular advances in transportation and communication, the old restrictions have melted away. But the freedom we all take for granted, to do things around the clock and pretty much wherever we want, is actually an extraordinarily new feature of human existence. In the largely agrarian societies of pre-modern times (and still in much of the world) people's lives were tied to the patterns imposed by nature, by day and night and the cycles of the seasons, and individuals rarely had the means or reason to travel far from home. This remained true until very recently. We must remember, for example, that the first commercial non-stop flight across the Atlantic, from the United States to Ireland, did not happen until 1939, and a trip that now takes three to five hours took twenty-nine hours to complete then. Before that, crossing the Atlantic by boat took weeks, and was very expensive and still reasonably dangerous.

This progressive "disembedding" of our lives, as Giddens calls it, frees us from the restraints of time and space but also tends to strip us of the hold of tradition. Traditional ways of doing things are strongly affiliated with specific times, places, and people, with the repetition of activities in specific contexts. But now when it is common for the members of a family to be spread over vast distances, within a nation or across the world, this simple but important linkage is broken. Everyone in such families may still celebrate Christmas, Diwali (Hindu festival of lights), or whatever, but the circumstances differ, and it does not take much imagination to realize the negative effects this has on the continued transmission of religious traditions across generations and around the world.

The process of disembedding was facilitated by our growing dependence on what Giddens calls "expert systems." By this he means systems of knowledge and practice, ranging from meteorology, aeronautics, the law, surgery, international finance, and computer science, to all the innumerable other advanced institutions operating in modern societies. It is these systems, Giddens asserts, that now "provide 'guarantees' of expectation across distantiated time-space" (1990: 28). In other words, they provide the sense of order and regularity required for social relations in the absence of shared experiences, places, and traditions. Our "trust" in the successful operation of these many interrelated expert systems, Giddens stresses, lies at the core of social life today. Every day in myriad ways we depend on the efforts and honesty of countless others, in ways we know but do not fully understand. We rely on those who build and maintain our vehicles or our roads, or the furnaces that heat our homes in the dead of winter, or manage the hard-earned money we have deposited in the banks, or educate our children, or operate the communication satellites we now seemingly cannot live without. The mesh of practical interdependencies at work in our late modern societies is vast and unprecedented. As Durkheim predicted at the dawn of sociology ([1893] 1964), it is our integration into an almost infinitely complex division of labour that is becoming the primary source of our fragile social cohesion, bridging the growing gaps in the beliefs, values, and experiences that we share.

Globalization

All of these developments result from, on the one hand, and contribute to, on the other, the process of globalization. In the words of international relations scholar Jan Aart Scholte (2000: 46): "Globalization refers to the emergence and spread of a supraterritorial dimension of social relations." Or more simply, as sociologist Roland Robertson states, it is the process by which the world is becoming a "single place" (Robertson and Chirico 1985: 220; Robertson, 1992). There are many aspects to this process and we will focus on a few key developments (see Waters, 2001).

First, globalization is strongly associated with the spread of capitalism from Europe to the rest of the world. It is about the rise of companies and economic relationships that operate on a transnational and, in many cases, a truly global scale. It is about the fabrication and distributing of goods, the provision of services, and the movement of labour across international boundaries. Second, this economic development was accompanied by the rise of nation-states and the governmental apparatus required to protect and to control the economy, as well as the interests of ordinary citizens. Through centuries of war, rebellion, treaties, and other political activity, nations have replaced kingdoms and tribal societies. Third, the very spread of nationalism in turn brought into being the system of international relations and all the political, social, and cultural institutions designed to foster co-operation and assistance among nations. Lastly, globalization is also about, and in fact was made possible by, the creation and spread of worldwide systems of transportation and communication. By radically reducing the time it takes to travel between places or to know what is happening almost anywhere, the perceived distance between places shrank. The world got smaller.

We can illustrate these changes in countless ways. An historical example comes to mind. On 25 June 1876, the troops of the Seventh Regiment of the United States army, under the command of General George Custer, were massacred by the combined forces of the Lakota, Northern Cheyenne, and Arapaho Indians at the famous Battle of the Little Bighorn in Montana. It took over a week, however, for news of this stunning defeat to find its way into the pages of the newspapers of New York City. Today, more often than not, cameras are at the ready when newsworthy events happen, providing live feed to the entire globe. We all watched in real time, sharing the horror, when the twin towers of the World Trade Center collapsed on 9/11. In a world of 24-hour global markets, worldwide production systems, easy international travel, and 24/7 news coverage, the pace of change is brisk and it is accelerating with each new push for more economic growth and technological innovation.

The changes to the material and social conditions of our lives under globalization are being matched by a change in our consciousness. What is local and what is global are becoming interlaced as never before, as is readily manifest in daily aspects of our lives—in the foods we eat, the music we listen to, and the clothes we wear, and in our entertainment, news, vacations, and even our careers. Within hours of stocks crashing on the markets of Hong Kong or Tokyo, jobs are lost on Bay Street in Toronto, and not long after on Main Street as well. The drama of miners trapped in Chile, riots in the Middle East, mudslides in California, or earthquakes in Japan can capture the attention of Canadians every day as they listen to their local news. We are amongst the first people to be exposed to events happening around the world every day, and the exposure is bridging the differences and the distance between us and the rest of the world. "They" are starting to become part of our imagined "us."

One of the more profound effects of this situation, Robertson stresses, is the "thematization" of "humanity" (Robertson and Chirico, 1985). By this he means that questions about the very nature and potential of humankind—what it means to be human, and not just Greek, French, Chinese, Hindu, Jewish, black, white, or whatever—are being considered in a fairly consistent and systematic way. Most conspicuously, this development is apparent in the relatively new concern with the formulation and institutionalization of "human rights"—rights for all humans and not just protections for the interests of this or that group of people. In work and play many of us now interact with people half a world away; they are our friends and colleagues, our competitors and partners. We have a concern for their health and welfare, and are coming to realize more and more that our individual fates are subject to threats happening on a global scale: global warming, international financial instability, terrorism, the threat of nuclear war, or a pandemic.

In these and other ways the process of globalization, as fact and consciousness, is often associated with the increased homogenization of life. Our local worlds are all becoming more alike, as aptly captured by George Ritzer's popular notion of the "McDonaldization" of society (Ritzer, 1993). In truth the economic, political, and cultural triumph of Western ways of living across the globe has dramatically reduced the differences among cultures and increased the standardization and uniformity of products and practices. The heightened competition of corporations and nations in international markets has required, ironically, the ever greater integration of societies at all levels.

Expressive Individualism and the New Tribalism

But there is a deeper dialectic at work, on two levels, that complicates the social conditions brought on by globalization. This is the less recognized flip-side of the globalization coin.

First, the very rise of nation-states and industrial economies developed hand-in-hand with the increased differentiation of individuals from society. Individualism is the hallmark of modernity; with the demise of tradition, one's identity is increasingly a personal and achieved phenomenon, and not a social and ascribed one. In modern societies, who we are is a subjective and accomplished aspect of life that exceeds the bare lineaments of identity provided by the families and groups into which we are born. This impetus to what has been called "expressive individualism" (Bellah et al., 1985; Roof and McKinney, 1987) is, in part, the inevitable by-product of a set of simple but profound social changes which are typical of modernity. With the survival of more children due to the improvements in the physical and social conditions of life, and advances in medical science, people started having fewer children, about whom they cared more. This demographic trend, combined with the movement of people into urban and even more suburban environments, shifted the focal point of life to the nuclear family and away from the traditional reliance on an extended family. More time, energy, and money were invested, because it could be invested, in learning and meeting the needs of each child, with the aim of maximizing the development of his or her intrinsic potential. Consequently, in late modern societies the drive to be a unique individual, to express one's "self" became paramount.

Much of the economy is dedicated to satisfying this urge, or at least sustaining the illusion that we can do so, by offering a staggering array of seemingly different products and services to choose from and express ourselves. Our social relations are patterned increasingly by rules of exchange premised on the mutual satisfaction of our identity needs. In other words, the homogenizing force of globalization is countered by a drive to increased heterogeneity, a massive indulgence in celebrating individual differences, though often at a rather superficial level. This tendency is manifested socially in everything from the notion that every child should have his or her own bedroom to the phenomenal success of Facebook or the modern cult of celebrity.

Second, and similarly, at the level of societies, and in terms of other kinds of persistent group identities, whether ethnic or religious, the heightened relativization of social identities in the face of global comparisons has induced a renewed search for distinctiveness as well—in part as an act of resistance to the homogenizing trends of globalization. This renewal of interest in cultural, ethnic, and religious differences, sometimes called the new tribalism, can be seen in everything from the strident efforts of the French government to protect French culture, language, and cuisine from the incursions of American mass culture, to our own growing anti-Americanism and Quebecois nationalism, to the rising tide of Islamic fundamentalism. Differences of identity are being celebrated, even invented in some cases, to counteract the strong economic forces working to obliterate the differences. This is the cross-cutting dialectic of globalization. At the level of the individual and the group it works to make everything the same, while simultaneously stimulating a new awareness of the need to retain or find new ways of being different.

The Risk/Trust Dialectic

The heightened global awareness and reliance on expert systems of late modernity brings us to two other closely inter-related aspects of Giddens' conception of the social structural changes that mark late modernity: the institutionalization of reflexivity and the risk/trust dialectic. The emergence of a global consciousness is exhilarating on the one hand, as it liberates us from traditional constraints. But it is disconcerting on the other hand, since it relativizes who we are and what we know, and burdens us with global problems we feel ill-equipped to handle. We are being pressed to be ever more critically self-aware and incessantly rational in our analysis of most aspects of our lives. This reflexivity, which is the hallmark of our creation, use, and reliance on expert systems, is the downside of our new freedom. The systems of knowledge embodied in our expert systems, in our major institutions, are premised on the ceaseless retrieval and examination of new data to effect improvement. But the pace of institutionalized change, let alone the other kinds of unanticipated and uncontrolled change brought on by the very scope and interdependency of our social and physical systems, can be disconcerting.

In the face of the relativizing effects of our increased global awareness and the reflexive imperative to court change, it is becoming harder and harder to find an abiding sense of security in the routines of everyday life and our taken-for-granted assumptions about the way things are and should be. For millennia, however, that is exactly what humans have done.

Today everything is subject to the spiralling imperative of critical self-study and justification. In our places of work, social programs, education, careers, and even our most intimate relationships we are being systematically encouraged and pressured to constantly monitor and change the way things are done. As Giddens comments, for example, "marriage and family would not be what they are today were they not thoroughly 'sociologised' and 'psychologised'" (1990: 43). Even the most private spheres of life have been penetrated by the gaze of the professionals. We are bombarded with books, magazine articles, and television shows offering advice from "experts" on how to fix or improve our relationships, turning the most natural foundations of social life into creative projects of self-expression and fulfillment. There is a disjuncture, in other words, between the sweeping and accelerating structural changes we are experiencing, and the imperative to embrace change itself, and our basic natures—our ingrained need for a significant measure of stability, sameness, personal control, and order in our lives.

This source of anxiety is aggravated by a change in the risk profile of late modern life. We are freed increasingly from many of the ills and threats that plagued our predecessors, and experiencing more materially prosperous and far less painful lives. It was once very common, for example, for women to die giving birth to their children; now this is rare in the developed world. While famine was a recurrent threat experienced by all people, killing tens of thousands, it is now confined to the poorest parts of the globe. But, as Giddens argues, the reality of our situation is more complex. Building on insights from Ulrich Beck (Beck, [1986] 1992), he suggests that both the "objective distribution of risks" and our "perception of perceived risks" have changed for the worst (Giddens, 1990: 124–5).

The distribution of risks has been altered in at least four ways. The first two have to do with the "scope" of the risks we face: (1) in a globalized world we are confronted with "high consequence risks" that threaten the whole planet (e.g., nuclear holocaust, global warming, or the loss of bio-diversity), and (2) there is an expanding array of contingent events that have an impact on people far and wide (e.g., a political decision made in Beijing about labour regulations can throw people out of work in Oshawa). The other two ways the distribution of risks has changed have to do with the "types" of threats people are exposed to: (3) we are being victimized increasingly by the unanticipated consequences of our own interventions into nature (e.g., oil spills from offshore drilling rigs or the importation of new species into environments), and (4) we have developed our own "institutionalized risk environments," like investment markets, that affect the life chances of millions.

The perception of risks has altered in at least three ways: (1) there is an ever wider awareness of the risks to which humanity is subject; (2) there is less confidence that the risks can be averted by supernatural or magical means; and (3) there is a growing awareness of the limits of expert systems in coping with the risks, even those created by the expert systems. Think in this regard of the disastrous effects of hurricane Katrina for New Orleans, or the likelihood that the global extinction of the dinosaurs resulted from an asteroid colliding with the Earth sixty-five million years ago.

For these and other reasons, it could be argued that we live in times of unprecedented doubt and anxiety. We seek to offset this uncertainty with

**Box
6.1**   The Faith of Henry Paulson and the Financial Crisis of 2008

On 13 September 2008 the world was on the brink of the biggest financial melt-down the global markets had experienced since the Great Depression of the 1930s. Lehman Brothers, the fourth largest investment bank in the United States and a major player in global financial transactions, was about to become insolvent. The bankruptcy of such a large firm could set off a cascade of panic that would cripple Wall Street and costs thousands of corporations and their ordinary investors bil-lions of dollars. In fact, in the worst case scenario—which regrettably happened—their fall could precipitate the failure of other even larger investment banks and many other kinds of financial organizations (e.g., AIG). Henry Paulson, ex-Chairman and Chief Executive Officer of Goldman Sachs, and the Secretary of the Treasury of the United States, was working feverishly with an elite team of experts to assess the situation, find a buyer for Lehman's, and avert a financial fiasco. But by the eve-ning of 14 September, their plans were unravelling and things were looking worse. The next day the turmoil hit the equity/bond markets and banks began freezing credit, sending businesses around the world into crisis. In his book *On the Brink: Inside the Race to Stop the Collapse of the Global Financial System* (Paulson, 2010), Paulson provides a fascinating account of these heady and stressful days, in the midst of which is the following moving passage about the evening of 14 September:

> Back in my temporary office . . . a jolt of fear suddenly overcame me as I thought of what lay ahead of us. . . . With the US sinking deeper into reces-sion, the failure of a large financial institution would reverberate through-out the country—and far beyond our shores. It would take years for us to dig ourselves out from under such a disaster.

trust in our expert systems. We have no other choice in our highly interde-pendent, globalized, and technological societies. But the very reflexivity of those systems, the consciousness they inevitably create in us of the highly contingent nature of our existence, works against placing full confidence in our systems. Rather, we are pushed by circumstances into an ever more problematic social space (Dawson, 2006b: 110–11):

> On a day-to-day basis we can cobble together the prerequisite trust in our own fate and that of our societies by the skilled cultivation of routine watchfulness in combination with calculated indifference. This curious blend has become a constituent element of socialization into adulthood. We are taught to have faith in the expert and abstract systems that guide

All weekend I'd been wearing my crisis armour, but now I felt my guard slipping. I knew I had to call my wife, but I didn't want to do it from the land line in my office because other people were there. So I walked around the corner to a spot near some windows. Wendy had just returned from church. I told her about Lehanan's unavoidable bankruptcy and the looming problems with AIG.

"What if the system collapses?" I asked her. "Everybody is looking to me, and I don't have the answer. I am really scared."

I asked her to pray for me, and for the country, and to help me cope with this sudden onslaught of fear. She immediately quoted from the Second Book of Timothy, verse 1:7—"For God hath not given us the spirit of fear, but of power, and of love, and of sound mind."

The verse was a favourite of ours. I found it comforting and felt my strength come back with this reassurance. With great gratitude, I was able to return to the business at hand. I called [White House chief of staff] Josh Bolten and New York City Mayor Michael Bloomberg to alert them that Lehman would file for bankruptcy that evening.

This simple passage goes to the heart of religion in all of its complexity and its perplexing efficacy. One might dismiss Paulson's confession of faith at this critical juncture as a passing nod to the conventions of faith in America, but that would be disingenuous and unhelpful. An individual steeped in a culture of practiced rationalism, and engrained to the tensions of the risk/trust dialectic at work in the modern global economy, continued to find a profound and instrumental benefit in the wisdom and solace offered by the ancient and poetic words of a preacher touching on the universal fate of humanity. But he had to be socialized to this tradition of wisdom to be able to exploit it for his benefit and the rest of us.

our societies, and we learn to fashion an immediate life-world of regularised activities that is comforting. We learn not to question certain aspects of our social systems too closely, and to deflect the fears invoked by the risks with which we chose to live by distracting ourselves with technologically sophisticated entertainments and the consumption of luxury goods. We are compelled to assume that our food, water, medicines and machines are safe. But as individuals we know little about them, and our conflicting expert systems are always raising doubts.

In other words, we are trapped in a dilemma which keeps getting worse. We need to achieve and sustain trust in our expert systems to feel secure in the face of our growing awareness of ever greater risks that are difficult to manage. But this awareness of risk is in large part either generated by the actual operation of the expert systems themselves or a by-product of the increased reflexivity and knowledge that comes with the creation and implementation of expert systems. We are damned if we do rely on our expert systems, and damned if we don't (see Box 6.1).

The Transformation of Intimacy

The processes of de-traditionalization and globalization, and the orientation to expressive individualism, in the context of a mounting sense of living with risks, all help to explain, Giddens and others argue (e.g., Beck and Beck-Gernsheim, 2002), one last prominent feature of late modern life: the new social significance of personal relationships, especially romantic ones. The sheer complexity of late modern life, combined with the rationalizing, relativizing, and disenchanting impact of our global consciousness and reliance on expert systems, has unintentionally brought about the progressive "de-moralization" of our societies (Wilson, 2001). For millennia humans have lived in relatively small and stable communities where a traditional and authoritative moral context existed for coping with what Giddens calls the "fateful moments" of life—the unexpected deaths, illnesses, accidents, and natural and human-made disasters. For many today there are few, if any, clear and external sources of authority in which to place one's faith. Rather, in the fragmented plurality of our social relations and activities we are faced with a contest of alternative knowledge claims from conflicting experts when seeking to deal with an almost overwhelming set of choices. In these circumstances we are thrown back on our personal experiences, on our inner resources, to cope. We are asked to rely on the results of what Giddens calls **the reflexive project of identity construction** that has become the new norm of our societies. We must find our "selves," our true natures, to acquire the strength and resilience to cope with adversity and to carve out a path to success. Under this conceptual regime of expressive individualism, adolescence has become an extended and ambiguous rite of passage and the entire lifespan has been reconceived as an endless opportunity to learn. We are always on our way somewhere, in terms of our development and fulfilment, and rarely seem to arrive anywhere in particular, because the socially prescribed endpoints keep changing and receding into the future.

But, as Giddens stresses, we are not quite the autonomous world creators our society often encourages us to imagine. Our condition remains profoundly social, if different from earlier times:

> [W]hile the regimes of self-development marketed today create the impression that our identity depends on some Herculean feat of self-analysis and motivation, our sense of self is no less intersubjective than in the past. We

are still dependent on our interactions with others to tell us who we are. But, in line with the freedom of choice so characteristic of modernity, the primary reference group for our project of identity construction has shifted from the social bodies into which we are born to the most intimate and emotional relationships we create. People are now socialised to the pursuit of a new ideal, the "pure relationship," through which they will find happiness, security, and psychological well-being (Dawson, 2006b: 112).

Friendships and romantic relationships, as never before, have become the focal point of the quest for a stable base of operations in ever-changing times. Here we seek to fashion and enjoy the trust that can provide the emotional sustenance for our life journey and our relationships under conditions of risk. This is abundantly apparent in the exaggerated mythology of romantic love that pervades our popular culture.

Regrettably, of course, the reality of our lives rarely lives up to the myth of "pure relationships" and this inconsistency is the subject of endless exploration in the literature, plays, films, and magazines of our culture. Yet, on the whole, the romantic vision of how things are persists and we staunchly maintain our preference for stories with happy endings, where the loving couple triumphs over adversity and lives happily ever after.

Religion in the Late Modern World

This understanding of our new social situation, of living under the conditions of "late modernity" is far from definitive. One can easily imagine other ways of conceptualizing things. In this context our objective is not to convince you of the specific veracity of Giddens's vision of the social forces shaping life today, though his theory incorporates and corresponds with the insights from many other social theorists. Rather, we are content with being suggestive. The objective is to get you thinking about the new social realities that religion must interact with and to see if you can locate your own experience in this new set of social conditions. At the core of the new situation is a dynamic with serious implications for religion, implications that have been charted in diverse and fragmentary ways by many sociologists of religion. Religion, like all other aspects of social life, is embroiled in the many cross-cutting currents of late modernity. On the one hand, we see this in the turn from traditional religions to more individualistic and experimental forms of spiritual quests, in the rise of a vast array of alternative religions and spiritual-therapeutic gurus and groups (e.g., Roof, 1999; Lynch, 2007; Heelas, 2008). On the other hand, we see it in the surprising resurgence of the more socially and theologically conservative forms of religious expression, from American evangelicalism to Islamic fundamentalism and Hindu religio-nationalism (e.g., Balmer, 1989; Marty and Scott, 1991;

Box 6.2   The Global Spread of Ayahuasca Religions

In the 1990s several new religions from Brazil that used a hallucinogenic compound as a sacrament began to find new converts in North America and Europe. The two best-known groups are União do Vegetal and Santo Daime, and the sacrament is ayahuasca, a tea brewed from the blend of two plants from the Amazon rain forest. The psychoactive substance in the tea is dimethyltryptamine (DMT), a proscribed drug in most of the Western world. In both religions, members consume ayahuasca in ritual contexts to experience profound and life-changing visions of an array of spiritual entities at work in the natural world and to gain deeper insight into their own selves. The substance, called *hoasca* in União do Vegetal and *daime* in Santo Daime, is known for its unique capacity to cathartically reveal unresolved, repressed, and often painful past experiences to participants. The drug has long been used by various shamans for medicinal and spiritual purposes; however, these two new religions have welded the visions induced by the drug to syncretistic spiritual systems of thought drawn from folk Catholicism, Kardecist Spiritism, and African and indigenous South American forms of animism present in Brazil. Each religion was founded by uneducated but charismatic men who were introduced to the shamanistic uses of ayahuasca while working as rubber collectors deep in the Amazon jungles. Raimundo Irineu Serra founded Santo Daime in the 1930s, and José Gabriel da Costa created União do Vegetal in the 1950s.

Of the two groups, Santo Daime is still the simpler and better known religion, with a more pronounced Christian tone. It members engage in long and silent

Smith, 1998; Brekke, 2012). Both of these seemingly contrary developments are probably being driven by the dynamics of globalization and the new risk profile of late modernity. But precise connections have yet to be established and we are admittedly engaging in speculation about the relationship.

Until recently most sociologists of religion have tended to limit religion in the late modern world to one of two options: they can accommodate themselves to the new social order and achieve a stable but extremely modest existence as a component of the growing leisure and service economy, or they can entrench themselves behind whatever traditional socio-religious structures they think they can maintain or construct, profess the old beliefs, and act as if nothing has happened. "In other words, they can either survive, yet more or less disappear as distinctive social entities with a unique purpose, or they can remain distinct but more or less disappear, surviving only at the margins of society, where they will become more and more difficult to sustain, both economically and symbolically" (Dawson, 2006a: 182). We suspect, however, that the reality is more complex and messy, with religion continuing in collective rituals of mediation called "concentrations" and more communal ceremonies called "hymnals" that involve slow rhythmic dancing and singing, accompanied by a few musical instruments. União do Vegetal has developed into a more complex and hierarchical religion of secret initiatory levels with a more New Age character. But both have attracted the attention of religious seekers from outside Brazil and been carried by these converts to the United States, Canada, the Netherlands, England, and elsewhere.

In these countries there have been several legal struggles with authorities over the importation of ayahuasca, which these groups believe can be prepared only under special circumstances using plants from the Amazon that are imbued with the spirits of the region. After careful investigation the Brazilian authorities approved the right of believers to use the substance long ago, but other countries have been more resistant. Legal victories in the Netherlands and the United States, however, have now assured that same right elsewhere. Careful restrictions have been imposed, though, to prevent the distribution of ayahuasca for non-religious uses. The substance is available online, however, and a small but thriving tourist trade exists to take people to Brazil for week-long therapeutically guided group sessions using ayahuasca.

The successful adoption of this exotic and originally illegal religious practice by average Americans, Canadians, and Europeans is indicative, we suspect, of the continued and sometimes quite intense interest in spiritual concerns in late modern societies. Moreover, this kind of religious activity aligns well with the de-traditionalism, expressive individualism, and even greater pragmatism so characteristic of life in the West today. Certainly the spread of the ayahuasca religions is itself a manifestation of the processes of globalization at the core of late modern life and indicative of the new religious pluralism that we are going to have to learn to live with.

a variety of forms with variable levels and kinds of social significance. Many sociologists see evidence that religion is changing and adapting to the new conditions, in part by developing ways of being religious that transcend the church-oriented or congregational forms of religious life dominant in the early modern and modern periods of Western society. The churches may be dying in most of Europe, Canada, Australia, and parts of the US, but religion *per se* is not. At this point, however, this discussion may be more cryptic than helpful. In the rest of this chapter we provide some indication of what we have in mind, by delineating what Giddens thought about the future of religion and sampling the views of several sociologists about the nature of the new forms of religiosity arising in late modern times. As the rest of this book unfolds the larger picture will become clearer (see Box 6.2).

Giddens on Religion

Giddens was not much concerned with religion in his work and he makes only scattered, though suggestive, comments on the place of religion in the late modern social order. He clearly understands that the dominant institutions of religion, at least in the West, are being marginalized by the combined effects of the processes of de-traditionalization, globalization, and individualization. People are turning their backs on the traditional religions of their parents and grandparents, in part because they no longer feel that these ways of being religious are congruent with their more reflexive approach to the world and the stresses and strains of their busy late modern lives. With their heightened awareness of the range of plausible, yet often clashing, religio-cultural perspectives present in their pluralistic and globalizing societies, educated people no longer simply assume that the religion they happen to have grown up with is intrinsically more virtuous and true. Nonetheless Giddens is not surprised that many religious groups and activities continue to develop and spread in the late modern era (Giddens, 1991: 207). Why? Two reasons can be gleaned from his analyses, which parallel the bifurcated developments noted by most sociologists of religion.

First, Giddens observes that some resistance to the processes of rapid change associated with the emergence of the late modern social order is inevitable. This comes, he states (1991: 206), in the form of "a burgeoning preoccupation with the reconstruction of tradition." Many segments of society have become more explicitly conservative in their social values, advocating political policies and cultural norms designed to turn back the hands of time to the social practices they identify with some idealized period from the past. Religiously this urge is manifested in the resurgence of forms of fundamentalism around the world (e.g., Christian, Jewish, Muslim, Hindu, even Buddhist). The fundamentalists are trying to forge a new and stable identity, one based on the prioritization of a limited set of very particular religious tenets and commitments, which they hope will be resistant to the homogenizing incursion of the more universal values of the new global economic, political, and social order (e.g., individualism, materialism, rationalism, and relativism). Giddens recognizes the appeal and power of such efforts to re-invent traditions, but he is skeptical. In his eyes they are irrational attempts to deny or suppress processes of change that are more or less irreversible (Giddens, 1990: 150, 206). Moreover, they stem from the exercise of the very reflexivity that is a hallmark of the late modern social order, and make sense only in the face of a growing awareness of the globalized nature of our world. In this ironic sense religious fundamentalism, as others have noted (Lechner, 1985; Robertson and Chirico, 1985), is actually a very modern phenomenon.

Second, while Giddens, like most sociologists, can no longer place his faith in religion to resolve the important issues in life, whether personal or societal, he recognizes that people in late modern societies are faced with moral dilemmas and fears with which science and reason alone cannot cope. Something like the commitments and convictions traditionally wielded by religion, for example, is required to motivate and guide the self-sacrifices needed to promote the collective good. Pragmatically, societies benefit from the ultimate assurances provided by religious beliefs that good deeds will be rewarded and that there is more to life than just staying alive and securing pleasure (e.g., Giddens, 1990: 141). Late modern society is essentially a "de-moralized" society yet people continue to need guidance, ethical and moral standards, to cope with the fateful moments in life when disturbing experiences intrude, such as "madness, criminality, sickness and death, sexuality, and nature" (1991: 156). This is another reason Giddens is not surprised that religion persists in the late modern era (1991: 207):

> We see all around us the creation of new forms of religious sensibility and spiritual endeavour. The reasons for this concern quite fundamental features of late modernity. What was due to become a social and physical universe subject to increasingly certain knowledge and control instead creates a system in which areas of relative security interlace with radical doubt and with disquieting scenarios of risk. Religion in some part generates the conviction which adherence to the tenets of modernity must suspend: in this regard it is easy to see why religious fundamentalism has a special appeal. But this is not all. New forms of religion and spirituality represent in a most basic sense a return of the repressed, since they directly address issues of the moral meaning of existence which modern institutions so thoroughly tend to dissolve.

New forms of religious life, Giddens indicates, are part of the wider set of social movements associated with the rise of identity or life politics in late modern societies. They are part of the effort to create, disseminate, and assert new ethical and moral standards in areas of life previously controlled by society that have now become subject to choice—too much choice. Parts of our lives that are crucial to our identity have been penetrated by the reflexive, disembedding, globalizing, and individualizing gaze of the expert systems of late modernity (e.g., sex, abortion, homosexuality, reproductive technologies, gender relations, race relations, health, and ecology), but are without, as yet, a corresponding sense of individual control.

Giddens's reflections on religion are limited to these speculative insights, which we think have merit. But are they congruent with the observations sociologists have made about changes in the basic nature of religion in late modern societies?

The New Religious Consciousness

In the late 1980s and early 1990s many sociologists began to observe the kinds of changes in religion that we are associating with the emergence of late modernity. For example, James Beckford, the British sociologist of religion, was one of the first to comment on the types of changes in religious sensibility we are addressing (1984, 1989, 1992). Reflecting on the data available on religion in contemporary Britain, he saw reason to reject the still-dominant thesis that modernization leads to the inevitable demise of religion. His colleague Grace Davie (1994) coined the now popular phrase "believing without belonging" to capture what had been happening in Britain and the rest of Europe for many decades. On the one hand, church attendance and membership figures had been plummeting and the cultural and political power of the mainline denominations was waning rapidly. Western European societies were secularizing, and religious institutions and leaders were losing their positions of prestige and influence in society. On the other hand, surveys continued to show relatively high levels of personal belief (e.g., Lambert, 1999; Stark, Hamberg, and Miller, 2005; Houtman and Aupers, 2007). The majority of Western Europeans continued to believe, for example, in a personal God or at least some spirit or vital force guiding the universe. They still accepted the inspired character of the Bible and the potential efficacy of prayer. They continued to express the general importance of having some kind of spiritual orientation, even if they rarely, if ever, attended traditional religious services.

It is widely agreed that the new expressive individualism, so characteristic of late modern societies, has long been the key social development driving people away from continued confidence in the traditional religious denominations and churches. But as the French sociologist of religion Danièle Hervieu-Léger argues (2003), this same individualism was fuelling a new kind of religiosity and secularization was being matched by at least the nascent elements of a new sacralization (2006: 59):

> The "rational disenchantment" characteristic of modern societies does not mark the end of religion. It has not caused the disappearance of the need to believe—far from it. This assertion—which nowadays would sound self-evident—formed the starting point, thirty years ago, of a theoretical revival in the sociology of religions. It paved the way for a major re-evaluation of the secularization process, a task still far from complete. One point has now been established, however: it has become clear that belief proliferates in proportion to the uncertainty caused by the pace of change in all areas of social life. But we also know that it sits less and less easily within the dogmatic frameworks offered by institutional religions. In societies that have developed the autonomy of individuals as a principle, individuals create, in an increasingly independent manner, the small systems of belief that fit their own aspirations and experiences.

But can a religiosity that is so highly individualistic ever be "socially" significant? Or will the ethos of individualism lead to views that are too diffuse and mutable, perhaps even trivial, to warrant serious attention? Steve Bruce (2002, 2011) has his doubts, but Hervieu-Léger (2003; 2006), along with others (e.g., Lambert, 1999; Dawson, 2004, 2006b; Houtman and Aupers, 2007; Aupers and Houtman, 2010), thinks that the new forms of religion can be socially significant. But before we can explore the more optimistic views of Hervieu-Léger we need a better sense of the new religious orientation that many sociologists see emerging in tandem with late modernity.

Starting in the 1980s, Beckford and others began to realize that a new set of religious sensibilities was becoming dominant, both amongst those drawn to new and alternative forms of spirituality and amongst many practitioners of conventional religion. Modern societies, he argued (1992), were undergoing a shift toward a kind of "transcendent humanism" with three common characteristics. First, people were turning to a more "holistic" perspective on life and the world. They wished to emphasize the interconnectedness of all things, of "human and non-human, the personal and the public, the physical and the mental, [the] national and international" (1992: 17). This meant they preferred to focus on religious and spiritual practices, such as meditation, dealing with what he calls the "little transcendence" of the limitations of the "mundane world" rather than the supernatural or "great transcendences" of the great salvation religions of the world (see Luckmann, 1990 as well). Second, people believe they can access and release "new sources of power" through this more holistic worldview and related practices. They can unlock the hidden potential of humans to fulfil a spiritually enlightened agenda of activities leading to improved health, an uncontaminated natural environment, better human relationships, and more social justice and peace. Third, this new spiritual orientation is "compatible with a wide range of specific ideologies and practices." It is an ethos and not a specific program of social and moral reform or religious practice. Those experiencing the shift, that is, see little inconsistency in identifying with Christ, practising Buddhist meditation, respecting the wisdom of the Qur'an, and using Ayurvedic medicine to treat their ills. Their focus is on the perceived similarities between traditions, which they see as essential, and not the historical differences, which they think are accidental. They are not concerned with keeping the traditions pure and favour creatively borrowing whatever ideas ring true.

Building on the insights of several other similar discussions of an emergent new religious consciousness, one of us (Dawson, 1998: 138–40) framed things a bit more elaborately, arguing that many people now approach religion with an orientation that is marked by six key features:

1. There is a pronounced religious individualism, and in two senses: "[p]eople's participation is motivated by the development of personal

identity, and correspondingly the locus of the sacred is often seen to be within the individual and not outside. . . . Immanence is stressed over transcendence" (138).

2. There is an emphasis on religious experience. Faith and personal, essentially transformative, experiences are valued more than belief and doctrine.

3. This encourages a more pragmatic approach to questions of religious authority and practice. Leaders and groups are recognized and esteemed for their capacity to induce, exemplify, develop, and perpetuate the kinds of transformative experiences people crave, and not their traditional credentials.

4. The new religious consciousness "is remarkably more syncretistic, accepting of relativism, and tolerant of other religious perspectives and systems than the religions dominant in the West in the past" (139).

5. Likewise, the new orientation is more "holistic," or as others prefer to say, "monistic." "Dualisms, on almost all fronts, are rejected or diminished in scope and significance: the traditional dualisms of God and humanity, the transcendent and the immanent, humanity and nature, the spiritual and material, the mind and the body, the subjective and the objective, male and female, good and evil, and even cause and effect" (139).

6. Lastly, the concern with each of these foci results in a preference for greater organizational openness and flexibility. People think of themselves first and foremost as clients seeking and receiving services, rather than committed members of a particular group or tradition. Even when they become devotees seeking truth, transformation, and salvation from one source, they still wish to exercise their right to choose how, and to what extent, they will participate in any prescribed activities.

Neither Beckford nor Dawson thinks that this new orientation is likely to culminate in a specific religious movement or a practice that will achieve prominence in the West. Only a small but growing minority of people are explicitly engaged in some alternative spiritual activity today. But some scholars think the data available suggest the tide is turning in this direction and more people will soon be engaged in such practices rather than attending traditional religious services (see e.g., Lambert, 1999; Heelas and Woodhead, 2005; Lynch, 2007; Heelas, 2008). Whatever the case, Dawson and Beckford are content to stress that the influence of the new set of religious or spiritual sensibilities can be detected throughout contemporary life, in new ways of thinking about medicine, education, sport, leisure, ecology, dying and grieving, self-help, gender, and even work (Beckford, 1992: 18; Dawson, 1998: 148). Even more fundamentally, as Beckford (1989, 1992) proposes and Dawson (1998; 2006a, 2006b) reiterates, the new orientation is indicative of an entire shift in the basic nature and role of religion, one

that parallels the shift to late modernity. Today, Beckford proposes, "it is
. . . better to conceptualize **religion as a cultural resource** . . . than a social
institution" (1992: 23). Religion has "come adrift from its former points of
social anchorage" (1992: 22) because the social structural changes wrought
by de-traditionalization, globalization, and expressive individualism have
eaten away at the conventional communal, familial, and organizational bas-
es of religion. But, Beckford argues, this change does not mean that religion no longer matters. "[R]eligious and spiritual forms of sentiment, belief
and action have survived as relatively autonomous resources. They retain
the capacity to symbolize, for example, ultimate meaning, infinite power,
supreme indignation and sublime compassion" (1992: 23). Consequently,
as free-floating cultural resources they will continue to play a pivotal role
in how people engage in identity politics, understand their personal needs,
resolve social conflicts, and conceptualize what it means to be human in late
modern societies.

Hervieu-Léger and the Paradoxes of Late Modern Religion

One of the most prominent sociologists of religion struggling to understand the significance of the changes in late modern religion in the West is
Danièle Hervieu-Léger. At the core of the changes sweeping through the
religious world of the contemporary West she sees a shift in the legitima-
tization of beliefs "from religious authorities, [as the] guarantors of the
truth of belief, to individuals themselves, who are responsible for the authenticity of their own spiritual approach." This means, she says, that religious modernity involves "the individualized dissemination of convictions
and the collapse of the religious codes [and institutions] that organized
shared certainties within believing communities" for centuries (2006: 60).
But, she asserts, paradoxically the increasingly "do-it-yourself" nature of
religion does not mean "we are entering into an era of spiritual fragmentation and radical change in perspective on shared certainties. . . . Things
are not so simple" (2006:61). She does not accept that the triumph of
individual choice means that religious beliefs and practices have lost their
social significance.

Two social developments, Hervieu-Léger proposes (2006: 62–3), primarily account for the rise of this increasingly individualized, subjectivized,
and privatized style of religiosity: the weakening of "the family structures
of religious transmission" and the phenomenal expansion in the availability
of "multifarious symbol stocks" from religious traditions across the globe.
The socialization of the young has long been the primary means by which
religions have perpetuated themselves, yet in today's culture of individual
choices and rights parents are ever more reluctant to compel their children
to accept their views (see Chapter 7). The new norm is increasingly that
"each individual must choose for him- or herself the lineage of belief with

which he or she identifies" and this renders many young people structurally open to the influence of other ideas and religious choices. This cognitive opening is occurring precisely at a time when higher education, mass media, global travel, popular culture, and the Internet are making a wide range of religious beliefs and practices—no matter how partially or superficially— available to everyone. To illustrate her point she notes, for example, that the vast majority of French Catholics "no longer associate a belief in sin with the idea of possible damnation" and the idea of "a paradise after death . . . is [being] out-distanced—among practicing Catholics—by belief in reincarnation" (2006: 60).

But there are real limits to the way people can select and reuse items plucked from the vast market of beliefs, symbols, and practices available to them. First, the use is conditioned "by the way the social environment represents and interprets the different contributing traditions" (2006: 61). The appeal of reincarnation in the contemporary West, for example, rests with a decidedly modern and this-worldly notion of mastering one's own fate and having a chance to start over, to do things right the next time, a view that conveniently ignores the much more pessimistic and other-worldly ontology of escape from the ceaseless torments of countless lives that is more characteristic of the traditional conceptions of reincarnation and rebirth in Hinduism and Buddhism. Second, "in this game of individualized belief composition, individuals display varied do-it-yourself skills, corresponding to differentiated social aptitudes. A forty-year-old graduate from a renowned university who lives in central Berlin and spends one-third of his time on business trips will not cobble ideas together in the same way as a thirty-year-old woman who has just arrived from the Caribbean and who works as a cleaner" (2006: 62).

In addition, a significant measure of order and limit is placed on the subjective fashioning of religious worldviews and spiritual practices by "the general laws of the market" (2006: 63–4). Both the material goods available worldwide and the process of symbol production in late modern societies are subject to a process of **standardization and marginal differentiation** that has a "homogenizing" effect (see in this regard the discussion of Berger's theory of secularization in Chapter 5). This is part of the paradoxical nature of recent religious developments, as Hervieu-Léger reads things. As with shampoos, cars, or political leaders, people crave the sense of choice and the appearance of variety. But in most important respects the products, beliefs, and leaders that succeed in our societies cleave pretty close to a set of recognized and standardized expectations, with only marginal variations. In most cases the degree of conformity to a common and winning pattern far exceeds any actual novelty. Thus, she argues, even though Charismatic and Pentecostal forms of Christianity have been sweeping the world for the last fifty years, achieving levels of success never imagined, and in places never imagined (e.g., Brazil, Nigeria, Korea), this success stems from the reduction of Christianity to a minimalist and standardized creed with a strong emotional appeal: "God loves you, Jesus saves, and you can be healed" (2006: 64). This simple, affective, and personalized rendering of the complexities of Christian theology adapts the message to the demands of modern individuals seeking quick access to a transformative experience and means of self-fulfillment. Similar reductive and homogenizing tendencies are at work in the spread of Eastern religions in the West, and more and more people are at home in justifying their religious preferences by simply voicing the new norm that at heart "we are all saying and seeking the same thing," and the religions of the world are all just espousing the same truths somewhat differently (2006: 65).

With the increased homogenization of beliefs comes the increased "migration of believers," who ignore traditional denominational and communal boundaries in their serial quest for the most personally fulfilling mixture of beliefs and practices. As spiritual leaders and ordinary believers expand their horizons and cobble together disparate views, paradoxically some innovations do occur; some of these syncretistic developments and cultural inventions gain popularity and spread, with rapidity and range, through the unprecedented means of mass communication now available, most notably the Internet (see Chapter 8).

But "the most striking paradox of this situation is this: the more beliefs circulate, the less they determine tangible affiliations and the more they further a desire for community liable to evolve into intensive forms of religious socialization" (2006: 66). This insight is at the heart of Hervieu-Léger's argument for the continued social significance of religion. "The extreme circulation of beliefs, in particular by the media," she observes, "stretches the connection between belief and belonging almost to the breaking point. The belief choices of individuals are more and more dissociated from the processes of socialization that ensure the introduction, however limited, of individuals into tangible groups. The bond that one chooses to preserve with some kind of spiritual family is now supported by no more than, one could almost say, minimal references, shared on a worldwide scale" (2006: 66-7). But in truth this state of affairs is unsatisfactory for the creation of the minimal certainties that people crave in order to construct their personal identity. Without abandoning the basic ethic of individualized choice people do seek community, or at least "niche communities," where they can enter into the dialogue with others of like mind to fashion the common "narrative" that helps to turn their personal experiences into something more meaningful. "In other words, there is no possible rendering of spiritual experience as a narrative unless the individual, at some point, meets another individual able to confirm it for [them]: 'What has meaning for you also has meaning for me'" (2006: 67).

Further, this dialogue requires access to, and acceptance of, some "means of authentication of belief," which usually involves resort to past religious tradition or synthesis of traditions. In this way things have changed for religion in the late modern world, yet in some ways they have also stayed the same. As Hervieu-Léger concludes (2006: 67–8):

> Invoking the continuity of a lineage received from the past, and qualified to set a course for the future, constitutes the structural axis of any "religious identity." If, in the contemporary context of fluidity of belief, the paths of religious identification follow unpredictable and continually amendable courses, they nevertheless still come across as the construction of an imaginary positioning system of individuals within a symbolic genealogy. It is this construction that ensures the integration of successive and fragmented experiences of the present into a duration endowed with meaning.

Ironically, as Hervieu-Léger (2003, 2006), Dawson (2004, 2006a), and others have noted, in the new conditions of religious volunteerism, when people are free to craft their own religious identities, and concomitantly when most of the institutional structure of society is secular, the engagement with others on the basis of the shared affirmation of intense personal experiences that the rest of society views as unusual, or even deviant, can produce religious commitments that surpass those achieved through the mere socialization of the next generation by such conventional means as Sunday schools. In this way, "paradoxically, at the very breaking point of tangible socio-religious links" we find people engaged in "the constitution, activation, and even invention of small community identities, which are compact, substantial, and compensatory" (Hervieu-Léger, 2006: 68), as demonstrated by the proliferation of new religious movements, fundamentalist and other traditionalist groups, house churches, intensive yoga, and other contemporary religious and spiritual innovations.

Conclusion

It does not really matter whether we live in "late modern" societies or not. The veracity of the overall theory or any of its parts is not necessarily important in this context. The theory seems very plausible to us, but we are interested in it as a heuristic device—in the manner of much theorizing in the social sciences. It is a way of focusing our thoughts about how the religious lives of contemporary Canadians, and others throughout the Western world, are changing, and how these changes may be rooted in broader patterns of social change. We are not saying societal changes dictate religious changes. Religions, like all social institutions and cultural systems, have acquired a certain key measure of autonomy over the centuries. Rather, it is important to understand the dialectical character of the relationship. Societies influence religions and religions influence societies, and this is happening in continuous and complex ways. In many cases changes in religious preferences and practices may be harbingers of what is to come in the rest of society, since religious ideas are used to think about the big issues, about what ultimately makes life worth living and protecting. Both Émile Durkheim and Max Weber realized this (see Chapter 4), but they also recognized that religions only succeed when the demands they make on people and their promises for the future resonate with the current stresses and strains, joys and ambitions, of people in their daily lives.

In line with Giddens's theory of late modernity we have suggested that Canadians, and most other citizens of advanced industrialized societies, are leading increasingly de-traditionalized and disembedded lives. This is due in part to the progressive intrusion of expert systems into almost every aspect of our lives, in conjunction with the compression of time and space, and the interpenetration of the local and the global, fostered by the processes of globalization. These processes have been accompanied by a turn away from the social and group forms of identity, which structured most social relations until recently, in favour of a heightened individualism and preoccupation with personal forms of identity, based on the reflexive construction of an individual narrative, especially in terms of our most intimate relationships. In other words, we are being driven by social forces and trends largely beyond our control into an increasingly bifurcated existence focused, more than ever before, on the dialectical interplay of actions and meanings at the two extremes of the spectrum of human activity and meaning: the personal and the human.

But our need for more concrete and communal forms of social guidance and legitimacy, especially in the face of the mounting uncertainties born of living in a risk society, and of our growing awareness of the formidable and global threats we face, leaves many in need of some greater measure of spiritual, moral, and social structure and meaning. The resurgence of fundamentalist and other conservative forms of religion worldwide serves this need by simplifying and re-inventing traditional worldviews that clarify what is required of individuals to be saved, and to keep the world safe. The re-invention of these traditional worldviews is selective, however, to avoid forfeiting the basic material and technological benefits of modernity. The rise of do-it-yourself spiritualities, and new religions, serves the same need for those even more personally wedded to the liberties and benefits of modernity, by framing systems of meaning that correlate key aspects of people's personal journeys of development with the progressive transformation of humanity. Religions have always done this, of course, but almost always through the mediating lens of group identities, actions, and prospects. The cosmic plans of the gods were supported and implemented by the acts of individuals, but primarily in their roles as members of groups—as Hebrews, Greeks, Hindus, Christians, Muslims, and so on. Now a more direct link is being forged between fulfilling the potential of each person, as an individual, and the fulfillment of the potential of humanity and the creation of a new cosmic order and destiny. This re-ordering of priorities, from the groups into which we are born or socialized, to our existence as unique individuals, on the one hand, and as members of humanity on the other hand, reflects the shifts in social realities working their way through societies globally, which are reconfiguring what matters to us most every day.

Critical Thinking Questions

1. Are you a citizen of the late modern world? Can you explain some of the ways in which the theorized features of this era have had an impact on your life? Or is there little correspondence between these ideas and your experience?

2. In the reflexive construction of your personal identity, what social factors, statuses, or beliefs still matter? Do any religious or spiritual beliefs, involvements, or concerns play a role?

3. Can very individualistic sets of religious or spiritual beliefs and practices continue to play an influential role in determining the social actions of groups, governments, and societies? How would this happen?

Suggested Readings

Giddens, Anthony. 1990. *The Consequences of Modernity*. Cambridge: Polity. This is the first of several books, by this well-known British social theorist, on the sweeping social changes affecting our society. This classic overview of the issues provides a comprehensive and engaging introduction to the new problems being posed by the impact of technological innovations and expert systems, the processes of globalization, and the loss of more traditional ways of life, for individuals living in late modern societies.

Brekke, Torkel. 2012. *Fundamentalism: Prophecy and Protest in the Age of Globalization*. Cambridge: Cambridge University Press. This book provides a comprehensive and yet concise overview of the historical and social origins of religious fundamentalism, in Christianity, Islam, Hinduism, and elsewhere, in terms of globalization theory. It also surveys the ways in which fundamentalists have specifically struggled to exert an influence on the state, the law, education, the sciences, and women.

Dawson, Andrew. 2007. *New Era-New Religions: Religious Transformation in Contemporary Brazil*. Aldershot: Ashgate. This excellent little book provides a fascinating look into the origins, nature, and significance of many of the syncretistic new religions rising in one of the most rapidly modernizing nations of the world—some of which are now spreading to Europe and North America. The case studies are set against the backdrop of a sociological analysis based on late modernity theory.

Related Websites

www.iasc-culture.org/research_program_religion_late_modernity.php

As a subset of The Institute for Advanced Studies in Culture at the University of Virginia, the Program on Religion and Late Modernity seeks to understand the dynamics and impact of late modern culture on the beliefs and practices of religious believers in Christianity, Judaism, and Islam. This website documents current research projects associated with this initiative, including key researchers involved and all events and publications to arise from this research.

http://cmrc.colorado.edu

The Center for Media, Religion, and Culture is a multidisciplinary initiative to explore the ways that media and religion influence one another and our daily lives in the twenty-first century. Special emphasis is given to the intersection of religion and identity in areas of politics, the economy, and social and cultural life, both nationally and globally. Blogs, conference information, past and present research projects and publications, and other external links and resources are features of this website.

7 The Religious Life of Contemporary Canadians

Learning Objectives

In this chapter, you will learn:

◎ To trace the changing religious landscape of Canada, from the pre-1960s period through to today.

◎ To critically evaluate recent interpretations of the religious life of contemporary Canadians, in particular Reginald Bibby's discussion of secularization, religious revitalization, and the polarization of the religious and non-religious in Canada.

◎ To understand the research findings and implications of a relatively new and prominent area of study in the sociology of religion: the religious views and practices of young people.

◎ To contemplate the possible future of religion in Canada, in light of what we are learning about the transmission of religious beliefs and practices across the generations.

Introduction

In this chapter we bring together the insights we have acquired into the theories and methods of the sociology of religion to understand the religious life of contemporary Canadians. Where have we been religiously, where are we now, and where are we going? We begin by looking at the state of religion in Canada prior to the 1960s, a pivotal time of change in Canadian society. Religion once thrived in Canada and Christian groups exerted a strong influence on public opinion. Religious denominations took a leading role in the operation of hospitals, social service programs, schools, and universities, and Christian leaders regularly lobbied the various levels of government to advance Christian values and interests. As few now realize, Canadians were even more religious than Americans, when measured by religious affiliation and church attendance figures. The state of religion in Canada changed significantly, however, after the social turmoil and cultural changes of the 1960s. This is perhaps nowhere more obvious than in Quebec, where the Quiet Revolution stripped the Roman Catholic Church of its prominent role in the delivery of many social services. But in a more general way, when the Baby Boomer generation came of age there was a mass exodus of young people from most Canadian congregations, both mainstream Catholic and Protestant churches and Jewish synagogues.

The changes set in motion then have been mapped across the succeeding decades by one of Canada's most influential sociologists of religion, Reginald Bibby, from the University of Lethbridge in Alberta. Every five years since 1975 (with the exception of 2010), Bibby has conducted national surveys with adult Canadians on their social and religious values and behaviours. Every eight years since 1984, he has conducted national surveys with Canadian teenagers. These have provided us with a uniquely comprehensive and valuable longitudinal survey of the changing attitudes and behaviours of Canadians. Over the years Bibby's interpretation of his findings has shifted, progressing from an initial emphasis on the secularization of Canada to some talk of a possible revitalization of religion, and most recently the polarization of views on religion in the Canadian populace. An examination of Bibby's data and interpretations provides us with a convenient window into the religious life of Canadians. It also highlights the ongoing problems in making sense of the findings.

We will also examine two other topics that have recently garnered a lot of attention among sociologists of religion and have clear implications for how we should think about the prospects of religion in Canada today and in the future. The first topic is the religious views of teenagers and young adults, those born into the conditions of late modernity. Not only are Canada's young less religious today than in years gone by, they also live in a society characterized by levels of diversity, pluralism, and relativism never seen before. This means they have a unique opportunity to construct their religious identities—an opportunity, however, that can be challenging and disconcerting. The young tend to embody the highly subjective and individualistic approaches to religion that Peter Berger, Steve Bruce, and others predicted would be typical of people in late modern societies, and such approaches are detrimental to participation in more conventional forms of religion. But the data in hand is multi-faceted and limited, so more work is needed to know what it means for the future of religion in Canada.

The second related topic is the transmission of religious beliefs and practices across generations. The changing attitudes and behaviours of the young in Canada and the United States raises questions about the religious socialization of the next generation in the context of a society marked by pluralism and individualism. Recent studies tell us quite a bit about the relative impact of age, period, and cohort effects on the way people are or are not religious in our societies.

The analysis of each of these topics is related to a further issue: the growing religious diversity of our societies, including the noticeable rise in those claiming "**no religion**." But these are topics we will consider at greater length in Chapter 8.

Religion in Canada before the 1960s

Even prior to its formation, Canada was a religiously diverse place, characterized by conflict and co-operation among and within religious groups. Prior to European settlers coming, Aboriginal life was guided by its own forms of spirituality, including beliefs and practices unique to individual nations and clans. In general, Aboriginals believed that the material and spiritual worlds were harmoniously connected and that the Earth and all that was in it ought to be respected, so as to not offend the spirits and the Creator of all things. Individuals, particularly young people, were encouraged to seek personal encounters with the spirit world, typically in the form of guiding animal spirits, and everyone regularly turned to shamans to help interpret their dreams and to cure illnesses. They also placed great importance on various symbols and ritual objects that they believed infused the ordinary with sacred meaning. In a related manner, Aboriginal custom included exchanging stories and myths of how the world was created and how people ought to live. Taken together, Aboriginal spiritual beliefs centred on community life and respect for self, land, and others, and in many ways reflected a highly traditional and pre-modern way of viewing the world (Lewis, 1993; Choquette, 2004).

Tensions arose in Canada with the arrival of European Christian missionaries who wanted to convert and "civilize" Canadian Aboriginals. Believing the Aboriginal way of life to be backward and sinful, the missionaries sought to suppress the Aboriginal traditions, languages, spiritual beliefs, and practices. The efforts to do so culminated in the residential school system, which began in the 1840s. Aboriginal children were separated from their parents and transferred to schools, often at a great distance, that were run by the Roman Catholic, Anglican, and United Churches. These religious schools attempted to "kill the Indian in the child," while they promoted Christian teachings, the English language, and modern farming practices. In the end many Aboriginals converted to Christianity, others rejected it, and some adopted a syncretistic expression of Aboriginal and Christian spirituality. The last residential school, in Saskatchewan, closed its doors only recently, in 1996. Canadians as a whole are far more sensitive now to the legitimacy of Aboriginal beliefs and practices, but our knowledge is limited and there are many misunderstandings that continue to feed into the mistreatment of Aboriginals.

From the beginning, however, there has also been friction between the two religious solitudes of the Canadian nation, the Catholics and the Protestants. Historically, with the notable exception of the French Catholics in Quebec, the English Protestants have dominated the drive to turn Canada into a Christian nation, into **"His Dominion"** (Clifford, 1977). The vision played upon the traditional sources of theological tension between the

Catholic and Protestant worldviews, including, but not limited to, the primacy of Scriptural versus Papal authority, the authority of personal religious experience versus Church teachings, and salvation by grace versus salvation by works. These theological differences influenced public life and disputes in Canada, as Catholics and Protestants disagreed about how their Christian faith ought to inform the exercise of political power, and the promotion of public order and social conformity. Divisions arose over public funding for separate religious schools, the influence of religious institutions on political candidates, and government involvement in the provision of social services to the citizens of the country. Further, driven by their fear of being reduced to a minority, each group actively sought to evangelize members of the other, heightening the existing strains in their relationship. Sometimes even street brawls broke out between members of the two religions, especially when the religious differences were compounded by ethnic ones, such as the enmity between the Irish and the English (Nock, 1993; Grant, 1998; Choquette, 2004; Christie and Gauvreau, 2010). Even in the 1960s, as a child growing up in small-town Ontario, one of the authors experienced the unthinking animosity of the Protestant and Catholic kids in the neighbourhood, expressed through taunts, tricks, sporting competitions, and snowball fights.

Still, Roman Catholics and Protestants pressed forward with attempts to realize what they believed a Christian nation ought to look like, doing so in their respective regions of the country: the French Canadian Catholics in Quebec, the Acadian areas of New Brunswick, and scattered French settlements in the West, and the English Protestants (Anglicans, Presbyterians, Baptists, and Methodists) in Ontario, the Atlantic provinces, and eventually most of the West. Roman Catholics created separate schools for their children and seminaries to train their priests. They established hospitals and asylums and a variety of social service agencies to care for orphans and the poor. Protestants, driven by the overarching goal of evangelism, started their own confessional schools and social service programs, and they organized to pressure political leaders to change society in ways they thought were in keeping with their Christian values (e.g., to improve the working conditions and rights of labourers). These initiatives were endorsed by most Canadians, given their strong personal piety and the shared desire to place a Christian stamp on the behaviour of individuals and institutions in Canada (Hewitt, 1993; O'Toole, 1996; Choquette, 2004; Christie and Gauvreau, 2010).

Just as differences between Roman Catholics and Protestants posed challenges for shaping a common Christian Canada, so did divisions with these groups. Although Roman Catholics were united, by and large, by a shared theology and the authority of the Pope, they were divided along ethnic lines, with tensions between the French Catholics in Quebec and elsewhere and the Irish Catholics dominant in most of the Maritimes and many parts of Ontario. Later the tensions were exasperated by the great influx of Catholic immigrants from Italy, Poland, and the Ukraine, and since the 1960s, the noticeable increase of Spanish, Portuguese, and Filipino Catholics (see Bramadat and Seljak, 2008). In line with their experience in their home countries, each ethnic group practised its Catholicism in distinctive ways, and each held different views about how it should interact with the Protestants and engage society at large. Irish Catholics, whose views had been shaped by the centuries of sectarian conflict with English and Irish Protestants, tended to be fiercely independent. Italian Catholics, who had not previously known what it meant to be a religious minority, maintained strong ties with their homeland and the Vatican in Rome.

In contrast, Protestantism by its very nature is riddled with denominational variation in beliefs and practices. Protestant traditions in Canada's early years included traditional groups with ties to Britain, such as the Anglicans and Presbyterians, and more revivalist and independent groups such as the Methodists and Baptists. These groups competed for the hearts and souls of those who settled Canada's frontiers. Protestants in nineteenth-century Canada struggled to balance respect and appreciation for tradition with the need to find new ways of inspiring personal piety and infusing society with religious ideals. It was this struggle that fostered the most notable attempt at innovation in the effort to fashion a Christian nation, the founding of the United Church of Canada in 1925.

The United Church of Canada grew out of the merger of the Methodists, two-thirds of the Presbyterians, the Congregationalists, and some smaller union churches in Canada. Established in part to cope with the burden of carrying the Christian message to the far-flung settlements of Western Canada, many believed the United Church would help Canada to realize the goal of creating a Christian nation, stretching from "sea to sea" (invoking the phrase from Psalm 72:8 that is etched into the Canadian coat of arms). Many envisioned a Canada filled with pious individuals, guided by public policy and social justice initiatives based on the perceived Christian principles of tolerance, diversity, and care for the poor and marginalized (see Graham, 1990; Milton, 1991; Noll, 1992; O'Toole, Campbell, Hannigan, Beyer, and Simpson, 1993; Best, 1994; Bibby, 1994; O'Toole, 1996). For decades the United Church was the largest Protestant denomination in Canada and its leaders were long associated with "progressive" causes and socialist politics. But the dream of a united Christian Canada never really materialized, and since the 1960s the active affiliates of the United Church of Canada have been in steady decline (Bibby, 2011: 30, 32). As with many of the Protestant denominations, the United Church has experienced internal dissent as members have disagreed on how liberal or conservative their theology should be and how best to respond to the liberalizing tendencies of late modern society. The ordination of homosexual clergy has been a particularly divisive issue for both the United and Anglican churches in Canada, with some conservative congregations formally separating from both denominations over the issue.

All the same, until the 1960s Canada was a pretty religious nation. At the societal level religion played an important role in Canadian public life (see O'Toole, 1996; Grant, 1998; Noll, 2006), and at the level of the individual Canadians conformed to the expectations of their faiths. Throughout the nineteenth and early twentieth century, around 90 percent of Canadians identified with one of the five major religious denominations: the Methodists or the United Church, the Presbyterians, the Anglicans, the Baptists, or the Roman Catholics (Bibby, 1987: 14–15, 28; 2011: 8–9; Beyer, 1997: 276; O'Toole, 2000: 43). These high rates of affiliation meant that new churches were built at a rapid pace, with a 250-percent increase taking place, for example, in Ontario and Quebec between 1851 and 1901 (Beyer, 1997: 277). Every town and city in these provinces bears ample witness to this past success with many large stone and brick churches that now far outstrip the needs of the dwindling members. Affiliation figures remained strong well into the middle of the twentieth century (Beyer, 1997: 278). In 1961 Statistics Canada reported that 47 percent of Canadians identified themselves as Roman Catholics, 49 percent as Protestants, and 1 percent as Eastern Orthodox. Only 2 percent of the population were affiliated with non-Christian traditions, and less than 1 percent claimed to have "no religion" (Bibby, 2011: 9). In 1946, 83 percent of Roman Catholics and 60 percent of Protestants claimed to have attended church in the past seven days. Overall these figures represented 67 percent of all Canadians. By comparison, only 58 percent of Americans reported attending church in the last seven days (Bibby, 1987: 17; 2011: 10). Ninety-five percent of Canadians claimed to believe in God and 84 percent believed in life after death.

To summarize, religion played a prominent role in the life of Canadians prior to the 1960s. In the public discourse of the nation Roman Catholics and Protestants openly pursued their respective visions of what a Christian nation might look like, and privately most Canadians strove to believe, belong, and behave as good Christians. In light of the high levels of religiosity, religious tensions and conflicts, both among and within religious groups, were a reasonably common feature of life in Canada. For the most part Catholics did not marry Protestants, but neither did Methodists marry Baptists. Denominational differences mattered in ways that most of us can no longer appreciate, while unbelief was exceptional and stigmatized.

Religion in Canada since the 1960s

How has the face of religion in Canada changed since the 1960s? Are Canadians more religious, less religious, or the same, and what do we have in mind when we say "religious"? What impact, if any, have changes in the broader social and cultural milieu had on Canadian religiosity? In his most recent book on religion in Canada, *Beyond the Gods and Back: Religion's Demise and Rise and Why it Matters*, Reginald Bibby (2011) summarizes the evolution of his own seminal research on religion in Canada. Over the years he has called upon three interpretive themes to encapsulate what the data reveal about the course of the religious lives of Canadians: secularization, revitalization, and polarization. As indicated, we will use an analysis of these themes to summarize the changes that have occurred and we will question how they should be understood.

Secularization

Returning to the multi-level approach to secularization proposed by Dobbelaere (2002), secularization occurred in Canada at the societal, organizational, and individual levels (see Chapter 5). Canada, like other modern Western nations, faced the emerging reality of a de-traditionalized, structurally differentiated, and institutionally specialized social order based on the Enlightenment ideals of progress and rationalism. As more and more facets of society—education, the legal system, healthcare, and the family—operated free of the formal influence of religion, Christian groups and leaders struggled to maintain some authority in Canadian society.

Nowhere was this felt more than in Quebec, after the **Quiet Revolution** of the 1960s (see e.g., Noll, 1992; Baum, 2000). With the election of the Liberal government of Jean Lesage in 1960, Quebeckers signalled their desire to distance themselves from the dominant and socially oppressive traditions and ideals of the Roman Catholic Church, in favour of a decidedly more open, plural, and liberal social system. The active role of the Roman Catholic Church in running the schools and hospitals of the province was curtailed as public systems of education and healthcare emerged, while labour unions and other social organizations severed their ties with the Church. Similar developments had been happening across Canada. As the demand for higher education grew, for example, the religiously founded universities of the nation were converted into secular public institutions (e.g., Queen's, which was Presbyterian; Acadia and McMaster, which were Baptist; Mount Allison, which was Methodist; Ottawa and Windsor, which were Catholic; Western Ontario, which was Anglican; and Wilfrid Laurier, which was Lutheran). Most Canadians today display a marked preference for keeping religion a private matter and out of the public forums of education or politics. Characteristically, Canadian Alliance party leader Stockwell Day was accorded a rough ride by the media in the 2000 national election when his opponents called attention to his strong affiliations with the Christian Right and their negative views of homosexuality and abortion and support for creationism. Canadian politicians, unlike many of their

American counterparts, do not wear their religion on their sleeves, even though some may be quite unexpectedly pious privately (e.g., former Prime Minister Pierre Elliott Trudeau).

As Berger (1967) and Bruce (2002) predict, secularization at the societal level increases the likelihood of secularization at the other levels, and aspects of organizational secularization soon followed in Canada. The touchstone event for the Roman Catholic Church was the Second Vatican Council or Vatican II (1962–1965), in which the church attempted to systematically respond to the challenges of modernity with the intent of keeping the church relevant. The basic changes introduced included using the vernacular language rather than Latin in services, moving the altar closer to the congregation, re-positioning the priest to face the congregation, and adopting a greater openness to ecumenical dialogue. A segment of the church, worldwide and in Canada as well, lamented the changes as dangerous concessions to trends of the time. In truth it was, in part, the beginning of a process of internal de-traditionalization which many found disconcerting. In Protestant settings, similar modernizing changes were underway, from abandoning the King James Version of the Bible in favour of more recent and accessible translations, to the inclusion of modern music, guitars, and bands in worship services, and more relaxed expectations for Sunday morning attire. Doctrinal shifts were afoot as well, with the ordination of women as ministers, for example, and greater acceptance of homosexuality. Again, many within these traditions interpreted the changes as unwarranted capitulations to the secular values and pressures of modern life, and some congregations have chosen to go their own way in protest.

Bibby refers to these aspects of secularization, but in conformity with the narrative of secularization itself, he concentrates his attention on the changes occurring in religion as a personal phenomenon. In other words, his work is focused on religion (and hence secularization) at the individual level, using survey methods. In *Unknown Gods* (1993) Bibby documented that regular church attendance and levels of membership had decreased steadily between the 1960s and 1990s. This was true no matter what factors were taken into consideration, whether gender, education, age, community size, or region. In 1957, 53 percent of Canadian adults attended religious services on a weekly basis, compared with 31 percent in 1975, and only 23 percent in 1990 (Bibby, 1993: 6). In terms of membership in a local congregation, 82 percent of Canadians claimed to have official membership status in 1957, versus 48 percent in 1975 and only 29 percent in 1990 (1993: 8). For those who attended regularly over this period things were deteriorating: the congregations were getting older, they had fewer religious leaders for each congregation, and it was getting more expensive to keep the doors of the church open (1993: 5). As few as 26 percent of Canadians during this time claimed that religion was "very important" to them (1993: 83), and another 18 percent said that religion was an "important" influence on how they thought and acted (1993: 80).

What was possibly even more problematic for religious organizations was the decreasing confidence that Canadians had in them. In the 1980s the confidence of Canadians in their religious leaders dropped from 60 percent to 37 percent, largely due to the negative publicity generated by a series of scandals related to allegations of abuse, rape, and marital and fiscal misconduct, as well as the tensions caused by the accommodation made for homosexuals within many religious organizations (1993: 73).

Symptomatic of the larger societal shifts that Berger and Bruce discuss in their theories of secularization (e.g., increasing pluralism, relativism, and individualism), Bibby (2006, 2011) identifies several social-structural shifts among Baby Boomers that contributed to the heightened secularization of Canadian society. He discusses these shifts in terms of themes, namely the shifts from dominance to diversity, obligation to gratification, deference to discernment, and homes to careers.

The shift from dominance to diversity is about the problem of pluralism. In the emerging age of information and globalization Canadians were exposed to an unprecedented degree of choice about what they could believe and how they could behave, and this worked to the detriment of traditional religious commitments. As Bibby summarizes (2011: 19):

> Such milieus in which options were emerging everywhere and truth was increasingly viewed in relativistic terms were hardly conducive to any religions that proclaimed absolutes and exhibited intolerance for things different. In fact, any religion that did not champion flexibility and freedom could expect to see its market share shrink. Yet, ironically, religions that aligned themselves with social change ran the risk of becoming indistinguishable from culture.

The change from obligation to gratification refers to the fact that people no longer attended religious services or joined religious groups out of any sense of social and familial obligation. Instead, individuals either stopped joining or participating because it became socially acceptable to do so, or they continued to participate because they found it personally gratifying to do so. Being religious started to differ little from other acts of consumption. The focus shifted to the needs, preferences, and feelings of individuals.

The turn from deference to discernment emphasizes this state of affairs by highlighting the new significance accorded to people's feelings and intuitions over the judgement of experts and traditional authorities. In an age of hyper-individualism the reflexive discernment of one's needs and the pragmatic payoffs of involvement took precedence over any trust in the traditional understanding of the reasons for belonging to a church.

Finally, the growth of women working for pay outside the home dealt a severe blow to traditional forms of religion. With both parents working and an escalation in the organized activities of children (e.g., dance classes and various team sports) families lacked the time or energy to struggle out of bed on Sunday mornings to attend religious service with any regularity—no matter how sincere their intentions to do so.

In light of these observations, Bibby made several suggestions for how religious leaders might lessen the growing gulf between religious organizations and Canadians. He argued that religious groups needed to pay closer attention to the ways they supplied religion to consumers, and in recent years some groups have devised some controversial ways to attract members (see Box 7.1 for some examples). At the time Bibby focused on certain structural, promotional, and distribution problems common to many groups. Structurally, he (1993: 183–220) cautioned religious groups not to rely so heavily on untrained volunteers, who potentially lacked the knowledge, time, and level of excellence expected by contemporary religious consumers. He also advised groups to be more mindful of the growing negative social perceptions of religion, born of the many sexual and financial scandals afflicting religious leaders. When it came to the ways that religious groups promoted their message, Bibby (1993: 222–30) encouraged them to give more attention to less conventional religious concerns and questions, to the interest in such things as reincarnation, psychic powers, communicating with the dead, and out-of-body experiences, as revealed by his surveys. Alongside mining these unconventional religious themes, he urged them to more forthrightly offer people self-affirmation and hope in the face of their troubled lives. In terms of marketing and distributing religion, Bibby (1993: 276) prompted religious leaders to target their product more to those people who either attended religious services infrequently (for religious holidays and rites of passages) or who did not attend at all, rather than to those who regularly attended. Talk less about church growth, churching planting, finances, and volunteerism, he advised, and more about the value of being religious in our secular age.

Revitalization

Bibby's work was popular with religious leaders in Canada and perhaps his suggestions had some impact on levels of religiosity in Canada, but he surprised many when he argued in his next book, *Restless Gods* (2002: xii), that "organized religion is making something of a comeback, and that it is all to be expected." Drawing on empirical findings about Protestant, Roman Catholic, and "Other" faith groups, Bibby pointed to some reasons for optimism about the continued role of religion in the lives of many Canadians. For instance, among 18- to 34-year-old Protestant affiliates there was a 6 percent increase in weekly attendance (from 20 percent to 26 percent), and there was a 5 percent increase among those aged 55 and older between 1990 and 2000 (2002: 77).

Box 7.1

Marketing Religion

Rational choice theorists may not have the following in mind when they argue that the supply of religion is critical to getting people to attend religious services more frequently; however, these recent examples show religious groups trying to market themselves in a way that will attract outsiders to join. A church in Minnesota gives newcomers an opportunity to win things like a flat-screen television, a video game system, movie passes, or NFL season tickets, just for showing up to church. A church in Texas gave away fifteen cars one Easter Sunday, along with $300 "goodie bags" for every person in attendance. In Daytona Beach, Florida, there is a drive-in church where individuals hear the choir on an FM radio station and receive communion in the comfort of their cars, as the pastor drives around on a golf cart to greet congregants. In the United Kingdom, a Church of England Bishop encouraged members to host lingerie parties to attract newcomers who might eventually attend the church. In Canada, an Anglican congregation in Winnipeg held a public wrestling event in the church basement, with several Christian wrestlers, in hopes of drawing non-believers to their church. Many congregations have also created floor hockey, dodge ball, and softball leagues, or offer some variation of "Theology on Tap" gatherings at a local pub where people converse about theology over a pint of beer, all with the aim of attracting and evangelizing possible converts.

The question is, does this work? Do such initiatives attract non-religious people into the fold? Regardless of whether they do or not, are these examples of the organizational secularization of religious groups, of their capitulation to the "secular" values of consumerism and individualism? Or is there little difference from the strawberry socials and revival tent meetings of our past? What do you think?

Some religious leaders are quick to suggest that such initiatives are highly effective, pointing to significant growth in their congregations, often over a short period of time. While this may be true, we lack any good sociological studies to know if this is in fact the case. In all likelihood, the significant growth that some churches experience as a result of these efforts is transfer growth, when people leave one church for another or when churchgoers move into a new city and look for a new church. Often those who transfer are attracted to a charismatic leader, relevant and dynamic preaching, high quality music, or programs for children and youth. Contrary to public perception, especially in larger congregations, sociological estimates suggest that only about 10 percent of most congregations are converts to the group (Bibby, 1987: 29). As for whether these initiatives are too "secular," that is a religious or theological concern, and not something for sociologists to determine, but the examples cited indicate that the traditional boundaries between the sacred and the secular appear to be blurring. Once more this highlights the importance and challenge of clarifying what we mean when we say something is "religious."

Conservative Protestants had held a consistent 8 percent share of the Canadian religious market since the 1950s (2002: 73), and they experienced a 7 percent increase (from 51 percent to 58 percent) in weekly attendance among adults between 1957 and 2000 (2002: 73), and a 19 percent increase (from 51 percent to 70 percent) among teenagers between 1984 and 2000 (2002: 88). Mainline Protestants who attended at least monthly increased from 26 percent to 31 percent between 1995 and 2005 as well (2006: 199).

Going back to 1871, when the first Canadian Census was conducted, about 45 percent of the Canadians who claimed a religious affiliation have been Roman Catholics (2002: 78). In 2000, roughly 2.5 million individuals attended Catholic mass each week, comparable to figures from the 1950s (2002: 78), and monthly attendance figures had increased from 50 percent to 53 percent between the 1990s and 2005 (2006: 196). Overall the percentage of Catholics attending mass regularly, relative to the population, which had grown, was lower. But the real number in regular attendance was still impressive.

Nearly two million Canadians identified with non-Christian religious traditions in 2000 (e.g., Muslims, Buddhists, or Jews), as compared with only 500,000 in the 1950s (2002: 83). Just three percent of teenagers identified with "Other" faith groups in 1984, yet by 2000 14 percent did (2002: 86). From 1984 to 2000, weekly attendance at religious services by Canadian teens in non-Christian traditions rose from 13 percent to 21 percent (2002: 88).

If we widen the focus of our attention beyond religious organizations, we find a high level of spirituality among Canadians, even if they fail to attend religious services. Since his first survey in 1975, Bibby documented that between 80 and 90 percent of all Canadians ask ultimate questions about happiness and suffering, life after death, the purpose of life, or the existence of God or the supernatural (Bibby, 1987: 63; 1993: 145; 2002: 93–136; 2006: 182–3). Canadians continue to espouse many conventional religious beliefs as well. Roughly 90 percent believe in God or a higher being; approximately 70 percent believe Jesus is divine; and nearly 60 percent believe in life after death. Almost 75 percent say they pray on occasion, and surprisingly, around 50 percent claim they have experienced God or the supernatural in their lives (Bibby, 1987: 65–71; 1993; 2002; 2006). In addition, Canadians subscribe to an array of unconventional religious beliefs and practices. Depending on the survey, between 20 and 75 percent of Canadians believe in astrology, extrasensory perception, communicating with the dead, or the power to predict events (Bibby, 1987: 74; 1993: 117–37; 2002: 27–30; 2006: 188).

There also are signs that many Canadians, even if they do not regularly attend religious services, maintain some relationship with religious groups. In Bibby's 1985 survey, for instance, almost 90 percent of Canadians either had turned or planned to turn to a religious group for a baptism or wedding. Around 50 percent of Canadians had turned to their religious group to observe a confirmation or a funeral, and 13 percent intended to do so in the future for a confirmation, and 45 percent for a funeral (1987: 76–7). Bibby captured this ongoing tie between Canadians and their religious groups by posing the following survey question (1987: 84):

> Some observers maintain that few people are actually abandoning their religious traditions. Rather, they draw selective beliefs and practices, even if they do not attend services frequently. They are not about to be recruited by other religious groups. Their identification with their religious tradition is fairly solidly fixed, and it is to these groups that they will turn when confronted with marriage, death and, frequently, birth. How well would you say this observation describes you?

In 1985, 45 percent of Canadians who attended monthly or less (representing 75 percent of the population) responded "very accurately" and 33 percent indicated "somewhat accurately." The figures were similar during the 1990s.

According to Bibby (2002: 220), some of these individuals actually desire to be more involved in their religious group:

> 55 percent of adults who are currently attending services less than monthly say they would "consider the possibility of being more involved in a religious group if [they] found it to be worthwhile for themselves or their families." . . . 15 percent offer an unequivocal "yes" to the receptivity query, while 40 percent say, "perhaps." However the good news for religious groups is that only 45 percent of Canadians who attend services less than once a month say they are not open to the possibility of greater involvement.

In line with his supply-side approach, Bibby suggests (2002 and 2004) that Canadians would consider greater involvement in their religious organization if certain ministry, organizational, and personal factors were addressed. People claim they would entertain becoming more involved when they got married or had children, or had less busy schedules (Bibby, 2002: 222–4). Whether this will happen is not something religious groups can count on, but they can seek to turn the odds more in their favour by better focusing their ministry on meeting the personal, spiritual, and relational needs of individuals (2002: 220). In other words, like the rational choice theorists, he suggests there is evidence of some real and ongoing demand for religion. Thus if religious groups can make their product more appealing, if they can effect some selective changes in the way religion is supplied, then many more Canadians might become involved again.

Polarization

In his latest book Bibby (2011) combines aspects of both the secularization and revitalization theses to describe his findings. Now he argues, however, that we have experienced a further shift in our religious beliefs and practices that is best captured by the term **polarization**. This point of view arises from his analysis of three common measurements of religiosity: church attendance, religious identification, and religious belief (see Table 7.1).

Beginning with church attendance, teenage patterns changed markedly between Bibby's surveys in 1984 and 2008. In 1984, 23 percent of Canadian teens attended religious services on a weekly basis and 28 percent never attended religious services. Fast forward to 2008 and 21 percent attend weekly and 47 percent never attend (Bibby, 2011: 45). Canadian adult survey findings between 1975 and 2005 show similar but subtler trends, as 31 percent attended weekly in 1975 and 18 percent never attended, compared with 25 percent and 23 percent respectively in 2005 (2011: 46).

When asked about whether they identify with a religion, and which religion, Canadian teens once more show notable changes. In 1984, 50 percent identified as Roman Catholic, 35 percent as Protestant, and 3 percent as aligned with non-Christian traditions, while 12 percent claimed to have "no religion." In 2008, 32 percent identified with the Roman Catholic Church, 13 percent with Protestant traditions, and 16 percent with non-Christian groups, while 32 percent said they had "no religion" (Bibby et al, 2009: 176). Among Canadians aged fifteen or older, the 2001 Canadian census data reveals that 43 percent identify as Roman Catholic (this was 45 percent in 1991), 29 percent as Protestant (down from 35 percent in 1991), 6 percent with non-Christian traditions (this was 4 percent in 1991), and 16 percent state they have "no religion" (this was 12 percent in 1991). Moving in a similar direction, the percentage of Canadian adults who say

Table 7.1 Polarization in Canada (%)

	Adults		Teenagers	
	1975	**2005**	**1984**	**2008**
Attendance				
Weeklys	31	25	23	21
Nevers	18	23	28	47
Identification				
Yes	91	85	88	68
No	9	15	12	32
Belief in God				
Theists	61	49	54	37
Atheists	6	7	6	16

Source: Bibby, Reginald. 2011. *Beyond the Gods and Back: Religion's Demise and Rise and Why it Matters.* Lethbridge, AB: Project Canada Books. Page 51.

that they have "no religion" rose steadily from 4 percent in 1971, the first time this category was an option on the Canadian census, to 16 percent in 2001, to 24 percent in the latest (2011) Statistics Canada data (Statistics Canada, 2013).

Two things stand out in terms of Canadian religious identification. The first is the gradual rise of those who identify with various non-Christian religious traditions. This corresponds, of course, with changing patterns in Canadian immigration, and we will examine this change and its implications in the next chapter. Second, the rise in the "no religion" category is noteworthy, and it will be addressed more fully in the next chapter as well.

Belief in God is another measure that Bibby (2011: 49) uses to support his new polarization argument. When asked in 1984 if they believe in God or a higher power, 54 percent of teens responded, "Yes, I definitely do," and 6 percent said "No, I definitely do not." In 2008, 37 percent stated, "Yes, I definitely do" and 16 percent indicated, "No, I definitely do not." In 1985, 61 percent of adults replied "Yes, I definitely do," while 6 percent said they definitely did not believe in God or a higher power. In 2005 these figures were 49 percent and 7 percent respectively. Combined, these findings suggest that Canadians are less confident that God or a higher power exists, and in the case of teenagers, are more likely to adopt an atheistic position.

To summarize, Bibby asserts that when talking about religion in Canada, it is inaccurate to simply measure or analyze one "extreme" of the religiosity continuum. The divide between religious and non-religious Canadians is greater than ever before, at least as far as we can tell. On the whole Canadians are not as religious as they were prior to the 1960s. But they are also not as secular as the data initially seemed to indicate in the 1980s and 1990s. There are still strong signs of religiosity in Canada today, and there are still reasons for optimism for religious groups in the future. For instance, 38 percent of teens who currently attend religious services less than monthly would be open to more involvement in their religious group if they found it to be worthwhile, and 84 percent of teens would turn to a religious group for a wedding, 83 percent for a funeral, and 65 percent for a birth-related rite of passage (Bibby, 2011: 212). Canadian adults show similar desires, with 62 percent saying in 2005 that they were receptive to greater involvement in their religious group (Bibby, 2006: 202). Beyond these indices, Bibby's work reinforces the common premise of scholars who study religion (see Chapter 1) that people turn to religion to provide meaning and purpose in their life and to help make sense of death. This does not mean that people will turn to religion only to resolve their concerns. But religion continues to be a leading source of answers and comfort for people who face these basic realities of life. Simply put, religion is not about to disappear in Canada. But it seems Canadians are more likely than ever to be sharply divided on the relevance of religious beliefs and practices.

Which is More Accurate:
Secularization, Revitalization or Polarization?

Bibby's arguments for the revitalization of religion in Canada appear to have some merit. Closer examination, however, reveals some methodological and theoretical reasons for being less certain (see Thiessen and Dawson, 2008 for a fuller account). Most notably, Bibby is overly charitable in the interpretation of his data. Consider the following important finding, reported above (2002: 220):

> 55 percent of adults who are currently attending services less than monthly say they would "consider the possibility of being more involved in a religious group if [they] found it to be worthwhile for themselves or their families." . . . 15 percent offer an unequivocal "Yes" to the receptivity query, while 40 percent say, "perhaps."

Combining the 15 percent and 40 percent figures creates the impression that many less-than-monthly attenders desire to be more involved. But it is difficult to know for sure whether those who answer "perhaps" (40 percent) really desire greater involvement. Without further data, from studies that press the point, how can we know if they do or do not? So how much confidence can we place in Bibby's claim that 55 percent of **marginal religious affiliates** have some desire to be more involved?

The limited data available casts doubt on this assertion. During in-depth interviews with a small sample of Canadians who attend religious services for religious holidays or rites of passage (i.e., "marginal religious affiliates"), Joel Thiessen (2010, 2012) discovered that few truly desire greater involvement. Most interviewees stated they were quite content with their current fragmented consumption of religion, which includes some combination of attending church for special occasions, an ongoing belief in God or a supernatural being, and occasional prayer or scripture reading in private. Still, there were a few individuals who expressed some type of interest in greater involvement if certain features of the supply of religion changed or barriers to their participation were removed.

With respect to supply-side issues, they say they might participate more if a church was closer by, a midweek service was offered, or a different style of church service was available (e.g., livelier music, relevant preaching, and better programming). A more representative national survey of marginal affiliates might well uncover additional issues. But if these are truly pertinent concerns shouldn't they be reflected in people's behaviour? Is there any evidence, for example, that these marginal affiliates sought to find a church that fits their preferences? In most communities there are churches that provide mid-week services, contemporary music, and dynamic and relevant sermons, and these churches pretty much run the gamut of theological orientations, from liberal to conservative. The individuals Thiessen (2010, 2012) interviewed admitted they had done little or nothing to locate a suitable group, and when presented with the reality that many such congregations exist in their community, they admitted they probably would not make the effort to pursue greater involvement. This admission does not bode well for the rational choice supposition that church attendance levels would increase if religious groups would only change the way they supply religion. In many cases the supply-side explanations offered by marginal affiliates appear to be rationalizations for their inaction more than explanations for why so many churches are failing.

In terms of barriers to greater involvement, or what might be termed demand-side reasons, interviewees told Thiessen that if their friends and family members were more supportive, or they were less busy, or they were at a different stage of life (e.g., having children), then they would consider greater involvement (see Figure 7.1). These things, however, are beyond the control of the churches and, given their prominence in explaining low levels of participation, even more doubt is cast on the adequacy of the supply-side arguments emphasized by Bibby and others.

In general sociologists need to do more to understand the meaning of religious beliefs and practices for these people. If they continue to attend religious services once or twice a year, but do so primarily for non-religious reasons, should their behaviour even be interpreted as "religious"? As Bibby (2002: 29) notes: "Such a pursuit of religious rites [could] reflect the pressures of relatives and friends." Conversely, it could be "driven by a sense that

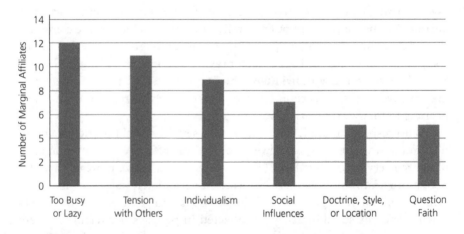

Figure 7.1 Reasons why marginal affiliates decreased their levels of church attendance
Source: Thiessen, Joel. 2010. "Churches are Not Necessarily the Problem: Lessons Learned from Christmas and Easter Affiliates." *Church and Faith Trends* 3 (3): 1–24. Page 3.

somehow 'God needed to be brought in' on what was happening." Bibby (1993: 167–8) favours the latter interpretation, declaring that individuals *"are there and something is happening.* Identity is being reaffirmed; life is being given meaning; memories are being constructed." But can we know? Surprisingly, the right kind of research has yet to be done. We need to investigate the motivations of Canadians much more thoroughly to be able to evaluate the secularization and revitalization theses.

In Thiessen's (2010, 2012) interviews with marginal affiliates, he asked them why they attend religious services once or twice a year. They provided an array of responses, ranging from maintaining their membership status, so they can obtain reduced funeral and burial rates, to a fear of going to hell, avoiding the commercialism of Christmas, or reinforcing their morals and belief in God, and feeling good about themselves. The top three reasons for maintaining some involvement were following tradition, family pressures, and feeling a sense of connection with a higher power in a sacred place. Regardless of the reason, many marginal affiliates state they do not find the religious services they attend very meaningful or significant. Is this because of their initial motivation or some failing in the delivery of the religious services? More work is needed, of a finer quality, to answer this basic question. Of course investigation of the issue throws us back again into considerations about the nature of religion and how it is measured.

In *Beyond the Gods and Back* (2011) Bibby brings in the additional theme of polarization (see Thiessen, 2011). How apt is that term? Many more Canadians appear to be either highly religious or irreligious, but almost 50 percent of those sampled avoid either end of the spectrum. This strong presence in "the middle" challenges the argument that Canadians are by and large polarized. The longitudinal data available call the polarization thesis into question as well. Without exception, the longitudinal measures of church attendance, religious affiliation, and belief in God or a supernatural being point to decreases on the "religious" end of the continuum and increases on the "non-religious" end. Canadian teens and adults are attending religious services less today, more individuals are never attending services, increasing percentages of Canadians claim to have "no religion," fewer individuals "definitely" believe in God or a supernatural being, and more individuals "definitely do not" believe in God or a supernatural being. In one sense these data lend support to the polarization thesis, but how accurate is it to speak of polarization when one of the poles is clearly still in decline and the other is on the rise? The secularization thesis, then, still provides a better guide to the future of religion in Canada, without denying that religious and spiritual beliefs and practices will continue to play an important role in the lives of many Canadians. But much depends on the trends we can detect in the generation coming of age in our societies.

Religion, Teens, and Young Adults

As a young person, how would you describe your religious orientation? Do you believe in the existence of something supernatural beyond yourself? Do you pray, read religious books, or meditate, and if so, how often? Are you a member of a religious group? Do you attend religious services of any kind? What role does religion play, or do you think it ought to play, in your life? What role should religion play in society?

Since 2005 several landmark studies have been published that help us to understand how teens and young adults respond to questions such as these, and offering us sociological explanations of the findings. Young people to-day, these studies stress, face an array of experiences that past generations did not, and these changes have shaped their approach to matters of faith and spirituality. These studies are American, but the findings are pertinent, with some caution, for understanding Canadian youth as well.

In his book *After the Baby Boomers* (2007), Robert Wuthnow delineates the ways in which young people's worlds are filled with uncertainty and transition. Young adults are getting married later in life. They are having fewer children and having them later in life. They are pursuing higher education at unprecedented rates. They are uncertain about work and money as they pay back student loans, think about buying a house, and so on. During their twenties they change jobs frequently, taking longer to settle into a career. They are living in a world being transformed by globalization and the rapid spread of technology. This in turn is influencing how they understand the world, in particular their relationships, which are loosening, thanks in part to geographic mobility and the rise of social media. They are experiencing a fundamental change in how people establish and maintain social ties. They are experiencing a degree of "uprootedness" that is unprecedented.

Christian Smith and Patricia Snell, in their book *Souls in Transition* (2009), echo many of Wuthnow's findings, adding that young people are overwhelmed with the volume of things they need to learn in order to eventually stand on their own. Consequently, they are uncertain of their life goals and purpose, other than to fulfil the middle-class dream of finishing their education, getting a good job and attaining financial security, getting married and having children, buying a nice house, driving reliable vehicles, taking vacations, and enjoying good relationships.

In facing these transitions young adults are setting religion aside for a time, since they are consumed with the pragmatic this-worldly concerns of life (see Clydesdale, 2007; Smith and Snell, 2009). For instance, young people adopt a rather private approach to their faith, claiming that religion operates in the backgrounds of their lives rather than as a guide for making daily decisions (Smith and Denton, 2005; Smith and Snell, 2009). Bibby,

Russell, and Rolheiser (2009: 25) found that 74–86 percent of Canadian teenagers believe that friendship, freedom, and a comfortable life are among the most important things in their lives, in contrast with the 27 percent who identify spirituality as being very important, or the 13 percent who indicate religious group involvement.

The themes of choice, identity, relativism, subjectivity, and individualism emerge when studying religion and young people in the late modern world. Many of these themes are present in Wuthnow's data (2007), leading him to identify young adults as "tinkerers" or "bricoleurs," an idea reinforced by the findings of other scholars (see Smith and Denton, 2005; Smith and Snell, 2009; Cush, 2010; Flory and Miller, 2010; Shepherd, 2010). Many young people are not keen on accepting the religious beliefs and practices handed down to them by their parents and religious traditions. They prefer to tailor their faith to their needs on a case-by-case basis. On the whole they believe that individuals should decide for themselves what they believe. They endorse an à la carte approach to their faith, "piecing together ideas about spirituality from many sources" (Wuthnow, 2007: 135). They emphasize personal religious experience over religious doctrine and argue that no religious beliefs or practices apply to all people in all places. They claim to be open-minded about different values, ideas, and lifestyles, and assert that issues of morality are not black and white.

As Giddens (1991) and Beck and Beck-Gernsheim (2002) point out, features of late modern society such as choice necessitate that individuals enter a reflexive process of identity construction. In many ways identity is no longer ascribed but is rooted in the many choices that individuals make throughout their lives. Some see this process as a welcome challenge, revelling in the freedom, while others are filled with fear at the prospect of the unknown. There are many people that I could marry, but will I marry the right one? I can pursue any career I want, but will I make the right decision? Is this move for a job a wise one? At the same time, our choices are situated in what the French sociologist Pierre Bourdieu (1977) identifies as "habitus." One's culture as well as aspects of the social structure into which we are born, such as race, socioeconomic status, or national background, exert a profound influence on the range of options we consider, sometimes resulting in conformity to one's group (e.g., choosing to be religious in ways that are close to those of their parents) and other times in deviance (e.g., choosing to be nonreligious or religious in ways that are at odds with one's parents).

The young are forced as never before to juggle the pressures of reflexivity and habitus, as illustrated by Pia Karlsson Minganti's (2010) study of young Muslim women in Sweden. Raised in devout Muslim homes, these young women encounter a hostile and discriminating non-Muslim world that forces them to actively choose how they will construct their identity. In their adopted society these first- and second-generation immigrants encounter different perspectives on gender, sexuality, and race, causing them to question their families' more traditional views of gender roles, the division of labour, dress, and sexuality. One way they respond is by connecting with Muslim youth organizations in Sweden, a subcultural context that provides a safe haven in which they can formulate their own identity and which still respects the major tenets of Islam but allows them to adopt some of the values and practices of the "outside" world, such as working outside the home, attending university, or driving a car. In effect they begin to practice a new form of Islam, for as Minganti (2010: 121) notes:

> The women admitted to adhering to several religious leaders simultaneously and to taking independent decisions on whose teachings to rely on. This is, undeniably, a break with the tradition to hold on to one single Islamic law school given to any individual Muslim by birth into a certain family and nationality.

This approach inevitably leads to an element of subjectivity and individualism both in how one practises and how one passes along one's faith to the next generation, as Minganti's conclusion suggests. Naturally, these are all manifestations of the larger social changes in late modern society discussed in Chapter 6, including de-traditionalization, globalization, expressive individualism, and the risk/trust dialectic (for an example of how young Christians in the United Kingdom balance the demands of reflexivity and habitus see Shepherd, 2010).

The same theme comes to the fore in Christian Smith and Melinda Lundquist Denton's book, *Soul Searching: The Religious and Spiritual Lives of American Teenagers* (2005). They use the phrase "Moralistic Therapeutic Deism" to describe the way most teenagers view religion. By this they mean that teens believe in being good moral beings, and they have largely reduced religion to a means of achieving this goal. Religion is also about making people feel good, happy, secure, and at peace with themselves and others. As for beliefs about God, many American teens believe that God exists and created the world and moral order, but is distant from people's individual affairs. Accordingly, Smith and Denton (2005: 173) conclude, religion has become a highly subjective phenomenon guided by an ethic of therapeutic individualism that "defines the individual self as the source and standard of authentic moral knowledge and authority, and individual self-fulfillment as the preoccupying purpose of life. Subjective, personal experience is the touchstone of all that is authentic, right, and true." This is less so for the young Muslim women in Sweden, and elsewhere, and the difference matters. Yet the overall trend in each case is the same.

Religious Socialization and the Future of Religion in Canada

No one can say for certain what the future holds. Will Canadians be even less religious, will there be some measure of religious revival, or will things stay pretty much the same? The information in hand is not encouraging for those who would like Canada to be a more religious nation once again. But we have yet to discuss another key consideration, the process of religious socialization. Do children take on the religious attitudes and behaviours of their parents when they become adults? Is the transmission of religion impacted by whether parents are likeminded in their religious outlook? Questions like these are important in pondering the future of religion, given the growth in the "no religion" category and the shift of young people toward more choice, relativism, and individualism in their approach to religion. Should we expect these trends to continue or even accelerate in the years to come?

The longitudinal studies of David Voas and Alasdair Crockett (Voas and Crockett, 2005; Crockett and Voas, 2006; Voas, 2009) and Sarah King-Hele (King-Hele, 2009) are informative in this regard. In their examination of religion in Britain, Europe, and Canada they explore whether the signs of decline in the areas of religious affiliation, church attendance, and the importance of religion to one's life can be attributed to age, period, or cohort effects. "Age effects" refer to changes in one's religious beliefs and practices over the course of life (assuming one's society stays the same). "Period effects" stem from significant social events that may influence entire societies (e.g., the Second World War), and the term "cohort effects" identifies changes in society that seem to be linked to the passing of generations, more than anything else.

It has long been commonly held that people tend to be more religious at certain times in their lives. Having children, for example, is very commonly thought to bring people back to religion, out of a desire to help raise their children with good morals and values. Others believe that when people turn old they tend to become more religious to help them cope with the prospect of their impending death. In some cases this is undoubtedly true. But Voas, Crockett, and King-Hele show that, on the whole, individuals do not become noticeably more or less religious with age. Michele Dillon and Paul Wink's (2007) examination of religion over the course of lifetimes reaches the same conclusion. While there is an ebb and flow to people's religious practices, such as during the times noted, people's level of religiosity in their old age is rarely higher than the levels experienced during their years as young adults. Christian Smith and Patricia Snell (2009: 208) likewise conclude that "the default of most people's lives is to continue being what they have been in the past."

Thinking of the impact of specific events, here too we find the common assumption that levels of religiosity will increase after personal or collective

Box 7.2   Woodhead's Typology of the Relationship of Religion and Gender Inequality

As noted in Chapter 3, the relationship between women and religion is more complicated than first appears to be the case, and this holds true in the late modern Canadian context. On the one hand, women are significantly over-represented in the ranks of the religious worldwide (Beit-Hallahmi and Argyle, 1996: 139–42; Inglehart and Norris, 2003: 58). On the other hand, most of the religions of the world are markedly patriarchal and out of step with the rising equality of the sexes. This is certainly the case for Catholicism, Eastern Orthodoxy, and most conservative forms of Protestantism, for conservative forms of Judaism, and for most traditional Muslim, Hindu, and Buddhist communities. How, then, should we understand this seeming paradox? Why are women more religious when these religions tend to reinforce their subservient status? Should we simply assume that many women fail to understand their best interests—that they are victims of what Marxists would call "false consciousness"? Building on the existing scholarship about how women are religious, the British scholar Linda Woodhead (2007b) provides a typology of the basic ways in which contemporary women differ in their religious involvements with regard to the established power differentials between men and women. The typology helps to clarify the diversity of ways in which women may negotiate the relationship between their gender status and their religiosity.

Her classic fourfold typology is based on variations along two axes: the vertical axis refers to the religion's situation relative to existing distributions of gender power in society, and runs between the poles of "mainstream" and "marginal"; the horizontal axis refers to religion's strategy relative to these gender power differentials and varies between the poles of "confirmatory" religion and "challenging" religion (see Figure 7.2). Mainstream religion is respectable and supports the status quo. Marginal religion is more out of step with the dominant social and gender order and "will therefore be treated as socially deviant by those who accept the dominant distribution of power" (Woodhead, 2007b: 569). "Confirmatory religion seeks to legitimate, reinforce, and sacralise the existing distribution of power in society, particularly the existing gender order, whilst challenging religion seeks to ameliorate, resist, or change this order" (Woodhead, 2007b: 569). The two axes give us four main types of religion relative to the gender relations issue: "consolidating," "tactical," "questing" and "counter-cultural." Before summarizing the features of these types we should note that Woodhead qualifies her generalizations carefully. Her comments are too elaborate to reiterate in full here. But she recognizes, for example, that there may be no single dominant religious or gender order in any society, and likewise within any one religious tradition or single community all four types of relationships may exist between the religion and some of its women members. All the same, the typology serves a very useful heuristic function, so let us sketch the differences between the types.

Consolidating
In the face of spreading secularization, which is positively correlated with growing gender equality, the link between gender inequality and religion has actually become more conspicuous in the late modern societies of the West. In the second half

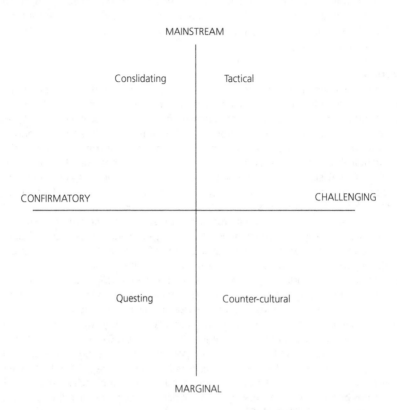

MAINSTREAM

Conslidating   Tactical

CONFIRMATORY   CHALLENGING

Questing   Counter-cultural

MARGINAL

Figure 7.2 The Relationship of Women, Gender Inequality, and Religion.
Source: Woodhead, Linda. 2007b. "Gender Differences in Religious Practice and Significance," in James A. Beckford and N.J. Demerath III, eds., *The Sage Handbook of the Sociology of Religion*. Los Angeles: Sage. Page 570.

of the twentieth century conservative religious movements around the globe have fixed on the preservation of traditional gender roles as a hallmark of their faith, con-solidating identity with these roles. "Deberg (1990) and Bendroth (1993) convinc-ingly demonstrate that hostility to changing gender roles and the rise of feminism were central factors in the rise of Christian fundamentalism in the USA, and that consolidation of 'traditional' gender roles is as essential and defining a compo-nent of fundamentalism as belief in God and theological ideas (Brasher, 1998: 11)" (Woodhead, 2007b: 572). But why would women affiliate with these religious move-ments in such great numbers? As Lynn Davidman's (1991) fascinating study of pro-fessional women converting to Orthodox Judaism in America suggests, two signifi-cant factors are the resolution of the tensions felt by women ambiguously striving to be both successful professionals and devoted mothers, and the corresponding clarification and reinforcement of the paternal responsibilities of men. "Davidman's data suggests that women are attracted by the whole package of nuclear familial domesticity which is advocated by contemporary forms of Orthodox Judaism, in-cluding the idea of a husband who will be a compassionate protector-provider and

continued

protect women from the dangers posed by family breakdown" (Woodhead, 2007b: 572). On the male side this same push to resolve this kind of normative conflict is reflected in the surprising rise and success of movements like the Promise Keepers (Williams, 2001).

Tactical

For many women their daily interaction with one another through the church, mosque, or temple takes precedence over the more formal and male-dominated ritual and organizational aspects of religious life. It is the sense of community and ongoing social support, especially from the other women, that is satisfying and underwrites their continued acceptance of traditions that are intrinsically patriarchal. As Brenda Brasher's (1998) study of two conservative mega-churches and Marie Griffith's (1997) study of the evangelical-charismatic Women's Aglow movement demonstrate, women often create a sort of parallel religious world of small support groups and activities that appear to be focused on Bible study and other traditional activities but whose primary focus is the discussion of personal and familial issues. These weekly or more-than-weekly meetings provide "an opportunity for the exploration, expression, healing and disciplining of emotions" (Woodhead, 2007b: 574). They also provide quite independent forums for the development and expression of confidence, authority, and significant involvement in public action. This contemporary finding is in line with the evidence of numerous historical studies of the strong role women played in the charitable, mission, temperance, and social reform movements of the late nineteenth century and early twentieth century in Britain, America, and Canada (e.g., Rendall, 1985; Mumm, 1999; Gray, 2008). Women have found tactical ways to offset and compensate for their subordinate status in the formal structures of their religions, and as Elizabeth Ozorak's (1996) interviews reveal, they are not deterred by the male dominance of the ecclesiastical power structures because they are seeking different benefits from church adherence than men (Woodhead, 2007b: 574–5).

Questing

Questing forms of religiosity carry us into more marginal ways of being religious, but ways that are seeking greater advantage within the existing gender order and not complete change. Woodhead identifies two types of recent religious activity with this point of view: the revival and practice of forms of witchcraft amongst teenage girls in the West and the diverse forms of self-spirituality associated with the New Age Movement. As Helen Berger and Douglas Ezzy (2007) and others have documented, and as is abundantly apparent in the popular culture of the 1990s and early twenty-first century (e.g., the hit television shows *Charmed, Buffy the Vampire Slayer, True Blood*), an interest in magic and the supernatural has surged to the fore in the youth cultures of North America, Europe, and elsewhere (Clark, 2003). Aided by the Internet (Cowan, 2005) and guided by a plethora of popular books (e.g., RavenWolf, 1999), a surprising number of young women have turned to the practice of rituals and spells, either as "solitary witches" or in "covens." Woodhead (2007b: 575) argues that the reversion to magic entails an attempt to "shift the balance of power" or "at least allow the actor to maximize her advantage" within a tacitly accepted dominant gender order. This holds as well for the more pervasive and adult movements of alternative spirituality arising in Western culture, with their emphasis on seeking fulfilment through an inner quest to find one's and/or gaining esoteric knowledge of other dimensions of reality (e.g., Findhorn, Yoga, Vipassana Meditiation, Eckankar). Heelas and Woodhead's (2005) study of this self-spirituality in the UK found that 80 percent of those involved were women. Elsewhere Woodhead (2007a) and Dick Houtman and Stef Aupers (2008) explain this preponderance of women in terms of the same "unresolved clash" of traditional and professional roles and expectations advanced by Davidman (see above). Woodhead concludes (2007b: 576):

> Self-spiritualities address this condition by encouraging the construction of new modes of selfhood in which identity is not dictated by social position and expectation, but discovered from within. Although this project of selfhood may have socially radical implications . . . it is more likely to render women successful in coping with the contradictions and costs of the unequal distribution of power and unpaid care work in contemporary Western societies than in changing these conditions.

Counter-Cultural

Some forms of self-spirituality and other new religions in general have a more explicitly oppositional nature or agenda of reform. Woodhead focuses on the goddess feminist movement within neo-paganism, as emblematically captured by Starhawk's highly influential book *The Spiral Dance* (1979). The many variants of this movement seek to highlight, honour, and promote the role of the "divine feminine" in our lives and in society. This is done through the creation of rituals and communities designed to empower women and reverse the established gender order. This can take the form of cells, circles, or covens operating on evenings and weekends, while conventional life continues, utopian experiments in communal living, or movements of political protest focused on women's issues (e.g., abortion and reproductive technologies), environmental problems, or anti-war campaigns. One of the best studies of this counter-cultural expression of women's religiosity is Jone Salomonsen's *Enchanted Feminism: The Reclaiming Witches of San Francisco* (2002). Other instances of religious efforts to overturn the gender status quo are provided by new religious movements not mentioned by Woodhead, such as the Barhma Kumaris and the Rajneesh/Osho movement. These neo-Hindu movements, which emerged from India and spread around the world, actively promote gender equality, the feminine character of the divine, and the role of women in positions of both practical and spiritual leadership (Goldman, 1999; Walliss, 2002). In fact, sociologists have investigated the ways in which many new religious movements have engaged in social experiments with gender relations in general (e.g., Palmer, 1994; Dawson, 2006a: 136–41).

Of course none of this is meant to explain why individual women adopt the religious/spiritual views they do. Gender concerns, whether explicit or implicit, constitute only one aspect of what matters, and to variable degrees from person to person. Our religious affiliations, let alone deeper spiritual identifications, are the result of a complex matrix of social and biographic influences, of cognitive, intuitive, and emotional experiences, capacities, and inclinations. But gender is what sociologists call a "master status," and as such it tends to play a preponderant role in all our activities, one that sociologists of religion have yet to explore as fully and consistently as would be desirable.

tragedies. Many, for example, mistook the sudden increase of religious rhetoric, praying, and church attendance in the immediate wake of the 9/11 terrorist attacks in the United States as evidence of a national return to religion. But as quickly as people flooded into the churches, to express their grief and solidarity, they ebbed away. Within a month church attendance rates returned to normal. During the massive financial crisis and recession of 2008–09, to cite another example, many sociologists of religion were contacted by the media with questions about the possible implications of the crisis for levels of religious activity. Surely people would turn to religion in a time of such great uncertainty and anxiety? Wouldn't they seek, as Marx surmised, the opiate-like solace of religion? The premise seems plausible, and many individuals may have done so, at least for a time. But as the economist David Beckworth (2007) argues, the empirical evidence does not support the supposition. In fact, longitudinal research has failed to detect any point in time since the early twentieth century when there was a marked increase or decrease in the levels of religiosity that affected all generations (Voas and Crockett, 2005; Crockett and Voas, 2006; King-Hele, 2009; Voas 2009).

Rather, the longitudinal data point to a cohort explanation for changes in the levels of religiosity, with each generation (in modern times) in the United Kingdom and Canada being less religious than the previous one (Voas and Crockett, 2005; Crockett and Voas, 2006; King-Hele, 2009; Voas, 2009; Bruce, 2011). Without exception, each cohort has been less likely to believe in God, to identify with a religious group, or to attend religious services regularly. In another study Reginald Bibby, Sarah Russell, and Ron Rolheiser (2009: 162–87) show the same cohort effect in Canada among "pre-Boomers," "Boomers," and "post-Boomers," and findings in the United States are similar (Pew Forum on Religion and Public Life, 2010).

It is the intergenerational transmission of religious beliefs and behaviours, or should we say the failure to transmit these beliefs and practices across the generations, that lies at the heart of the decline of conventional religious beliefs and practices in most Western societies (Voas and Crockett, 2005). In other words, there appears to be a strong correlation between the process of secularization and the process of socializing children to the religious orientations of their parents. In families where both parents claim to have "no religion," over 90 percent of the children also describe themselves as such (see Wuthnow, 2007: 86–7). When both parents are religious, regardless of whether they belong to the same religious group or not, roughly 50 percent of the children are also religious, identifying with the religions of one or both parents. When only one parent is religious, about 25 percent of the children follow suit.

Focusing on religious nones, Kosmin and Kaysar (2008: 6-8) suggest that approximately one-quarter come from households where one or both parents claim to have "no religion." Depending on the survey, between 21 and 32 percent of American nones claim they were raised in households with no religion (Kosmin and Kaysar, 2008: 8; Pew Forum on Religion and Public Life, 2008: 27). This suggests that many in the "no religion" category are "(de)converts" from other religious traditions, with Roman Catholicism being the main "feeder" into the religious none group. Findings in Canada of large Roman Catholic declines (see Bibby, 1987, 1993, 2002, and 2011) suggest that this shift could be a reaction to the more authoritarian and hierarchical structure of Catholicism in an age dominated by an emphasis on individual autonomy. Concerns on this front come to the fore in the resistance to the church's conservative views on birth control, abortion, and women in leadership. Many think the Catholic Church is out of step with the egalitarian and democratic spirit of the twenty-first century on these issues. The lack of what some characterize as relevant preaching, contemporary music, and interesting programming may be contributing to these Catholic defections as well (see Thiessen, 2010).

But these explanations do not necessarily account for the specific cohort effects detected in the longitudinal data. David Voas (2010) asserts that a more specific logical explanation lies with the attitudes of parents towards the religious socialization of their children. Parents are apparently much less committed to ensuring that their children adopt the parents' religious beliefs and values. In support of this view Voas points to the changing values of the parents, the shift in emphasis from obedience and loyalty to independence and tolerance. He also highlights that even for parents who regularly attend religious services there has been a sizeable decrease in the number of their children who do so as well. The same point cropped up repeatedly in Thiessen's (2010) interviews with marginal affiliates in Canada: they first stopped participating when they were teenagers because their parents gave them the option of doing so. This liberal approach to religious socialization contrasts starkly with the dominant practice only fifty years ago. As many people over the age of fifty-five in Thiessen's sample indicated, attending church weekly, getting baptized, and marrying in a church were non-negotiable facets of life. Church attendance was a socially desirable activity that was normalized in the home, at school, and in the broader community.

As Stephen Warner and Rhys Williams (2010) highlight in their research with Christians, Muslims, and Hindus in the United States, parents who wish to transmit their faith to their children must realize that religion is no longer a taken-for-granted part of social and family life; on the contrary, they need to be intentional and work hard to pass on their faith. This includes involving the extended family as part of a child's religious formation, fostering religious practices in the home, developing intergenerational ties outside the home for the purposes of religious instruction, and providing young people with leadership opportunities in their religious institutions. In

Canada intentional religious instruction occurs less today than in the past. In 1975, Bibby reports (2011: 13), 36 percent of parents said their children regularly attended either Sunday school or took classes in religion (outside of regular school days). Yet by 2005 only 19 percent did. Similarly, in 1975 only 23 percent of children never attended some type of religious instruction, and by 2005 the figure was 51 percent.

The more relaxed approach to religious socialization is both one of the causes of, and a product of, the diminished significance given to church attendance as a socially desirable activity. Religion has become firmly associated with a plethora of other personal choices, and as such it is valued, but the choice to be religious is no longer viewed as being intrinsically more virtuous than the choice to not be religious. Young people are granted a high degree of autonomy in constructing this aspect of their identities, though they still do not tend to venture far from the views of their parents. This increased autonomy is especially present in mixed religion marriages, where parents are even more likely to encourage the children to explore the religious options available and decide for themselves (see Arweck and Nesbitt, 2010).

So being raised in a religious home does not guarantee that a child will remain religious throughout his or her life. But we know that there is a stronger chance of someone being religious in their adult life if they were raised in a religious home (see Dillon and Wink, 2007). With this simple fact in mind, what does the data suggest about the future of religion in Canada? If we consider the current patterns of religious attendance, with two-thirds of Canadians attending religious services only yearly or less, the growing percentage of people claiming to have "no religion," and the significantly weakened patterns of religious socialization, then it is easy to see why many think continued secularization, especially at the individual level, is the most likely future.

Conclusion

Prior to the 1960s, Canadians were fairly religious, privately and publically. In some respects these higher levels of religiosity fuelled many of the tensions that shaped the emergence of our nation, between Aboriginals and European Christians, Roman Catholics and Protestants, and within the Roman Catholic and Protestant traditions. Strong religiosity also facilitated the prolonged attempt to fashion Canada as a Christian nation, through the missions to convert and church those on our frontiers and the infusion of our educational, health, and judicial institutions with Christian values. Yet the dream of a fully Christian nation, stretching from sea to sea, never fully materialized, and the surge of religiosity after the Second World War was soon followed by a retreat from religious commitments by the baby boomers, beginning in the 1960s. As religious institutions were pushed to the periphery of public life, and new forms of immigration and higher levels of educational attainment fostered an unprecedented degree of religious pluralism and freedom, fewer people attended traditional religious services with regularity, and more and more Canadians either ceased to be religious or sought to meet their spiritual needs more privately, picking and choosing from an expanding array of religions, both old and new.

In the midst of this change, Bibby suggested in 2002 that Canada might experience a renaissance of religion, given the continued evidence of belief in God, loyalty to specific religious traditions, and attendance at religious services for religious holidays and rites of passage. Calling on aspects of the rational choice theory of religion, he posited there is an ongoing demand for the things that religion provides and that if religious groups improved the way they supplied religion, more Canadians would be sitting in the pews. A decade later, Bibby continues to advance a similar argument, though he has tempered his views, arguing that the religious life of Canada is becoming increasingly polarized between the highly religious and the irreligious.

We raised several doubts about both the revitalization and polarization arguments, suggesting that there is little real reason to believe that many Canadians desire to be more involved in their religious groups, that the demand for religion in general is exaggerated, and that even when people attend services, they often do so for non-religious reasons. These criticisms reiterate the need, however, to develop a better understanding of the definition, nature, and measure of religion and of secularization in the late modern context. Equally, they shine a spotlight on the urgent need to engage in more far-reaching and careful qualitative research into why many Canadians continue to profess an interest in religious and spiritual questions, ideas, and practices.

In the struggle to better discern what is happening to religion in the Western world, sociologists of religion have turned their attention to a relatively neglected group, the young. The lives of young people today are filled with transition and uncertainty. They feel the need to engage in the project of the self, as Giddens calls the quest for identity, and they must do so in an environment flooded with ever more information and choices. In the face of this complexity they are staying in school longer, getting married and having children later, and starting their careers later too. In the rush of this-worldly activities many are also setting religion aside. When they do choose to be religious, or to develop a spiritual aspect to their lives, they are breaking the boundaries of traditional religions and fashioning sets of beliefs and practices suited to their own inclinations. In part there should be no surprise in any of this since the parents of today's young adults ceased, on the whole, to feel they had either the right or the need to force their children to learn about and practise their beliefs, if they had any. The demise of religious socialization and secularization has gone hand-in-hand so far.

What does the future hold for religion in Canada? The existing trends do not bode well for many traditional and mainstream forms of religion. Secularization is likely to continue at the societal, organizational, and individual levels. Yet as sociologists have been saying for some time, a religious-like element of life persists for most Canadians, even amongst those who claim to have no religion (see Chapter 8). We are surrounded with an unprecedented religious diversity, new religious movements keep arising every day, and the Internet is suffused with sites dedicated to the promotion, study, and debate of religious ideas. Is this residual and often new kind of religious life socially significant? Or has religion become nothing more than another product to be consumed selectively for amusement or perhaps some kind of relief from the pressures of late modern life? These are some of the themes broached in the next and final chapter.

Critical Thinking Questions

1.   Were you aware that Canada was once a much more religious society? What led you to think so?

2.   Perhaps the religious views of Canadians are becoming more polarized. If so, will this be problematic for Canadian society? If so, in what ways?

3.   Do any of the research findings about the religious views and practices of the young resonate with you? Which ones and in what ways? How might you explain those experiences, sociologically?

Suggested Readings

O'Toole, Roger. 1996. "Religion in Canada: Its Development and Contemporary Situation." *Social Compass* 43 (1): 119–34. This article provides one of the most succinct and yet comprehensive overviews of the history of religion in Canada through to the 1990s. It is highly recommended as an introduction to the topic.

Bibby, Reginald. 2011. *Beyond the Gods and Back: Religion's Demise and Rise and Why it Matters.* Lethbridge, AB: Project Canada Books. The fourth in a series of books devoted to the topic of religion in Canada, this book clearly summarizes Bibby's core arguments and research findings since 1975. It also provides global comparisons for many measurements of religiosity and is a must-read for those interested in religion in Canada.

Collins-Mayo, Silvia and Pink Dandelion, eds. 2010. *Religion and Youth.* Burlington, VT: Ashgate. A global comparison and discussion of religion and youth, this book captures the dominant themes of choice, identity, relativism, subjectivity, and individualism that young people of all religious traditions currently face. It draws on quantitative and qualitative research studies conducted by the leading experts in different fields from around the world.

Thiessen, Joel. 2010. "Churches Are Not Necessarily the Problem: Lessons Learned from Christmas and Easter Affiliates." *Church and Faith Trends* 3 (3): 1–24. This article contains some of the most direct criticisms of Reginald Bibby's work. In contrast to a supply-side argument, Thiessen notes that there are many demand-side factors that limit people's involvement in churches. It also includes several recommendations for church leaders in light of a demand-side argument.

Related Websites

www.reginaldbibby.com
> Reginald Bibby's personal website contains information and attachments to his publications, media stories, conference presentations, and speaking engagements, and access to the raw data from his national surveys since 1975.

www.wondercafe.ca
> Designed by the United Church of Canada, primarily to engage younger Canadians, this website includes various discussion topics, blogs, articles, and merchandise, all intended to help Canadians to grapple with contemporary issues in the world today.

8 The New Religious Diversity

Learning Objectives

In this chapter, you will learn:

◎   To understand how immigration patterns are changing the religious composition and landscape of Canada.

◎   To know how religious minority groups are adapting to Canada and how Canadian society, in turn, is responding to the new religious diversity.

◎   To examine and consider the significance of another new form of religious diversity: the surge in Canadians claiming to have no religion.

◎   To think about the nature and implications of the proliferation of new and small, yet often global and controversial, religious movements in late modern societies.

Introduction

The religious landscape of Canada is changing in obvious and less obvious ways. Those living in larger urban areas have witnessed the rise of Muslim mosques, Hindu and Buddhist temples, and Sikh gurdwaras. They may have watched them grow, moving from the old store fronts, warehouses, or abandoned churches where they first appeared to magnificent new facilities downtown or in the suburbs. On any street in Montreal, Toronto, Winnipeg, Edmonton, or Vancouver, a Catholic church is now as likely to have a Gurjarati Hindu temple as its neighbour as a Lutheran Church. This is the most conspicuous aspect of the new religious diversity in Canada, born of the changing patterns of immigration. Canada was already well on its way to becoming a post-Christian nation when the changes began, and most Canadians now think of their nation as multicultural, and hence implicitly multi-religious. As Canadian life is increasingly infused with the practices of cultures from around the world, and as people are exposed to distant lands through mass communications, air travel, and business contacts, a new and unparalleled religious diversity is slated for our future. There are other less conspicuous forms of diversity, though, which are emerging in our society as well, and they may have an equally significant impact on our religious landscape. We discuss two of them in this chapter: the growth of the religious "nones" (i.e., those checking the box for "no religion" on surveys), and the proliferation of new religious movements.

Religion and Immigration in Canada

Canada has always been a religiously diverse nation and it is becoming more so. Immigration patterns are a major explanation for this reality (see Beyer, 2005, 2008; Bramadat and Seljak, 2005, 2008). The immigrants from France, Great Britain, and the United States who founded this nation in the seventeenth, eighteenth, and nineteenth centuries brought their rather antithetical Catholic and Protestant convictions with them, and the Protestants were divided further by their denominational differences as Anglicans, Presbyterians, Methodists, and Baptists vied for members and influence in Canada. These imported religious views were imposed on the pre-existing diversity of Aboriginal religious beliefs and practices. Massive immigration from other parts of Europe in the first half of the twentieth century brought even more diversity, as thousands of Lutheran, Mennonite, Eastern Orthodox, and Jewish people arrived. These first waves of immigration to Canada, then, were overwhelmingly Christian. Prior to 1961, Statistics Canada data shows that 39 percent of immigrants were Roman Catholic, 39 percent were Protestant, 11 percent had no religion, and only 3 percent identified with a non-Christian religious tradition (Bibby, 2011: 31).

But, as indicated, some real diversity existed among and within these forms of Christianity (see Bramadat and Seljak, 2008). Denominational differences mattered in ways we now find hard to understand. In the nineteenth and early twentieth centuries, no self-respecting Methodists, for example, would want one of their children to marry a Baptist, let alone a Catholic, and vice versa. The Catholics were also diverse and ethnic differences led to tensions and struggles for dominance, most notably between the large French and Irish Catholic communities in Canada (McGowan, 1999; Fay, 2002). Ethnic variation contributed to an array of theological and political differences dealing with how people believed and practised their faith and viewed their relationship with the rest of Canadian society.

Immigration patterns and religious identification trends began to change when Prime Minister Pierre Elliott Trudeau endorsed a new policy of "multiculturalism" in 1971. With the passage of The Multiculturalism Act in 1988 Canada became the first country in the world to formally adopt a policy of multiculturalism, aimed at fostering the diversity and equality of all Canadians. The accompanying shift of immigration policy allowed more people from the rest of the world to come to Canada, with significant implications for religion in Canada.

Table 8.1 Major Religious Denominations in Canada: 1991[1] and 2001.

	2001		1991		Percentage Change 1991–2001
	Number	%	Number	%	
Roman Catholic	12,793,125	43.2	12,203,625	45.2	4.8
Protestant	8,654,845	29.2	9,427,675	34.9	−8.2
Christian Orthodox	479,620	1.6	387,395	1.4	23.8
Christian, not included elsewhere[2]	80,450	2.6	353,040	1.3	121.1
Muslim	579,640	2.0	253,265	0.9	128.9
Jewish	329,995	1.1	318,185	1.2	3.7
Buddhist	300,345	1.0	163,415	0.6	83.8
Hindu	297,200	1.0	157,015	0.6	89.3
Sikh	278,415	0.9	147,440	0.5	88.8
No religion	4,796,325	16.2	3,333,245	12.3	43.9

[1]For comparability purposes, 1991 data are presented according to 2001 boundaries.

[2]Includes persons who report "Christian," as well as those who report "Apostolic," "Born-again Christian" and "Evangelical."

Source: Statistics Canada. 2001. "2001 Census: Analysis Series. Religions in Canada." Retrieved 3 March 2010. (www12.statcan.ca/english/census01/products/analytic/companion/rel/pdf/ 96F0030XIE2001015.pdf).

The Religious Implications of New Immigration

We will consider four of the religious implications of the new patterns of immigration. First, the new policy of multiculturalism resulted in many immigrants from Asia, Africa, Latin America, and the Middle East coming to Canada, greatly expanding the diversity of religious identifications, beliefs, and practices present in the nation. Just over 30 percent of immigrants currently arrive in Canada identifying with a non-Christian religious tradition (Bibby, 2011: 31). As of 2011, just over 1 million Canadian adults identified themselves as Muslim, nearly 500,000 said they were Hindu, 455,000 professed to be Sikh, roughly 367,000 declared themselves to be Buddhist, and almost 330,000 claimed to be Jewish (Statistics Canada, 2013). Each of these groups is growing numerically, as well as in proportion to the Canadian population, partly through immigration and partly through their somewhat higher rates of fertility. The number of immigrants who are first generation varies from group to group. Seventy-three percent of the Buddhists in Canada are foreign born, compared with 72 percent of the Muslims, 72 percent of the Hindus, 63 percent of the Sikhs, and 31 percent of the Jews. When these and other smaller non-Christian religious groups are combined they constitute 8.2 percent of the Canadian adult population. In 1991 the figure was 3.8 percent (Bibby, 2011: 6; Statistics Canada, 2013). Recent Statistics Canada data projects that by 2017, Muslims, Jews, Hindus, Sikhs, and Buddhists will comprise 10 percent of the adult population of Canada (Valpy and Friesen, 2010), and by 2031, 8 percent of

Canadians could be Muslim (Friesen and Martin, 2010; Statistics Canada, 2010). In fact, Muslims are the fastest-growing religious group in Canada. But this fact is less impressive when one considers the relatively small size of the Muslim community, numerically and proportionately, to the entire Canadian population.

Fewer immigrants identify themselves as Christian today, but Christians, particularly Roman Catholics and evangelical Protestants, are still the leading religious groups coming to Canada, with 23 percent of immigrants identifying as Roman Catholic and 11 percent as Protestant (2001 Canadian Census data; see Beyer, 2008). The character of the Christianity practised in Canada, and elsewhere in the West, is being changed, however, by the newest waves of immigration. This is a second implication of the changing patterns of immigration for religion in Canada.

All traditions are being impacted by immigration. Fourteen percent of all Roman Catholics in Canada today were born outside of Canada, and over 61 percent of those people have arrived in Canada since 1971. Over 17 percent of Protestant evangelicals are foreign born, and nearly 71 percent of those immigrated after 1971 (Bramadat and Seljak, 2008: 440). The newer forms of Christianity that originated in North America, such as The Church of Jesus Christ of Latter-day Saints (i.e., Mormons), the Seventh-day Adventists, The Jehovah's Witnesses, and the Pentecostals, are being impacted even more dramatically. These new forms of Christianity have grown at a phenomenal pace around the world, and now many of their converts are immigrating to the United States and Canada. This is a less often recognized aspect of religious globalization. Imperialism carried Western cultures and their religions to the rest of the world, and many of these religions, modified by their new host cultures (e.g., South Africa, South Korea, China, Guatemala), are now sending emissaries back. These immigrants are reshaping the traditions in line with their preferences in leadership and practices (see e.g., Lawson, 1998; Wilkinson, 2006).

The influence of these immigrants stems in part from the fact that they tend to display higher levels of religiosity than Christians born in Canada (Bowen, 2004: 56–7; Bramadat and Seljak, 2008). In part this is because they have learned in their homelands to take their religion more seriously. More often than not they are far more traditional in their approach to their religious beliefs and practices, and their conservative values are creating tensions between foreign-born and Canadian-born Christians (see Bramadat and Seljak, 2008). But their greater religiosity is also because religion acts as a stabilizing force in their lives as they cope with the challenges and upheavals of coming to a new and strange land. The churches of their co-religionists provide a safe haven for the cultural gatherings, language training, and social and financial assistance essential to their settlement in Canada (Ebaugh and Chafetz, 2000: 55–8; Bramadat and Seljak, 2008).

This is equally true, of course, for immigrants from non-Christian backgrounds. They too tend to be far more religious than native-born Canadians in these traditions (Friesen and Martin, 2010). These immigrants can no longer take their religion for granted, as they often did in their homelands (e.g., in India, China, Egypt, Indonesia). Finding themselves in the minority in Canada, they work much harder to observe and protect their religious identity (see Warner and Williams, 2010). Even more than the Christian immigrants, these immigrants rely on the everyday support of their co-religionists in making their transition to Canada, turning to the temple or mosque to make friends, find mates, make business contacts, share ethnic food, and speak their native tongues. They also tend, at least for a time, to protectively isolate themselves from the wider and strange society by prohibiting intermarriage, for example, with those outside their faith, and providing faith-based education, media, and medical care. In fact in many cases religious organizations are at the heart of an array of activities in ethnic enclaves fostering what sociologists call **institutional completeness**: allowing immigrants to live for a time in an environment that is culturally almost totally familiar and self-sufficient.

These conservative trends in religion are being replicated within the dominant Christian traditions as well. Overall, as Philip Jenkins (2002) and others warn, we must realize that the global centre of gravity of Christendom has shifted to the southern hemisphere. Demographically this is where most Christians live and it is where the religion is growing. With time the Christians from these developing societies will seek to exert greater control over the traditional seats of religious power in Europe and North America (e.g., Pope Francis is the first ever non-European pope). As the churches of the South seek to exercise more influence they will try to impose their more traditional views on the more liberal ways of being Christian dominant in Western Europe and most of North America. Tensions and conflicts will arise over such social issues as gay marriage and ordination and the role of women in the churches. Some schisms in these older denominations may well be in the offing. The flow of immigrants from the developing South to the more prosperous North is augmenting this process, while it is also adding to the diversity of modes of religious expression in Canada.

A third, and opposite, consequence of changing immigration patterns is the increasing number of immigrants arriving with no religious commitments (21 percent) (Bibby, 2011: 31). In part this simply reflects the increased immigration from eastern Asia, where it is less common for people to identify with a specific religious group, even though they may participate in a variety of religious practices (Lai, Paper, and Paper, 2005; Beyer, 2008: 27–8). There is little research, however, on this trend and its possible implications, other than recognizing its contribution to the overall rise in the number of religious "nones" (see next page).

Fourth, we must remember that it is inaccurate to talk about Jews, Hindus, Buddhists, or Muslims as homogeneous groups (Hoodfar, 2006; Beyer, 2008; Bramadat and Seljak, 2008). There are Sunni Muslims and Shi'ite Muslims, Theravadin and Mahayanist Buddhists, and Orthodox Jews and Reform Jews, each holding distinct beliefs and practices, and often long-standing grievances with one another. These intra-religious differences, rivalries, and conflicts are being imported to Canada. These groups are also divided along racial, ethnic, national, and class or caste lines, and there are tensions between groups with differing views about accommodating to Canadian customs. The Sikh community in Canada, for instance, has experienced sharp tensions between the clean-shaven descendants of earlier periods of immigration, who sought to blend in, and the more conservative and even militant religious practices of many later immigrants, who insist on maintaining a more conspicuous and traditional Sikh identity. For the latter, a male Sikh in good standing must not cut his hair, and he should wear traditional Punjabi clothing and a turban (Johnston, 1999; Jakobsh, forthcoming). For the former group, chairs can be used in the temple; for the traditionalists they are forbidden.

Religious Adaptations in Canada

Members of religious minority groups in Canada rarely, if ever, simply transplant their religious beliefs and practices into the Canadian context. As Bramadat and Seljak (2005: 13) remind us, "religion is never relocated (like baggage), but rather is always re-created." Several examples typify this point. Canadian Hindus have adapted their death rituals to Canadian customs by hiding the body of the deceased inside a casket or cremating it, rather than burning it in full public view, as is normally done in India. This makes the grieving process, however, much more abstract and removed than the custom that Hindus are familiar with and prefer (Banerjee and Coward, 2005). Canadian Muslims are breaking with tradition in forming multiethnic congregations. They are also asking their Imams to take on new roles—offering pastoral counselling, providing religious education, and making public appearances on behalf of the Muslim community. Emulating Christian and other religious groups, Muslims are forming voluntary associations to run sports leagues, engage in charity, lobby the government, and work for social justice (McDonough and Hoodfar, 2005: 134). To appear more "Western" many Buddhist groups in Canada mimic churches by holding their religious gatherings on Saturdays or Sundays, and not during the week as is customary in the countries they come from. In Canada Buddhist monks and nuns share monasteries, and monks often spend much more of their time performing ceremonies than studying and meditating (Boisvert, 2005). In these and many other ways the culture and practices of non-Christian traditions are changing in Canada.

In adapting, the members of religious minorities are confronted with several challenges. Two of the most prominent are gender issues and intergenerational differences. In Canada many women from much more staunchly patriarchal societies are confronted with new expectations to get an education, perhaps a job, and to participate in public activities. Consequently, with time some immigrant women seek to exert more influence in their religious communities, to assume positions of leadership. While this is still rare, most women are taking on greater responsibility and authority, especially with regard to the new activities in these communities involving children and youth, religious instruction, missionary work, and other social services (Ebaugh and Chafetz, 2000: 62-9; Boisvert, 2005: 78-9; Wuthnow, 2005: 59-63). Some immigrant men feel threatened by these changes. The new status and prominence of women cuts against the grain of the prerogatives traditionally enjoyed by the men, and in some cases it magnifies the loss of dignity they feel as they struggle to learn a new language, understand strange customs, and find suitable work. Some men are inclined to seek compensation for their loss of self-esteem by stressing their traditional sources of their power and status in the religious communities and repressing and coming into conflict with the women around them (also see Minganti, 2010).

Issues of adaptation and gender also come to the fore in disputes about religious attire in religious minorities (see Minganti, 2010; Singh, 2010). These kinds of debates highlight tensions within many communities and between the community and the rest of society. For instance, many Canadians assume that Muslim women who wear a hijab (head covering) or a burka (full body cloak) are suppressing themselves at the bidding of their fathers and husbands. It is assumed these women long to be "free" to dress and behave like other women in the Western world. The same assumption, by the way, often informs views of women in ultra-conservative Christian and Jewish sects as well, such as the Old Order Mennonites, Hutterites, and Hasidic Jews. No doubt in some cases this is true, and conflicts erupt between daughters, mothers and fathers over whether the children will or will not wear the more traditional clothing. Some daughters will resist wearing the symbols of their faith in public because they wish to fit in with their Canadian peers. In others cases, however, it is the children who want to assert their personal religious identity by wearing the traditional attire and the parents resist because they fear doing so will lead to discrimination. Many Canadians fail to realize that some women choose to wear head coverings not only out of obedience to religious teachings about modesty, but as a symbol of their freedom and independence in a liberal society (McDonough and Hoodfar, 2005: 142; Hoodfar, 2006).

These and many other similar situations reveal that despite our attempts in the late modern world to confine religion to the private sphere, religious concerns will continue to be the focus of some ongoing public debate in Canada, especially as we seek to sort out our not always consistent commitments to the ideals of multiculturalism, equality, and national unity. This is most noteworthy in contexts where religious clothing sparks an overt clash of cultural norms and expectations, such as wearing head coverings in employment settings, especially in jobs where there are uniform requirements (e.g., as a police or RCMP officer), or where issues of public safety arise, such as wearing a turban instead of a motorcycle helmet or removing a veil before boarding an airplane.

A second challenge that exists among immigrants pertains to intergenerational approaches to religion, especially when it comes to the language used in religious settings (Ebaugh and Chafetz, 2000: 105–11; Bramadat and Seljak, 2005). First-generation immigrants tend to prefer religious services that are offered in their native tongue. Their children prefer English or French services. The result is that second-generation immigrants feel alienated when English is not used, while their parents feel equally estranged when English or French are used. Younger Buddhists in Canada, in particular, are attending religious services less and less because few priests know English or French (Boisvert, 2005: 80). Some groups respond to this dilemma by offering multiple services, some in English and some in the native tongue, while others even offer generation-specific services adapted to their language and worship style preferences.

In addition to language, first-generation immigrants are frequently concerned that their children will stray from their traditional and conservative religious roots, particularly in areas of drugs, alcohol, sex, marriage, and violence (Ebaugh and Chafetz, 2000: 122–30; Bramadat and Seljak, 2005). Strict rules, close supervision, and the pursuit of "institutional completeness" are some of the ways parents respond to these concerns, especially with regard to their daughters, dating, and marriage arrangements. Conversely, children are fearful that they will be estranged from the surrounding culture if they are isolated in their ethnic and religious enclaves, a sentiment that is magnified when they believe that their religion is boring and irrelevant to their everyday experiences. Some communities have created youth groups and camps, an innovation in these traditions, to offer young people a safe context for discussing identity questions with their peers, free of any interference from the wider society.

Another point of tension between immigrant children and their parents is religious authority. Like most youth in Canada, second-generation youth in religious minorities tend to take a highly individualistic approach to their faith (Beyer, 2008: 30–1). They compare traditional sources of authority such as religious texts, leaders, and their parents with their personal experiences and religious quests, and they want to choose which beliefs and practices they will accept or discard. This is not to suggest that parents or other sources of religious authority do not continue to play an important role in the decisions they make. But in the end they will do the identity work themselves before deciding the nature of their religious commitments. Interestingly, as the Canadian sociologist of religion Peter Beyer reports (2008: 34–7), despite taking a more individualist approach, young Muslims are fairly consistently choosing to adopt a similar set of core beliefs and practices, while there is more variation in the beliefs and practices of Hindu and Buddhist youth in Canada. This is in line with the turn of Muslims throughout the West to a more generic, de-cultured, and universal expression of Islam, one that is often touted as being a purer form of the faith (see, e.g., Roy, 2004).

Canadian Response to Religious Diversity

In her book *A New Religious America: How a "Christian Country" Has Become the World's Most Religiously Diverse Nation*, Diana Eck (2001: 47) outlines three common social responses to religious diversity: exclusion (i.e., people with non-traditional beliefs should not be allowed in the country), assimilation (i.e., everyone is welcome, but they must leave their culture and religion behind), and pluralism (i.e., everyone can come and be as they are). Similarly, Robert Wuthnow in *America and the Challenges of Religious Diversity* (2005) discusses three possible individual responses to religious diversity. Some embrace religious diversity, to the point of fusing beliefs and practices from different traditions into their personal spiritual lives. Others accept or tolerate diversity, either keeping their distance from people of different faiths or intentionally building bridges with members of other religious groups. They recognize that different religions are equally valid, or at least that there are many good and valuable aspects to different religious traditions. Finally, some reject religious diversity, typically holding to the view that their religion is right and all other religions are wrong. The latter tend to think that other faith groups pose a threat to the fundamental Western values of democracy, individualism, and free thought.

With Canada's multicultural background, many might assume Canadians are open to immigration and welcoming to people of different faiths. There is some truth to this assumption, with the partial exception of Quebec where there is a pervasive fear that multiculturalism and religious diversity will jeopardize the majority French culture in its struggle to survive as a minority in English-speaking North America (see Box 8.1). However, the evidence to support the "nice Canadian" narrative is less conclusive than is commonly assumed. (For a comparable discussion of the situation in the United States, see Putnam and Campbell, 2010.) The history of Canada is replete with contrary examples of times when Canadians have discriminated against non-Christian and non-Western groups out of fear of the "other" (see Beaman, 2008b; Cowan, 2008; Lefebvre, 2008). In the late 1800s Canada and the United States passed laws specifically designed to stem the tide of immigration from

Asia, and in the aftermath of the Japanese attack on Pearl Harbour in 1941 Japanese Canadians were forcibly removed from their homes on the west coast and relocated to internment camps in the interior of Canada. For many years before and afterward, Japanese Buddhists were shunned in Canadian society. In the middle of the twentieth century anti-Semitism was more or less acceptable and actively supported by members of the social and religious elites of Canada. Jews were barred from being members of many prominent social institutions (e.g., social and golf clubs), and during the Second World War many Jewish refugees fleeing the Holocaust were shamefully turned away from the shores of Canada (Davies and Nefsky, 1997).

In the wake of 9/11 many Canadian Muslims have been victimized, in subtle and not so subtle ways, by the "Islamophobia" rising in much of the Western world. As the Canadian sociologist Jasmin Zine comments (2012: 46):

> I became particularly aware of the precariousness and fragility of the narrative of Canadian national identity for Muslims after the tragic terrorist attacks of 9/11. Muslims tend to talk about life in terms of a critical rupture—"pre-9/11" or "post-9/11"—that created an ontological as well as a temporal shift. In the West, peaceful citizens were transformed overnight into threats to national security. Ten years and the deaths (by some estimates) of almost 1 million Muslims in Iraq and Afghanistan in US-led war on terror have not changed this perception or assuaged the Western desire to root out the Muslim fanatic maybe disguised as the neighbour next door.

This and other kinds of prejudice manifest themselves in direct and indirect ways, ranging from bullying in the schoolyards to the rulings of city councils and zoning boards. Regulations of the latter sort are often used to obstruct new religions or force religious minorities to adjust their religious practices to the norms of the dominant society (Eck, 2001: 308–28). When the Laos Buddhist community of the greater Toronto area, for example, sought to build its first traditional temple in the hills of Caledon (just north of Toronto), the vociferous complaints of some residents prompted authorities to force the Buddhists to change the architecture of their temple and to plant a row of trees between it and the road, to reduce the visibility of the temple. Yet only months later a large Christian church was built down the road with no restrictions on its size, location, or visibility (White, 2012). Taken together, ongoing and subtle forms of discrimination can have a negative impact on members of religious minorities, lowering their self-esteem, increasing rates of suicide, and reducing the educational performance of children (McDonough and Hoodfar, 2005: 137–8; Seljak, 2005).

So the overall picture in Canada, past and present, is mixed. On the one hand, 78 percent of Canadians recently said that on the whole immigration is

**Box
8.1**

Multiculturalism and the Perceived Threat to Western Values

On 22 July 2011, an obscure Norwegian captured the attention of the world. Anders Behring Breivik set off bombs at several government buildings in downtown Oslo, and then went on a shooting rampage at a political youth camp on Utoya Island. He killed 76 people in total. These shocking acts were done in protest against the government's immigration and multiculturalism policies. Breivik is a right-wing, Christian, anti-Muslim extremist who carried out his attacks because he believed that the Muslims coming to Norway were going to undermine Norwegian culture and open the door to Islamist radicals bent on suppressing the traditional values of Western Europe. In the 1,500-page manifesto he posted online before his attack, Breivik recycles many of the outlandish claims and fears espoused by leaders of the radical right in Europe, the United States, and Canada about the threats posed by Muslim immigration.

While few fully share his views, let alone accept the way Breivik chose to express them, the underlying sentiments have been gaining ground in Europe and elsewhere, fuelling the surprising electoral success of some politicians and movements opposed to Muslim immigration and the accommodation of religio-cultural differences (e.g., Geert Wilders' Party for Freedom in the Netherlands; the National Front in France, founded by Jean-Marie Le Pen and now led by his daughter Marine; and to some extent the Parti Québécois, as evidenced by statements made during the election campaign of 2012). In fact, multiculturalism was falling out of favour with most of the reigning conservative leaders of Europe when Breivik struck. German Chancellor Angela Merkel, French President Nicolas Sarkozy, and British Prime Minister David Cameron all declared multiculturalism to be an abject failure, largely because of the persistent tensions between the large Muslim immigrant populations in their countries and the nominally Christian majorities. Fear of the "Muslim tide" in France has led to bans on wearing outward symbols of religion in the schools and public places (e.g., crucifixes, the burka, and turbans), something that several leaders in Quebec have proposed as well.

Is this fearful reaction justified? Multiculturalism, as Canadians understand the policy and practice, has really never been instituted in most of Europe. In Germany, France, and England, "multiculturalism" means treating the Muslims and others as formally equal but essentially separate. This approach has left much of the Muslim population isolated and marginalized. Little effort has been made to cultivate the sense of inclusion so essential to the success of the Canadian policy of multiculturalism. The difference has fostered resentment in the second generation of European Muslims, with some of the children of immigrants becoming susceptible to the messages of violent religious extremists. And the mounting tensions are swelling the ranks of the radical right, anti-immigration movements, especially in the hard economic times following the 2008 financial disaster. Could something similar happen here? While there is evidence that hate crimes do happen in Canada based on religious differences (see Bramadat and Seljak, 2005), outside of Quebec we have not experienced the same sense of mutual alienation. But just how well insulated are we by our more favourable experience of multiculturalism?

In Quebec the policy of multiculturalism has been subjected to relentless attacks, and it is often misrepresented and associated with the misadventures of European "multi-cul-de-sacism" (Mistry, 1995). As Louise Beaudoin, the Parti Québécois critic for Secularism, declared in January 2011, "Multiculturalism may be a Canadian value, but it is not a Quebec value" (Montpetit, 2011; Patriquin, 2011). The Bouchard-Taylor Commission on Reasonable Accommodation (2008) in Quebec came to a similar conclusion: federal multiculturalism is a governance model that cannot be duplicated in Quebec. The so-called central assumption of multiculturalism—that there is no dominant culture in Canada and the sanctity of differences must be respected—is unacceptable, argues Gerard Bouchard (cited in Montpetit, 2011). Francophone culture is the majority culture of Quebec and any governance model for managing diversity must begin by acknowledging this reality. As the Bouchard-Taylor Commission noted, English Canada can afford a looser concept of multiculturalism as governance because of its privileged status as the majority. By contrast, the French majority in Quebec is a distinct minority in Canada and the rest of North America. This militates against promoting the more permissive policy of multiculturalism. It would be tantamount to linguistic and cultural suicide, the Commission argued. While being critical of the tendency to indulge in simplistic and distorted caricatures of federal multiculturalism in Quebec (2008: 121, 192), in the final analysis, the Commission was adamant that the province must support an alternative policy of "interculturalism," to allay the anxieties of the beleaguered French-speaking cultural minority in an English-speaking North America.

But what is this "interculturalism"? While the cultural concerns of the Québécois have some validity, would the governance logic of interculturalism really make any difference? Both models constitute political acts whose primary goal is to foster an inclusive society by managing the integration of newcomers without ruffling the status quo. Both are predicated on the assumption that the central authorities possess the right to define what counts as differences, and what differences count, so that newcomers can be different, but only in the same and limited ways (Fleras, 2012). There is little that is unique about interculturalism except its greater openness in defining the limits of pluralism and drawing the line about what is and is not acceptable. Rather, interculturalism appears to be just an alternative label, one used to differentiate Quebec further from the rest of Canada (Patriquin, 2011)—little more than old wine in new bottles. To be sure, Canada's official multiculturalism is less "multi" than widely perceived, while Quebec's interculturalism is less "inter" than many propose. But neither the proponents of multiculturalism nor those of interculturalism have a knack for meaning what they say or saying what they mean (see Canadian Diversity, Spring 2012). So it is easy to anticipate that debates over these competing governance models will remain lively for years to come, and this may spark some radicalization on the part of Canadians with opposing views.

good for Canada, as compared with only 66 percent in 1950 (Bibby, 2006: 25). Ninety-four percent of Canadians claim to be tolerant, while 82 percent say that diversity is a good thing for Canada (Reimer, 2008: 110). Young Canadian Muslims, Buddhists, and Hindus similarly voice their strong support for multiculturalism and the vast majority reject any form of politicized religion (Beyer, 2008: 36–7). Yet, on the other hand, as an Angus Reid poll (2009) indicates, 62 percent of Canadians oppose changing or modifying laws and norms to accommodate minorities, including 72 percent of those questioned in Quebec (Geddes, 2009). The same poll also reveals that 72 percent of Canadians have a favourable opinion of Christianity, while the figures for other religions is much lower: 57 percent for Buddhism, 53 percent for Judaism (36 percent in Quebec), 41 percent for Hinduism, 30 percent for Sikhism (15 percent in Quebec), and 28 percent for Islam (17 percent in Quebec). Similarly, while only 10 percent of Canadians believe that Christian beliefs encourage violence, the figures for other faiths are higher: 13 percent for Hinduism, 14 percent for Judaism, 26 percent for Sikhism, 45 percent for Islam (57 percent in Quebec). In the post-9/11 world suspicions are running high. But it is reasonable to think that things will get better on this front. As almost every study of religious diversity argues, people become more accepting of the beliefs and practices of others with exposure (e.g., Wuthnow, 2005; Geddes, 2009; Putnam and Campbell, 2010), and interaction with members of these relatively new religions in Canada is on the rise.

The backdrop to all discussions of religion in Canada is the broader tendency to "privatize" religion. This is the term sociologists use to identify the modern view that religion is essentially a private matter and thus religious views should play no role in the creation or exercise of public policy. A privatized conception of religion grows naturally out of the desire to protect everyone's right to freedom of expression, conscience, and religion. It is part of the process by which religions became dis-established, in Canada and elsewhere in the Western world (see Chapter 7). In Canada, unlike Saudi Arabia or Iran, no single religion can dictate how people should lead their lives. The process of privatization is also a reflection of the increasingly subjective conception people now have of religion (see Chapter 5). Seeing religion as an essentially private matter, however, has led many Western governments to move towards a more or less complete ban on the public expression of religion, which can amount at times to actual discrimination against religion and the religious. Moreover, it has resulted in the neglect of the very real role religious commitments continue to play in shaping the cultural practices and social relations of most societies. John Biles and Humera Ibrahim (2005) argue that Canada's official "diversity model," which stresses the coming together of those with different cultural backgrounds in a spirit of inclusion, equality, and accommodation, tends to ignore the critical role religion should play in any discussion of diversity. For many immigrants, as indicated, religion is integral to their adjustment to Canada, including their sense of self, their networking opportunities, and the provision of many of the social services, schools, and cultural centres many new Canadians rely on. These aspects of the religious lives of many immigrants provide them with the sense of belonging and attachment that is imperative to their successful transition into life in Canada. For these reasons, Biles and Ibrahim call on the government and all Canadians to pay more attention to religion in our ongoing dialogue about our growing diversity and its consequences.

But why is religion so often left out of the Canadian discussion? Biles and Ibrahim conjecture that most Canadians tend to still to assume that Canadians are Christian (at least nominally), and thus it is simply not necessary to consider religious diversity. While the assumption is somewhat justified, the religious composition of Canada is changing and in many communities, such as the so-called GTA (Greater Toronto Area), Montreal, and Vancouver, the substantial presence of growing non-Christian communities warrants a shift in our reasoning. Another possible reason is that many Canadians suspect that religious groups and views are inherently problematic because they are intolerant, and giving religion a significant role in the public discourse on multiculturalism will lead to too much contention. But the failure to consider religion also stems from the misperception that the religious orientation of immigrants is simply a less important marker of their identity than race and ethnicity. In many instances, however, religion is just as important if not more so. The recognition of cultural differences and conflicts has not impaired the public discussion of multiculturalism. On the contrary, it is part of the rationale for having the discussion. Similarly, Biles and Ibrahim contend, religion as a phenomenon needs to be freed from the constraining conceptual box imposed by privatized conceptions of religion, and Canadians as a whole need to be drawn into open dialogue and debate with the religious about the place of religion in Canadian society. To this end the public needs to be better educated about the beliefs and practices of different religious groups, something that is sadly lacking in Canada today.

Ironically, in many educational settings across Canada religion is being eliminated from the curriculum and program offerings out of respect for the growing diversity of Canadians. For example, until 1997 all schools in Newfoundland and Labrador were operated by church-run boards. Now they are secular and public. It is illegal at present to provide religious instruction in public schools, at least in the form of overt indoctrination to a particular religion. Religious activities (e.g., prayers) are also prohibited in schools, in case some students who abstain are stigmatized. Christmas concerts are now called "winter concerts" in many public schools. The province of Alberta went so far as to pass Bill 44 in 2009 that granted parents the right to pull their children out of classes where religion will be discussed. Yet there are many contradictions in how Canadians deal with religion and public education. Ontario provides public funding to Catholic schools, as does Quebec for Protestant schools. This is a legacy of the political conditions in existence when the British North America Act was framed in 1867 (Thiessen, 2001:13). The calendars of virtually all public schools are still dictated by Christian holidays, and while Muslims are denied dedicated prayer rooms or student clubs, some schools still permit Christian groups to form student clubs and to hold worship services on school grounds.

So, as David Seljak (2005) laments, the Canadian approach can have the unintended and ironic effect of discriminating against religious minorities—and by extension immigrants—when its stated objective is actually to foster their inclusion by suppressing religious differences. At a more general level, the lack of religious instruction in schools means that many children are religiously illiterate. In the name of not supporting the promotion of one religion, religion itself has simply disappeared from the curriculum of most public school systems. Many children now lack a basic comprehension of the beliefs and practices of the new religious groups emerging in Canada and, more importantly, their own neighbourhoods, in part because they lack an adequate understanding of any religion. This is problematic in a country dedicated to multiculturalism and in which people will be encountering more people of different religious persuasions in their daily dealings with businesses, governments, and the educational, legal, and medical systems. In most instances, Seljak concludes, the way Canadians handle religion in educational settings is anything but neutral: in fact, it is largely anti-religious.

Some religious minorities are equally disappointed with the decision to abandon religious instruction in public schools, even if Christianity is the dominant or only religion taught, because they value the moral training associated with religious instruction. They also believe that the secular humanist worldview dominant in the public schools is at odds with the values promoted by their religions. Consequently, some religious minority groups have set up their own religious schools. British Columbia, Alberta, and Quebec have decided to assist these independent religious schools, providing up to 60 percent of the funding given to public schools. But education is a provincial jurisdiction in Canada and there are significant inconsistencies. In Ontario, where Catholic schools are publicly funded, there is no financial support for other religious schools. In the eyes of some Canadians all these religious schools are problematic because they are indicative of attempts to resist full integration into the broader society. In the view of many religious minority groups, however, the right to establish independent religious schools embodies the core values of a democratic, diverse, and pluralistic society like Canada.

In conclusion, it is worth considering the distinction between "**diversity**" and "**pluralism**" drawn by both Diana Eck (2001) and Robert

Wuthnow (2005). Diversity designates the existence of a multiplicity of different beliefs and practices. Pluralism entails that people understand their own beliefs, actively seek to understand the beliefs and practices of others, and are open to meaningful dialogue and interactions with other groups. Canada is certainly a diverse society, but are we a pluralistic one? The growing religious minorities in our midst desire to be shown more respect and greater understanding. They want Canadians to abandon the negative stereotypes so often perpetuated in the media (Eck, 2001: 24; Wuthnow, 2005: 65; Fleras, 2011; Zine, 2012; Saunders, 2012). In this vein, Lori Beaman (2008a) encourages Canadians to stop using words like "tolerance" or "accommodation" to address the situation because these terms imply obliging a minority group that is of lesser status and not really of part of "us." Instead, she favours speaking about a shared struggle for "equality," thereby embodying a value that most Canadians hold dear and encouraging the development of a more truly pluralistic Canadian society.

The Religious "Nones"

To discern the future of religion sociologists have turned their attention to the study of the growing number of people choosing the "no religion" category on surveys, also referred to as religious "nones" or, more prosaically, as the "unaffiliated." As we learned in Chapter 7, 24 percent of Canadians claim to have "no religion" (Statistics Canada, 2013). In the United States, the most religious country in the Western world, the figure is slightly lower. Data from the Pew Forum on Religion and Public Life, the American General Social Survey, and the American Religious Identification Survey all indicate that approximately 15 percent of Americans claim to have "no religion," and one recent study estimates as many as one in five Americans (19 percent) may be nones (Grossman, 2012). Only about 8 percent could be described as such in 1990. That is a substantial change in a relatively brief time. Treated as an integral part of the Canadian religious landscape, the nones could be seen as the second largest "religious" grouping in Canada (i.e., bigger than any Protestant denomination). This is an important point, because while many assume that Canada is becoming an ever more religiously diverse nation, they rarely take this particular category into consideration.

Who are these people, and why is there a surge in the percentage of people making this still rather controversial claim? As we will see, this category is not exclusively tied to atheists (those who do not believe in a god) and agnostics (those who are unsure whether a god exists or not); rather, it represents a more complex grouping of people with a variety of attitudes and behaviours. Even more, the "no religion" category is tied, in part, to the larger movement of people who wish to distance themselves from the resurgence of conservative and fundamentalist forms of religiosity, especially the aggressive evangelical Protestantism that has received so much public attention in the United States. To know who Canadians are, religiously, it is becoming apparent that we need a better grasp of this growing, and until recently fairly unexamined, new element of diversity in the population.

The religious nones, in Canada and the United States, stand out demographically in some respects. They are disproportionately found, for example, in the younger cohorts. Seventy-four percent of those who claim "no religion" in Canada are 44 years old or younger, and 39 percent are less than 24 years old (Statistics Canada, 2001: 20). In the United States, 60 to 70 percent of the unaffiliated are under the age of 49, including 30 percent who are under the age of 30 (Pew Forum on Religion and Public Life, 2008: 37; Kosmin and Keysar, 2008: 1). This suggests that some of the growth in this category is generational, and sociologists are aware that insufficient attention has been given to the views of the young. Their take on religion has not been differentiated adequately from that of their families and in recent years this has led to several studies of this group (e.g., Smith and Denton, 2005; Wuthnow, 2007; Bibby et al. 2009; Smith and Snell, 2009; Zuckerman, 2012: see Chapter 7). This research documents the sizable increase in the number of young people claiming to have no religion, with some estimating that over 50 percent of 15- to 29-year-olds in Canada have no religion or never attend religious services (Valpy, 2010). In the United States, 23 percent of young adults aged 18 to 29 claim to have no religion, compared with just 12 percent in the 1970s (Pew Forum on Religion and Public Life, 2010: 5).

The unaffiliated are also far more likely to be male than female. In the United States, nearly 60 percent of the unaffiliated are males (Kosmin and Keysar, 2008: 1; Pew Forum on Religion and Public Life, 2008: 63). Correlations exist as well with immigration patterns. Between 1991 and 2001, 21.3 percent of the immigrants to Canada claimed to have no religion, second only to those claiming to be Roman Catholics (23 percent; Statistics Canada, 2001: 19). Since 1961 there has been a steady decline in the number of Roman Catholic immigrants, while the "no religion" category has consistently increased. If the trend continues, the religious nones will become the leading "religious" group immigrating to Canada in the near future. In the United States, 16 percent of those who are foreign born are unaffiliated, and Canada accounts for the second highest percentage of these immigrants (24 percent). The immigrants with the highest percentage of unaffiliated (27 percent) are those from East Asia (Pew Forum on Religion and Public Life, 2008: 49).

In other respects, however, the "nones" in the United States are not demographically much different from their fellow Americans. This is true for their marital status, racial and ethnic composition, educational attainment, and household income (Kosmin and Keysar, 2008: 2-5). In these significant and somewhat surprising ways, Barry Kosmin and Ariela Keysar (2008: 5), conclude, "Nones in the U.S. have grown increasingly similar to the general U.S. population in the last two decades." There is no strong support here, then, for the common presumption that the turn away from religion is linked to rising levels of education and prosperity.

Understandably, we might be inclined to think that those claiming to have "no religion" are either atheists or agnostics, but this is not necessarily the case. Bibby (2011: 48–9) reports that only about half of Canadian adults and teens who say they have "no religion" are in fact atheists. While the "no religion" category is growing quickly, only 2–4 percent of the American population say they are atheists or agnostics (Kosmin and Keysar, 2008: 5; Pew Forum on Religion and Public Life, 2008: 5). How then should we think about all the other unaffiliated people?

Table 8.2 American Religious Nones and Belief in God

Response	Category	Percentage Nones (N = 1.106)	Percentage US Adults (N = 1.1015)
There is no such thing	Atheist	7	2
There is no way to know	Hard Agnostic	19	4
I'm not sure	Soft Agnostic	16	6
There is a higher power but no personal God	Deist	24	12
There is definitely a personal God	Theist	27	70
Don't Know/Refused	N/A	7	6
TOTAL		100%	100%

Source: Kosmin, Barry and Ariela Keysar. 2008. "American Nones: The Profile of the No Religion Population," page 11. Retrieved 17 February 2010. (http://commons.trincoll.edu/aris/files/2011/08/NONES_08.pdf).

There is a growing consensus amongst sociologists that there is a great deal of variation in those captured by the "no religion" category. Michael Hout and Claude Fischer (2002), who study religion in the United States, and David Voas and Abby Day (2010), who primarily study religion in the United Kingdom, both demonstrate that many of these people are nonetheless religious in various ways. For instance, some believe in God, the afterlife, or in the importance of religion, while others even attend religious services or participate in private religious practices (e.g., prayer), and some are religious in all of these ways. Kosmin and Keysar (2008: 11) show that over half of Americans who are unaffiliated believe in either a higher power or a personal God, and many turn to religious groups for rites of passage, such as baptisms, weddings, or funerals. Accordingly, a Pew Forum on Religion and Public Life report (2008: 6, 20) differentiates between the **secular unaffiliated** and the **religious unaffiliated**. The first group (6.3 percent of Americans) constitutes those who say religion is not important to their lives, and the second group (5.8 percent of Americans) includes those who say that religion is somewhat or even very important to their lives. In sum, individuals who claim that they have "no religion" are not necessarily irreligious, and this points to the complexity of people's religious identities in the late modern world. Being "religious" (or "spiritual") no longer means one must even identify with, let alone belong to, a specific religious group or tradition (Davie, 1994).

In a recent article Chaeyoon Lim, Carol Ann MacGregor, and Robert Putnam (2010) argue that the "no religion" category is a fluid one, with people flowing in and out of this self-identification. Based on two sets of surveys done one year apart, they found that only 70 percent of the Americans who claimed to have "no religion" on the first survey did so on the second survey. That means 30 percent of the religious nones claimed a religious affiliation one year after stipulating that they had none. But the overall percentage of religious nones in the population remained stable because an equal number of people must have moved in the opposite direction. By way of comparison, 90 percent of those who declared themselves to be Protestants or Catholics on the first survey held to their religious identification on the second one. The authors argue that the data suggests we should draw a distinction between "secular religious nones" (i.e., those who stably remain nones) and "liminal nones" (i.e., those who fluctuate in their identification). Examining the religiosity of the two groups, they discovered that the liminal nones "are, on average, significantly more religious than the stable nones in all measures of religiosity." But by the same token they are "significantly less religious than the people who consistently identify with a religious group" (2010: 614). There is variation among "liminal nones" in their rates of church attendance and belief in God, and their propensity to say that religion is important to them, or that they are spiritual. Their overall levels of religiosity, though, did not change much, if at all, in the process of becoming or ceasing to be a religious none.

This distinction brings some clarity to debates about the meaning of the rise in the number of religious nones. Lim, MacGregor, and Putnam (2010: 614) reject the suggestion often made by opponents of secularization theory that religious nones are just "unchurched believers" waiting to find the right religious organization or they are "spiritual seekers" pursuing their religious interests privately. This is clearly not the case for the secular or stable nones, and there is little evidence that the liminal nones are engaged in any active search for religious answers either in or outside of traditional religious organizations. Does this mean that the rise in religious nones is indicative of secularization? Lim et al. (2010) have their doubts. The liminal nones may well be on their way to not being religious at all, but most claim that their levels of church attendance have been constant for the previous five years, and their levels of religiosity did not fluctuate in the year between their contrary claims about their religious identification. "In other words, despite the instability of their reported religious preferences, their marginal involvement in religion appears to be enduring" (Lim et al. 2010: 614). The nature of these liminal nones, then, remains rather obscure.

Why are people increasingly self-identifying as non-religious, even if only for a time? We lack the research, especially in Canada, to say anything with certainty. Perhaps it is just that people now feel freer to do so. As Berger predicted, in our increasingly plural and diverse societies the dominance of any single sacred canopy has been shattered. This sharply reduces the stigma associated with being non-religious in Canada and the United States. The social value attached to the individual's right to choose and express oneself authentically has trumped the value of demonstrating one's virtue through conformity to the dictates of a dominant belief system. Of course this is more transparently so in Canada than the United States, where an overarching Christian religious narrative continues to frame many aspects of their national identity (see Box 4.2).

In fact the strong resurgence in religious rhetoric in the American public realm since the 1980s may be another reason why the ranks of the religious nones have swelled. Perhaps it reflects a reaction to the strong fusion of religious conservatism, even fundamentalism, and right-wing politics in the United States and elsewhere. As Hout and Fischer (2002: 168) first argued, "The growing connection made in the press and in the Congress between Republicans and Christian evangelicals may have led Americans with moderate and liberal political views to express their distance from the Religious Right by saying they prefer no religion." Tim Clydesdale (2007: 196–7), in his examination of American university students, also references youth who are put off by the strong ties between faith and politics in the United States. The main point of contention for those who adopt a "no religion" stance is the evangelical led support for so-called "family values" in America, in terms of mobilizing political action against abortion, gay marriage, stem-cell research, and euthanasia.

In their book *unChristian* (2007), David Kinnaman and Gabe Lyons report that many non-Christians hold the following six negative perceptions of Christians, particularly evangelicals who attend church regularly: they are thought to be hypocritical, anti-homosexual, sheltered within a Christian subculture, too political, too judgmental, and motivated to make friends with non-Christians only to convert them. Putnam and Campbell (2010: 499–501) reinforce these findings, noting that the most religious people in America are also perceived to be the most intolerant. According to Hout and Fischer (2002), the result of such perceptions is a strong backlash against the belief that being religious means adopting conservative values. Some are simply choosing to have no religion rather than get caught up in the broader social perception of religion as a source of contention and division in

America. The geographic proximity of Canada and the United States, combined with the strong American media influence in Canadian homes, might partially explain why there has been an increase in the "no religion" category north of the border as well. Certainly Thiessen (2010, 2012) discovered that many marginal affiliates in Canada are influenced by their disdain for the behaviour of American televangelists and other American religious figures to whom they have been exposed through the media.

Research into the religiously unaffiliated is gaining ground in the United States and Europe, yet much more work is needed, especially in Canada. Why, for example, do some self-declared religious nones adopt religious or spiritual beliefs and practices? What beliefs and practices are adopted and how? Why do some people move in and out of this category? How does this occur? Is there a correlation between patterns of religious socialization and the adoption of this ambiguous "religious" identity? If there is, what is it and how might it impact the future of this group? How might a better understanding of the nones contribute to our grasp of the place of religion in late modern societies? Can the rise in their numbers be used as a reliable indicator of secularization? Overall should we expect the nones to decrease, stabilize, or increase in the years to come?

New Religious Movements

Beginning in the late 1960s and continuing through to the late 1990s, a new kind of "diversity" challenge surged to the forefront of public awareness: the seemingly sudden rise and prominence of numerous new and exotic religious movements. Young Americans, and to a lesser extent Canadians and Europeans, were leaving their families, friends, and educations behind to pursue new and unusual lives as devotees of various self-proclaimed gurus, prophets, and messiahs. These so-called "cults," the term used to stigmatize the groups, seemed suddenly to be cropping up everywhere as people began to encounter the followers of The Children of God/The Family, Krishna Consciousness, the Divine Light Mission, the Unification Church, Scientology, Transcendental Meditation, the Process, Eckankar, the Rajneesh movement, the Raelians, and many other groups too numerous to mention, on the streets of their cities (see, e.g., Partridge, 2004). Many people were perplexed and offended by the way many of these groups began to aggressively canvass for donations and converts in parks and airports and on the street corners of their communities. The cultural clash between the nominally Christian and yet largely materialist sensibilities of mainstream society and the more strident, other-worldly, moralistic and often simply foreign demands placed on the young new converts to these religious movements set off a social panic, **"the great cult scare"** (e.g., Bromley and Shupe, 1981; Singer, 1995). As the mass media fanned the flames with sensationalistic stories of "cult" oddities and abuses (Beckford, 1999; McCloud, 2004) an organized anti-cult movement formed (e.g., Citizens Freedom Foundation, Council on Mind Abuse, Cult Awareness Network, American Family Foundation), leading to calls for government inquiries and new forms of regulation, and to multiple court cases (e.g., Hill, 1980; Bromley and Shupe, 1993; Richardson and Introvigne, 2001). As parents and their allies in the anti-cult movement sought to discredit the new religions and rescue, often forcibly, their children from these supposedly "dangerous cults," sociologists of religion found themselves drawn into the fray. The study of new religions soon became an abiding concern of the field as many scholars sought to provide more reliable information on these groups to offset the rumours and atrocity tales circulating in the media and the courts. Many sociologists soon recognized the imperative to defend the constitutional rights of these new religious minorities in order to protect the broader religious freedoms of everyone (Robbins and Anthony, 1982; Young and Griffith, 1992; Richardson, 2004). In the process much was learned about the birth and demise of religions, the process of conversion, the changing religious sensibilities of late modern societies, especially amongst the young, and the relationship between religious innovation and various forms of social deviance and experimentation. The overall gains in knowledge are too sweeping and complex to survey here, but we will briefly examine three important and relevant sets of findings: (1) some of the probable reasons for the rise of this new type of religious diversity; (2) the insights gained from study of two of the main foci of the controversy surrounding "cults," namely the debates about **brainwashing** and charges of sexual deviance; and (3) thoughts on the longer-term social significance of the very emergence of this kind of new religious diversity (for a more comprehensive coverage of these and other related issues see either Lewis, 2004 or Dawson, 2006a).

The Emergence of New Religious Movements

The new religions that emerged after the 1960s drew special attention from the public and researchers because they were more numerous, more exotic in form, and more prominent. But most of all it was because they were recruiting their members from amongst the best and the brightest and not the dregs of society. In ways not well appreciated until quite recently, the United States and to a lesser extent Canada have long been hotbeds of new religious activity (Jenkins, 2000; Albanese, 2007). But most of these older new religious movements, such as the Church of Jesus Christ of Latter-day Saints, the Seventh-day Adventists, the Christian Scientists, the Jehovah's Witnesses, the Pentecostals, and many more less prominent groups, were Christian sects born out of dissatisfaction with the dominant denominations. They came into being largely out of the desire to practise what they thought to be a purer form of Christianity. They represented attempts to reform the

status quo. These groups also tended to attract their followers, at least initially, from the poorest and most marginalized segments of the society, and
it was commonly assumed that the members were seeking some compensation for their reduced material and social circumstances (e.g., Niebuhr,
1929; Pope, 1958). Jesus, after all, had promised that the humble yet virtuous would be granted life ever after and that with his Second Coming they
would inherit the Earth. In these small groups individuals could acquire the
respect, status, and power they lacked in the rest of society. They could also
enjoy the more immediate psychic rewards of participating in the intense,
emotionally rousing, and sometimes even ecstatic religious practices characteristic of many of these groups.

But the new religions that arose in the 1960s broke this mould. The
converts to these groups came largely from college and university students.
They were the children of privilege, coming from middle- and upper middle-
class families. Most of the religions in question, moreover, were either
non-Christian (e.g., The International Society for Krishna Consciousness,
Vajradhatu) or more or less wholly new creations (e.g., Scientology, Urantia),
in essence seemingly invented religions. Even when the new groups were
Christian (e.g., The Children of God or the Unification Church), they practised a form of Christianity deemed to be highly heretical and unconventional, even by the standards of previous sectarian groups. The Reverend
Sun Myung Moon, founder of the Unification Church, for instance, was believed to be the next messiah, Christ incarnate come back to earth to lay the
physical foundation for the coming Kingdom of God. David Berg, the leader
of The Children of God, advocated the promiscuous enjoyment of sex as one
of God's primary blessings, and its liberal use in promoting the Christian
message and winning converts. The increased strangeness of many of the
teachings and practices of these new religions, at least from the perspective
of most Americans and Canadians, and the sense of loss and confusion experienced by parents whose children abandoned school to join these groups,
sowed the seeds of suspicion and resentment in the mind of the public, a
suspicion liberally fanned by the sensationalistic exposés penned by journalists and aggrieved ex-members of these groups. Misunderstanding was rife
and clashes were common.

Four larger social structural conditions, however, really account for why
these fears culminated in such a pervasive social panic, one that captured
the attention of many sociologists of religion for decades and ultimately
helped to reshape the religious landscape of the Western world. These conditions are intertwined in complex ways but for clarity we will discuss them
separately.

First, the cult scare became consequential because it coincided with
and was fed by the baby boom that followed the Second World War. This
youthful bulge in the population was the largest, most materially well-off,

best educated, and most media-aware generation the world has ever seen (Roof, 1993). As they came of age the entire society became re-oriented to the needs and preferences of the young, setting off another social problem called "the generation gap." The sheer demographic reality of the situation assured two things: first, that there were simply more young people, with time on their hands, to be recruited to the new religions and, second, that their conversions would be subject to greater scrutiny than ever before.

This brings us to the second social condition: all this was transpiring at a time when the mass media and their role in our societies were exploding. Newspapers, magazines, radio, and television were entering into the golden age of their popularity and influence and the repeated tales of ordinary young kids suddenly abandoning the pursuit of the American dream to swear allegiance to strange gurus from foreign lands sold papers and attracted audiences. This media frenzy magnified the seeming significance of what was happening. In truth only a small fraction of Americans or Canadians ever became involved with a new religious movement: less than 1 percent in Canada and never more than 3 percent in the United States. But the seemingly pervasive presence of the groups and the repeated accounts of conversions led most people to assume these new religions were much more successful. Soon a feedback loop was established by which the new religions used the media exposure to exaggerate their claims of success to attract more followers, while the exaggerated claims were uncritically repeated by the media to justify their continued attention to the story, further stoking the flames of resistance in the broader public, which became yet another reason for more media attention.

Third, the more recent wave of new religious movements was both a product of and a response to the youthful counterculture that swept North America and much of the rest of the world in the late 1960s and early 1970s. As the younger generation "turned on and tuned out," as they used drugs, adopted the Hippie lifestyle, protested against the Vietnam war, became feminists, and went to the streets to fight for the civil rights of blacks in America, they also began to "turn East" (Cox, 1977; Gitlin, 1987). Through their mass participation in higher education and the media, and the greater ease of international travel, many in the Baby Boomer generation were exposed to the religious beliefs and practices of other cultures. The mystical and philosophical systems of India (e.g., Yoga) and the Far East (e.g., Zen Buddhism) appeared to offer a highly evolved spiritual antidote to the excessive materialism, military aggression, and staid church-based religious conformism of contemporary Western (i.e., American) culture. Moreover, these traditions appeared to place their primary focus on the individual quest for happiness through an inner journey of meditative discovery, unlocking secrets of human nature and the world that had been overlooked in the Western rush to world supremacy. This metaphysical alternative resonated with the growing expressive individualism and rebelliousness of this generation (Tipton, 1982). In other words, as Dawson (2006a: 43) concludes, "the clamour for change, the experience of disruption, the rising educational levels, and the emergence of new ideals of personal authenticity in the sixties opened the door to a much greater interest in alternative world-views and ways of living." It created a cognitive opening for Westerners to seriously entertain non-Christian understandings of the world and our ultimate purpose in it.

But equally, many have argued, the eventual failure of much of the social agenda set by this generation, exemplified by the prolongation of the Vietnam War, the tragic assassinations of Robert Kennedy Jr. and Martin Luther King, and the infamous Watergate political scandal (1972–4), also swelled the ranks of the recruits to new religious movements. As some of the most engaged people in the social protest movements matured and became more cynical about politics, they sought to recentre themselves spiritually. Soon many were dedicating themselves to changing the world more gradually and intrinsically, one person at a time, by converting others to alternative paths to enlightenment and salvation (Bellah, 1976; Kent, 2001).

Fourth and finally, all of this was made possible, in some respects, by a crucial change in the immigration laws of the United States: the quiet repeal in 1965 of the policies of Asian exclusion. In Canada similar laws had been removed in 1947, but in practice Asian immigration had also been very restricted until well into the 1960s. This removed a significant impediment to the natural development of Eastern religious traditions in the West, allowing an influx of spiritual and religious leaders to foster and guide the growth of these traditions both in the communities of immigrants and amongst Western converts. This helped to advance the "normalization" of Hinduism and Buddhism in the West (e.g., Fields, 1981; Prebish, 1999).

We are now well past the peak level of new religious movements in the West and the corresponding cult scare. But the "cult wars" of the 1970s and 80s added a new and permanent element of diversity and pluralism to our societies. Today there are thousands of new religious movements operating in North America. The vast majority now receive little attention as they go quietly about their business. But certain events, such as the conversion of celebrities or prophecies of the imminent end of the world, can catch the attention of the public and bring them, for good or bad, into the news. In the largely post-Christian context of late modern societies, however, people feel much more free to be "metaphysical and spiritual seekers" (Roof, 1999) and a burgeoning new cultural industry exists to meet their needs (Forbes and Mahan, 2005).

Accusations of Brainwashing and Sexual Deviance

Legally the opponents of new religious movements, of specific groups and "cults" in general, recognize that they cannot take action against them on

the basis of the unorthodox, strange, or morally suspect nature of their belief and practices. This would violate the fundamental constitutional right
to religious freedom, and governments and the courts have no interest in
adjudicating between different religious teachings. But if it could be proven
that the beliefs and practices of these groups were harming people, especially in ways that violated existing laws, then the state could be called upon
for assistance in suppressing these new religions. Two kinds of accusations
in particular have figured prominently in the efforts to do this: converts to
new religious movements have been brainwashed, and many members, and
especially juvenile ones, are being encouraged to engage in sexually deviant
activities. These are complex issues that we can only address summarily
here, but the research spawned by these accusations has helped us to better
understand the processes of religious change and innovation and the hostility it often evokes, especially in a late modern social context.

The initial, most common, and still recurrent charge made against
new religious movements is that converts have been psychologically man-
ipulated into joining new religious movements through the illicit use of
techniques of brainwashing or mind control (Clark et al., 1981; Singer,
1995). The use of this term is specifically meant to suggest the loss of voli-
tion on the part of converts. If individuals have not freely chosen to belong,
then it can be argued that they are no longer competent to determine what
is in their best interests and either the parents of the young converts or
agencies of the government can circumvent the constitutional guarantee
of their freedom of religious expression and be granted the right to forcibly remove them from the religions in question and hold them against
their will to re-educate or "deprogram" them. In the 1970s and 80s quasi-
professional cult deprogrammers began to offer their services to families
and several court decisions initially supported their actions (e.g., Patrick
and Dulak, 1976; Hassan, 1988; www.rickross.com). But as more reliable
research became available and sociologists, psychologists, and religious
studies scholars started to provide expert testimony to the courts, this
trend was reversed (Young and Griffith, 1992). The notion that people
could be "brainwashed" to undertake actions against their will was dis-
missed as "unscientific"—it lacked the credibility required by the courts
(Anthony, 1990; Anthony and Robbins, 1992). In fact, the study of converts to the new religions tended to substantiate the opposite interpretation
of what was happening. Researchers came to understand that the process
of religious conversion is more active and interactive than previously recognized. People are not so much converted as they convert. This process
often involves some experimentation and role-playing prior to deciding to
become fully committed to a group. The conversion is the end point of a
gradual process, though often it may appear to outsiders that it is sudden,
and it involves an ongoing negotiation between the potential convert and

representatives of the religion (Lofland and Stark, 1965; Barker, 1984; Levine, 1984; Richardson, 1985).

This does not mean, however, that many new religions do not employ intense forms of social pressure to influence, recruit, and manipulate people. They do, and in ways that make most of us uncomfortable. In fact it is clear that many movements exploit the youthful enthusiasm of their converts, working them long and hard as volunteers for the cause. In principle and practice, however, the social manipulation of the converts is on a continuum with that characteristic of many other social institutions that we tend to accept as legitimate, ranging from school fraternities, competitive sporting teams, and the military to traditional religious orders and seminaries. In each case we must come to a judgement about the objectionable nature of the social pressure applied based on our estimation of the degree to which it violates some implicit ideal or conventional standard of personal autonomy. This is a difficult thing to determine without reverting to some form of prejudice—literally making a pre-judgement about the validity of the beliefs and practices of the religion. But in every case we need to develop a better understanding of the processes of resocialization and reconditioning (Wilson, 1984) that produce the dramatic changes witnessed in the behavior and lives of converts, and little is gained by belittling the participants by saying they have been brainwashed (see Dawson 2006a for a fuller discussion of this debate).

As accusations about brainwashing started to be stymied by the courts, more attention turned to the prevalent concerns about the sexual behavior of "cult" leaders and members. Through the ages it has been commonplace to discredit new religious ideas and groups by accusing them of sexual impropriety and debauchery (Jenkins, 2000). Some of the leaders of these new religious movements did experience controversial falls from grace when members found that they had indulged in sexual dalliances that violated their own teachings, and some women in particular came to feel that they had been sexually exploited by the gurus to whom they had dedicated their lives (Jacobs, 1984; Puttick, 1997). But these real abuses were occurring amidst the mounting controversy over the epidemic of child molestation charges levelled at priests in the Catholic Church (Jenkins, 1996), and the many high-profile sex scandals rocking the congregations of famous American televangelists and several large mega-churches (Shupe, 1998). We must guard against assuming, then, that new religions are in any way more susceptible to these moral failings than other more conventional religions.

In truth, however, they are more susceptible to the accusations, since new religions are more likely to experiment with alternative sexual relations. As Dawson observes (2006a: 131):

> Sexuality is a profoundly personal matter closely associated with our deepest self-understanding. In groups seeking to refashion the self to save the

world it is logical that sexuality should be a focal concern. The power relations in society are commonly reflected in its sexual customs, while the intimacy and ecstasy of sexual life itself has long been used to symbolically express human relations with the divine (e.g., from the arrows of Christ's love penetrating the heart of the great Spanish mystic Teresa of Avila to the erotic tales of the young Krishna in Hinduism). In controlling people's sexual activity, new religions are seeking to challenge conceptions of social power and relations with the divine. Sexuality provides a means of access to the human psyche, a means of redirecting attention from the limited rewards and worries of this world to the greater promise of another.

Ironically, while some new religions are taken to task for their experiments with so-called "free love," others are criticized for being too ascetic. Some groups seek to bring people closer to realizing their true natures, the purpose of life, and a proper relationship with God by encouraging them to engage in acts of sexual liberation designed to break the shackles of psychological repression imposed by the dominant Christian culture (e.g., The Farm, the Rajneesh movement, The Children of God/The Family). In the communal contexts common to these groups people are encouraged to couple more openly and widely, to indulge their fantasies, and use sex to commune with the power of the divine feminine that has been suppressed by centuries of religious patriarchy. Others advocate the opposite, stressing the spiritual virtue of practising strict chastity (e.g., the Unification Church, International Society for Krishna Consciousness, the Brahma Kumaris). Either way, it is deviation from the dominant middle class norms of American and Canadian society that is objectionable and invites ridicule.

But the controversies sparked by the challenges the new religions posed to the dominant conventions of sexual propriety and gender relations only served in the long run to heighten everyone's awareness of the dilemmas of moral relativity. As Dawson argues (2006a: 129), "[i]n the pluralistic context of life today there is no satisfactory way to identify the relevant standards of normalcy for determining the deviancy of any religiously justified sexual practice without running the risk of arbitrarily favouring one religious tradition over another."

Of course the most heated and damaging debates involve accusations of child abuse, sexual and otherwise, and throughout the last few decades individual parents and religious leaders have been accused and sometimes convicted of the neglect, molestation, manslaughter, and even murder of children in their care. These cases are rare and often the result of misguided efforts at corporal punishment, spiritual healing, or exorcisms. Accusations of sexual abuse often arise in contentious custody disputes, when a parent who has left a new religion is seeking to remove children from the care of the other who is still part of the group. Beginning in the 1980s, however, the anti-cult movement started making claims that all of the children in certain new religious movements were at risk. At their instigation, for example, several mass raids were made on the communal homes of The Children of God, later called The Family, in Argentina, Australia, France, Spain, and the United States. These raids traumatized hundreds of children and wrongfully imprisoned their parents. In each instance after many months of investigation the charges were dropped against the Children of God for lack of evidence, and in some cases the courts rebuked the officials involved for perverting the course of justice. But by then massive damage had been done to this new religion, first by the worldwide negative publicity, and second, through the draining-away their meagre funds to cover mounting legal expenses. Moreover, as Richardson comments (1999: 181), in these situations new religions "must adjust [their] priorities and alter [their] very shape, a short-term process that may well have long-lasting repercussions. In this way, the . . . organizational life [of the groups] becomes 'deformed' by the necessity of dealing with such pervasive external pressures."

On the other hand, David Berg, the prophetic leader of the Children of God, had foolishly cast propriety to the wind, as religious fanatics are inclined to do, and invited censure by publishing and promoting tracts extolling the natural sexuality of children and religiously sanctioning the sexual interaction of children and adults within the Children of God community. Few members in fact acted on Berg's suggestion, but some children were hurt and the group soon repudiated the views. The sheer audacity of entertaining such religious teachings, however, is but an extreme instance of the tendency to engage in the transgression of norms that is typical of most new religious movements, like Jesus associating with publicans (tax collectors for the Romans) and prostitutes to shock and invert the staid moral standards of the Jewish religious elites of his day or the Buddha forfeiting his legacy as a prince to wander the countryside, living on charity, to bring enlightenment to the masses.

In these and other ways too diverse to discuss here, new religions often court opposition and their opponents often succeed in discrediting and derailing them. But other groups seem to spring up with alacrity to take their place, and to the surprise of many, religious innovation is rife in the late modern world (see Box 8.2).

The Social Significance of New Religious Movements

We are discovering that there have been many more new religious movements throughout the course of Western history than was commonly appreciated (Jenkins, 2000; Albanese, 2007). The difference is that, in the modern context of state secularism and *de facto* religious pluralism, people can be more open in expressing their alternative views. They do not need to fear being systematically persecuted, imprisoned, or even killed for their unconventional beliefs. As indicated, however, misunderstanding and suspicion are still prevalent and members of new religions run the risk being stigmatized, ridiculed, and sometimes even prosecuted. This very reality points to the first of several ways in which the existence and spread of new religious movements is socially significant, despite the relatively small size of almost all these religions. The social problem of "cults"—to use the more popular and pejorative term—raises doubts about the place of religion in late modern societies. Deep and sincere religious commitments make people uncomfortable in our age of reason, leisure, prosperity, and technology. "The numerous legal disputes involving charges of brainwashing against cults," Dawson observes (2007: 118), "have been prompted by a perceived violation of the norms of everyday life in modern societies. These societies highly value freedom and individual choice, yet not when it is exercised in a manner that defies expectations about what is 'normal.' Young people are to pursue education and prepare for jobs, not dedicate their lives to the study of esoteric religious texts, meditation, or the saving of souls." As Émile Durkheim theorized long ago, however, deviants serve an indispensable social function: their identification reveals and reinforces the contours of the values really shaping a society, and given this mirroring function societies will always find people to identify as deviants to help distinguish what matters most to the rest.

It could also be said that new religions actively court this deviant label and social role because they represent, in many ways, either forms of protest against the deficiencies of late modern societies or laboratories for social experimentation linked to broader processes of social change. These functions are not fully separate, but we will treat them as the second and third ways of understanding the social significance of new religious movements.

Many of the scholars studying new religions have assumed, with some justification, that when people turn to these groups they are driven by a desire to escape some of the anomic and alienating effects of life in modern societies. Most often it is thought that converts are looking for the greater normative clarity and comradeship associated, rightly or wrongly, with a bygone and more religious era. Unhappy with the plethora of choices we face in fashioning a sense of ourselves in the late modern context, and sensing that many of the choices available are contrived and superficial, converts are said to be seeking to "resacralize daily life by anchoring [their] private activities and identities, and to some extent even public ones, in institutions conceived once again as reflections of the natural, cosmic, or divine order" (Dawson, 2007: 119). They are seeking to resurrect Berger's "sacred canopy" (see Chapter 4). They want firm guidance in determining how best to deal with issues of courtship, sexuality, gender roles, marriage, childrearing, consumption, vocations, education, and health. They want their choices to be undergirded and unified by a higher sense of purpose and of permanence (Hunter, 1981).

Box
8.2

The Fiery Fate of the Solar Temple

On the morning of 4 October 1994 a blaze engulfed a complex of luxury condominiums in the resort town of Morin Heights, in the Laurentian Mountains just north of Montreal. Firefighters found the bodies of a Swiss couple, Gerry and Collette Genoud, in the ruins. At first it was thought that the fire was accidental; then news arrived from Switzerland of another decidedly odd set of fires at homes owed by the same men who owned the Quebec condominiums. On 5 October, in the burned remains of a farmhouse at Cheiry, the Swiss police found 23 bodies of people who had been shot once in the head after taking some kind of sedative. Most of the bodies were found in several hidden and obviously ceremonial chambers. They were dressed in silk capes and arranged in a circle, and many had plastic bags over their heads. One hundred kilometres away at fires in three vacation chalets in Granges-sur-Salvan, Swiss authorities found 25 more bodies burned beyond recognition. All of the fires had been set with improvised incendiary devices, and the police knew they were dealing with a rare incidence of mass murder-suicide. Returning to the condominiums in Morin Heights on 6 October the Quebec police detected evidence of the same improvised devices and a further search uncovered three more bodies hidden in a storage closet. Antonio Dutoit, a Swiss citizen, had been stabbed 50 times. His British wife had been stabbed 13 times, including once in each breast. Their baby, three-month-old Christopher Emmanuel, had been stabbed six times, particularly in the heart. In addition, the police reported that Mrs. Dutoit and the baby had been "bled white" (Hall, 2000: 112).

Soon it became apparent that all of the dead were members of an esoteric religious group known as The Solar Temple. The group had been founded in the early 1980s by the Swiss owner of a chain of jewellery stores, Joseph Di Mambro, and was co-led by Luc Jouret, a successful Belgian homeopathic doctor. Di Mambro, long steeped in the study of Western esoteric traditions, was the ideological leader of the group; the charismatic Jouret was the front man. They were participating in a movement of groups imaginatively tracing their origins back to the Knights Templar, a medieval mystical order of warriors, which in turn formed a subset of a larger movement focused on Rosicrucianism, a neo-Christian mystical brotherhood of supposedly ancient lineage. The Solar Temple never had more than a few hundred members, drawn largely from the middle classes and the well-to-do of Switzerland, France, and Quebec, but tens of thousands of Europeans and North Americans participate in the larger Rosicrucian movement. After its success in recruiting new members in Quebec, the Solar Temple relocated much of its activity there, establishing a farming commune outside of Quebec City.

From the recorded and written message left behind by the group it is clear that the leaders felt it was time to effect what they called a "transit" to another reality associated with Sirius, the Dog Star, in order to escape mounting persecution. In fact the group had drawn the attention of police and anti-cult activists in several countries. But the significance of the threat had been exaggerated by the leaders to inflate the group's sense of self-importance and to deflect growing dissension in its ranks. Those killed at Morin Heights and Cheiry were dissenters calling into question the legitimacy of the leadership and practices of Di Mambro and Jouret, and it is suspected this internal struggle helped to pre-cipitate the tragic events of October 1994 (for a fuller account see Mayer, 1999; Introvigne, 1999; Hall, 2000). The murder of the Dutoit baby, for example, was like-ly rooted in the belief that he was a competitor for the messianic role given to Di Mambro's "cosmic child" Emmanuelle.

In a surprising further testament to the strength of the beliefs and commit-ments of members of this new religion, however, sixteen more people took their own lives in a similar "transit" ceremony on the winter equinox of 1995 in a wooded moun-tain area of France, and five more committed suicide near Quebec City around the spring equinox of 1997. These deaths attracted massive media attention. They were part of a series of similar cult-related episodes of mass violence in the last quarter of the twentieth century, beginning with the death of 914 members of the Peoples Temple in 1978, then the 80 people who died in the Branch Davidian fiasco of 1993, the deaths of 12 and injury of thousands in the terrorist attack perpetrated by Aum Shinrikyo in 1995, the suicide of 39 members of Heaven's Gate in 1997, and finally the murder-suicide of 780 members of the Movement for the Restoration of the Ten Commandments in 2000.

In examining these complicated and shocking incidents, scholars stress how exceptional this kind of violence is, since there are tens of thousands of new re-ligious movements around the world. Further, each tragedy is rooted in a unique set of events and contexts. But it is possible to detect a similar dynamic at work that provides important information about why some new religions become vio-lent. In each case the movement towards extremism was precipitated by an intense focus on apocalyptic beliefs, an excessive dependence on precarious forms of char-ismatic authority, and the near complete social encapsulation of the groups. The apocalyptic beliefs helped to imbue the groups with a sense of urgency, set them in opposition to much of the rest of society, and dehumanized their enemies. The focus on often unstable charismatic leaders set in play an internal dynamic of one-upmanship as the leaders perpetually sought to bolster their authority by increas-ing the demands of the followers, isolating them, and increasing their commit-ment through the invention of threats and enemies. The resultant encapsulation cut off the groups from the healthy negative feedback that all systems, biological, mechanical, and social, need to maintain the balance of perspectives and actions required to adapt to changing circumstances.

No one of these factors accounts for the radicalization to violence that occurred in these new religious movements. It is their combination, in conjunction with ag-gravating responses from the rest of society, which fostered the sense that there was no recourse other than violence. The analysis of the nature and interaction of these three factors far exceeds the scope of this book. But it is important to realize that even these highly unusual and sensational socio-religious phenomena can be explained, in large measure, by the careful acquisition of a detailed understanding of the groups' histories, their ways of seeing the world, and what transpired, in com-bination with the judicious use of existing theoretical and empirical insights from other areas of sociology and social psychology (see e.g., Bromley, 2002 and Dawson, 2006a). With this knowledge in hand, perhaps other tragedies can be averted.

"Marriage, for example, is less likely to be followed by divorce if it is understood again as a religious and eternal commitment and not merely a personal act" (Dawson, 2007: 119). This essentially "demodernizing" impulse, to the extent that it is present in new religions, can provide us, then, with some insights into the ways in which are current societies are failing to meet the fundamental needs of some people.

On the other hand, and sometimes even simultaneously, new religions "function as forums for a vital degree of quasi-legitimate social experimentation in a pluralistic society" (Dawson, 2007: 122). Thomas Robbins and David Bromley (1992, 1993) argue that many new religious movements are exploring alternative kinds of sexuality and gender relations, economic and social organization, proselytizing and persuasion, and healing and therapy. While some new religions are seeking to alleviate the uncertainty of living in late modern times by reasserting patriarchal patterns of authority, for example (e.g., Krishna Consciousness; the Unification Church, the Happy-Healthy-Holy movement, and most Christian splinter groups), many others are trying to drive the last nail into the coffin of patriarchy, as found in most of our traditional religions (e.g., Theosophy, the Church Universal and Triumphant, the neo/pagan and Wiccan movement, the Rajneesh/Osho movement, and many aspects of the New Age movement). These new religions glorify and celebrate the divine feminine in their beliefs and rites, and they elevate women into positions of leadership and authority (see Aidala, 1985; Palmer, 1994). On the economic and organizational front, to cite another example, many new religions have shattered the traditional normative boundaries (if not real ones) separating the worlds of business and religion. Operating in an age of global consumerism, they have forged international corporate empires to support their religious missions, manufacturing and/or selling a diverse range of products, spiritual and otherwise, to support their religious activities (e.g., The Church of Jesus Christ of Latter-day Saints, the Unification Church, the Church Universal and Triumphant, Transcendental Meditation, Scientology, Soka Gakkai, and many forms of New Age and neo-pagan religion and splinter Christian groups). In fact, they have been very inventive in revising ways of tying the process of recruitment and conversion and the progression of members through the faith to the provision and purchase of books, taped lectures, DVDs, music, jewellery clothing, art, ritual instruments, and other religious paraphernalia (see Richardson, 1988). In this regard, many groups also are surprisingly adept at harnessing new communication technologies to spread their message (e.g., radio, television, the Internet, smartphone applications), even when this message is anti-modern in its ideological thrust. This means they are willing to have their members trained in the technology and to pour their resources into the creation and support of the infrastructure needed to succeed. Unlike many of the older sectarian forms of new religion (e.g., the Amish, certain orthodox Jewish groups), and contrary to popular expectations, they see no contradiction between their moral and spiritual impetus and the exploitation of cutting-edge technology. Many new religions have been in the vanguard, then, in the adaptation of cutting-edge communication technologies to age-old religious purposes (Dawson and Cowan, 2004).

Conclusion

People living in late modern societies must learn to cope with, or perhaps even embrace, a degree of religious pluralism that is unprecedented. Since religions speak to the most personal and ultimate concerns of individuals, and often provide the legitimation for the core values used to identify and differentiate groups, they are frequently the source of division and dissension in society. They pit people against one another, especially if the religious commitments are taken seriously. This potential is worrisome, and all the more so when a society is transitioning from a lived experience of near total identification with just one religious tradition (i.e., Christianity) to one where it can no longer be assumed that others share the same religious worldview—where it is conspicuous, in fact, that many do not. Mere tolerance will likely not be enough to sustain the social harmony and collaboration required to make Canada the kind of peaceful and prosperous society we desire in the face of a populace divided amongst mainstream Christians, sectarian Christians, Jews, Muslims, Buddhists, Hindus, and others, as well as various kinds of religious nones and new religious movements. The religious identity of Canada is in flux and we need to be tracking the changes and their consequences. A policy of public secularism, of acting as if religion is a strictly private matter, can serve to keep clashes based on blatant religious differences in check, but it is insufficient whenever greater numbers of people choose to assert their constitutional right to express their religious identities in meaningful and public ways.

Within Canada an interesting social experiment has begun. On the one hand, the province of Quebec, under the umbrella of interculturalism, is emulating the French model of *laïcité* (or secularism), enacting policies to directly regulate and suppress religious behaviour in public and encouraging more complete assimilation into the dominant French Canadian culture, while implicitly favouring the Catholic heritage of Quebec (e.g., refusing to remove the crucifix above the speaker's chair in the Legislative Assembly). On the other hand, the rest of Canada, with some variability, is committed for the foreseeable future to a quite robust policy of multiculturalism, whereby immigrants and others are helped to find ways to express their diverse cultural and religious identities while promoting the larger shared value of inclusion and acceptance of differences as something typically Canadian. Two quite different ways of responding to one of the most telling and unavoidable challenges of globalization are being pursued within the borders of one nation. This is an extraordinary situation, and yet both approaches are equally hard to delineate, manage, and assess; sociologists could play a key role in gathering and analyzing the data needed to bring greater clarity.

Overall, though, the institutions of Canada—legal, educational, medical, and political— need to adjust in more sophisticated ways to the diverse and even seemingly deviant yet protected forms of religious expression that will be demanding equal and fair treatment. Explicitly and implicitly, the traditional conceptions of religion (i.e., modern Christianity) which Canada inherited will no longer serve as reasonable guides for instituting the social control, social solidarity, and social change required to keep our society vibrant and progressive.

Critical Thinking Questions

1. Are Canadian government officials and educators rightfully fearful of discussing religion? If you think they are, then why? Are there ways of avoiding the problems you perceive?

2. What does multiculturalism mean, and is it a realistic public policy objective?

3. Are you a religious "none"? If so, in what sense and why?

4. Did the discussion in this chapter challenge your preconceptions about new religious movements? If so, how?

5. Do you think new religious movements are a social problem? If you do, what are your reasons? Or are they an inevitable part of life in late modernity?

Suggested Readings

Bramadat, Paul and David Seljak, eds. 2005. *Religion and Ethnicity in Canada*. Toronto, ON: Pearson. This book captures the lived realities and experiences of those in Canada's six "major minority" religious groups (Hindus, Sikhs, Buddhists, Chinese, Jews, and Muslims), as well as the implications of religious diversity for public policy, education, and health care.

Bramadat, Paul and David Seljak, eds. 2008. *Christianity and Ethnicity in Canada*. Toronto, ON: University of Toronto Press. This book uniquely examines the growing ethnic diversity within Christianity, giving particular attention to migration patterns, changing religious beliefs and practices, institutional completeness, racism and religious discrimination, the role of women, and intergenerational challenges.

Zuckerman, Phil. 2012. *Faith No More: Why People Reject Religion*. New York: Oxford University Press. This book summarizes findings from 87 face-to-face interviews with Americans who say they have "no religion" and documents leading explanations for conversion and de-conversion to this "religious" category.

Dawson, Lorne L. 2006. *Comprehending Cults: The Sociology of New Religious Movements*. 2nd ed. Toronto: Oxford University Press. Organized around many of the most common questions raised about new religions, such as why new religious movements emerged, who joins them and why, whether converts are brainwashed, and why some become violent, this book provides a comprehensive overview of the relevant social scientific literature.

Related Websites

http://religionanddiversity.ca

The Religion and Diversity Project, hosted by the University of Ottawa, is an interdisciplinary exploration into the contours of religious diversity in Canada, including how religious identities are socially constructed, how religious expression is defined and delimited in law and public policy, how and why gender and sexuality act as flashpoints in debates about religious freedom, and how Canada can respond to the various opportunities and challenges presented by religious diversity in ways that promote a just and peaceful society.

www.has.vcu.edu/wrs/index.html

The World Religions and Spirituality Project website provides comprehensive summaries, videos, and scholarly resources pertaining to contemporary religious and spiritual movements, established world religions, and historical religious and spiritual movements, including information about each group's beliefs, rituals, organization, and leadership, and current issues and challenges. This website is especially useful for learning about new religious movements.

9 Summary and Conclusions

The chapters of this book, with their array of diverse topics and debates, actually tell a pretty integrated tale, but one defined by a repeated tension between two points of view about what things mean and how they will end. On the whole it is a historical narrative of change across the generations, of decline, misfortune and even death. Yet there is a repeated subplot of curious and unexplained happenings that hint at some kind of partial redemption for some of the characters, and in the end a sense of mystery prevails. In the closing lines of this "story" there is a marked sense of nostalgia and sadness about what was prized and is now lost. But there is also an abiding sense that something more profound and pertinent persists, despite all that has changed. Our appreciation of some deeper element of the human condition may even have strengthened with the eclipse of old and comfortable ways of being religious and the emergence of new opportunities and ways of being religious. But we are not sure, for not enough information is available.

On the one hand, the numbers do not lie. Religion as it has been practised traditionally, which means primarily congregational forms of Christianity, has experienced steady decline and misfortune, and some denominations (e.g., the Anglican Church of Canada) may not be far from death, at least as significant institutions. Since the 1960s fewer and fewer Canadians are attending church services with regularity, or maintaining their membership in the churches. Canadian children, with the partial exception of those in Catholic schools, are no longer being socialized into these religions. The conventional forms of religious practice that played an important role in the lives of Canadians throughout the history of this country are disappearing, and the religious institutions that provided those services already have lost most of their social significance. Politicians no longer seek to establish their conventional religious credentials, as they still do in the United States, to curry favour with the electorate. On the contrary, for some time they have avoided any public displays of their religious commitments for fear of offending the dominant consensus that one's religion is a private matter and should have little bearing on the determination of public policy. This does not mean that traditional church-going forms of Christianity will disappear from Canada. We are not about to witness the complete secularization of the nation. But this form of religious expression, the one that set the template for how ordinary people and most sociologists conceive of religion, has been reduced to a minority position, with less than a quarter of the population continuing to care enough to attend and support the churches.

Of course in some ways many of these traditional churches, individually and as denominations, are not quite so traditional any more. Efforts have been made to adapt their liturgies and activities to the times. New forms of music, preaching, social activities, schedules, and services have been introduced to attract a younger crowd. But for the most part the hair of the parishioners just keeps getting greyer and the basic beliefs, structure, and expectations of the churches remain much the same. Too often the success of the innovations is variable, and much depends on the ingenuity and the charisma of individual leaders. The pervasive norm linking religious practice with social respectability and trustworthiness has evaporated from our society and been replaced, for many Canadians, by a suspicion that the proponents of more conservative forms of Christianity, whether Protestant or Catholic, are now dangerously out of step with the core values of tolerance, individualism, and freedom of expression so characteristic of an increasingly pluralistic and multicultural Canada.

In most respects these developments are in line with what the founding figures of sociology, Marx, Durkheim, and Weber, expected—pointing to the incompatibility of religion with the social structures and attitudes most characteristic of modernity. The decline of traditional religion is not unique in this regard. Rather, religion is simply being impacted, like many others aspects of our social lives (e.g., education, families, work), by the processes of de-traditionalization and globalization, and the rising tide of expressive individualism typical of late modern societies.

On the other hand, studies consistently reveal that Canadians, like the citizens of the other Western European nations that have experienced secularization at the societal and organizational levels, continue to claim an interest in the big questions about the meaning of life, life after death, and suffering—the questions that have driven religious thought and practice through the ages. We may now appear to be secularized at the personal level as well, since most Canadians select not to go to church on a Sunday morning (or any other time). There are so many other seemingly more important and interesting things to do. But belief in God remains high and Canadians continue to demand access to the religious rites that traditionally mark the major passages of life (e.g., birth, marriage, and death). Many Canadians also engage in alternative ways of meeting their more immediate spiritual needs, whether by reading and discussing such best-selling pop spirituality books as Deepak Chopra's *The Seven Spiritual Laws of Success*, Neale Donald Walsch's *Conversations with God*, and Eckhart Tolle's *The Power of Now*, or by taking up the practice of some popular form of yoga (e.g., Moksha Hot Yoga), meditation (e.g.,Vipassana) or alternative healing (e.g., Ayruvedic or Quigong). At this point we do not have an accurate sense of how pervasive these ideas and activities are in Canada. With a few exceptions (e.g., Emberley, 2002; Chandler, 2008, 2010, 2011), the relevant research has yet to be done. But the sheer frequency with which these new ways of being "religious" capture the attention of the pubic (through the media), and their successful commercialization, suggests that the religious landscape is changing. In line with developments elsewhere (e.g., see Roof, 1999; Heelas, 2008), many Canadians will continue to be religious, or, as they often prefer to say "spiritual," but in new, more diffuse, and personal ways.

Ironically this new religiosity is equally a product of the social structural changes and processes associated with the onset of late modernity. What has broken the old mould is shaping a new one. The disintegration of traditional ways, brought on in part by the rising educational levels and heightened geographic mobility of the population, has opened a cognitive space, so to speak, for the emergence of alternative religious beliefs and practices. This applies both to those religions that have always been with us but which have been suppressed, such as paganism and witchcraft, and those that have been imported, such as Islam, Buddhism, and Hinduism. Most people now are free to experiment with these new types of religious expression without fear of social rejection or stigma. In fact, in many social circles the quest for new spiritual experiences is actively encouraged. It is all part of appearing "with it" and enlightened. The religious changes are emblematic of the triumph of expressive individualism, and the pervasive quest to find one's true self or develop one's full potential has dramatically heightened the interest in new religious experiences. The presence of the alternative religions, of the ideas, groups, and leaders required to indulge the new spiritual appetites, is a straightforward and graphic manifestation of globalization.

In this regard, as we have seen, the very growth in those choosing to tell researchers that they have no religion is ambiguous. People drift in and out of the religious "none" category over the course of their lives and many of those claiming to have no religion actually hold certain religious beliefs or engage in religious activities. They are declaring their current unwillingness to be affiliated with traditional religious identities and groups, not their irreligiousness. But as this indicates, much depends on what we mean by "religious." It has always been difficult to differentiate religion from the welter of other kinds of social activities and commitments with which it shares some features, and the formal and informal conceptions of religion, those espoused by the state and by individuals, can be variant even in societies dominated by a single religious tradition (e.g., Hinduism in India, or Catholicism in Italy). Under the conditions of pluralism characteristic of globalized late modern societies, such as the large urban centres of Canada, the harmonization of subjective and objective conceptions of religion, which Berger theorizes is typical of traditional societies, is in fact atypical. Religion is almost by definition a subjective matter, a matter of choice, and a way of differentiating individuals. This tendency is recognized in the law of Canada through the application of the sincerity test to unconventional beliefs. If it can be indicated that someone holds an unusual religious position sincerely, then in most cases their behaviour, no matter how controversial, falls under the protections provided for the freedom of religious expression by the Canadian Charter of Rights and Freedoms.

How, though, is sincerity to be determined? More often than not the courts, like people in everyday life, must look to the presence of other signs of religiosity, such as participation in rituals, claims to extraordinary experiences, and whether the beliefs are shared and used to regulate social relations and interactions in some way. In other words, questions of definition, even in very practical circumstances, hinge on having some knowledge of the nature and range of the most basic elements of "religious" life. In these ways the patterns of behaviour associated with religion in the past continue to cast a defining shadow over the credibility of religious innovations today. Paradoxically, the secular courts of Canada, and elsewhere in the late modern world, must become more steeped in an understanding of the complex realities and ambiguities of religiosity in order to apply the constitution in cases involving religious claims to avoid simply reinforcing naive notions of orthodoxy or what constitutes religion.

The most pragmatic way to escape the seemingly endless debates over the definition of religion, we argue, is to apply Wittgenstein's notion of "family resemblance." In doing so, however, we must become finely attuned to the ethnocentric (i.e., largely Christocentric in Canada) legacy of the language and ideas we use to talk about "religion" in the popular and specialized discourses of the West. With the intrusion of many new forms of "spiritual" practice into our societies, including ones that look like religion but deny that they are, and ones that claim to be religious but are doubted by many, the need to be observant of our explicit and implicit prejudices will increase. This will hold true, in particular, for the many Canadians who simply are no longer religious or who have an antipathy to religion. The denial of all public expression of religion in order to prevent any one religion from supposedly gaining an advantage over others is a disingenuous way of suppressing all religions in the name of protecting them. Militant secularism is not a prerequisite for the preservation of civil rights, but moderation and civility in the expression of religion in the public sphere probably is necessary. In most Western societies the suppression of religious minorities by religious majorities, with the assistance of the state, is a thing of the past. But more often than not, religious rights are now offset by other rights, and absolute claims to religious freedom are being displaced by complicated assessments of the relative interests of the public.

The Church of the Universe, for example, has the right in Canada to treat marijuana as sacred and to use it, in private, as a sacrament. This does not give it the right, however, to violate the existing laws restricting the growth and distribution of marijuana (*R. v. Kharaghani and Styrsky*, 2011). In response to the constitutional challenge launched by the church the court found, given the flimsy standards of membership in the church, that these laws constitute a reasonable limit on the freedom of religious expression (Lewis, 2011). This and other legal disputes, however, have opened a can of worms, since they hinge on coming to a workable definition of religion, something that has yet to be achieved in the Canadian legal system. Someday another unconventional yet more developed religion will have reason to fight this fight again over some infringement of their activities (e.g., Santo Daime), and then there will be less practical wiggle room for a judge to render a decision based on the credibility of the group's religious activities.

The plight of the courts is not unique. Everywhere one looks in Canada the study of our own religious sensibilities and activities is hindered by a lack of appropriate primary data. Reginald Bibby, whom we have cited repeatedly in these pages, has provided us with a unique and longitudinal pool of quantitative data on the state of religion in Canada, and students interested in knowing where we are religiously should take full advantage of the findings of his repeated national surveys (see e.g., Bibby, 2011). We lack, however, the more fine-grained and comprehensive qualitative data, from interviews with individuals, required to really understand the meaning of many of Bibby's findings, as well as the results of other polls taken to capture the views of Canadians about religion. From the limited qualitative research available we know that there are many reasons why people choose to do similar things, such as attend religious services with regularity, or attend sporadically but nevertheless remain members of churches, or attend only for rites of passage and Christmas and Easter celebrations, or claim to have "no religion" (e.g., Thiessen, 2010, 2012). Likewise, there is no simple and consistent reason why growing numbers of Canadians claim to be "spiritual but not religious" or practise a wide array of alternative forms of spirituality (e.g., Chandler, 2011). Why, for example, was a novel like *The Celestine Prophecy*, rich in New Age ideas and imagery but largely seen as lacking literary merit, on the bestseller list of the *New York Times* for 165 weeks? Why was it translated into 34 languages? What is the nature of the appeal of this book? Is it merely entertainment and therefore unworthy of serious academic consideration? Or, in line with other aspects of popular culture, is the phenomenal success of this book indicative of a significant shift in the larger sensibilities of people, including the many millions of Canadians who read it and recommended it to their friends and family? We do not know, because we have not bothered to explore these and many related questions about the meaning of the experiences of Canadians with things religious or spiritual, whether great or small, in the course of their daily lives.

Better headway is being made with the study of the religion of immigrants to Canada and the resulting introduction of new religious beliefs and practices to Canada (Beyer, 2005). Most of this research is in the form of case studies, many of which are informed by participant observation in the communities and interviews with their members (e.g., McLellan, 1999, 2009; Bramadat and Seljak, 2005; Harding, Hori and Soucy, 2010; Campbell, 2011; Scott, 2012). Given the status of regular churchgoers in Canada today perhaps we should start to treat them as an exotic minority as well and hence worthy of more attention. We need to undertake an anthropological or micro-sociological analysis of the religious worldviews and activities of ordinary Canadians, on a par with studies of immigrants and followers of some new religions. To this end it is time for us to slough off the complacency toward religion implanted in our collective psyche by decades of experience with a dominant and, for the most part, nominal Christianity.

In the end, though, more and better data may only ameliorate and not resolve the basic interpretive tension in the sociology of religion over the meaning of the findings for the future of religion in Canada. The proclivities of the authors of this book reflect the complexities of the situation. Counter-intuitively, the author who is conventionally religious doubts the viability and significance of the many forms of private and popular religiosity detected amongst contemporary Canadians, while the author who never has been religious sees encouraging signs of the continued significance of religion as a guiding and motivating force in the lives of Canadians in the popular and unconventional spiritual interests and activities of many Canadians. It is likely that the clash of these interpretive options will continue to drive the sociology of religion forward for some time, but the debate will remain important only if we can turn from educated guesses about what is happening to detailed arguments about specific developments based on fuller data.

In thinking about religion in contemporary Canada we started with some of the seminal insights of Max Weber about religion in general and it is fitting to end on the same note. Reflecting on the role of religion in human affairs over the long course of history Weber wrote ([1915] 1958b: 280):

> The . . . idea of redemption . . . is very old, if one understands by it a liberation from distress, hunger, drought, sickness, and ultimately from suffering and death. Yet redemption attained a specific significance only where it expressed a systematic and rationalized "image of the world" and represented a stand in the face of the world. For the meaning as well as the intended and actual psychological quality of redemption has depended upon such a world image and such a stand. Not ideas, but material and ideal interests, directly govern [people's] conduct. Yet very frequently the "world images" that have been created by "ideas" have, like switchmen, determined the tracks along which action has been pushed by the dynamic

of interest. "From what" and "for what" one wished to be redeemed and, let us not forget, "could be" redeemed, depended upon one's image of the world.

If we no longer require redemption, then religion will no longer have a function to serve for us, either individually or as a society. Certainly there is no longer one common world image or switchman in Canada today, or one shared notion of from what or for what we need to be saved. But as Weber also stressed, the world never fails to resist and confound our desires and rational expectations, and in the age of mounting global risks and heightened awareness of the liabilities of our own inventiveness, the urge for redemption may continue to inspire social creations that look like religions and that we will need to study and understand.

Glossary

Anomie and alienation In Berger's theory of religion people gain protection from anomie—a threatening sense of normlessness and lack of meaning—by believing in the teachings of religions and becoming alienated, estranged from and unaware of their own creative role, as members of their culture and society, in the creation of a meaningful world order.

Brainwashing New religious movements or "cults" are commonly accused of using brainwashing techniques to recruit and retain their members. This term stems from a crude transliteration of the Chinese characters used to designate the process of forced political education used by the Communist Chinese to bring dissents in line with the new regime instituted after the revolution of 1949—techniques later employed by the North Koreans on American prisoners of war during the Korean War (1950–53). The term popularly implies that converts to new religions have lost control over their own consciousness and become enslaved to the demands of the "cult" leaders.

Collective conscience and collective effervescence These are the two terms Durkheim coined to characterize the source of power people feel in the presence of the sacred and in the performance of rituals. *Collective conscience* refers to the cumulative knowledge and wisdom of a society as embodied in the teachings and symbols of religions. *Collective effervescence* refers to the excited state of mind experienced in the presence of large groups engaged in solemn or celebratory activities. The combined psychological effect of being exposed to the collective conscience and collective effervescence in the context of religious rituals generates the sense of strength people call upon to endure in the face of suffering and other hardships.

Compensators In the earlier version of Stark's theory, religion is identified with the supply of certain highly general compensations for the most scarce rewards sought by humans, such as the promise of immortality after death as reward for good behaviour in this life.

Diversity versus pluralism It has been argued that the term *diversity* should be restricted to designating the presence of different beliefs and practices in a society with regard to such things as religion, race, ethnicity, socioeconomic status, education, family background, or sexual orientation; while *pluralism* should be used to denote something more than mere diversity. It refers to a social condition in which people understand their own beliefs, actively seek to understand beliefs and practices of others, and are willing to engage in dialogue and interaction with members of other groups.

Elective affinity The insightful phrase used by Weber to identify the way in which ideas, often religious in nature, and material conditions combine in the course of human history to bring about fortuitous social changes with momentous and unanticipated consequences, as illustrated by the way the pursuit of salvation in Protestant Europe provided the motivational foundation for the rise of capitalism.

Exchange between humans and gods In the later version of Stark's theory, religious life is analyzed in terms of the conditions influencing the nature of the exchanges envisioned between humans and gods in terms of the relative rewards and costs of the different kinds of transactions imagined.

Family resemblance The reference in this case is to Wittgenstein's argument that there is no definitive list of criteria for defining anything; rather, we must operate as ordinary people do in life, recognizing that things share enough of a resemblance to warrant being classed together.

Functional definitions of religion Definitions that attempt to differentiate religion from other things by identifying what it primarily "does."

Globalization The process by which everyone on the planet is becoming socially integrated, intentionally or otherwise, with everyone else, through the worldwide spread of multinational economic, political, social, and cultural institutions, and other patterns of activity. It also designates the new identification people are developing with humanity as a whole and not just their more local group identities.

His Dominion This phrase describes the Protestant vision of the ideal society, in line with the supposed will of God and redolent with millennial overtones, that guided much of public life in Canada in the nineteenth and early twentieth centuries. As N. Keith Clifford states (1977: 24), it "implied a homogeneous population with a shared heritage of political democracy and evangelical Protestant Christianity," and it resulted in efforts to restrict and re-socialize any newcomers to Canada who did not share this vision, like the Chinese or the Ukrainians.

Homo religiosus The term coined by Mircea Eliade to designate just how thoroughly religious almost all humans were until the last few hundred years. It is widely used now by religious studies scholars to indicate the possibility that humans may be inherently religious because of their long evolutionary exposure to a religious worldview.

Individualism The belief that the desires, rights, and talents of the individual are of paramount social significance. For most of human history the daily life experiences of people were very similar. Social life was based on some rudimentary distinctions based on gender and some differences in abilities (e.g., those who could hunt well had more prestige). People understood their identity, consequently, in terms of the groups to which they belonged, and on which they depended for survival. As the material conditions of life improved and societies became more complex, more attention could be focused on the differences between individuals, and one's social identity was increasingly matched by the pursuit of a unique identity based on aspects of personality and individual achievements.

Institutional completeness This term refers to the capacity of some subgroups to be fairly self-sufficient and isolated from the broader society, to be capable of meeting the needs of their members in areas such as education, religion, employment, food, clothing, economic activity, medical care, and social assistance.

Marginal religious affiliates This is the label Bibby and Thiessen use to designate individuals who formally identify with a particular denomination or religion but normally attend religious services only irregularly, primarily on holidays and other special occasions. Today such marginal affiliates may well constitute the majority of people in Canada who still say they are religious. The question is, just how "religious" are they?

Mysterium tremendum The key descriptive phrase that Rudolf Otto used to describe the experience of the holy, the core irrational experience of religion, which distinguishes it, he claimed, from all other social and psychological phenomena.

No religion/religious nones These are the terms sociologists use to identify the people who check the "no religion" box for survey questions about their religious affiliation. For decades only a tiny minority of individuals did so, even if large numbers of people did not actually practise their religions. But in recent years the number choosing this option has grown dramatically, indicating a shift in sensibilities.

Nomos This is the Latin term Berger uses to identify the meaningful world order people are compelled to create to fend off the chaos and danger posed by the natural world into which we are born, individually and as a species.

"Opium of the people" This is the famous phrase used by Marx to characterize religion, referring to its role both in softening the blow of the hardships imposed on the lower classes of society by the ruling system and classes and in distracting people from identifying and addressing the political sources of their distress.

Pluralism This is the term used to designate the situation in which some singular or relatively unified set of ideas, practices, or groups is displaced by a more complex and fragmented interaction of multiple belief systems, ways of doing things, or social groups and organizations. This often also entails a change in values whereby no one set of beliefs, practices, or groups is thought to be intrinsically superior to another.

Polarization In this context the term refers to the tendency of people to gravitate to more extreme views about religion, primarily in terms of their being either very religious, representing one pole of a spectrum of possibilities, or utterly uninterested in or even actively opposed to religion, representing the other pole of the spectrum. The number of people occupying one of these poles is growing, suggesting we are entering a time marked by increased polarization with regard to religion.

Protestant ethic Weber argued that the ascetic impulse at the heart of early capitalism was derived from the influence of two religious doctrines, *calling* and *predestination*, on the heirs of the Protestant Reformation on Europe. These doctrines unintentionally created a pervasive ethical emphasis on the virtues of hard work and self-sacrifice.

Quasi- and para-religions These terms are used to identify forms of religious expression that diverge from conventional conceptions of religion and often involve a blurring of the distinctions used to separate the sacred and profane. Sociologists use the terms to call attention to forms of religious expression, change, and innovation that are unlikely to be incorporated into official statistical measures of religious activity and beliefs.

Quiet Revolution By most conventional measures of religiosity, the province of Quebec had long been one of the most religious societies in the world, comparable to Ireland and Italy. Catholicism was an integral part of the French Canadian identity in the face of the English and predominantly Protestant identity of the rest of Canada and the United States. But in the late 1950s and early 1960s a sweeping cultural revolution happened, dubbed the "Quiet Revolution," that incrementally transferred that sense of national identity to the French language itself. Consequently, Quebec, while still predominantly a Catholic society, has become one of the most socially liberal and secular societies in the Western world.

Rationalization This is the central interpretive theme of Weber's sweeping sociological work and his way of characterizing the processes that modernized the world. In Weber's view a social phenomenon or social system is more rational if: (i) there is greater intellectual clarification, specification, and systematization of ideas, (ii) there are more differentiated, flexible, yet comprehensive systems of normative control, and (iii) there are ever more complete and elaborate patterns of motivation. Over the long course of human history this has happened.

Reflexive project of identity construction This is the phrase Giddens uses to stress the central and uncertain role played by the quest for personal identity in late modern societies. Identity in the modern world is less about the features ascribed to us by the communities into which we are born (e.g., our race, ethnicity, class, and geographic location) and more about what

we achieve and create for ourselves—at least that is the ideal espoused by our societies. We are now being asked to think about who we really are, to be reflexive, throughout our lives in order to "improve" ourselves and succeed.

Religion as a cultural resource James Beckford used this phrase to capture the ways in which religious ideas and symbols have continued to be important in late modern societies, even though the size and role of traditional religious social institutions is shrinking. He argues that religious ideas, images, and aspirations have become detached from specific traditions and instead become significant aspects of the larger and eclectic popular culture many people call on to make sense of their lives, and hence that they continue to be influential.

Religiosity The cumulative and multiple dimensions of religion evidenced in an individual, group, or entire society, including, for example, religious experience, ritual, devotion, belief, knowledge, and community. Religiosity can be unique (or not) to a group and may or may not impact one's daily life.

Rewards and costs In his theory of religion Stark argues that we must understand religion, like everything else humans do, as the result of our attempts to maximize the rewards in life while minimizing the costs of securing those rewards.

Risk/trust dialectic Ulrich Beck and Anthony Giddens have introduced this idea to sociology to describe what they think is one of the new drivers of change in late modern societies: the need to strike a meaningful balance between a heightened awareness of a set of high-consequence risks and the need to have trust in the expert systems that govern society and manage these risks, when it is these same systems that have created many of the new risks.

Rites of passage Arnold van Gennep's name for one of the most common forms of ritual found in all societies: a tripartite process by which individuals and groups are guided through a major transition in life and the resulting change is sanctified by the community.

Sacralization Sociologists and religious studies scholars have begun using this term to capture the dynamic character of religious life and the ever-present nature of religious change. It refers to the often overlooked fact that new forms of the sacred are arising all around us while our attention tends to be focused on the more obvious demise, in terms of social significance, of older conceptions of what is sacred. As new people, places, things, activities, and values are sacralised, by design or more spontaneously, religion persists and mutates.

Secular unaffiliated and religious unaffiliated These are the terms used in a Pew Forum on Religion and Public Life report (2008) to acknowledge that those who declare they have no religion can actually be differentiated into a group that says religion is not important to them and one that says it is somewhat or even very important to them. In other words, when a person declares that they do not identify with any particular religion it does not mean necessarily that they are irreligious.

Secularization The term used to describe the decline in the influence and presence of religion in society, as well as the individual practice of religion. Those aspects of society that are not religious are called secular. No consensus exists, however, on a precise definition of the process of secularization.

Societal, organizational, and individual secularization It is widely recognized now that the process of secularization encompasses three separate but related sets of social changes with regard to religion, and changes at one level may not be matched at the others. For example, while the influence of religious institutions in society may be lessening in obvious ways, individuals may still be very fervent in their beliefs and practices. Consequently, sociologists must be careful to designate the kind of secularization they are talking about at any time.

Social differentiation This term refers to the changes in social relationships that accompanied the process of structural differentiation, since the rise of new institutions went hand in hand with a growing division of labour in society; in other words, the involvement of individuals in increasingly specialized forms of work. As people increasingly spent much of their time doing different things their sense of the world and their place in it diverged, giving rise to an additional form of pluralism at the individual level.

Standardization and marginal differentiation Danièle Hervieu-Léger uses this phrase, drawn from economics, to explain the paradox that as the market for religious ideas becomes more open and larger, allowing individuals to sample and use beliefs and symbols from around the globe in constructing their own spiritual worldviews, the ideas that become popular are usually quite homogeneous in nature. The term was first used in this manner in Peter Berger's theory of secularization (1967; see Chapter 5).

Structural differentiation This is the term sociologists use to identify the process by which societies become more complex as new types of social institutions with specific social functions arise. Historically, this process of differentiation has been marked by a reduction in the influence and practical role of religion in society since the first and most significant instances of structural differentiation involved the creation of political, economic, and social institutions that operated independently from the religious institutions that once dominated society. Structural differentiation constitutes one form of pluralism.

Substantive definitions of religion Definitions that attempt to delineate what religion "is" in some essential sense.

Sui generis This Latin expression, literally meaning "of its own kind/genus," is commonly used in discussions of religion to assert the relative autonomy of religious phenomena from other social, economic, and political motivations and processes at work in society.

The great cult scare This is the phrase used to identify the social panic that gripped much of the Western world, but particularly the United States, in response to the sudden growth and prominence of new religious movements in the period roughly from the late 1960s into the early 1990s.

Theodicy A term borrowed from theology to designate any attempt to explain and justify the presence of evil and suffering in the world, and in particular the seemingly senseless and immoral suffering of the innocent, especially in worlds created by omnipotent gods.

Thomas theorem Thomas stated, "If men define situations as real, they are real in their consequences." It is wise to keep this in mind in studying the subjective claims at the heart of religion as a social phenomenon.

Ultimate legitimation Building on elements of Marx and Durkheim, Berger argues that religion's primary social function is to provide the highest level of justification for the social systems we have created, creating the impression that the given social order is how things are meant to be.

References

Aidala, Angela. 1985. "Social Change, Gender Roles, and New Religious Movements." *Sociological Analysis* 46: 287–314.

Albanese, Catherine L. 2007. *A Republic of Mind and Spirit: A Cultural History of American Metaphysical Religion.* New Haven: Yale University Press.

Aldridge, Alan. 2000. *Religion in the Contemporary World: A Sociological Introduction.* Cambridge: Polity Press.

Allport, Gordon W. and J.M. Ross. 1967. "Personal Religious Orientation and Prejudice." *Journal of Personality and Social Psychology* 5: 432–43.

Althouse, Peter. 2010. "The Ecumenical Significance of Canadian Pentecostalism," in *Winds from the North: Canadian Contributions to the Pentecostal Movement,* edited by Michael Wilkinson and Peter Althouse. Leiden: Brill.

Anderson, Robert Mapes. 1979. *Vision of the Disinherited: The Making of American Pentecostalism.* New York: Oxford University Press.

Anthony, Dick. 1990. "Religious Movements and Brainwashing Litigation: Evaluating Key Testimony," in Thomas Robbins and Dick Anthony, eds., *In Gods We Trust: New Patterns of Religious Pluralism in America,* 2nd ed. New Brunswick, NJ: Transaction.

——— and Thomas Robbins. 1992. "Law, Social Science and the 'Brainwashing' Exception to the First Amendment." *Behavioral Sciences and the Law* 10 (1): 5–27.

Arweck, Elisabeth and Eleanor Nesbitt. 2010. "Growing Up in a Mixed-Faith Family: Intact or Fractured Chain of Memory?" in Sylvia Collins-Mayo and Pink Dandelion, eds., *Religion and Youth.* Burlington, VT: Ashgate.

Asad, Talal. 1993. "The Construction of Religion as an Anthropological Category," in *Genealogies of Religion: Discipline and Reasons of Power in Christianity and Islam.* Baltimore: Johns Hopkins University Press.

Atran, Scott. 2002. *In Gods We Trust: The Evolutionary Landscape of Religion.* New York: Oxford University Press.

Aupers, Stef and Dick Houtman eds, 2010. *Religions of Modernity: Relocating the Sacred to the Self and the Digital.* Leiden: Brill.

Balmer, Randall. 1989. *Mine Eyes Have Seen the Glory: A Journey into the Evangelical Subculture in America.* New York: Oxford University Press.

Banerjee, Sikata and Harold Coward. 2005. "Hindus in Canada: Negotiating Identity in a 'Different' Homeland," in Paul Bramadat and David Seljak, eds., *Religion and Ethnicity in Canada.* Toronto, ON: Pearson.

Barker, Eileen. 1984. *The Making of a Moonie: Choice or Brainwashing?* Oxford: Basil Blackwell.

Baudrillard, Jean. 1998 [1970]. *The Consumer Society: Myth and Structure.* Trans. by J.P. Mayer. Thousand Oaks, CA: Sage.

Baum, Gregory. 2000. "Catholicism and Secularization in Quebec," in David Lyon and Marguerite Van Die, eds., *Rethinking Church, State, and Modernity: Canada Between Europe and America.* Toronto, ON: University of Toronto Press.

Baumann, Zygmunt. 2000. *Liquid Modernity.* Cambridge: Polity Press.

———. 2007. *Consuming Life.* Cambridge: Polity.

Beaman, Lori. 2004. "Church, State and the Legal Interpretation of Polygamy in Canada." *Nova Religio: The Journal of Alternative and Emergent Religions* 8 (1): 20–38.

———. 2008a. "A Cross-National Comparison of Approaches to Religious Diversity: Canada, France and the United States." in Lori Beaman and Peter Beyer, eds., *Religion and Diversity in Canada.* Boston, MA: Brill.

———. 2008b. *Defining Harm: Religious Freedom and the Limits of the Law.* Vancouver, BC: University of British Columbia Press.

———. 2008c. "Defining Religion: The Promise and the Peril of Legal Interpretation," in Richard Moon, ed., *Law and Religious Pluralism in Canada.* Vancouver: University of British Columbia Press.

Beck, Urlich. 1992 [1986]. *Risk Society: Towards a New Modernity.* Trans. by Mark Ritter. London: Sage.

——— and Elisabeth Beck-Gernsheim. 2002. *Individualization: Institutional Individualism and its Social and Political Consequences.* London, UK: Sage.

Becker, Penny Edgell. 1999. *Congregations in Conflict: Cultural Models of Local Religious Life.* New York, NY: Cambridge University Press.

Beckford, James A. 1984. "Holistic Imagery and Ethics in New Religious and Healing Movements." *Social Compass* 31(2–3): 259–72.

———. 1989. *Religion in Advanced Industrial Society*. London: Unwin Hyman.

———. 1992. "Religion, Modernity and Postmodernity," in Bryan Wilson, ed., *Religion: Contemporary Issues*. London: Bellew.

———. 1996. "Postmodernity, High Modernity and New Modernity: Three Concepts in Search of Religion," in Kieran Flanagan and Peter C. Jupp, eds., *Postmodernity, Sociology and Religion*. New York: St. Martin's Press.

———. 1999. "The Mass Media and New Religions," in Bryan Wilson and Jamie Cresswell, eds., *New Religious Movements: Challenge and Response*. New York: Routledge.

Beckworth, David. 2007. "Praying for a Recession: The Business Cycle and Protestant Religiosity in the United States." Available at http://uweb.txstate.edu/~db52/praying_for_a_recession.pdf.

Beit-Hallahmi, Bemjamin and Micheal Argyle. 1996. *The Psychology of Religious Behaviour, Belief and Experience*. London: Routledge.

Bell, Catherine. 1992. *Ritual Theory, Ritual Practice*. New York: Oxford University Press.

———. 1997. *Ritual: Perspectives and Dimensions*. New York: Oxford University Press.

———. 2006. "Ritual," in Robert A. Segal, ed., *The Blackwell Companion to the Study of Religion*. Oxford: Blackwell.

Bell, Daniel. 1973. *The Coming of Post-Industrial Society: A Venture in Social Forecasting*. New York: Basic Books.

Bellah, Robert N. 1967. "Civil Religion in America." *Daedalus: Journal of the American Academy of Arts and Sciences* 96: 1–21.

———. 1976. "The New Religious Consciousness and the Crisis of Modernity," in Charles Glock and Robert Bellah, eds., *The New Religious Consciousness*. Berkely, CA: University of California Press.

———, Richard Madsen, William N. Sullivan, Ann Swidler, and Steven M. Tipton. 1985. *Habits of the Heart: Individualism and Commitment in American Life*. Berkeley, CA: University Of California Press.

Bendroth, Margaret L. 1993. *Fundamental-ism and Gender: 1875 to the Present*. New Haven: Yale University Press.

Berger, Helen A. and Douglas Ezzy. 2007. *Teenage Witches: Magical Youth and the Search for the Self*. New Brunswick, NJ: Rutgers University Press.

Berger, Ida. 2006. "The Influence of Philanthropy in Canada." *Voluntas* 17: 115–32.

Berger, Peter L. 1967. *The Sacred Canopy: Elements of a Theory of Religion*. New York: Doubleday.

———. 1969. *A Rumour of Angels: Modern Society and the Rediscovery of the Supernatural*. Garden City, NY: Doubleday.

———. 1979. *The Heretical Imperative: Contemporary Possibilities of Religious Affirmation*. Garden City, NY: Doubleday.

———. 1992. *A Far Glory: The Question of Faith in an Age of Credulity*. New York: The Free Press.

———. 1998. "Protestantism and the Quest for Certainty." *The Christian Century* 115 (23): 782–96.

———, ed. 1999. *The Desecularization of the World: Resurgent Religion and World Politics*. Grand Rapids, MI: Eerdmans.

———, Grace Davie and Effie Fokas. 2008. *Religious America, Secular Europe? A Theme and Variations*. Aldershot, Hampshire: Ashgate.

Best, Marion and Friends. 1994. *Will Our Church Disappear: Strategies for the Renewal of the United Church of Canada*. Winfield, BC: Wood Lake Books.

Beyer, Peter. 1994. *Religion and Globalization*. Thousand Oaks, CA: Sage.

———. 1997. "Religious Vitality in Canada: The Complementarity of Religious Market and Secularization Perspectives." *Journal for the Scientific Study of Religion* 36 (2): 272–88.

———. 1998. "The Emergence of Religions in a Global Social System of Religion." *International Sociology* 13: 151–72.

———. 2003a. "Conceptions of Religion: On Distinguishing Scientific, Theological, and 'Official' Meanings." *Social Compass* 50 (2): 141–60.

———. 2003b. "Defining Religion in Cross-National Perspective: Identity and Difference in Official Conceptions," in Greil, Arthur L. and David G. Bromley, eds., *Defining Religion: Investigating the Boundaries Between the Sacred and the Secular*. Religion and the Social Order, Vol. 10. New York: JAI.

———. 2005. "The Future of Non-Christian Religions in Canada: Patterns of Religious Identification among Recent Immigrants and their Second Generation, 1981–2001." *Studies in Religion/Sciences religieuses* 34: 165–96.

———. 2008. "From Far and Wide: Canadian Religious and Culture Diversity in Global/Local Context," in Lori Beaman and Peter Beyer, eds., *Religion and Diversity in Canada*. Boston, MA: Brill.

Bibby, Reginald. 1987. *Fragmented Gods: The Poverty and Potential of Religion in Canada*. Toronto, ON: Stoddart Publishing Co. Limited.

———. 1993. *Unknown Gods: The Ongoing Story of Religion in Canada.* Toronto, ON: Stoddart Publishing Co. Limited.

———. 1994. *Unitrends: A Summary Report prepared for The Department of Stewardship Services of The United Church of Canada.*

———. 2002. *Restless Gods: The Renaissance of Religion in Canada.* Toronto, ON: Stoddart Publishing Co. Limited.

———. 2004. *Restless Churches: How Canada's Churches Can Contribute to the Emerging Religious Renaissance.* Ottawa, ON: Wood Lake Books.

———. 2006. *The Boomer Factor: What Canada's Most Famous Generation is Leaving Behind.* Toronto, ON: Bastian Books.

———. 2007. "Good Without God, But Better With God?" Available at www.reginald bibby.com/images/PC_10_BETTER_WITH_GOD_OCT0807.pdf.

———. 2011. *Beyond the Gods and Back: Religion's Demise and Rise and Why it Matters.* Lethbridge, AB: Project Canada Books.

———, Sarah Russell and Ron Rolheiser. 2009. *The Emerging Millen-nials: How Canada's Newest Generation Is Responding to Change & Choice.* Lethbridge, AB: Project Canada Books.

Biles, John and Humera Ibrahim. 2005. "Religion and Public Policy: Immigration, Citizenship, and Multiculturalism—Guess Who's Coming to Dinner?" in Paul Bramadat and David Seljak, eds., *Religion and Ethnicity in Canada.* Toronto, ON: Pearson.

Block-Hoell, Nils. 1964. *The Pentecostal Movement: Its Origins, Development, and Distinctive Character.* London: Allen & Unwin.

Boisvert, Mathieu. 2005. "Buddhists in Canada: Impermanence in a Land of Change," in Paul Bramadat and David Seljak, eds., *Religion and Ethnicity in Canada.* Toronto, ON: Pearson.

Bouchard, Gerard and Charles Taylor. 2008. "Building the Future: A Time for Reconciliation. Report." Commission de Consultation sur Les Pratiques D'Accommodement Reliees Aux Differences Culturelles. Available at www. accommodements.qc.ca/documentation/rapports/rapport-final-integral-en.pdf.

Bourdieu, Pierre. 1977. *Outline of a Theory of Practice.* New York, NY: Cambridge University Press.

———. 2001. *Masculine Domination.* Cambridge: Polity.

Bowen, Kurt. 2004. *Christians in a Secular World: The Canadian Experience.* Montreal, QC: McGill-Queen's University Press.

Boyer, Pascal. 2001. *Religion Explained: The Evolutionary Origins of Religious Thought.* New York: Basic Books.

Bramadat, Paul and David Seljak, eds. 2005. *Religion and Ethnicity in Canada.* Toronto: Pearson Longman.

———. 2008. *Christianity and Ethnicity in Canada.* Toronto, ON: University of Toronto Press.

Brasher, Brenda. 1998. *Godly Women: Fundamentalism and Female Power.* New Brunswick, NJ: Rutgers University Press.

Brekke, Torkel. 2012. *Fundamentalism: Prophecy and Protest in the Age of Globalization.* Cambridge: Cambridge University Press.

Bromely, David G. 2002. "Dramatic Denouements," in David G. Bromley and J. Gordon Melton, eds., *Cults, Religion and Violence.* Cambridge: Cambridge University Press.

——— and Anson D. Shupe. 1981. *Strange Gods: The Great American Cult Scare.* Boston: Beacon.

——— and ———. 1993. "Organized Opposition to New Religious Movements," In David G. Bromley and Jeffry K. Hadden, eds., *The Handbook on Cults and Sects in America, Part A, Religion and the Social Order, Vol. 3.* Greenwich, CT: JAI Press.

Bromley, David G. and Jeffrey K. Hadden, eds, 1993. *Handbook of Cults and Sects in America, Parts A and B. Religion and the Social Order, Vol. 3.* Greenwich, CT: JAI Press.

Bruce, Steve. 1999. *Choice and Religion: A Critique of Rational Choice Theory.* New York: Oxford University Press.

Bromely, David G. 2002. *God is Dead: Secular-ization in the West.* Oxford: Blackwell.

———. 2011. *Secularization: In Defence of an Unfashionable Theory.* New York, NY: Oxford University Press.

Bullough, Vern L. and James A. Brundage, eds. 1982. *Sexual Practices in the Medieval Church.* Buffalo, NY: Prometheus.

Byrne, Peter. 1989. *Natural Religion and the Nature of Religion: The Legacy of Deism.* London: Routledge.

Campbell, David and Steven Yonish. 2003. "Religion and Volunteering in America," in Corwin Smidt, ed., *Religion as Social Capital: Producing the Common Good.* Waco, TX: Baylor University Press.

Campbell, Patricia Q. 2011. *Knowing Body, Moving Mind: Ritualizing and Learning at Two Buddhist Centers.* New York: Oxford University Press.

Campbell, Robert A. 2006. "Theodicy, Distribution of Risk, and Reflexive Modernization: Explaining the Cultural Significance of New Religious Movements," in James A. Beckford and

John Wallis, eds., *Theorizing Religion: Classical and Contemporary Debates.* Aldershot, UK: Ashgate.

Canadian Diversity. 2012 (Spring). *Multiculturalism, Inteculturalism and Cross-Cultural Understanding: Communities and Stakeholders.* Association for Canadian Studies/Association d'études canadiennes.

Canipe, Lee. 2003. "Under God and Anti-Communist: How the Pledge of Allegiance Got Religion in Cold War America." *Journal of Church and State* 45(2): 305–23.

Capps, Walter H. 1990. *The New Religious Right: Piety, Patriotism, and Politics.* Columbia, SC: University of South Carolina Press.

Casanova, Jose. 1994. *Public Religions in the Modern World.* Chicago, IL: University of Chicago Press.

———. 2007. "Rethinking Secularization: A Global Comparative Perspective." in Peter Beyer and Lori Beaman, eds., *Religion, Globalization, and Culture.* Koninklijke Brill NV, Leden, The Netherlands: Brill.

———. 2008. "Public Religions Revisited," in Hent de Vries, eds., *Religion: Beyond a Concept.* New York, NY: Fordham University Press.

Cha, Seong Hwan. 2000. "Korean Civil Religion and Modernity." *Social Compass* 47 (4): 467–85.

Chandler, Siobhan. 2008. "The Social Ethic of Religiously Unaffiliated Spirituality." *Religion Compass* Vol. 3, http://online library.wiley.com/doi/10.1111/j.1749-8171.2007.00059.x/abstract

———. 2010. "Private Religion in the Public Sphere: Life Spirituality in Civil Society," in Stef Aupers and Dick Houtman, eds., *Religions of Modernity: Relocating the Sacred to the Self and the Digital.* Leiden, The Netherlands: Brill.

———. 2011. *The Social Ethic of Religiously Unaffiliated Spirituality.* Dissertation, Wilfrid Laurier University.

Chaves, Mark and Philip Gorski. 2001. "Religious Pluralism and Religious Participation." *Annual Review of Sociology* 27: 261—81.

Choquette, Robert. 2004. *Canada's Religions: An Historical Introduction.* Ottawa, ON: University of Ottawa Press.

Christie, Nancy and Michael Gauvreau. 2010. *Christian Churches and Their Peoples, 1840–1965: A Social History of Religion in Canada.* Toronto, ON: University of Toronto Press.

Cimino, Richard and Don Lattin. 1998. *Shopping for Faith: American Religion in the New Millennium.* San Francisco: Jossey-Bass.

Clark, John, M.D. Langone, R.E. Schacter, and R. C. D. Daly. 1981. *Destructive Cult Conversion: Theory, Research, and Treatment.* Weston, MA: American Family Foundation.

Clark, Lynn S. 2003. *From Angels to Aliens: Teenagers, the Media, and the Supernatural.* New York: Oxford University Press.

Clarke, Peter B. and Peter Byrne. 1993. *Religion Defined and Explained.* New York: St. Martin's Press.

Clifford, N. Keith. 1977. "His Dominion: A Vision in Crisis," in Peter Slater, ed., *Religion and Culture in Canada.* Waterloo: Wilfrid Laurier University Press.

Clydesdale, Tim. 2007. *The First Year Out: Understanding American Teens after High School.* Chicago, IL: University of Chicago Press.

Cowan, Douglas E. 2005. *Cyberhenge: Modern Pagans on the Internet.* New York: Routledge.

———. 2008. "Fearing Planes, Trains, and Automobiles: Sociophobics and the Disincentive to Religious Diversity," in Lori Beaman and Peter Beyer, eds., *Religion and Diversity in Canada.* Boston, MA: Brill.

Cox, Edwin. 1967. *Sixth Form Religion.* London: SCM.

Cox, Harvey. 1977. *Turning East: The Promise and the Peril of the New Orientalism.* New York: Simon and Schuster.

———. 1995. *Fire from Heaven: The Rise of Pentecostal Spirituality and the Reshaping of Religion in the Twenty-First Century.* Reading, MA: Addison-Wesley.

Cristi, Marcella and Lorne L. Dawson. 2007. "Civil Religion in America and in Global Context," in James A, Beckford and N.J. Demerath III, eds., *The Sage Handbook of the Sociology of Religion.* Los Angeles: Sage.

Crockett, Alasdair and David Voas. 2006. "Generations of Decline: Religious Change in 20th Century Britain." *Journal for the Scientific Study of Religion* 45 (4): 567–84.

Cush, Denise. 2010. "Teenage Witchcraft in Britain," in Sylvia Collins-Mayo and Pink Dandelion, eds., *Religion and Youth.* Burlington, VT: Ashgate.

Daly, Mary. 1973. *Beyond God the Father: Toward a Philosophy of Women's Liberation.* Boston: Beacon.

Dark, Ken R., ed. 2000. *Religion and International Relations.* New York: St. Martin's Press.

Davidman, Lynn. 1991. *Tradition in a Rootless World: Women Turn to Orthodox Judaism.* Berkeley: University of California Press.

Davidson, James D. and Dean D. Knudsen. 1977. "A New Approach to Religious Commitment." *Sociological Focus* 10 (2): 151–73.

Davie, Grace. 1994. *Religion in Britain Since*

1945: Believing without Belonging. Oxford: Blackwell.

———. 1999. "Europe: The Exception that Proves the Rule?" in Peter L. Berger, ed., *The Desecularization of the World: Resurgent Religion and World Politics.* Grand Rapids, MI: Eerdmans.

Davies, Alan and Marilyn Nefsky. 1997. *How Silent Were the Churches? Canadian Protestantism and the Jewish Plight During the Nazi Era.* Waterloo: Wilfrid Laurier University Press.

Dawkins, Richard. 2006. *The God Delusion.* Boston: Houghton Mifflin.

Dawson, Andrew. 2007. *New Era, New Religions: Religious Transformation in Contemporary Brazil.* Aldershot, England: Ashgate.

Dawson, Lorne L. 1987. "On References to the Transcendent in the Scientific Study of Religion: A Qualified Idealist Proposal." *Religion* 17 (3): 227–50.

———. 1998. "Anti-Modernism, Modern-ism, and Postmodernism: Struggling with the Cultural Significance of New Religious Movements." *Sociology of Religion* 59 (2): 131–56.

———. 2004. "The Sociocultural Significance of Modern New Religious Movements," in James R. Lewis, ed., *Oxford Handbook of New Religious Movements.* New York: Oxford University Press.

———. 2006a. *Comprehending Cults: The Sociology of New Religious Movements.* 2nd ed. Toronto: Oxford University Press.

———. 2006b. "Privatization, Globaliza-tion, and Religious Innovation: Giddens' Theory of Modernity and the Refutation of Secularisation Theory," in James A. Beckford and John Wallis, eds., *Theorizing Religion: Classical and Contemporary Debates.* Aldershot, UK: Ashgate, 110–12.

———. 2007. "The Meaning and Significance of New Religious Movements," in David G. Bromley, ed., *Teaching New Religious Movements.* New York: Oxford University Press.

———. 2008. "Church-Sect-Cult: Constructing Typologies of Religious Groups," in Peter Clarke, ed., *Oxford Handbook of Sociology of Religion.* Oxford: Oxford University Press.

——— and Douglas E., Cowan, eds. 2004. *Religion Online.* New York: Routledge.

DeBerg, Betty A. 1990. *Ungodly Women: Gender and the First Wave of American Fundamentalism.* Minneapolis: Fortress.

Demerath III, N.J. 2007. "Secularization and Sacralization Deconstructed and Reconstructed," in James Beckford and N.J. Demerath III, eds., *The Sage Handbook of the Sociology of Religion.* London, UK: Sage.

Dillon, Michele and Paul Wink. 2007. *In the Course of a Lifetime: Tracing Religious Belief, Practice, and Change.* Berkeley, CA: University of California Press.

Dobbelaere, Karel. 1981. "Secularization: A Multi-Dimensional Concept." *Current Sociology* 29 (2): 1–213.

———. 2002. *Secularization: An Analysis at Three Levels.* Brussels, Belgium: Peter Lang.

Douglas, Mary. 1966. *Purity and Danger: An Analysis of Concepts of Pollution and Taboo.* London: Routledge and Kegan Paul.

Driver, Tom. 1997. *Liberating Rites: Understanding the Transformative Power of Ritual.* Boulder, CO: Westview Press.

Dubuisson, Daniel. 2003 [1998]. *The Western Construction of Religion: Myths, Knowledge, and Ideology.* Trans. W. Sayers. Baltimore, ML: Johns Hopkins University Press.

Durkheim, Émile. 1964 [1893]. *The Division of Labour in Society.* Trans. George Simpson. New York: The Free Press.

———. 1973 [1898]. "Individualism and the Intellectuals," in Robert N. Bellah, ed., *Émile Durkheim on Morality and Society.* Chicago: University of Chicago Press.

———. 1995 [1912]. *The Elementary Forms of Religious Life.* Trans. by Karen E. Fields. New York: The Free Press.

Ebaugh, Helen Rose Fuchs and Janet Saltzman Chafetz, eds., 2000. *Religion and the New Immigrants: Continuities and Adaptations in Immigrant Congrega-tions.* Walnut Creek, CA: AltaMira Press.

Eck, Diana. 2001. *A New Religious America: How a "Christian Country" Has Now Become the World's Most Religiously Diverse Nation.* San Francisco, CA: HarperSanFrancisco.

Eliade, Mircea. 1959. *The Sacred and the Profane: The Nature of Religion.* San Diego, CA: Harcourt Brace Jovanovich.

———. 1963 [1958]. *Patterns in Comparative Religion.* Trans. by Willard R. Trask. Princeton, NJ: Princeton University Press.

———. 1969. *The Quest: History and Meaning in Religion.* Chicago: University of Chicago Press.

Emberley, Peter C. 2002. *Divine Hunger: Canadians on Spiritual Walkabout.* Toronto: HarperCollins.

Fay, Terence J. 2002. *A History of Canadian Catholics.* Montreal: McGill-Queen's Press.

Feuerbach, Ludwig. 1957 [1841]. *The Essence of Christianity.* Trans. by George Elliot. New York: Harper and Row.

Fields, Rick. 1981. *How the Swans Came to the Lake: A Narrative History of Buddhism in America.* Boulder, CO: Shambhala Press.

Finke, Roger. 1997. "The Consequences

of Religious Competition: Supply-Side Explanations for Religious Change," in Lawrence Young, ed., *Rational Choice Theory and Religion: Summary and Assessment*. New York, NY: Routledge.

Finke, Roger, Avery M. Guest, and Rodney Stark. 1996. "Pluralism and Religious Participation: New York, 1855–1865." *American Sociological Review* 61: 203–18.

Finke, Roger and Rodney Stark. 2005. *The Churching of America 1776–2005: Winners and Losers in Our Religious Economy*. Piscataway, NJ: Rutgers University Press.

Fiorenza, Elisabeth Schüssler. 1983. *In Memory of Her: A Feminist Theological Reconstruction of Christian Origins*. New York: Crossroad.

Fitzgerald, Timothy. 1999. *The Ideology of Religious Studies*. New York: Oxford University Press.

Fleras, Augie. 2011. *The Media Gaze: Representations of Diversities in Canada*. Vancouver: University of British Columbia Press.

———. 2012. "'Differently the Same' Multi/Inter/Culturalism as Immigrant Governance Model." *Canadian Diversity* (Spring): 46–51.

Flood, Gavin. 1999. *Beyond Phenomenology: Rethinking the Study of Religion*. London: Cassell.

Flory, Richard and Donald Miller. 2010. "The Expressive Communalism of Post-Boomer Religion in the USA," in Sylvia Collins-Mayo and Pink Dandelion, eds., *Religion and Youth*. Burlington, VT: Ashgate.

Forbes, Bruce David and Jeffrey H. Mahan, eds. 2005. *Religion and Popular Culture in America*. Revised ed. Berkeley, CA: University of California Press.

Fraser, James George. 1922. *The Golden Bough: A Study in Magic and Religion*. Abridged ed. London: Macmillan.

Freud, Sigmund. 1950 [1913]. *Totem and Taboo*. London: Routledge and Kegan Paul.

Friesen, Joe and Sandra Martin. 2010 (October 5). "Canada's Changing Faith." *Globe and Mail*. Available at www.theglobe andmail.com/news/national/time-to-lead/multiculturalism/canadas-changing-faith/article1741422.

Fuller, Robert C. 20001. *Spiritual but not Religious: Understanding Unchurched Americans*. New York: Oxford University Press.

Galbraith, John Kenneth. 1958. *The Affluent Society*. Boston: Houghton Mifflin.

———. 1967. *The New Industrial State*. New York: Mentor Books.

Geddes, John. 2009. "What Canadians Think of Sikhs, Jews, Christians, Muslims . . ." *Macleans*. Available at www2.macleans .ca/2009/04/28/

what-canadians-think-of-sikhs-jews-christians-muslims.

Geertz, Clifford. 1973 [1966]. "Religion as Cultural System," in *The Interpretation of Cultures: Selected Essays*. New York: Basic Books.

Gennep, Arnold van. 1960 [1908]. *The Rites of Passage*. Chicago: University of Chicago Press.

Giddens, Anthony. 1990. *The Consequences of Modernity*. Cambridge: Polity.

———. 1991. *Modernity and Self Identity: Self and Society in the Late Modern Age*. Cambridge: Polity.

———. 1992. *The Transformation of Intimacy*. Cambridge: Polity.

———. 1994. "Living in a Post-Traditional Society," in Ulrich Beck, Anthony Giddens, and Scott Lash, *Reflexive Modernization*. Stanford, CA: Stanford University Press.

Gitlin, Todd. 1987. *The Sixties: Years of Hope, Days of Rage*. New York: Bantam.

Glock, Charles and Rodney Stark. 1965. *Religion and Society in Tension*. New York: Rand McNally.

Gluckman, Max. 1962. *Essays in the Ritual of Social Relations*. Manchester: Manchester University Press.

Goldman, Marion S. 1999. *Passionate Journeys: Why Successful Women Joined a Cult*. Ann Arbor, MI: University of Michigan Press.

Graham, Ron. 1990. *God's Dominion: A Sceptic's Quest*. Toronto, ON: McClelland & Stewart.

Grant, John Webster. 1998. *The Church in the Canadian Era: Updated and Expanded Edition*. Vancouver, British Columbia: Regent College Publishing.

Gray, Charlotte. 2008. *Nellie McClung*. Toronto: Penguin Canada.

Greeley, Andrew M. 1989. *Religious Change in America*. Cambridge, MA: Harvard University Press.

Green, Robert W. 1973. *Protestantism, Capitalism, and Social Science: The Weber Thesis Controversy*. 2nd ed. Lexington, MA: Heath.

Greil, Arthur L. 1993. "Explorations Along the Sacred Frontier," in David G. Bromley and Jeffrey K. Haddon, eds., *Handbook of Cults and Sects in America*. Vol. A. Greenwich, CT: JAI Press.

Greil, Arthur L. and David G. Bromley, eds. 2003. *Defining Religion: Investigating the Boundaries Between the Sacred and the Secular*. Religion and the Social Order, Vol. 10. New York: JAI.

Greil, Arthur L. and Thomas Robbins, eds. 1994. *Between the Sacred and the Secular*. Greenwich, CT: JAI Press.

Griffith, R. Marie. 1997. *God's Daughters:*

Evangelical Women and the Power of Submission. Berkeley: University of California Press.

Grimes, Ronald L. 1995 [1982]. *Beginnings in Ritual Studies*. rev. ed. Columbia, SC: University of South Carolina Press.

———. 2000. *Deeply into the Bone: Re-Inventing Rites of Passage*. Berkeley, CA: University of California Press.

Grossman, Cathy Lynn. 2012. "Survey finds 19 percent without religious affiliation." *USA Today*, July 20. Available at wwrn .org/articles/37779/.

Hadaway, C. Kirk, Penny Long Marler, and Mark Chaves. 1993. "What the Polls Don't Show: A Closer Look at U.S. Church Attendance." *American Sociological Review* 58 (6): 741-52.

Hadden, Jeffrey. 1987. "Toward Desacralizing Secularization Theory." *Social Forces* 65: 587–611.

——— and Anson Shupe, eds. 1989. *Secularization and Fundamentalism Reconsidered*. New York, NY: Paragon House.

Hall, John R. 2000. *Apocalypse Observed: Religious Movements and Violence in North America, Europe, and Japan*. New York: Routledge.

Hall, Michael, David Lasby, Steven Ayer, and William David Gibbons. 2009. "Caring Canadians, Involved Canadians: Highlights from the 2007 Canada Survey of Giving, Volunteering, and Participating." Available at www.giving andvolunteering.ca/files/giving/en/csgvp_ highlights_2007.pdf.

Hamburg Eva M. And Thorlief Pettersson. 1994. "The Religious Market: Denominational Competition and Religious Participation in Contemporary Sweden." *Journal for the Scientific Study of Religion* 33: 205–16.

———. 1997. "Short-Term Changes in Religious Supply and Church Attendance in Contemporary Sweden." *Research in the Social Scientific Study of Religion* 8: 35–51.

Hamilton, Malcolm. 1995. *The Sociology of Religion: Theoretical and Comparative Perspectives*. London: Routledge.

Hammond, Phillip E. 1980. "The Conditions of Civil Religion: A Comparison of the United States and Mexico," in Robert N. Bellah and Phillip E. Hammond, eds., *Varieties of Civil Religion*. San Francisco: Harper and Row.

Hanegraaff, Wouter J. 1996. *New Age Religion and Western Culture: Esotericism in the Mirror of Secular Thought*. Leiden, The Netherlands: Brill.

Hansen, Klaus J. 1981. *Mormonism and the American Experience*. Chicago: University of Chicago Press.

Happold, Fredrick C. 1970. *Mysticism: A Study and an Anthology*. Baltimore: Penguin Books.

Harding, John S., Victor Sogen Hori, and Alexander Soucy. 2010. *Wild Geese: Buddhism in Canada*. Montreal: McGill-Queen"s University Press.

Harris, Sam. 2004. *The End of Faith: Religion, Terror, and the Future of Reason*. New York: Norton & Co.

———. 2006. *Letters to a Christian Nation*. New York, NY: Knopf.

Harrison, Peter. 1990. *"Religion" and the Religions in the English Enlightenment*. Cambridge: Cambridge University Press.

Hassan, Steve. 1988. *Combatting Cult Mind-Control*. Rochester, VT: Park St. Press.

Heelas, Paul. 1996. *The New Age Movement*. Oxford: Blackwell.

———. 2008. *Spiritualities of Life: New Age Romanticism and Consumptive Capitalism*. Oxford: Blackwell.

———, Linda Woodhead, Benjamin Seel, Bronislaw Szerszynski, and Karin Tusting. 2005. *The Spiritual Revolution: Why Religion is Giving Way to Spirituality*. Malden, MA: Blackwell Publishing.

———, Scott Lash, and Paul Morris, eds. 1996. *Detraditionalisation: Critical Reflections on Authority and Identity*. Oxford: Blackwell.

Herbrechtsmeier, W. 1993. "Buddhism and the Definition of Religion: One More Time." *Journal for the Scientific Study of Religion* 32: 1–18.

Hervieu-Léger, Danièle. 2003. "Individualism, the Validation of Faith, and the Social Nature of Religion in Modernity," in Richard K. Fenn, ed., *The Blackwell Companion to Sociology of Religion*. Oxford: Blackwell.

———. 2006. "In Search of Certainties: The Paradoxes of Religiosity in Societies of High Modernity." *The Hedgehog Review*, Spring and Summer.

Hewitt, W.E. 1993. "The Quest for the Just Society: Canadian Catholicism in Transition," in W.E. Hewitt, ed., *The Sociology of Religion: A Canadian Focus*. Toronto, ON: Butterworths.

Hill, Daniel G. 1980. *Study of Mind development Groups, Sects and Cults in Ontario: A Report to the Ontario Government*. ISBN 0-7743-5266-3.

Hitchens, Christopher. 2007. *God is Not Great: How Religion Poisons Everything*. Toronto: McClelland and Steward.

Hoodfar, Homa. 2006. "More than Clothing: Veiling as an Adaptive Strategy," in Lori Beaman, ed., *Religion and Canadian Society: Traditions, Transitions, and Innovations*. Toronto, ON: Canadian Scholars' Press Inc.

Hout, Michael and Claude S. Fischer. 2002. "Why More Americans Have No Religious Preference: Politics and Generations." *American Sociological Review* 67: 165–90.

Houtman, Dick and Stef Aupers. 2007. "The Spiritual Turn and the Decline of Tradition: The Spread of Post-Christian Spirituality in 14 Western Countries, 1981–2000." *Journal for the Scientific Study of Religion* 46 (3): 305–20.

———. 2008. "The Spiritual Revolution and the New Age Gender Puzzle: The Sacralisation of the Self in Late Modernity, 1980–2000," in Kristin Aune, Sonja Sharma, and Giselle Vincett, eds., *Women and Religion in the West: Challenging Secularization*. Aldershot, Hampshire: Ashgate.

Hubert, Henri and Marcel Mauss. 1964 [1898]. *Sacrifice: Its Nature and Functions*. Trans. by W.D. Hall. Chicago: University of Chicago Press.

Hume, David. 1976 [1757] . "The Natural History of Religion," in A. W. Clover and J. V. Price, eds., *David Hume on Religion*. New York: Oxford University Press.

Hunter, James Davidson. 1981. "The New Religions: Demodernization and the Protest against Modernity," in Bryan Wilson, ed., *The Social Impact of the New Religious Movements*. New York: Rose of Sharon Press.

Iannaccone, Laurence. 1994. "Why Strict Churches are Strong." *American Journal of Sociology* 99 (5): 1180–211.

Idinopulous, Thomas A. and Edward A. Yonan, eds.1996. *The Sacred and Its Scholars: Comparative Methodologies for the Study of Primary Religious Data*. Leiden, The Netherlands: E.J. Brill.

Inglehart, Ronald and Pippa Norris. 2003. *Rising Tide: Gender Equality and Cultural Change Around the World*. Cambridge: Cambridge University Press.

Introvigne, Massimo. 1999. "The Magic of Death: The Suicide of the Solar Temple," in Catherine Wessinger, ed., *Millennialism, Persecution and Violence: Historical Cases*. Syracuse, NY: Syracuse University Press.

Ivins, Stanley S. 1992. "Notes on Mormon Polygamy," in Michael Quinn, ed., *The New Mormon History*. Salt Lake City, UT: Signature Books.

Jacobs, Janet Liebman. 1984. "The Economy of Love in Religious Commitment: The Deconversion of Women from Nontraditional Religious Movements." *Journal for the Scientific Study of Religion* 23: 155–71.

Jakobsh, Doris. Forthcoming. "The Sikhs in Canada: Culture, Religion and Radicalization," in Paul Bramadat and Lorne L. Dawson, eds., *Religion, Radicalization and Securitization in Canada and Beyond*. Toronto: University of Toronto Press.

James, William. 1994 [1902]. *The Varieties of Religious Experience: A Study in Human Nature*. New York: The Modern Library.

Jelen, Ted G. and Clyde Wilcox. 1998. "Context and Conscience: The Catholic Church as an Agent of Political Socialization in Western Europe." *Journal for the Scientific Study of Religion* 37 (1): 28–40.

Jenkins. Philip. 1996. *Pedophiles and Priests: Anatomy of a Contemporary Crisis*. New York: Oxford University Press.

———. 2000. *Mystics and Messiahs: Cults and New Religions in American History*. New York: Oxford University Press.

———. 2002. *The Next Christendom: The Coming of Global Christianity*. New York: Oxford University Press.

Johnston, Hugh. 1999. *The Encyclopedia of Canada's Peoples*. Available at http://multiculturalcanada.ca/Encyclopedia/A-Z/s4/1.

Juschka, Darlene M. 2005. "Gender," in John R. Hinnells, ed., *The Routledge Companion to the Study of Religion*. London: Routledge.

Katz, Steven, ed. 1983. *Mysticism and Religious Traditions*. New York: Oxford University Press.

Kent, Stephen A. 2001. *From Slogans to Mantras: Social Protest and Religious Conversion in the Late Vietnam War Era*. Syracuse, NY: Syracuse University Press.

Kim, Andrew. 1983. "The Absence of Pan-Canadian Civil Religion: Plurality, Duality, and Conflict in Symbols of Canadian Culture." *Sociology of Religion* 54: 257–75.

King-Hele, Sarah. 2009. "Generational Changes in Canadian Religiosity." Conference Presentation at the Society for the Scientific Study of Religion in Denver, CO.

Kinnaman, David and Gabe Lyons. 2007. *UnChristian: What a New Generation Really Thinks About Christianity . . . And why it Matters*. Grand Rapids, MI: Baker Books.

Kirkpatrick, Lee A. and Ralph W. Hood Jr. 1990. "Intrinsic-Extrinsic Religious Orientation." *Journal for the Scientific Study of Religion* 29: 442–62.

Kosmin, Barry and Ariela Keysar. 2008. "American Nones: The Profile of the No Religion Population." Available at http://commons.trincoll.edu/aris/files/2011/08/NONES_08.pdf.

Lai, David Chuenyan, Jordan Paper and Li Chuang Paper. 2005. "The Chinese in Canada: Their Unrecognized Religion," in Paul Bramadat and David Seljak, eds.,

Religion and Ethnicity in Canada. Toronto, ON: Pearson.

Lambert, Yves. 1999. "Religion in Modernity as a New Axial Age: Secularization or New Religious Forms?" *Sociology of Religion* 60 (3): 303–33.

Lanternari, Vittorio, 1963. *The Religions of the Oppressed: A Study of Modern Messianic Cults*. Trans. by Lisa Sergio. New York: Knopf.

Lawson, Ronald. 1998. "From American Church to Immigrant Church: The Changing Face of Seventh-day Adventism in Metropolitan New York." *Sociology of Religion* 59 (4): 329–51.

———. 1999. "Internal Political Fallout from the Emergence of an Immigrant Majority: The Impact of the Transformation of Seventh-day Adventism in Metropolitan New York." *Review of Religious Research* 41: 20–46.

Lechner, Frank J. 1985. "Fundamentalism and Sociocultural Revitalization in America: A Sociological Interpretation." *Sociology of Religion* 46 (3): 243–59.

Lefebvre, Solange. 2008. "Between Law and Public Opinion: The Case of Quebec," in Lori Beaman and Peter Beyer, eds., *Religion and Diversity in Canada*. Boston, MA: Brill.

Leuba, James H. 1921 [1916]. *The Belief in God and Immortality*. Chicago: Open Court.

Levine, Saul V. 1984. *Radical Departures: Desperate Detours to Growing Up*. New York: Harcourt Brace Jovanovich.

Lewis, Charles. 2011. "Updated: 'Pot church' member sentenced to three months in jail." *National Post*, 30 May. Available at http://life.nationalpost.com/2011/05/30/pot-churvh-members-to be-sentenced.

Lewis, David. 1993. "Canada's Native Peoples and the Churches," in W.E. Hewitt, ed., *The Sociology of Religion: A Canadian Focus*. Toronto, ON: Butterworths.

Lewis, James R. 2004. *The Oxford Handbook of New Religious Movements*. New York: Oxford University Press.

———, ed. 2009. *Scientology*. New York: Oxford University Press.

Liebman, Charles S. And Elizar Don-Yehiya. 1983. *Civil Religion in Israel*. Berkeley, CA: University of California Press.

Lim, Chaeyoon, Carol Ann MacGregor and Robert Putnam. 2010. "Secular and Liminal: Discovering Heterogeneity Among Religious Nones." *Journal for the Scientific Study of Religion* 49 (4): 596–618.

Lofland, John and Rodney Stark. 1965. "Becoming a World-Saver: A Theory of Conversion to a Deviant Perspective." *American Sociological Review* 30 (6): 863–74.

Luckmann, Thomas. 1967. *The Invisible Religion: The Problem of Religion in Modern Society*. New York: Macmillan.

———. 1990. "Shrinking Transcendence, Expanding Religion." *Sociological Analysis* 50 (2): 127–38.

Lynch, Gordon. 2007. *The New Spirituality: An Introduction to Progressive Belief in the Twenty-First Century*. London: I.B. Tauris.

Lyon, David. 1994. *Postmodernity*. Minneapolis: University of Minnesota Press.

Lyotard, Jean-Francois. 1984 [1979]. *The Postmodern Condition: A Report on Knowledge*. Trans. by Geoff Bennington and Brian Massumi. Minneapolis: University of Minnesota Press.

Malinowski, Bronislaw. 1948. *Magic, Science, and Religion, and Other Essays*. New York: Doubleday.

Martin, David. 1978. *A General Theory of Secularization*. New York, NY: Harper & Row.

———. 2005. *On Secularization: Towards a Revised General Theory*. Burlington, VT: Ashgate.

Marty, Martin and Scott Appleby, eds. 1991. *Fundamentalism Observed*. Chicago: University of Chicago Press.

Marx, Karl. 1957 [1844]. "Contribution to the Critique of Hegel's Philosophy of Right —Introduction," in *On Religion: Karl Marx and Friedrich Engels*. Moscow: Progress.

Masuzawa, Tomoko. 2005. *The Invention of World Religions*. Chicago: University of Chicago Press.

Mayer, Jean Francois. 1999. "'Our Terrestrial Journey is Coming to an End': The Last Voyage of the Solar Temple." *Nova Religio* 2: 172–96.

McCloud, Sean. 2004. *Making the American Religious Fringe: Exotics, Subversives, and Journalists, 1955–1993*. Chapel Hill, NC: University of North Carolina Press.

McCutcheon, Russell T., ed. 1999. *The Insider/Outsider Problem in the Study of Religion: A Reader*. New York: Cassell.

McDonough, Sheila and Homa Hoodfar. 2005. "Muslims in Canada: From Ethnic Groups to Religious Community," in Paul Bramadat and David Seljak, eds., *Religion and Ethnicity in Canada*. Toronto, ON: Pearson.

McGowan, Mark. 1999. *The Waning of the Green: Catholics, the Irish and Identity in Toronto, 1887–1922*. Montreal: McGill-Queen's Press.

McGuire, Meredith B. 1997. *Religion in Social Context*. 4th ed. Belmont, CA: Wadsworth Pub.

McKinnon, Andrew. 2002. "Sociological Definitions, Language Games, and the

'Essence' of Religion." *Method and Theory in the Study of Religion* 14: 61–83.

McLellan, Janet. 1999. *Many Petals of the Lotus: Five Asian Buddhist Communities in Toronto.* Toronto: University of Toronto Press.

———. 2009. *Cambodian Refugees in Ontario: Resettlement, Religion and Identity.* Toronto: University of Toronto Press.

Mellor, Phillip. 1993. "Reflexive Traditions: Anthony Giddens, High Modernity and the Contours of Contemporary Religiosity." *Religious Studies* 29: 111–27.

Melton, J. Gordon. 2000. *The Church of Scientology.* Salt Lake City: Signature Books.

Miller, Donald. 1997. *Reinventing American Protestantism: Christianity in the New Millennium.* Berkeley, CA: University of California Press.

——— and Tetsunao Yamamori, 2007. *Global Pentecostalism: The New Face of Christian Social Engagement.* Berkeley: University of California Press.

Mills, C. Wright. 1959. *The Sociological Imagination.* New York: Oxford University Press.

Milton, Ralph. 1991. *This United Church of Ours.* 2nd Edition. Winfield, BC: Wood Lake Books.

Minganti, Pia Karlsson. 2010. "Islamic Revival and Young Women's Negotiations on Gender and Racism," in Sylvia Collins-Mayo and Pink Dandelion, eds., *Religion and Youth.* Burlington, VT: Ashgate.

Mistry, Rohinton. 1995. *A Fine Balance.* Toronto: McClelland & Stewart.

Mol, Hans. 1976. *Identity and the Sacred: A Sketch for a Social Scientific Theory of Religion.* New York: Free Press.

Montpetit, Jonathan. 2011. "Will Interculturalism Replace Multiculturalism?" *Toronto Star* (Canadian Press) 6 March.

Moon, Richard, ed. 2008. *Law and Religious Pluralism in Canada.* Vancouver, BC: University of British Columbia Press.

Müller, Max. 1889. *Natural Religion.* London: Longmans.

Mumm, Susan. 1999. *Stolen Daughters, Virgin Mothers: Anglican Sisterhoods in Victorian Britain.* London: Leicester University Press.

Nason-Clark, Nancy. 1993. "Gender Relations in Contemporary Christian Organizations," in W.E. Hewitt, ed., *The Sociology of Religion: A Canadian Focus.* Toronto: Butterworths.

Nelsen, H. N. Cheek and P. Au. 1985. "Gender Differences in Images of God." *Journal for the Scientific Study of Religion* 24: 396–402.

Nemeth, Roger J. and Donald Al Luidens. 2003. "The Religious Basis of Charitable Giving in America: A Social Capital Perspective," in Corwin Smidt, ed.,

Religion as Social Capital: Producing the Common Good. Waco, TX: Baylor University Press.

Nicol, John Thomas. 1966. *Pentecostalism.* New York: Harper & Row.

Niebuhr, H. Richard. 1929. *The Social Sources of Denominationalism.* New York: Henry Holt.

Nietzsche, Friedrich. 1967 [1877]. *On the Genealogy of Morals.* New York: Vintage Books.

Nock, David. 1993. "The Organization of Religious Life in Canada," in W.E. Hewitt, ed., *The Sociology of Religion: A Canadian Focus.* Toronto, ON: Butterworths.

Noll, Mark. 1992. *A History of Christianity in the United States and Canada.* Grand Rapids, MI: William B. Eerdmans Publishing Company.

———. 2006. "What Happened to Christian Canada?" *Church History* 75 (2): 245–73.

Norris, Pippa and Ronald Inglehart. 2004. *Sacred and Secular: Religion and Politics Worldwide.* New York, NY: Cambridge University Press.

O'Toole, Roger. 1996. "Religion in Canada: Its development and Contemporary Situation." *Social Compass* 43 (1): 119–34.

———. 2000. "Canadian Religion: Heritage and Project," in David Lyon and Marguerite Van Die, eds., *Rethinking Church, State, and Modernity: Canada Between Europe and America.* Toronto, ON: University of Toronto Press.

———, Douglas F. Campbell, John A. Hannigan, Peter Beyer and John H. Simpson. 1993. "The United Church in Crisis," in Warren Edward Hewitt, ed., *The Sociology of Religion: A Canadian Focus.* Toronto, ON: Butterworths.

Olson and Hadaway. 1999. "Religious Pluralism and Affiliation among Canadian Counties and Cities." *Journal for the Scientific Study of Religion* 38 (4): 490–508.

Otto, Rudolph. 1958 [1917]. *The Idea of the Holy: An Inquiry into the Nonrational Factor in the Idea of the Divine and Its Relation to the Rational.* Trans. by John W. Harvey. Oxford: Oxford University Press.

Ozorak, Elizabeth Weiss. 1996. "The Power but not the Glory. How Women Empower Themselves Through Religion." *Journal for the Scientific Study of Religion* 35 (1): 17–29.

Palmer, Susan Jean. 1994. *Moon Sisters, Krishna Mother, Rajneesh Lovers: Women's Roles in New Religions.* Syracuse, NY: Syracuse University Press.

Partridge, Christopher H. 2004. *New Religions: A Guide.* New York: Oxford University Press.

Patrick, Ted and Tom Dulack. 1976. *Let Our Children Go!* New York: E.P. Dutton.

Patriquin, Martin. 2011. "Just What Does Quebec's Official Answer to Multicultural-ism Entail?" *Maclean's* 18 February.

Paulson, Henry M., Jr. 2010. *On the Brink: Inside the Race to Stop the Collapse of the Global Financial System.* New York: Business Plus.

Pew Forum on Religion and Public Life. 2008. "U.S. religious Landscape Survey." Available at http://religions.pewforum.org/pdf/report-religious-landscape-study-full.pdf.

———. 2010. "Religion among the Millennials: Less Religiously Active than Older Americans, but Fairly Traditional in Other Ways." Available at http://pewforum.org/newassets/images/reports/millennials/millennials-report.pdf.

Pew Research Center. 2002 (December 19). "Among Wealthy Nations: U.S. Stands Alone In Its Embrace of Religion." Available at www.pewglobal.org/2002/12/19/among-wealthy-nations/.

Piché, Eric. 1999. "Religion and Social Capital in Canada." MA Thesis, Department of Sociology at Queen's University, Kingston, ON.

Pope, Liston. 1958. *Millhands and Preachers: A Study of Gastonia.* New Haven, CT: Yale University Press.

Prebish, Charles S. 1999. *Luminous Passage: The Practice and Study of Buddhism in America.* Berkeley, CA: University of California Press.

Presser, Stanley and Mark Chaves. 2007. "Is Religious Service Attendance Declining?" *Journal for the Scientific Study of Religion* 46 (3): 417–23.

Prothero, Stephen. 2007. *Religious Literacy: What Every American Needs to Know—and Doesn't.* New York: Harperone.

Putnam, Robert and David Campbell. 2010. *American Grace: How Religion Divides and Unites Us.* New York, NY: Simon and Schuster.

Puttick, Elizabeth. 1997. *Women in New Religions: In Search of Community, Sexuality and Spiritual Power.* New York: St. Martin's Press.

Quinn, D. Michael. 1993. "Plural Marriage and Mormon Fundamentalism," in Martin E. Marty and R. Scott Appleby, eds., *Fundamentalisms and Society: Reclaiming the Sciences, the Family, and Education.* Chicago, IL: University of Chicago Press.

R. v. Kharaghani and Styrsky. 2011. Reasons for Decision. Ontario Superior Court of Justice. ONSC 836, Court File No.: 1-5972294.

Radcliffe-Brown, Alfred R. 1972 [1939]. "Taboo," in William Lessa and Evon Z. Vogt, eds., *Reader in Comparative Religion,* 3rd ed. New York: Harper and Row.

Rappaport, Roy A. 1999. *Ritual and Religion in the Making of Humanity.* Cambridge: Cambridge University Press.

RavenWolf, Silver. 1999. *Teen Witch: Wicca for a New Generation.* St. Paul, MN: Llewellyn Publications.

Redfield, James. 1994. *The Celestine Prophecy.* New York: Warner Books.

Reed, Paul and Kevin Selbee. 2001. "The Civic Core in Canada: Disproportionality in Charitable Giving, Volunteering, and Civic Participation." *Nonprofit and Voluntary Sector Quarterly* 30 (4): 761–80.

Reimer, Sam. 2003. *Evangelicals and the Continental Divide: The Conservative Protestant Subculture in Canada and the United States.* Montreal: McGill-Queen's University Press.

———. 2008. "Does Religion Matter? Canadian Religious Traditions and Attitudes Toward Diversity," in Lori Beaman and Peter Beyer, eds., *Religion and Diversity in Canada.* Boston, MA: Brill.

Rendall, Jane. 1985. *The Origins of Modern Feminism. Women in Britain, France and the United States, 1780–1860.* Basingstoke: Macmillan.

Research Council of Norway. 2006 (November 30). "World's Oldest Ritual Discovered—Worshipped the Python 70,000 Years Ago." *ScienceDaily.* Available at www.sciencedaily.com-/releases/2006/11/061130081347.htm.

Reuther, Rosemary Radford, ed. 1974. *Religion and Sexism: Images of Woman in the Jewish and Christian Traditions.* New York: Simon and Schuster.

Richardson, James T. 1985. "The Active vs Passive Convert: Paradigm Conflict in Conversion/Recruitment Research." *Journal for the Scientific Study of Religion* 24 (2): 163–79.

———. 1988. *Money and Power in New Religions.* Lewiston, NY: Edwin Mellen Press.

———. 2004. "Legal Dimensions of New Religions," in James R. Lewis, ed., *The Oxford Handbook of New Religious Movements.* New York: Oxford University Press.

———. 2006. "Religion, Constitutional Courts, and Democracy in Former Communist Countries." *The Annals of the American Academy of Political and Social Science* 603: 129–39.

———, G. Krylova, and Marat Shterin. 2004. "Legal Regulation of Religion in Russia: New Developments," in James T. Richardson, ed., *Regulating Religion.* New York: Kluwer.

——— and Massimo Introvigne. 2001. "'Brainwashing' Theories in European

Parliamentary and Administrative Reports on Cults and Sects." *Journal for the Scientific Study of Religion* 40: 143–68.

Riis, Ole and Linda Woodhead. 2010. *A Sociology of Religious Emotion*. New York: Oxford University Press.

Ritzer, George. 1993. *The McDonaldization of Society*. Thousand Oakes, CA: Pine Forge Press.

Robbins, Thomas and David G. Bromley. 1992. "Social Experimentation and the Significance of American New Religions," in Monty Lynn and David Moberg, eds., *Research in the Social Scientific study of Religion*. Vol.4. Greenwich, CT: JAI Press.

——— and ———. 1993. "What Have We Learned about New Religions? New Religious Movements as Experiments." *Religious Studies Review* 19: 209–16.

Robbins, Thomas and Dick Anthony. 1982. "Deprogramming, Brainwashing and the Medicalization of Deviant Religious Groups." *Social Problems* 29 (3): 283–97.

Robertson, Roland. 1992. *Globalization: Social Theory and Global Culture*. London: Sage.

Robertson, Roland and JoAnn Chirico. 1985. "Humanity, Globalization, and Worldwide Religious Resurgence: A Theoretical Exploration." *Sociological Analysis* 46: 219–42.

Roof, Wade Clark. 1993. *A Generation of Seekers: The Spiritual Journeys of the Baby Boom Generation*. San Francisco: Harper-Collins.

———. 1999. *Spiritual Marketplace: Baby Boomers and the Remaking of American Religion*. Princeton, NJ: Princeton University Press.

Roof, Wade Clark and William McKinney. 1987. *American Mainline Religion: Its Changing Shape and Future*. New Brunswick, NJ: Rutgers University Press.

Roy, Oliver. 2004. *Globalized Islam: The Search for a New Ummah*. New York: Columbia University Press.

Saler, Benson. 1993. *Conceptualizing Religion: Immanent Anthropologists, Transcendent Natives, and Unbounded Categories*. Leiden, The Netherlands: E.J. Brill.

Salomonsen, Jone. 2002. *Enchanted Feminism: The Reclaiming Witches of San Francisco*. New York: Routledge.

Saunders, Doug. 2012. *The Myth of the Muslim Tide: Do Immigrants Threaten the West?* Toronto: Alfred A Knopf.

Scholte, Jan Aart. 2000. *Globalization: A Critical Introduction*. Basingstoke, UK: Macmillan.

Schucman, Helen. 1996. *A Course in Miracles*. 2nd ed. New York: Viking Penguin.

Scott, Jamie, ed. 2012. *The Religions of Canadians*. Toronto: University of Toronto Press.

Segal, Robert A., Carol E. Burnside, William E. Paden, Thomas Ryba, and Michel Despland. 1991. "Symposium on the Sacred." *Method and Theory in the Study of Religion* 3 (1): 1–46.

Seljak, David. 2005. "Education, Multiculturalism, and Religion," in Paul Bramadat and David Seljak, eds., *Religion and Ethnicity in Canada*. Toronto, ON: Pearson.

Sered, Susan Starr. 1987. "Ritual, Morality and Gender: The Religious Lives of Oriental Jewish Women in Jerusalem." *Israel Social Science Research* 5: 87–96.

———. 1994. *Priestess, Mother, Sacred Sister: Religions Dominated by Women*. New York: Oxford University Press.

Sharf, Robert H. 1998. "Experience," in Mark C. Taylor, ed., *Critical Terms for Religious Studies*. Chicago: University of Chicago Press.

Shepherd, Nicholas M. 2010. "Religious Socialisation and a Reflexive Habitus: Christian Youth Groups as Sites for Identity Work," in Sylvia Collins-Mayo and Pink Dandelion, eds., *Religion and Youth*. Burlington, VT: Ashgate.

Shupe, Anson D. 1998. *Wolves within the Fold: Religious Leadership and Abuses of Power*. New Brunswick, NJ: Rutgers University Press.

Simmons, G. and Tony Walter. 1988. "Spot the Men: The Relation of Faith and Gender." *Third Way*, April: 10–12.

Singer, Margaret T. 1995. *Cults in Our Midst: The Hidden Menace in our Everyday Lives*. San Francisco: Jossey-Bass.

Singh, Jasjit. 2010. "British Sikh Youth: Identity, Hair and the Turban," in Sylvia Collins-Mayo and Pink Dandelion, eds., *Religion and Youth*. Aldershot, UK: Ashgate.

Smart, Ninian. 1989. *The World's Religions: Old Traditions and Modern Transformations*. Cambridge: Cambridge University Press.

Smidt, Corwin, John Green, James Guth and Lyman Kellstedt. 2003. "Religious Involvement, Social Capital, and Political Engagement: A Comparison of the United States and Canada," in Corwin Smidt, ed., *Religion as Social Capital: Producing the Common Good*. Waco, TX: Baylor University Press.

Smith, Christian. 1998. *American Evangelicalism: Embattled and Thriving*. Chicago: University of Chicago Press.

——— and Melinda Lundquist Denton. 2005. *Soul Searching: The Religious and Spiritual Lives of American Teenagers*. New York, NY: Oxford University Press.

———, Michael Emerson, Sally Gallagher, Paul Kennedy, and David Sikkink.

1998. *American Evangelism: Embattled and Thriving*. Chicago, IL: University of Chicago Press.

——— and Patricia Snell. 2009. *Souls in Transition: The Religious and Spiritual Lives of Emerging Adults*. New York, NY: Oxford University Press.

Smith, Huston. 2000. *Cleansing the Doors of Perception: The Religious Significance of Entheogenic Plants and Chemicals*. New York: Tarcher/Putnam.

Smith, Ian. 2011 (November 23). "B.C. Supreme Court Rules Polygamy Ban is Constitutional, but Flawed." *Vancouver Sun*. Available at http://news.nationalpost.com/2011/11/23/b-c-supreme-court-rules-polygamy-law-is-constitutional/.

Smith, Jonathan Z. 1982. *Imaging Religion: From Babylonia to Jonestown*. Chicago: University of Chicago Press.

———. 1998. "Religion, Religions, Religious," in Mark C. Taylor, ed., *Critical Terms for Religious Studies*. Chicago: University of Chicago Press.

Smith, Wilfred Cantwell. 1959. "Comparative Religion—Wither and Why?," in Mircea Eliade and Joseph M. Kitagawa, eds., *The History of Religions: Essays in Methodology*. Chicago: University of Chicago Press.

———. 1962. *The Meaning and End of Religion: A New Approach to the Religious Traditions of Mankind*. New York: Macmillan.

Smith, William Robertson. 1969 [1889]. *Lectures on the Religion of the Semites: The Fundamental Institutions*. 3rd ed. New York: KTAV.

Spencer, Herbert. 1886. *Principles of Sociology*. New York: D. Appleton, 3 vols.

Spiro, Melford. 1966. "Religion: Problems of Definition and Explanation," in Michael Banton, ed., *Anthropological Approaches to the Study of Religion*. London: Tavistock.

Staal, Fritz. 1983. *Agni: The Vedic Fire Ritual*. Berkeley, CA: Asian Humanities Press.

Stace, Walter Terence. 1960. *Mysticism and Philosophy*. Philadelphia: Lippincott.

Starhawk. 1979. *The Spiral Dance: A Rebirth of the Ancient Religion of the Great Goddess*. San Francisco: Harper and Row.

Stark, Rodney. 1991. "Normal Revelations: A Rational Model of Mystical Experiences," in David G. Bromley, ed., *New Developments in Theory and Research, Religion and Social Order*, Volume 1. Greenwich, CT: JAI Press.

———. 1997. "German and German-American Religion: Approximating a Crucial Experiment." *Journal for the Scientific Study of Religion* 36: 182–93.

———. 1999. "Secularization: RIP." *Sociology of Religion* 60: 249–73.

———, Eva Hamberg, and Alan.S. Miller.

2005. "Exploring Spirituality and Unchurched Religions in America, Sweden, and Japan." *Journal of Contemporary Religion*. 20 (1): 3–23.

——— and Laurence Iannaccone. 1994. "A Supply-Side Reinterpretation of the "Secularization" of Europe." *Journal for the Scientific Study of Religion* 33 (3): 230–52.

——— and Roger Finke. 2000. *Acts of Faith: Explaining the Human Side of Religion*. Berkeley, CA: University of California Press.

——— and William Sims Bainbridge. 1985. *The Future of Religion: Secularization, Revival and Cult Formation*. Berkeley, CA: University of California Press.

——— and ———. 1996 [1987]. *A Theory of Religion*. New Brunswick, NJ: Rutgers University Press.

Statistics Canada. 2001. "2001 Census: Analysis Series. Religions in Canada." Available at www12.statcan.ca/english/census01/products/analytic/companion/rel/pdf/96F0030XIE2001015.pdf.

———. 2010. "Projections of the Diversity of the Canadian Population: 2006–2031." Available at www.statcan.gc.ca/pub/91-551-x/91-551-x2010001-eng.pdf.

———. 2013. "Immigration and Ethnocultural Diversity in Canada." Available at www12.statcan.gc.ca/nhs-enm/2011/as-sa/99-010-x/99-010-x2011001-eng.pdf.

Stewart, Adam. 2010. "A Canadian Azusa? The Implications of the Hebden *Mission for Pentecostal Historiography*," in *Winds from the North: Canadian Contributions to the Pentecostal Movement*, edited by Michael Wilkinson and Peter Althouse. Leiden: Brill.

Sutton, Philip W. and Stephen Vertigans. 2005. *Resurgent Islam: A Sociological Approach*. Cambridge: Polity Press.

Thiessen, Elmer John. 2001. *In Defence of Religious Schools and Colleges*. Montreal, QC: McGill Queen's University Press.

Thiessen, Joel. 2010. "Churches are not Necessarily the Problem: Lessons Learned from Christmas and Easter Affiliates." *Church and Faith Trends* 3 (3): 1–24.

———. 2011. Book review of Reginald Bibby's *Beyond the Gods and Back: Religion's Demise and Rise and Why it Matters. Church and Faith Trends 4 (1): 1–4*.

———. 2012. "Marginal Religious Affiliates in Canada: Little Reason to Expect Increased Church Involvement." *Canadian Review of Sociology* 49 (1): 69–90.

——— and Lorne Dawson. 2008. "Is There a 'Renaissance' of Religion in Canada? A Critical Look at Bibby and Beyond." *Studies in Religion* 37 (3–4): 389–415.

Thomas, Scott. 2005. *The Global Resurgence*

of Religion and the Transformation of International Relations. New York: Palgrave.

Thomas, W.I. and D.S. Thomas. 1928. The Child in America: Behavior Problems and Programs. New York: Knopf.

Tillich, Paul. 1957. Dynamics of Faith. New York: Harper.

Tipton, Steven M. 1982. Getting Saved from the Sixties. Berkeley, CA: University of California Press.

Toft, Monica Duffy. 2011. God's Century: Resurgent Religion and Global Politics. New York: W.W. Norton & Co.

Tönnies, Ferdinand. 1957. Community and Society: Gemeinschaft and Gesellschaft. Translated and edited by Charles Loomis. East Lansing, MI: Michigan State University Press.

Turner, Bryan S. 1991. Religion and Social Theory. 2nd ed. London: Sage.

Turner, Ralph H. 1978. "The Role and the Person." American Journal of Sociology 84 (1): 1–23.

Turner, Victor W. 1969. The Ritual Process. New York: Aldine.

Tylor, Edward B. 1871. Primitive Culture: Researches into the Development of Mythology, Philosophy, Religion, Art, and Custom. London: J. Murray, 2 vols.

Valpy, Michael. 2010 (15 December). "Young Increasingly Shun Religious Institutions." Globe and Mail. Available at www.theglobeandmail.com/news/national/young-increasingly-shun-religious-institutions/article1837678/.

—— and Joe Friesen. 2010 (11 December). "Canada Marching from Religion to Secularization." Globe and Mail. Available at www.theglobeandmail.com/news/national/canada-marching-from-religion-to-secularization/article1833451/page1/.

Voas, David. 2009. "The Rise and Fall of Fuzzy Fidelity in Europe." European Sociological Review 25 (2): 155–68.

——. 2010. "Explaining Change over Time in Religious Involvement," in Sylvia Collins-Mayo and Pink Dandelion, eds., Religion and Youth. Aldershot, UK: Ashgate.

—— and Abby Day. 2010. "Recognizing Secular Christians: Toward an Unexcluded Middle in the Study of Religion." The Association of Religion Data Archives. Available at www.thearda.com/rrh/papers/guidingpapers/Voas.pdf.

—— and Alasdair Crockett. 2005. "Religion in Britain: Neither Believing Nor Belonging." Sociology 39 (1): 11–28.

Wacker, Grant. 2001. Heaven Below: Early Pentecostals and American Culture. Cambridge: Harvard University Press.

Walliss, John. 2002. The Brahma Kumaris as a "Reflexive" Tradition: Responding to Late Modernity. Aldershot, Hampshire: Ashgate.

Walsch, Neal Donald. 1997. Conversations with God. New York: Hodder and Stoughton.

Walter, Tony and Grace Davie. 1998. "The Religiosity of Women in the Modern West." British Journal of Sociology 49 (4): 640–60.

Warner, R. Stephen. 1993. "Work in Progress Toward a New Paradigm in the Sociology of Religion in the United States." American Journal of Sociology 98 (5): 1044–93.

—— and Rhys H. Williams. 2010. "The Role of Families and Religious Institutions in Transmitting Faith among Christians, Muslims, and Hindus in the USA," in Sylvia Collins-Mayo and Pink Dandelion, eds., Religion and Youth. Aldershot, UK: Ashgate.

Waters, Malcolm. 2001. Globalization. 2nd ed. London: Routledge.

Weber, Max. 1958a [1904]. The Protestant Ethic and the Spirit of Capitalism. Trans. by Talcott Parsons. New York: Charles Scribner's Sons.

——. 1958b [1915]. "The Social Psychology of the World Religions." In Hans Gerth and C. Wright Mills, eds., From Max Weber: Essays in Sociology. New York: Oxford University Press.

——. 1963 [1922]. The Sociology of Religion. Trans. Ephraim Fischoff. Boston: Beacon.

——. 1964 [1922]. The Theory of Social and Economic Organization. Trans. by A.M. Henderson and Talcott Parsons. New York: Free Press.

White, Marybeth. 2012. Enlivening the Buddha: Laying the Foundations for the Re-Creation of Lao Buddhism in Canada. PhD Dissertation, Religion and Culture, Wilfrid Laurier University.

Wilkinson, Michael. 2006. The Spirit Said Go: Pentecostal Immigrants in Canada. New York: Peter Lang.

Williams, Rhys H. ed. 2001. Promise Keepers and the New Masculinity: Private Lives and Public Morality. Lanham, MD: Lexington Books.

Wilson, Bryan. 1982. Religion in Sociological Perspective. New York, NY: Oxford University Press.

——. 1985. "Secularization: The Inherited Model," in Phillip Hammond, ed., The Sacred in a Secular Age. Berkeley, CA: University Of California Press.

——. 2001. "Salvation, Secularization, and De-Moralization," in Richard Fenn, ed., The Blackwell Companion to Sociology of Religion. Malden, MA: Blackwell Publishers.

Wilson, Stephen R. 1984. "Becoming a Yogi:

Resocialization and Deconditioning as Conversion Processes." *Sociological Analysis* 45 (4): 301–14.

Wittgenstein, Ludwig. 1974 [1921]. *Tractatus Logico-Philosophicus*. London: Routledge and Kegan Paul.

———. 1958 [1953]. *Philosophical Investigations*. Oxford: Basil Blackwell

Woodhead, Linda. 2007a. "Why so many Women in Holistic Spirituality," in Kieran Flanagan and Peter Jupp, eds., *The Sociology of Spirituality*. Aldershot, Hampshire: Ashgate.

———. 2007b. "Gender Differences in Religious Practice and Significance," in James A. Beckford and N.J. Demerath III, eds., *The Sage Handbook of the Sociology of Religion*. Los Angeles: Sage.

———. 2008. "Gendering Secularization Theory." *Social Compass* 55 (2): 187–93.

Worsley, Peter. 1968. *The Trumpet Shall Sound: A Study of "Cargo Cults" in Melanesia*. New York: Shocken.

Wuthnow, Robert. 2004. *Saving America? Faith-Based Services and the Future of Civil Society*. Princeton, NJ: Princeton University Press.

———. 2005. *America and the Challenges of Religious Diversity*. Princeton, NJ: Princeton University Press.

———. 2007. *After the Baby Boomers: How Twenty- and Thirty-Somethings Are Shaping the Future of American Religion*. Princeton, NJ: Princeton University Press.

Yinger, Milton J. 1970. *The Scientific Study of Religion*. London: Macmillan.

Young, John L. and Ezra E.H. Griffith. 1992. "A Critical Evaluation of Coercive Persuasion as Used in the Assessment of Cults." *Behavioral Sciences and the Law* 10: 89–101.

Young, Lawrence, ed. 1997. *Rational Choice Theory and Religion: Summary and Assessment*. New York: Routledge.

Zaehner, Robert C. 1972. *Drugs, Mysticism and Make-Believe*. London: Collins.

Zine, Jasmin. 2012. "Unsettling the Nation: Gender, Race, and Muslim Cultural Politics in Canada," in Jasmin Zine, ed., *Islam in the Hinterlands: Muslim Cultural Politics in Canada*. Vancouver: University of British Columbia Press.

Zinnbauer, Brian, Kenneth I. Pargament, B. Cole, M.S. Rye, E.M. Butter, T.G. Belavich, K.M. Hipp, A.B. Scott, and J.L. Kadar. 1997. "Religion and Spirituality: Unfuzzying the Fuzzy." *Journal for the Scientific Study of Religion* 36 (4): 549–64.

Zuckerman, Phil. 2008. *Society without God: What the Least Religious Nations Can Tell Us about Contentment*. New York, NY: New York University Press.

———. 2012. *Faith No More: Why People Reject Religion*. New York: Oxford University Press.

Zuzanek, Jiri, Roger Mannell and Margo Hilbrecht. 2008. "Leisure, Spirituality and Emotional Well-Being in the Lives of Teenagers." Conference Presentation at the Canadian Congress on Leisure Research in Montreal, QC.

Index